Bounded Rationality

The Adaptive Toolbox

Goal of this Dahlem Workshop:

To promote bounded rationality as the key to understanding how actual people make decisions without utilities and probabilities.

Report of the 84th Dahlem Workshop on
Bounded Rationality: The Adaptive Toolbox
Berlin, March 14–19, 1999

Held and published on behalf of the
President, Freie Universität Berlin: P. Gaehtgens

Scientific Advisory Board: G. Braun, F. Hucho, K. Labitzke,
R. Menzel, W. Reutter, K. Seppelt,
T. Trautner, L. Wöste

Acting Director: K. Roth

Series Editor: J. Lupp

Assistant Editors: C. Rued-Engel, G. Custance

Bounded Rationality

The Adaptive Toolbox

Edited by

G. Gigerenzer and R. Selten

Program Advisory Committee:
G. Gigerenzer and R. Selten, Chairpersons
R. Boyd, P. Hammerstein

The MIT Press

Cambridge, Massachusetts
London, England

First MIT Press paperback edition, 2002
© 2001 Massachusetts Institute of Technology

This book was in Times by Dahlem Konferenzen

Printed and bound in the United States of America.

Library of Congress Cataloging-in-Publication Data

Bounded rationality : the adaptive toolbox / edited by G. Gigerenzer and R. Selten.
    p. cm.
    Includes bibliographical references and indexes.
    ISBN 0-262-07214-9 (hc : alk. paper), 0-262-57164-1 (pb)
    1. Decision making—Congresses. 2. Reasoning—Congresses.
I. Gigerenzer, Gerd. II. Selten, Reinhard.

BF448 .B67 2001
153.4'3—dc21   00-064589

10 9 8 7 6 5 4

Contents

Contents

The Dahlem Konferenzen

In 1974, the Stifterverband für die Deutsche Wissenschaft[1] in cooperation with the Deutsche Forschungsgemeinschaft[2] founded the *Dahlem Konferenzen*. It was created to promote an interdisciplinary exchange of scientific ideas as well as to stimulate cooperation in research among international scientists. Dahlem Konferenzen proved itself to be an invaluable tool for communication in science, and so, to secure its long-term future, it was integrated into the Freie Universität Berlin in January, 1990.

As has been evident over recent years, scientific research has become highly interdisciplinary. Now, before real progress can be made in any one field, the concepts, methods, and strategies of related fields must be understood and able to be applied. Coordinated research efforts, scientific cooperation, and basic communication between the disciplines and the scientists themselves must be promoted in order for science to advance.

To meet these demands, Dahlem Konferenzen created a special type of forum for communication, now internationally recognized as the *Dahlem Workshop Model*. These workshops are the framework in which coherent discussions between the disciplines take place and are focused around a topic of high priority interest to the disciplines concerned. At a Dahlem Workshop, scientists are able to pose questions and solicit alternative opinions on contentious issues from colleagues from related fields. The overall goal of a workshop is not necessarily to reach a consensus but rather to identify gaps in knowledge, to find new ways of approaching controversial issues, and to define priorities for future research. This philosophy is implemented at every stage of a workshop: from the selection of the theme to its breakdown in the discussion groups, from the writing of the background papers to the formulation of the group reports.

Workshop topics are proposed by leading scientists and are approved by a scientific board, which is advised by qualified referees. Once a topic has been approved, a Program Advisory Committee of scientists meets approximately one year before the workshop to delineate the scientific parameters of the

---

[1] The Donors' Association for the Promotion of Sciences and Humanities, a foundation created in 1921 in Berlin and supported by German trade and industry to fund basic research in the sciences.

[2] German Science Foundation.

meeting, select participants, and assign them their tasks. Participants are invited on the basis of their scientific standing alone.

Each workshop is organized around four key questions, which are addressed by four discussion groups of approximately ten participants. Lectures or formal presentations are taboo at Dahlem. Instead, concentrated discussion — within a group and between groups — is the means by which maximum communication is achieved. To facilitate this discussion, participants prepare the workshop theme prior to the meeting through the "background papers," the themes and authors of which are chosen by the Program Advisory Committee. These papers specifically review a particular aspect of the group's discussion topic as well as function as a springboard to the group discussion, by introducing controversies or unresolved problem areas.

During the workshop week, each group sets its own agenda to cover the discussion topic. Cross-fertilization between groups is both stressed and encouraged. By the end of the week, in a collective effort, each group has prepared a report reflecting the ideas, opinions, and contentious issues of the group as well as identifying directions for future research and problem areas still in need of resolution.

A Dahlem Workshop initiates and facilitates discussion between a certain number — necessarily restricted — of scientists. Because it is imperative that the discussion and communication should continue after a workshop, we present the results to the scientific community at large in the form of this published volume. In it you will find the revised background papers and group reports, as well as an introduction to the workshop theme itself.

The difference between proceedings of many conventional meetings and this workshop report will be easily discernable. Here, the background papers have not only been reviewed by formal referees, they have been revised according to the many comments and suggestions made by *all* participants. In this sense, they are reviewed more thoroughly than scientific articles in most archival journals. In addition, an extensive editorial procedure ensures a coherent volume. I am sure that you, too, will appreciate the tireless efforts of the many reviewers, authors, and editors.

On their behalf, I sincerely hope that the spirit of this workshop as well as the ideas and controversies raised will stimulate you in your work and future endeavors.

Wedigo de Vivanco, Director
Dahlem Konferenzen der Freien Universität Berlin
Thielallee 66, D–14195 Berlin, Germany

List of Participants

W. ALBERS Institute for Mathematical Economic Research, University of Bielefeld, P.O. Box 10 01 31, D–33501 Bielefeld, Germany

Experimentally based boundedly rational models of games, auctions, and individual decision making under risk

R. BOYD Dept. of Anthropology, University of California, Los Angeles, CA 90024, U.S.A.

The models of cultural evolution and social behavoir; empirical models of the same

I. EREV Faculty of Industrial Engineering + Management, Israel Institute of Technology, TECHNION, Haifa 32000, Israel

Cognitive psychology (with focus on learning among decision strategies)

D.M.T. FESSLER Dept. of Anthropology, University of California, Los Angeles, CA 90095–1553, U.S.A.

Anthropology/evolutionary psychology: the evolution of emotion; topics: shame, pride, disgust, emotion and risk-taking behavior; emotion and sexual behavior/incest, cultural and time preference

G. GIGERENZER Center for Adaptive Behavior and Cognition, Max Planck Institute for Human Development, Lentzeallee 94, D–14195 Berlin, Germany

Rationality, reasoning, and risk

D.G. GOLDSTEIN Center for Adaptive Behavior and Cognition, Max Planck Institute for Human Development, Lentzeallee 94, D–14195 Berlin, Germany

Models of bounded rationality for inference: when and why simple heuristics work

W. GÜTH Institute for Economic Theory, Humboldt University, Spandauer Str. 1, D–10178 Berlin, Germany

Game theory; experimental economics; models of bounded rationality

P. HAMMERSTEIN   Innovationskolleg Theoretische Biologie, Humboldt University, Invalidenstr. 43, D–10115 Berlin, Germany

Theoretical problems in evolutionary biology; evolutionary game theory

S. HARNAD   Cognitive Sciences Centre, ECS, Southampton University, Highfield, GB–Southampton SO17 1B5, U.K.

Origin of language, neural nets, sensorimotor grounding of symbols; categorical perception; categorization bias

C.K. HEMELRIJK   Artificial Intelligence Laboratory, Dept. of Computer Science, University of Zurich, Winterthurerstr. 190, CH–8057 Zurich, Switzerland

Process-oriented approach to social behavior; self-structuring effects of social behavior as a tool to hypothesis generation about animals

J. HENRICH   University of Michigan Business School, 701 Tappan Rd. D3276, Ann Arbor, MI 48109–1234, U.S.A.

Cross-cultural economic behavior and cultural transmission

R. HERTWIG   Center for Adaptive Behavior and Cognition, Max Planck Institute for Human Development, Lentzeallee 94, D–14195 Berlin, Germany

Research in judgment and decision making (e.g., how simple heuristics can exploit environmental structures); methodological issues in experimental psychology and experimental economics

U. HOFFRAGE   Center for Adaptive Behavior and Cognition, Max Planck Institute for Human Development, Lentzeallee 94, D–14195 Berlin, Germany

Judgment and decision making: simple heuristics, representation of information; risk-taking behavior

R.M. HOGARTH   Dept. of Economics and Management, University Pampeu Fabra, Ramon Trias Fargas, 25–27, E–08005 Barcelona, Spain

Psychology of judgment and decision making: processes of intuition and insight

A. KACELNIK   Dept. of Zoology, Oxford University, GB–Oxford OX1 3PS, U.K.

Animal decision making; risk sensitivity; integration of evolutionary and psychological theories of behavior

Y. KAREEV   Goldie Rotman Center for Cognitive Science and Education, School of Education, The Hebrew University, Jerusalem 91905, Israel

The relation between limited working memory capacity and the perception of contingency and variability

G. KLEIN   Klein Associates, Inc., 1750 Commerce Center Blvd. North, Fairborn, OH 45324, U.S.A.

Psychology – cognition, decision making, human factors, industrial/organizations

B. KUON   Laboratory for Experimental Economic Research, University of Bonn, Adenauerallee 24–42, D–53113 Bonn, Germany

Experimental economics, bounded rationality, game theory

K.N. LALAND   Sub-Department of Animal Behaviour, University of Cambridge, Madingley, GB–Cambridge CB3 8AA, U.K.

Animal social learning, gene–culture coevolution and niche construction

L. MARTIGNON   Center for Adaptive Behavior and Cognition, Max Planck Institute for Human Development, Lentzeallee 94, D–14195 Berlin, Germany

Statistics of neural interactions; Bayesian inference; mathematical analysis of fast and frugal strategies

K.A. MCCABE   Economic Science Laboratory, University of Arizona, McClelland Hall, 116, P.O. Box 210108, 1130 E. Helen, Tucson, AZ 85721–0108, U.S.A.

Experimental studies of the evolutionary and neurological foundations of economic behavior

B.A. MELLERS   Dept. of Psychology, Ohio State University, 142 Townshend Hall, 1885 Neil Ave. Mall, Columbus, OH 43210, U.S.A.

Individual decision making, with special emphasis on the emotional and cognitive processes that underlie choice

B.R. MUNIER   GRID, École Normale Supérieure de Cachan, 61, Avenue du président Wilson, F–94235 Cachan cedex, France

Risk theory, experimental economics, risk management, decision making, bounded rationality

A. OCKENFELS   Morgan Hall T25, Harvard Business School, Soldiers Field Road, Boston, MA 02163, U.S.A.

Experimental economics, motivations, game theory; cross-culture and framing effects in social interaction

J.W. PAYNE   Fuqua School of Business, Duke University, Durham, NC 27708, U.S.A.

Information processing and decision making

A. SADRIEH   Dept. of Economics, Tilburg University, P.O. Box 90153, NL–5000 LE Tilburg, The Netherlands

Experimental economics, bounded rationality, game theory

K.R. SCHERER   Dept. of Psychology, University of Geneva, 9, route de Drize, CH–1227 Carouge/GE, Switzerland

Psychology of emotion, in particular cognition and emotion, emotion-antecedent appraisal, expression of emotion

K.H. SCHLAG   Dept. of Economic Theory III, University of Bonn, Adenauer Allee 24–26, D–53113 Bonn, Germany

Selection among simple learning rules using boundedly rational principles and evolutionary dynamics in order then to make predictions in games

T.D. SEELEY   Dept. of Neurobiology and Behavior, Cornell University, Mudd Hall, Ithaca, NY 14850, U.S.A.

Social organization of insect societies: group decision making in honey bee colonies as they decide where to live, how to forage, and how to build their combs

R. SELTEN   Juridicum, University of Bonn, Adenauerallee 24–26, D–53113 Bonn, Germany

Experimental and theoretical research on economic behavior

P.E. TETLOCK   Dept. of Psychology, Ohio State University, 142 Townshend Hall, 1885 Neil Avenue, Columbus, OH 43210–1222, U.S.A.

Impact of social/political context on judgment and choice; clarifying the concept of good judgment

P.M. TODD   Center for Adaptive Behavior and Cognition, Max Planck Institute for Human Development, Lentzeallee 94, D–14195 Berlin, Germany

Evolutionary psychology of simple decision-making heuristics; interactions between behavior, learning, evolution, and environment structure

M. WARGLIEN   Dept. of Economics and Business Administration, University ca' Foscari of Venice, Ca' Bembo S. Trovaso-Dorsoduro 1075, I–30123 Venice, Italy

Mental models of games; disjunctive reasoning; organizational routines

M. WEBER   Dept. of Economics and Business Administration, L5, 2, University of Mannheim, D–68131 Mannheim, Germany

Behavioral finance

H.P. YOUNG   Dept. of Economics, Johns Hopkins University, Mergenthaler Hall, 3400 North Charles Street, Baltimore, MD 21218–2685, U.S.A.

Game theory, learning, social norms

1

Rethinking Rationality

Gerd Gigerenzer[1] and Reinhard Selten[2]

[1]Center for Adaptive Behavior and Cognition, Max Planck Institute for Human
Development, Lentzeallee 94, 14195 Berlin, Germany
[2]Juridicum, University of Bonn, Adenauerallee 24–42, 53113 Bonn, Germany

Visions of rationality do not respect disciplinary boundaries. Economics, psychology, animal biology, artificial intelligence, anthropology, and philosophy struggle with models of sound judgment, inference, and decision making. These models evolve over time, just as the idea of rationality has a history, a present, and a future (Daston 1988). Over the last centuries, models of rationality have changed when they conflicted with actual behavior, yet, at the same time, they provided prescriptions for behavior. This double role — to describe and to prescribe — does not map easily onto a sharp divide between descriptive and normative models, which plays down the actual exchange between the psychological and the rational (Gigerenzer et al. 1989). Herbert Simon's notion of bounded rationality was proposed in the mid-1950s to connect, rather than to oppose, the rational and the psychological (Simon 1956). The aim of this book is to contribute to this process of coevolution, by inserting more psychology into rationality, and vice versa.

This book, however, cannot and will not provide a unified theory of bounded rationality. Rather, its goals are (a) to provide a framework of bounded rationality in terms of the metaphor of the *adaptive toolbox*, (b) to provide an understanding about why and when the simple heuristics in the adaptive toolbox work, (c) to extend the notion of bounded rationality from cognitive tools to emotions, and (d) to extend the notion of bounded rationality to include social norms, imitation, and other cultural tools.

To reach these goals, this book adopts a broad interdisciplinary perspective. Bounded rationality needs to be, but it is not yet, understood. Before we look into the future of models of rationality, however, let us have a glance back into the past.

THE RATIONAL AND THE PSYCHOLOGICAL

The Aristotelian distinction between the realm of demonstrative proof (that is, the things people were absolutely certain about, such as matters of mathematics and religion) and that of mere probable knowledge has shaped millennia of Western thought. The empire of demonstrative proof and certainty, however, narrowed in Europe after the Reformation and the Counter-Reformation. In the mid-17th century, a new and more modest standard of reasonableness emerged that acknowledged the irreducible uncertainty of human life. God, as John Locke (1690/1959) asserted, "has afforded us only the twilight of probability." The theory of probability that emerged at that time became the major guide for reasonableness. Its birth-year has been dated at 1654, when Blaise Pascal and Pierre Fermat exchanged letters about gambling problems (Hacking 1975). The initial definition of reasonableness was to choose the alternative that maximizes expected value (in modern notation, $\Sigma p_i v_i$, where p_i and v_i are the probability and value, respectively, of the ith consequence of a given alternative). Pascal's *wager* illustrates that this newly conceived rationality was not only a cognitive revolution, but a new form of morality as well. Pascal pondered on whether to believe in God or not. He reasoned that even if the probability that God exists were small, the expectation is infinite: infinite bliss for the saved and infinite misery for the damned. Therefore, Pascal argued that rational self-interest dictates that we forego our certain but short-lived worldly pleasures and bet on the uncertain but infinite prospect of eternal salvation. The new brand of calculating rationality replaced faith with moral expectation.

The definition of reasonableness in terms of expected value soon ran into problems: it conflicted with the intuition of educated people. The first in a series of conflicts was the so-called St. Petersburg paradox, based on the following monetary gamble. Pierre offers Paul a gamble in which a fair coin is tossed. If the coin comes up heads on the first toss, Pierre agrees to pay Paul $1; if heads do not turn up until the second toss, Paul receives $2; if not until the third toss, $4, and so on. What is the fair price Paul should pay to play this game? The fair price is defined by the expected value, $\Sigma p_i v_i$, which is the sum of all possible outcomes (values) times their probability. This sum is $1/2 \times \$1 + 1/4 \times \$2 + 1/8 \times \$4 + \dots + 1/2^n \times \$n + \dots$, which is infinitely large. However, reasonable people offer only some $5 to $10 to play this game rather than a very large amount of money. This discrepancy was labeled a paradox, the "St. Petersburg paradox," not because it is a logical paradox, but because the mathematical theory was so at odds with the dictates of good sense. The theory of rationality was thought of as a description of human behavior as well as a prescription for it. To resolve the discrepancy between theory and good sense, Daniel Bernoulli proposed changing the theory: from maximizing expected value to maximizing expected utility, that is, through incorporating the psychological facts that money has diminishing returns (which he modeled by a logarithmic function between monetary value and utility) and that this utility depends on the amount of money a person already has (Bernoulli 1738/1954).

The St. Petersburg paradox was the first in a series of monetary gambles — such as the Allais paradox and the Ellsberg paradox in the 20th century — that led to changes, or at least to proposed changes, in the theory of rationality. By the early 19th century, it was realized that there are several definitions of expectation, not just one (e.g., arithmetic mean, geometric mean, and median; as well as several measures of variability around the expected value to model risk). This ambiguity was perceived as a defeat for the program to arrive at the *one* mathematical definition of reasonableness, and became one of the reasons why the program was abandoned by most mathematicians around 1840 (Daston 1988). The program, however, was revived in the mid-20th century. Like Bernoulli, many contemporary researchers attempted to resolve discrepancies between description and prescription by tinkering with the utility or probability function, while at the same time retaining the ideal of maximization or optimization.

In this book, we pursue a more radical alternative to connect the rational with the psychological. The theory of bounded rationality, as we understand it, dispenses with optimization, and, for the most part, with calculations of probabilities and utilities as well.

BOUNDED RATIONALITY

In the 1950s and 60s, the Enlightenment notion of reasonableness reemerged in the form of the concept of "rationality" in economics, psychology, and other fields, usually referring to the optimization (maximization or minimization) of some function. Before that time, economists assumed that people were motivated by "self-interest," whereas the term "rationality" was used only occasionally (Arrow 1986). Similarly, psychologists, before 1950, assumed that thinking can be understood by processes such as "restructuring" and "insight," whereas the calculation of probabilities and the notion of optimization played little, if any, role. This situation changed after 1950. In psychology, for instance, tools for statistical inference became institutionalized in the 1950s and, once entrenched in the daily routine of the laboratory, were proposed by the researchers as models of cognitive processes. Fisher's analysis of variance turned into a mechanism of causal attribution, and Neyman-Pearson decision theory became a model of stimulus detection and discrimination (Gigerenzer and Murray 1987). By this tools-to-theories heuristic, cognitive processes came to be seen as involving the calculation of probabilities, utilities, and optimal decisions. But this is not the only route by which the ideal of optimization entered the behavioral sciences. Animal biologists developed optimal foraging theory, and the emerging field of artificial intelligence bet on designing rational agents similar to the "optimal" animals, that is, pursuing the ideal of providing artificial agents with a complete representation of their environment and extensive computing capacities for calculating optimal behavior.

About the same time as the notion of rationality as optimization became entrenched in theory and research across many disciplines, the competing notion of "bounded rationality" emerged (Simon 1956; Sauermann and Selten 1962). Herbert Simon, who coined the term "bounded rationality," used the metaphor of a pair of scissors, where one blade is the "cognitive limitations" of actual humans and the other the "structure of the environment." Minds with limited time, knowledge, and other resources can be nevertheless successful by exploiting structures in their environments. In Simon's (1956) words, "a great deal can be learned about rational decision making ... by taking account of the fact that the environments to which it must adapt possess properties that permit further simplification of its choice mechanisms" (p. 129). Studying only one blade is not enough; it takes both for the scissors to cut.

Thus, models of bounded rationality describe how a judgment or decision is reached (that is, the heuristic processes or proximal mechanisms) rather than merely the outcome of the decision, and they describe the class of environments in which these heuristics will succeed or fail. These models dispense with the fiction of optimization, which in many real-world situations demands unrealistic assumptions about the knowledge, time, attention, and other resources available to humans. Note that dispensing with optimization (as a model of cognitive processes) does not imply that the outcome of a nonoptimizing strategy is bad. For instance, optimization is often based on uncertain assumptions, which are themselves guesswork, and as a consequence, there may be about as many different outcomes of optimizing strategies as there are sets of assumptions. In these real-world cases, it is possible that simple and robust heuristics can match or even outperform a specific optimizing strategy.

Simon's original vision, however, has met with only limited success. In particular, bounded rationality has become a fashionable label for almost every model of human behavior. In the following, we sketch our vision of bounded rationality, which is an elaboration of Simon's original concept. We begin with two prominent interpretations that are both inconsistent with our vision of bounded rationality.

WHAT BOUNDED RATIONALITY IS NOT

Bounded rationality is neither optimization nor irrationality. Nevertheless, a class of models known as *optimization under constraints* is referred to in the literature as "bounded rationality," and a class of empirical demonstrations of so-called errors and fallacies in judgment and decision making has also been labeled "bounded rationality." The fact that these two classes of models have little if anything in common reveals the distortion the concept of bounded rationality has suffered.

Optimization Under Constraints

A key process in bounded rationality is limited search. Whereas in models of un-bounded rationality all relevant information is assumed to be available already, real humans and animals need to search for information first. Search can be for two kinds of information: alternatives (such as for houses and spouses) and cues (that is, for reasons and predictors when deciding between given alternatives). Search can be performed inside the human mind (memory) or outside it (e.g., library, internet, other minds). Internal search costs time and attention, and exter-nal search may cost even further resources, such as money. Limited resources constrain institutions, humans, animals, and artificial agents, and these limita-tions usually conflict with the ideal of finding a procedure to arrive at the opti-mal decision.

One way to model limited search without giving up the ideal of optimization is known as optimization with decision costs taken into account, also referred to as *optimization under constraints*. Stigler (1961) used the example of a person who wants to buy a used car, and stops searching when the costs of further search would exceed the benefit of further search. This is known as an optimal stopping rule. The problems with this form of optimization as a model of actual cognitive processes are well known. First, reliable estimates of benefits and costs, such as opportunity costs, can demand large degrees of knowledge; second, there is an infinite regression problem (the cost-benefit computations themselves are costly, and demand a meta-level cost-benefit computation, and so on); and fi-nally, the knowledge and the computations involved can be so massive that one is forced to assume that ordinary people have the computational capabilities and statistical software of econometricians (Sargent 1993).

All in all, this attempt to model limited search leads to the paradoxical result that the models become even less psychologically plausible. The reason is that the desire for optimization is retained. Because optimization under constraints is often referred to as "bounded rationality" (e.g., Sargent 1993), this confusion has led to the dismissal of bounded rationality as a hidden form of optimiza-tion — one that just makes everything more complicated. As we will see, this in-terpretation is inappropriate and misleading. Models of bounded rationality use fast and frugal stopping rules for search that do *not* involve optimization.

Irrationality

Since the 1970s, researchers have documented discrepancies between a "norm" (e.g., a law of probability or logic) and human judgment. Unlike in Bernoulli's proposal, the blame was put on the human mind rather than on the norm. The dis-crepancies were labeled "fallacies," such as the base-rate fallacy and the con-junction fallacy, and attributed to humans' "bounded rationality," in the sense of limitations on rationality. This interpretation was put forward in psychology (e.g.,Kahneman et al. 1982, p. xii), experimental economics (Thaler 1991, p. 4), and the law (Jolls et al. 1998, pp.1548–1549).

Bounded rationality is, however, not simply a discrepancy between human reasoning and the laws of probability or some form of optimization. Bounded rationality dispenses with the notion of optimization and, usually, with probabilities and utilities as well. It provides an alternative to current norms, not an account that accepts current norms and studies when humans deviate from these norms. Bounded rationality means rethinking the norms as well as studying the actual behavior of minds and institutions.

The interpretation of fallacies as bounded rationality focuses on one blade of Simon's scissors (the cognitive limitations), but neglects the other blade (the structure of environments). Several of the so-called fallacies are based on norms that have been put forth without analyzing the structure of environments. For instance, what has been interpreted as base-rate neglect turns out to be a reasonable strategy under plausible assumptions about the environment (e.g., Birnbaum 1983; Mueser et al. 1999). Moreover, when information is represented in natural frequencies rather than probabilities, base rate neglect is perfectly rational (Gigerenzer and Hoffrage 1995). To sum up, bounded rationality is not an inferior form of rationality; it is not a deviation from norms that do not reflect the structure and representation of information in environments. Theories of bounded rationality should not be confused with theories of irrational decision making. The label "bounded rationality" signifies a type of theory, not outcomes.

MODELING OMNISCIENCE VERSUS HEURISTICS: AN ILLUSTRATION

In cricket, baseball, and soccer, players need to catch balls that come in high. Our thought experiment is to build a robot that can catch the ball. (No such robot exists as yet.) For the sake of simplicity, we consider only cases where a ball comes in front of or behind a player, but not to his left or right. One team of engineers, which we call the optimizing team, proceeds by programming the family of parabolas into the robot's mind (in theory, balls fly in parabolas). To select the proper parabola, the robot needs to be equipped with instruments that can measure the distance from which the ball was thrown or shot, as well as its initial velocity and projection angle. Yet in the real world, balls do not fly in parabolas due to air resistance and wind. Thus, the robot would need further measurement instruments that can measure the speed and direction of the wind at each point of the ball's flight, and compute the resulting path. Yet in a real game, there are myriad further factors, such as spin, that affect the flight of the ball, and the robot would need instruments to measure the initial direction and strength of the spin, and knowledge of how the various factors interact. Thus, the optimization team's program is to develop reliable measurement instruments that supply the robot with all the relevant knowledge, and powerful computer software that can compute from these measurements where the ball will land. All this would have to be calculated within one or two seconds — the usual time a ball is in the air. Then the robot would run to this point and catch the ball.

A second team of engineers, which we call the boundedly rational team, makes a different start. They first study what experienced players actually do. (The optimizing team had discussed this option, but dismissed it because the visual measurements and computations players are assumed to perform are unobservable and unconscious; thus, observing and interviewing players would mean wasting time. Have you ever interviewed a soccer player?) Based on these observations, the heuristic team programs the robot not to move during the first half second or so but to make a crude estimate of whether the ball is coming down in front of or behind it, and then start running in this direction while fixating its eye on the ball. The heuristic the robot uses is to adjust its running speed so that the angle of gaze — the angle between the eye and the ball — remains constant (or within a certain range; see McLeod and Dienes 1996). By using this simple gaze heuristic, the robot will catch the ball while running. Note that this boundedly rational robot pays attention to only one cue, the angle of gaze, and does not attempt to acquire information concerning wind, spin, or the myriad of other causal variables, nor perform complex computations on these estimates. Note also that the gaze heuristic does not allow the robot to compute the point where the ball will land, run there, and wait for the ball. However, the robot does not need to make this difficult calculation; it will be there where the ball lands — just as actual players do not first calculate the landing point and then run there and wait for the ball. They catch the ball while running.

This thought experiment can illustrate several more general points. First, contrary to conventional wisdom, limitations of knowledge and computational capability need *not* be a disadvantage. The heuristic tools of humans, animals, and institutions can be simple, but nevertheless effective in a given environment. The optimizing robot that needs a complete representation of the environment (some AI researchers have fed their programs more than a million facts to approximate this ideal) and bets on massive computation, may never finish its analysis before the ball has hit the ground. Simplicity, by contrast, can enable fast, frugal, and accurate decisions. Second, a simple heuristic can exploit a regularity in the environment. In the present case, the regularity is that a constant angle of gaze will cause a collision between the ball and the player. Third, boundedly rational heuristics are, to some degree, domain-specific rather than universal strategies. These heuristics are middle-ranged, that is, they work in a class of situations (e.g., pilots are taught a similar heuristic to avoid collisions with other planes), but they are not general-purpose tools such as the ideal of an all-purpose optimization calculus. What we call the "adaptive toolbox" contains a number of these middle-range tools, not a single hammer for all purposes.

MODELS OF BOUNDED RATIONALITY

We mentioned at the beginning that, so far, there is no complete theory of bounded rationality. Nevertheless, we can specify three classes of processes that models of bounded rationality typically specify:

1. *Simple search rules*. The process of search is modeled on step-by-step procedures, where a piece of information is acquired, or an adjustment is made (such as to increase running speed to keep the angle of gaze constant), and then the process is repeated until it is stopped.

2. *Simple stopping rules*. Search is terminated by simple stopping rules, such as to choose the first object that satisfies an aspiration level. The stopping rule can change as a consequence of the length of search or other information, as in aspiration adaptation theory (Selten 1998). Simple stopping rules do not involve optimization calculations, such as computations of utilities and probabilities to determine the optimal stopping point.

3. *Simple decision rules*. After search is stopped and a limited amount of information has been acquired, a simple decision rule is applied, like choosing the object that is favored by the most important reason — rather than trying to compute the optimal weights for all reasons, and integrating these reasons in a linear or nonlinear fashion, as is done in computing a Bayesian solution.

The process of search distinguishes two classes of models of bounded rationality: those that search for alternatives (e.g., aspiration level theories such as satisficing, see Chapters 2 and 4), and those that search for cues (e.g., fast and frugal heuristics, see Chapters 3, 4, and 9). The chapters in this book describe and discuss models of both kinds in detail. Here, we will address the four questions that, in our opinion, pose a challenge for research on bounded rationality and around which this book is organized.

FOUR BIG QUESTIONS

The goal of this book is to promote bounded rationality as the key to understanding how actual people make decisions without calculating utilities and probabilities — that is, without optimizing.

1.   Is There Evidence for an Adaptive Toolbox?

As mentioned above, models of bounded rationality consist of simple step-by-step rules that function well under the constraints of limited search, knowledge, and time — whether or not an optimal procedure is available. The repertoire of these rules or heuristics, available to a species at a given point in its evolution is called its "adaptive toolbox." The concept of an adaptive toolbox, as we see it, has the following characteristics: First, it refers to a collection of rules or heuristics rather than to a general-purpose decision-making algorithm (as was envisioned in Leibniz's dream of a universal calculus or in versions of subjective expected utility theory). Second, these heuristics are fast, frugal, and computationally cheap rather than consistent, coherent, and general. Third, these heuristics are adapted to particular environments, past or present, physical or social. This "ecological rationality"— the match between the structure of a heuristic and the structure of an environment — allows for the possibility that heuristics can be fast, frugal, and accurate all at the same time by exploiting the structure of information in natural environments (Gigerenzer et al. 1999). Fourth, the bundle of heuristics in the adaptive toolbox is orchestrated by some mechanism reflecting the importance of conflicting motivations and goals. This mechanism is not yet well understood.

2. Why and When Do Simple Heuristics Work?

Bounded rationality is sometimes interpreted as suboptimal or even irrational in comparison with nonbounded rationality. However, evidence exists showing that fast and frugal rules can be about as accurate as complex statistical models (e.g., multiple regression, Bayesian networks), while demanding less information and computational power (e.g., Martignon and Laskey 1999). One reason simple heuristics work is that they can exploit structures of information in the environment. That is, their rationality is a form of ecological rationality, rather than of consistency and coherence. A second reason is the robustness of simple strategies compared to models with large numbers of parameters, which risk overfitting. Third, there are real-world situations involving multiple goals (e.g., accuracy, speed, frugality, consistency, accountability) that have no known common denominator, which poses serious problems to optimization, but can be handled by models of bounded rationality (e.g., Chapter 2).

3. What Role Do Emotions and Other Noncognitive Factors Play in Bounded Rationality?

Emotions are often seen as obstacles to rationality. However, emotions like disgust or parental love can provide effective stopping rules for search and a means for limiting search spaces. In particular, for important adaptive problems such as food avoidance, an emotion of disgust, which may be acquired through observation of conspecifics, can be more effective than cognitive decision making. Similarly, in social species, imitation and social learning can be seen as mechanisms that enable fast learning and obviate the need for individual calculations of expected utilities. For instance, a monkey may be prepared to acquire a fear of snakes the moment it sees another conspecific exhibit signs of fear in the presence of a snake (one-trial learning), or a child may make choices by imitating parents and peers.

Thus, many decisions seem to be made on the basis of factors other than cognitive ones, that is, factors other than estimations of probabilities, gains, costs, and the like. In general, the questions are: What noncognitive factors allow humans and animals to make fast and accurate decisions and to learn more efficiently than from mere experience? In what situations are noncognitive factors indispensable for adaptive decision making?

4.   What Is the Role of Culture in Bounded Rationality?

Models of bounded rationality have been focused not only on cognitive factors but also on individual decision making. However, just as emotions can lead to sensible decisions and commitments, so can social norms and institutions. Social norms can be seen as fast and frugal behavioral mechanisms that dispense with individual cost-benefit computations and decision making. For instance, culture (as a system of values and beliefs) can help actual humans diminish the problem of combinatorial explosion and the related problem of how to make an infinite number of possible decisions in real time, which has tormented attempts at building intelligent machines and robots. Cultural systems of belief need not be "correct" to work. For instance, navigational systems were successful long before our present-day astronomical knowledge was available, and they worked often on the basis of false cultural beliefs about the movement of the earth and heavenly bodies (Hutchins 1995). The point is that humans do not need to wait until all knowledge is acquired and all truth is known (which probably will never be the case). Adaptive solutions can be found with little knowledge; the price for this is that they are not general, but do work in a specific environment, culture, or time.

INTERDISCIPLINARITY

Bounded rationality is a genuinely interdisciplinary topic: its subject matter is the proximal mechanisms (the heuristics) that animals, humans, institutions, and artificial agents use to achieve their goals. The common denominator is that decisions need to be made with limited time, knowledge, and other resources, and in a world that is uncertain and changing. Thus, the framework of bounded rationality — the building blocks of heuristics; the notion of ecological rationality; the cultural acceleration of learning by social norms and imitation — may help to integrate fields that, so far, have been dissociated and did not access relevant knowledge outside their disciplines.

The lack of information flow between disciplines can hardly be underestimated. A brilliant example is the sunk cost fallacy (e.g., an agent has a choice to invest either in A or B, where B is the more promising option; however, because the agent had previously invested in A but not in B, he chooses A). Hundreds of papers were written in economics and psychology on the sunk cost fallacy, and hundreds of papers were written in evolutionary biology (by some of the most eminent biologists) on the Concorde fallacy — which is the same fallacy. There is not a single cross reference in these hundreds of papers, nor any awareness that both fields came to opposite conclusions: in economics and psychology, it is taken for granted that humans often commit the sunk cost fallacy, in animal biology, no conclusive evidence has been found that a single animal species would commit the sunk cost fallacy (Arkes and Ayton 1999). Bounded rationality and the study of the adaptive toolbox may help to shift discipline-oriented research toward more problem-focused research.

Optimization is an attractive fiction; it is mathematically elegant, and one can draw on a well-developed calculus. Compared to the beauty of optimization, the actual proximal mechanisms of humans and animals resemble the tools of a backwoods mechanic. The pleasing ideal of a universal calculus may have distracted researchers in many fields from exploring the contents of the adaptive toolbox. However, there is also another sense of beauty: the aesthetics of simplicity. There is a sense of wonder in how simplicity can produce robustness and accuracy in an overwhelmingly complex world. The gaze heuristic, the adaptation of aspiration levels, Tit-for-Tat, the recognition heuristic, Take the Best, and many other smart heuristics described in this book can produce this sense of wonder.

REFERENCES

Arkes, H.R., and P. Ayton. 1999. The sunk cost and Concorde effects: Are humans less rational than lower animals? *Psych. Bull.* **125**:591–600.

Arrow, K.J. 1986. Rationality of self and others in an economic system. *J. Business* **59**:S385–S399.

Bernoulli, D. 1738/1954. Specimen theoriae novae de mensura sortis. *Commentarii academiae scientarum imperialis Petropolitanae* **5**:175–192. (Engl. transl. by L. Sommer, Exposition of a new theory on the measurement of risk. *Econometrica* **22**:23–26.)

Birnbaum, M.H. 1983. Base rates in Bayesian inference: Signal detection analysis of the cab problem. *Am. J. Psych.* **96**:85–94.

Daston, L.J. 1988. Classical Probability in the Enlightenment. Princeton, NJ: Princeton Univ. Press.

Gigerenzer, G., and U. Hoffrage. 1995. How to improve Bayesian reasoning without instructions. Frequency formats. *Psych. Rev.* **102**:684–704.

Gigerenzer, G., and D.J. Murray. 1987. Cognition as Intuitive Statistics. Hillsdale, NJ: Erlbaum.

Gigerenzer, G., Z. Swijtink, T. Porter, L. Daston, J. Beatty, and L. Krüger. 1989. The Empire of Chance. How Probability Changed Science and Everyday Life. Cambridge: Cambridge Univ. Press.

Gigerenzer, G., P.M. Todd, and the ABC Research Group. 1999. Simple Heuristics That Make Us Smart. New York: Oxford Univ. Press.

Hacking, I. 1975. The Emergence of Probability. Cambridge: Cambridge Univ. Press.

Hutchins, E. 1995. Cognition in the Wild. Cambridge, MA: MIT Press.

Jolls, C., C.S. Sunstein, and R. Thaler. 1998. A behavioral approach to law and economics. *Stanford Law Rev.* **50**:1471–1550.

Kahneman, D., P. Slovic, and A. Tversky, eds. 1982. Judgment under Uncertainty: Heuristics and Biases. Cambridge: Cambridge Univ. Press.

Locke, John. 1690/1959. An Essay Concerning Human Understanding, ed. Alexander Campbell Fraser. New York: Dover.

Martignon, L., and K.B. Laskey. 1999. Bayesian benchmarks for fast and frugal heuristics. In: Simple Heuristics That Make Us Smart, G. Gigerenzer, P.M. Todd, and the ABC Research Group, pp. 169–188. New York: Oxford Univ. Press.

McLeod, P., and Z. Dienes. 1996. Do fielders know where to go to catch the ball or only how to get there? *J. Exp. Psych.: Human Percep. Perf.* **22**:531–543.

Mueser, P.R., N. Cowan, and K.T. Mueser. 1999. A generalized signal detection model to predict rational variation in base rate use. *Cognition* **69**:267–312.

Sargent, T.J. 1993. Bounded Rationality in Macroeconomics. Oxford: Oxford Univ. Press.

Sauermann, H., and R. Selten. 1962. Anpassungstheorie der Unternehmung. *Z. ges. Staatswiss.* **118**:577–597.

Selten, R. 1998. Aspiration adaptation theory. *J. Math. Psychol.* **42**:191–214.

Simon, H.A. 1956. Rational choice and the structure of environments. *Psych. Rev.* **63**:129–138.

Stigler, G.J. 1961. The economics of information. *J. Pol. Econ.* **69**:213–225.

Thaler, R.H. 1991. Quasi Rational Economics. New York: Russell Sage.

2

What Is Bounded Rationality?

Reinhard Selten

Juridicum, University of Bonn, Adenauerallee 24–42, 53113 Bonn, Germany

ABSTRACT

This chapter discusses the concept of bounded rationality as it is understood in the tradition of H.A. Simon. Fundamental problems and theoretical issues are presented, with special emphasis on aspiration adaptation theory. Further remarks concern basic modes of decision behavior (like learning and expectation formation), reasoning, and the connection between bounded rationality and motivation.

INTRODUCTION

Modern mainstream economic theory is largely based on an unrealistic picture of human decision making. Economic agents are portrayed as fully rational Bayesian maximizers of subjective utility. This view of economics is not based on empirical evidence, but rather on the simultaneous axiomization of utility and subjective probability. In the fundamental book of Savage (1954), the axioms are consistency requirements on actions, where actions are defined as mappings from states of the world to consequences. One can only admire the imposing structure built by Savage. It has a strong intellectual appeal as a concept of ideal rationality. However, it is wrong to assume that human beings conform to this ideal.

Origins

At about the same time that Savage published his book, H.A. Simon created the beginnings of a theory of bounded rationality (Simon 1957). He described decision making as a search process guided by aspiration levels. An aspiration level is a value of a goal variable that must be reached or surpassed by a satisfactory decision alternative. In the context of the theory of the firm, one may think of goal variables like profit and market shares.

Decision alternatives are not given but found, one after the other, in a search process. In the simplest case, the search process goes on until a satisfactory alternative is found that reaches or surpasses the aspiration levels on the goal variables, and then this alternative is taken. Simon coined the word "satisficing" for this process.

Often, satisficing is seen as the essence of Simon's approach. However, there is more to it than just satisficing. Aspiration levels are not permanently fixed but are rather dynamically adjusted to the situation. They are raised if it is easy to find satisfactory alternatives, and lowered if satisfactory alternatives are hard to acquire. This adaptation of aspiration levels is a central idea in Simon's early writings on bounded rationality.

Three features characterize Simon's original view of bounded rationality: search for alternatives, satisficing, and aspiration adaptation.

Aim of This Essay

It is difficult to gain an overview of the literature on bounded rationality accumulated since Simon's seminal work, and no attempts in this direction will be made here. Instead, I discuss only a few selected topics with the aim of conveying insights into the essential features of bounded rationality.

I approach the subject matter from the point of view of economic theory. I am convinced of the necessity of reconstructing microeconomics on the basis of a more realistic picture of economic decision making. Moreover, I think that there are strong reasons for modeling boundedly rational economic behavior as nonoptimizing, and the material presented here reflects this conviction. More about the nonoptimizing character of boundedly rational decision making will be said in the remaining sections of the introduction.

A comprehensive, coherent theory of bounded rationality is not available. This is a task for the future. At the moment we must be content with models of limited scope.

Bounds of Rationality

Full rationality requires unlimited cognitive capabilities. Fully rational man is a mythical hero who knows the solutions to all mathematical problems and can immediately perform all computations, regardless of how difficult they are. Human beings are in reality very different. Their cognitive capabilities are quite limited. For this reason alone, the decision-making behavior of human beings cannot conform to the ideal of full rationality.

It could be the case that, in spite of obvious cognitive limitations, the behavior of human beings is approximately described by the theory of full rationality. Confidence in this conjecture of approximate validity explains the tenacity with which many economists stick to the assumption of Bayesian maximization of subjectively expected utility. However, there is overwhelming experimental evidence for substantial deviations from Bayesian rationality (Kahneman et al. 1982): people do not obey Bayes's rule, their probability judgments fail to satisfy basic requirements like monotonicity with respect to set inclusion, and they do not have consistent preferences, even in situations involving no risk or uncertainty. (For a more detailed discussion, see Selten 1991.)

The cognitive bounds of rationality are not the only ones. A decision maker may think that a choice is the only rational one (e.g., to stop smoking) but nevertheless not take it. Conclusions reached by rational deliberations may be overridden by strong emotional impulses. The lack of complete control over behavior is not due to cognitive bounds of behavior but rather to motivational ones.

Concept

In this chapter, the use of the term *bounded rationality* follows the tradition of H.A. Simon. It refers to the rational principles that underlie nonoptimizing adaptive behavior of real people. However, bounded rationality cannot be precisely defined. It is a problem that needs to be explored. Nevertheless, to some extent it is possible to say what it is *not*.

Bounded rationality is not irrationality. A sharp distinction should be made here. The theory of bounded rationality does not try to explain trust in lucky numbers or abnormal behavior of mentally ill people. In such cases, one may speak of irrationality. However, behavior should not be called irrational simply because it fails to conform to norms of full rationality. A decision maker who is guided by aspiration adaptation rather than utility maximization may be perfectly rational in the sense of everyday language use.

Sometimes the term bounded rationality is used in connection with theories about optimization under some cognitive bounds. An example of this is the game theoretic analysis of supergames under constraints on the operating memory (Aumann and Sorin 1989). The task the players have to solve is much more complicated with these constraints than without them. The paper by Aumann and Sorin is a remarkable piece of work, but it is not a contribution to the theory of bounded rationality. The same must be said about the recent book on "bounded rationality macroeconomics" (Sargent 1993). There, the assumption of rational expectations is replaced by least square learning, but otherwise an optimization approach is taken without any regard to cognitive bounds of rationality. Here, too, we see a highly interesting theoretical exercise that is, however, far from adequate as a theory of boundedly rational behavior.

Subjective expected utility maximization modified by some isolated cognitive constraints does not lead to a realistic description of boundedly rational decision making in a complex environment. Moreover, there are reasons to believe that an optimization approach fails to be feasible in many situations in which not only an optimal solution must be found but also a method of how to find it. More will be said about this in the next section.

Boundedly rational decision making necessarily involves nonoptimizing procedures. This is a central feature of the concept of bounded rationality proposed here. Other features will become clear in later parts of this chapter.

Much of human behavior is automatized in the sense that it is not connected to any conscious deliberation. In the process of walking, one does not decide after each step which leg to move next and by how much. Such automatized routines can be interrupted and modified by decisions, but while they are executed they do not require any decision making. They may be genetically preprogrammed (e.g., involuntary body activities) or they may be the result of learning. Somebody who begins to learn to drive a car must pay conscious attention to much detail, which later becomes automatic.

One might want to distinguish between bounded rationality and automatic routine; however, it is difficult to do this. Conscious attention is not a good criterion. Even thinking is based on automatized routine. We may decide what to think about, but not what to think. The results of thinking become conscious, but most of the procedure of thinking remains unconscious and not even accessible to introspection. Obviously the structure of these hidden processes is important to a theory of bounded rationality.

Reinforcement learning models have a long tradition in psychology (Bush and Mosteller 1955) and have recently become popular in research on experimental games (Roth and Erev 1995; Erev and Roth 1998). These models describe automatized routine behavior. Reinforcement learning occurs in human beings as well as animals of relatively low complexity, and one may therefore hesitate to call it even boundedly rational. However, a theory of bounded rationality cannot avoid this basic mode of behavior (see section on Reinforcement Learning).

The concept of bounded rationality has its roots in H.A. Simon's attempt to construct a more realistic theory of human economic decision making. Such a theory cannot cover the whole area of cognitive psychology. The emphasis must be on decision making. Learning in decision situations and reasoning supporting decisions belong to the subject matter, but visual perception and recognition, a marvelously powerful and complex cognitive process, seems to be far from it.

Undoubtedly, biological and cultural evolution as well as the acquistion of motivational dispositions in ontogenetic development are important influences on the structure and content of decision behavior. However, boundedly rational decision making happens on a much smaller time scale. For the purpose of examining decision processes, the results of biological and cultural evolution and ontogenetic development can be taken as given. The emphasis on decision making within the bounds of human rationality is perhaps more important for the concept of bounded rationality than the boundaries of its applicability.

Impossibility of Unfamiliar Optimization When Decision Time Is Scarce

Imagine a decision maker who has to solve an optimization problem in order to maximize utility over a set of decision alternatives. Assume that decision time is scarce in the sense that there is a deadline for choosing one of the alternatives. The decision maker has to do his best within the available time.

It is useful to distinguish between familiar and unfamiliar problems of this kind. A problem is familiar if the decision maker knows the optimal way to attack it, i.e., knows what to do through prior training or mathematical investigation, or perhaps the problem is so simple that a suitable method immediately suggests itself.

In the case of an unfamiliar problem, the decision maker must devise a method for finding the alternative to be chosen before it can be applied. This leads to two levels of decision-making activities which both take time:

Level 1: Finding the alternative to be chosen.
Level 2: Finding a method for Level 1.

What is the optimal approach to the problem of Level 2? One can hardly imagine that this problem is familiar. Presumably a decision maker who does not immediately know what to do on Level 1 will also not be familiar with the task of Level 2. Therefore, some time must be spent to find an optimal method for solving the task of Level 2. Thus we arrive at Level 3.

It is clear that in this way we obtain an infinite sequence of levels $k = 2, 3, \ldots$ provided that finding an optimal method for Level k continues to be unfamiliar for every k.

Level k: Finding a method for Level $k - 1$.

It is reasonable to assume that there is a positive minimum time which is required for the decision-making activities at each Level k. Obviously this has the consequence that an optimization approach is not feasible when decision time is scarce.

Admittedly, the reasoning that has led to the impossibility conclusion is not based on a precise mathematical framework and therefore cannot claim the rigor of a formal proof. Nevertheless it strongly suggests that a truly optimizing approach to unfamiliar decision problems with constrained decision time is not feasible.

Trying to optimize in such situations is like trying to build a computer that must be used in order to determine its own design — an attempt doomed to fail. The activity of optimizing cannot optimize its own procedure.

The impossibility of unfamiliar optimization, when decision time is scarce, would not be of great importance if most optimization problems faced by real people were familiar to them in the strict sense explained above. It is clear that the opposite is true.

ASPIRATION ADAPTATION THEORY

There are reasons to believe that unfamiliar optimization is impossible within the cognitive bounds of rationality, when decision time is scarce. This raises the following question: How can we model the nonoptimizing behavior of boundedly rational economic agents? Earlier, I was involved in an attempt to answer this question (Sauermann and Selten 1962). Only recently has this *aspiration adaptation theory* been made available in English (Selten 1998a). This sign of a continued interest in the theory has encouraged me to present a condensed exposition here. Experiences with a course on bounded rationality suggest that aspiration adaptation theory is a good starting point for conveying insights into the problem area and the modeling possibilities.

Aspiration adaptation theory cannot claim to be an empirically validated description of decision-making behavior. Experimental evidence points to a need of extensions and modifications. However, the basic ideas have been fruitful in experimentation (e.g., in the development of descriptive theories of two-person bargaining [Tietz and Weber 1972; Tietz 1976]) and may continue to be valuable in the future.

The Aspiration Scheme

One of the features of aspiration adaptation theory is that it models decision making as a multi-goal problem without aggregation of the goals into a complete preference order over all decision alternatives. The decision maker has a number of real-valued goal variables. For each goal variable, more is better. This is a convenient modeling convention. If, for example, one of the goals is to keep costs low, then this can be modeled by negative costs as a goal variable. Consider two different vectors of values for the goal variables. If one of them has a higher or equal value for each goal variable, then this vector is preferred to the other; however, if this is not the case, then there is no comparability. We refer to this feature as *goal incomparability.*

In aspiration adaptation theory, an *aspiration level* is a vector of values for the goal variables. These values, the *partial aspiration levels*, vary in discrete steps. The possible aspiration levels form a grid in the space of the goal variables. We refer to it as the *aspiration grid*. Aspiration adaptation takes the form of a sequence of *adjustment steps*. An adjustment step shifts the current aspiration level to a neighboring point on the aspiration grid by a change of only one goal variable. An *upward* adjustment step is an increase and a *downward* adjustment step is a decrease of a goal variable.

Aspiration adaptation takes the form of a sequence of adjustment steps. Upward adjustment steps are governed by an *urgency order,* a ranking of the goal variables without ties. Downward adaptations decrease a *retreat variable*. The retreat variable is not necessarily the least urgent one. Urgency order and retreat variable may depend on the grid point. The aspiration grid, together with the assignment of an urgency order and a retreat variable to every grid point, forms an *aspiration scheme.*

In aspiration adaptation theory, the aspiration scheme takes the place of the preference order in the usual decision theory. Goal incomparability is not removed. Urgency order and retreat variable do not express global preferences over decision alternatives but *local procedural preferences* over adjustment steps. There is an asymmetry between upward adjustment steps and downward adjustment steps. One needs an urgency order to select among different feasible upward adjustment steps, but one can always choose the least painful downward adjustment and continue the adaptation process from there.

Aspiration adaptation theory offers a coherent modeling approach to bounded rationality. It provides a first orientation in the problem area. Therefore, a condensed exposition will be presented in this and the following sections with some minor extensions of previously published material.

As we have seen, aspiration adaptation models two features that seem to be important ingredients of bounded rationality: *goal incomparability* and *local procedural preferences.*

Selection of One of Many Given Alternatives

The exposition of aspiration adaptation theory given here restricts itself to the case of a *borderless* aspiration grid without maximal or minimal values for partial aspiration levels. This avoids tedious detail without loss of important aspects of the theory.

Imagine a decision maker who has to select one of a finite number of alternatives with specified values for all goal variables. The vector of these values for an alternative is called its *goal vector.* The aspiration levels, satisfied by the goal vector of at least one alternative, are called *feasible.* The decision maker starts with a *previous aspiration level* taken over from the past. The selection is made by an *adaptation process* which generates a sequence of *intermediate aspiration levels* with the initial aspiration level as the first one and a *new aspiration level* as the last one. At the end, a choice is made that satisfies the new aspiration level.

An upward adjustment step is *feasible* if it leads to a feasible aspiration level. The *most urgent* feasible upward adjustment step among all feasible ones is the one that raises the most urgent goal variable. The adaptation process is governed by three adaptation rules:

1. *Downward rule*: If an intermediate aspiration level is not feasible, the downward adjustment step is taken which lowers the partial aspiration level of the retreat variable.
2. *Upward rule*: If an intermediate aspiration level is feasible and an upward adjustment step is feasible, then the most urgent feasible upward adjustment step is taken.
3. *End rule*: If an intermediate aspiration level is feasible and no upward adjustment step is feasible, then this aspiration level is the new one.

The process may involve a first phase of downward adjustment steps until a feasible aspiration level is reached followed by a second phase of upward adjustments leading to the new aspiration level.

Search for Alternatives with Integrated Decisions on Decision Resources

Imagine a decision maker engaged in a sequential search for decision alternatives. The search generates a sequence of alternatives with specified goal vectors. Some of the goal variables may be stocks of decision resources like *decision cost resources* out of which decision costs must be paid or *decision time reserves*, i.e., time saved compared to maximum decision time. These *decision resource stocks* diminish with search.

The decision maker knows the first alternative, the *default alternative*, before she has the opportunity to start searching, and she can stop searching at any time. The search may also be stopped exogenously by the end of decision time. The decision maker starts with an *initial aspiration level*. Consider the situation after k alternatives have been found, including the default alternative. For $k = 1$, the *previous aspiration level* is the initial one. An *adaptation process* running through intermediate aspiration levels, like the one mentioned above, leads to a *new aspiration level* that becomes the next *previous aspiration level*.

Dissimilar to the previous section, the term "feasible" will now be used in a dynamic sense: an aspiration level is *feasible* if it is satisfied by the goal vector of at least one alternative which has already been found. An aspiration level that is not feasible at the moment is *potentially feasible*, if it is possible for it to become feasible through further searching and *recognizably infeasible* otherwise. To clarify this classification into three nonoverlapping categories, I must explain what is meant by "possible" in this context. It is assumed that everything is possible as far as goal variables other than decision resource stocks are concerned. However, decision resource stocks are diminished by search. As soon as some of them become so low that they exclude further search at the current aspiration level, this aspiration level becomes recognizably infeasible.

An upward adjustment step is *permissible* if it leads from a feasible aspiration level to another feasible one or to a potentially feasible one. The definition of the *most urgent* permissible upward adjustment step is analogous to that of the most urgent feasible upward adjustment step in the preceding section. We now define *permissible* aspiration levels by the following three conditions:

1. A feasible aspiration level is permissible.
2. A potentially feasible aspiration level is permissible if it is the previous aspiration level or if it can be reached by a permissible upward adjustment step.
3. Aspiration levels other than those permissible by Pts. 1 or 2 are not permissible.

In this section, the permissible aspiration levels have the same role as the feasible ones in the preceding section. Aspiration adaptation is analogous with the sole difference that everywhere in the three adaptation rules, "feasible" has to be replaced by "permissible." The following *continuation rule* determines whether search is continued or not.

Continuation rule: If the new aspiration level is potentially feasible, then search is continued; otherwise search ends with the new aspiration level as the *final aspiration level* and an alternative is chosen whose goal vector satifies this final aspiration level.

Since permissible aspiration levels are either potentially feasible or feasible the final aspiration level is feasible.

The definition of permissibility embodies a *principle of cautious optimism*. Only recognizable infeasibility is a reason to lower the previous aspiration level, not just lack of feasibility. As long as an aspiration level is potentially feasible, one can hope to satisfy it through further search. However, upward adjustment should not lead more than one step away from what is feasible now. Therefore, upward adjustment steps from potentially feasible aspiration levels are not permissible. Caution is thereby imposed on the optimism necessary for search.

The model of this section shows how aspiration adaptation theory simultaneously deals with the choice of a decision alternative and decisions on decision resources. We refer to this feature as *integrated decisions on decision resources*. This feature seems to be a necessary ingredient of rational behavior within the cognitive bounds of human beings.

Aspiration Adaptation on the Basis of Qualitative Expectations

Boundedly rational decision makers do not necessarily form quantitative expectations. Instead, they may rely on qualitative expectations connected to decision alternatives. This means that the decision maker has expectations about the direction of change compared with the present state of affairs. A decision alternative may be expected to raise a goal variable, or to lower it, or to have a negligible influence on it. We use the symbols "+," "–," and "0" to represent these three possibilities formally. In this way, aspiration adaptation theory describes the qualitative expectations connected to a decision alternative by a *qualitative goal vector* with +, –, or 0 as possible entries.

In a simple model, called the "routine model," a firm makes period-by-period decisions on a number of *instrument variables*, like price, production, advertising, etc. The decision alternatives are a finite number of possibilities of change, e.g., "increase price by 5% and advertising by 10%." For each alternative, the firm has a qualitative expectation in the form of a qualitative goal vector.

We refer to the goal vector realized in the last period as the *realization*. One of the alternatives is *doing nothing*, i.e., leaving the instrument variables at their last period's values. For this alternative a quantitative expectation is formed, namely the realization. The decision maker expects that nothing is to be changed if nothing is done. The realized aspiration level is the highest aspiration level (highest in each component) that is satisfied by the realization.

The decision maker constructs an *expected feasible aspiration level* for each alternative. The realized aspiration level is the expected feasible aspiration level for doing nothing. For other alternatives, four *expectation rules* determine the *expected feasible aspiration level* by relating its partial aspiration level for a goal variable to the corresponding entry of the qualitative goal vector:

1. If the entry is +, then the partial aspiration level is one step above that of the realized aspiration level.
2. If the entry is − and the value of the goal variable in the realization is above that in the realized aspiration level, then the partial aspiration level is that of the realized aspiration level.
3. If the entry is − and the value of the goal variable in the realization is equal to that in the realized aspiration level, then the partial aspiration level is one step below that of the realized aspiration level.
4. If the entry is 0, then the partial aspiration level is that of the realized aspiration level.

Aspiration adaptation follows after the construction of the expected feasible aspiration levels. Starting with the previous aspiration level taken over from the last period, the procedure for selecting one alternative out of many is applied for this purpose (see section on Selection of One of Many Given Alternatives) with the only difference being that now the expected feasible aspiration levels take the place of the feasible ones. This yields a new aspiration level for the current period. An alternative to this expected feasible aspiration level is chosen. If there are several such alternatives, the choice is narrowed by the successive application of two criteria:

1. Minimization of the number of entries "−" in the qualitative goal vector of the alternative.
2. Maximization of the number of entries "+" in the qualitative goal vector of the alternative.

In the preceding section, upward adjustment steps from feasible aspiration levels to potentially feasible ones were modeled as permissible. The expected feasible aspiration levels are similar to the potentially feasible aspiration levels reached in this way. One can hope that the chosen alternative will result in a new realization that satisfies its expected feasible aspiration level, but one cannot count on this. Choosing an alternative on this basis of qualitative expectations requires the optimism expressed by expectation rules 1 and 2. The partial aspiration levels of expected feasible aspiration levels are at most one step away from the realized ones. This adds an element of caution.

Cautious optimism seems to be a necessary feature of boundedly rational behavior where there is ignorance about the consequences of decisions. This includes a costly search for new alternatives as well as situations in which alternatives have to be tried out on the basis of qualitative expectations.

Decision making largely based on only qualitative information seems to be an important mode of boundedly rational behavior. Aspiration adaptation theory offers a modeling approach for this.

Risk-related Goal Variables

Everyday experience suggests that risky decisions are rarely based on explicit probability judgments. In some special contexts, probability estimates are found on the basis of frequency information. Life insurance companies use mortuary tables for this purpose. However, their customers usually do not even think of the relevant probabilities. Thus a buyer of life insurance may decide that he wants to be insured for an amount that enables his family to survive for three years if this can be done for a premium not higher than 5% of his income. This involves a two-dimensional aspiration level with premium and amount as goal variables, but no probability estimates.

In some cases, probability judgments are also formed on the basis of a priori considerations. However, this seems to be restricted to very special contexts like that of a gambling house. In practical business and daily life there is usually no opportunity for such a priori judgments.

The risk of a catastrophe, such as bankruptcy, can be limited by paying attention to goal variables with the property that the greater the value of this variable, the smaller the risk . We call such goal variables *risk related*. Thus a firm may use a liquidity ratio (liquid assets as a percentage of obligations) as a risk-related goal variable.

An interesting example of a risk-related goal variable is the safety margin applied in engineering computations. On static computations for buildings or bridges one requires that the structure withstands k times the maximal forces expected in use, where k is an integer like 2 or 3. The computations are based on a deterministic model. Nevertheless, the risk of breakdown can be limited by a partial aspiration level on k.

Safety margins may be imposed by law. In this case they are the result of collective rather than individual aspiration adaptation.

Features of Bounded Rationality Modeled by Aspiration Adaptation Theory

The decision behavior modeled by aspiration adaptation theory has some features that seem to be of significance for the description of bounded rationality independently of modeling details. These features are listed below:

1. goal incomparability,

2. local procedural preferences,
3. integrated decisions on decision resources,
4. decisions based on qualitative expectations,
5. cautious optimism in the search for alternatives and the use of qualitative expectations,
6. risk-related goal variables.

Aspiration adaptation theory models decision making in a multi-goal frame-work with goal incomparability and local procedural preferences. These properties are embodied in the aspiration scheme. Integrated decisions on decision resources are modeled by aspiration adaptation involving decision resource stocks as goal variables. Aspiration adaptation theory also describes the use of qualitative expectations on the directions of change as the basis of a cautiously optimistic construction of expected feasible goal vectors for alternatives and aspiration adaptation among them. Search for alternatives is also modeled as cautiously optimistic. Risk-related goal variables explain how risks can be limited without probability judgments.

Questions Not Answered by Aspiration Adaptation Theory

Aspiration adaptation theory is a coherent approach to rational decision making; however, it has its weaknesses. Extensions and modifications are necessary. Moreover, the way in which aspiration adaptation is modeled could be brought into closer agreement with the behavioral theory of the firm (Cyert and March 1963). This mainly concerns aspiration adaptation as an organizational process, a problem area intentionally avoided here in order to concentrate attention on features of bounded rationality already found on the individual level.

It is possible that experimental research will lead to a fundamentally different theory of nonoptimizing decision making. However, it seems to be more likely that aspiration adaptation in a multi-goal framework will have to be a part of a comprehensive theory of boundedly rational decision making, even if the modeling details are different. Aspiration adaptation theory suffers from its neglect of aspects of boundedly rational behavior, which often are indispensible for the explanation of experimental results. These aspects are relevant for a number of questions not answered by aspiration adaptation theory, at least not in its present form.

Decision makers do not always know what they want. In new situations, goals must be formed. Where does the aspiration scheme come from? Often only a finite number of decision alternatives is considered, even if in principle an infinite number are available. How is this selection made? If quantitative or qualitative expectations about goal variables need to be formed, how is this done? Aspiration adaptation theory leaves processes of *goal formation*, *construction of alternatives*, and *expectation formation* largely unmodeled.

SOME BASIC MODES OF CHOICE BEHAVIOR

Human decision making seems to involve a multitude of basic modes of choice behavior. One can think of them as forming an "adaptive toolbox" with many special instruments used for different purposes, alone or in combination with others. Probably we do not yet know more than a small fraction of the contents of this toolbox. Without any claim of completeness, the following sections will loosely describe examples of what is known. These examples are basic modes of choice behavior used for the performance of tasks of judgment, expectation formation, and learning. One approach to bounded rationality, the study of "fast and frugal heuristics" (Gigerenzer et al. 1999), will not be discussed here because it is described in detail elsewhere (see Gigerenzer, Todd, and Martignon, all this volume).

Prominence in the Decimal System

The theory of prominence in the decimal system is based on Albers and Albers (1983). Roughly speaking, it is a theory of the perception of degrees of roundness of numbers. Recently, Wulf Albers has developed a new version of the theory which is more powerful, but also more complex. In this chapter, it is not possible to describe even the old version in detail. Instead, I sketch a process of selecting a spontaneous response, which makes it understandable why such responses tend to be rounder numbers than randomly expected.

Consider a person who has to guess the number of inhabitants of Islamabad. The first step is the perception of a broad range in which the answer must be, say between zero and 20 million. Attention is then focused on the midpoint, 10 million, and the person ponders the question whether the number of inhabitants is higher or lower than 10 million. If the person feels that she cannot answer this question, then the process stops here and her response is 10 million.

Suppose that this person decides that the number is lower: this narrows the range to the numbers between zero and 10 million. Again, attention is focused on the midpoint, 5 million, and the person asks herself whether the number is lower or higher. If she cannot decide, 5 million is the spontaneous response. Suppose she thinks that the number is greater. In this situation, some people will focus on 7.5 million while others will focus on 7 or 8 million, since they perceive these as rounder. Suppose that she focuses on 7 million; she then decides that the number is smaller, considers the new midpoint, and ends up with a response of 6 million, since she feels that she is unable to judge whether the number of inhabitants is smaller or greater.

In this way it becomes understandable that direct numerical responses tend to be round: the rounder the number, the less is known about the subject matter. The question arises as to how judgments acquired by this process are made. Maybe these judgments are based on a procedure like "Take The Best," in which one criterion after the other is checked, e.g., whether the person knows the name, whether the town is a capital, etc. (Gigerenzer 1997). The first criterion that points in one direction decides the issue unless the criteria are exhausted and the process stops. Presumably, different criteria are used at different midpoints.

A much better elaborated theory about how rough estimates are made is the procedure known as "QuickEst" (Hertwig et al. 1999). Here, the estimates are restricted to a predetermined scale of prominent numbers. Each number on the scale is connected to a criterion. Beginning with the smallest number, one criterion after the other is examined until one of them leads to a negative answer. Then the process stops with the associated number on the scale as the estimate.

Expectation Formation

O. Becker and U. Leopold (1996) have developed an interesting experimentally based theory of expectation formation in an environment in which a subject predicts the next value of a univariate time series on the basis of past observations. In the experiments, the time series was generated by a stochastic second-order difference equation. The average forecasts of the subjects are well described by a surprisingly simple rule, which they call the "bounds and likelihood procedure." To explain this rule, we need some definitions and notations.

Let x_t be the value of the time series at period t and let f_{t+1} be the forecast for period $t + 1$. The average variation b_t is the average of all absolute changes $|x_j - x_{j-1}|$ for $j = 2, ..., t$. The average variation is an upper bound for the absolute value of the predicted change. This bound is modified by the likelihood h_t of the event that x_t will be a turning point. (h_t will be defined below.) Let M_t be the number of local maxima of the time series observed up to period t, and let m_t be the number of those local maxima among them which are smaller than or equal to x_t. Similarly, let N_t be the number of local minima up to period t, and let n_t be the number of those among them which are greater than or equal to x_t. The *likelihood*, h_t, is defined as follows:

$$h_t = \frac{1 + m_t}{2 + M_t} \quad \text{for } x_t > x_{t-1}, \tag{2.1}$$

$$h_t = \frac{1 + n_t}{2 + N_t} \quad \text{for } x_t < x_{t-1}. \tag{2.2}$$

The *bounds and likelihood procedure* specifies the following forecast:

$$f_{t+1} = x_t + b_t(1 - 2h_t) \ \text{sign} \ (x_t - x_{t-1}), \tag{2.3}$$

where sign $(x_t - x_{t-1})$ is +1, −1, and 0 for $x_{t+1} > x_t$, $x_{t+1} < x_t$, and $x_{t+1} = x_t$ respectively.

The more previous local maxima are surpassed by x_t, the less likely is a continuation of an increase. An analogous statement applies to the continuation of a decrease. This is the rationale of the procedure. It is very interesting to note that the variance of the best prediction based on an exact knowledge of the stochastic difference equation is 87% of the variance of the bounds and likelihood procedure. This shows that this procedure is surprisingly efficient, in spite of the fact that it is very different from, and much simpler than, the usual forecasting techniques. However, one must bear in mind that it describes average forecasts rather than individual behavior. Nevertheless, it suggests that the spontaneous response of individuals is also guided by the recent direction of the time series, by past average variation, and by comparisons of the present value with past local extrema.

Reinforcement Learning

In this chapter there is no room for a thorough discussion of reinforcement learning models. The *payoff sum model* has been very successful in experimental game research (Roth and Erev 1995). In the simplest version of this model, the probability of choosing an alternative is proportional to its *payoff sum*, defined as follows: Before period 1, the payoff sum is equal to a positive *initial value*. The payoff sum of an alternative is increased by the period payoff just obtained after a period in which the alternative has been chosen; otherwise it remains unchanged.

This model is applicable to situations in which payoffs are always nonnegative; however, modifications also cover the case that payoffs may be negative. The behavior described by the payoff sum model is characterized by *information parsimony* in the sense that it uses no other information than the feedback about payoffs. This is a remarkable property which makes this model applicable to situations in which the decision maker is ignorant about his environment.

Learning Direction Theory

Learning direction theory (Selten and Stoecker 1986; Selten and Buchta 1999) is another surprisingly successful approach to learning that is quite different from reinforcement theory. The basic idea can be illustrated through a simple example: Consider an archer who repeatedly tries to hit the trunk of a tree with a bow and arrow. After a miss he will have the tendency to aim more to the left if the arrow passed the trunk on the right-hand side and more to the right in the opposite case.

The example is not as trivial as it may seem to be. The archer is guided by a qualitative causal model of his environment. This model relates changes of the angle at which the bow is held to changes of the direction in which the arrow flies. After a miss he sees on which side of the trunk the arrow has passed. This feedback and the qualitative causal model enable the archer to draw a qualitative conclusion about what would have been better in the previous period. He can determine in which direction a better alternative could have been found.

The term *ex post rationality* refers to the analysis of what could have been done better, in contrast to *ex ante rationality* which reasons about future consequences of possible actions. Learning direction theory is based on *ex post* rationality. It requires reasoning, but only about the past, not about the future.

Learning direction theory can be applied to repeated decision tasks in which a parameter p_t has to be chosen in a sequence of periods $t = 1, ..., T$, provided that the decision maker has a qualitative causal model and receives feedback, which enables him to infer in which direction a better choice could have been found.

The theory predicts that the parameter tends to be changed in the direction indicated by the inference, if it is changed at all. This is a weak prediction which, however, has proved to be successful in about a dozen experimental studies (see Selten 1998a).

Learning direction theory differs from reinforcement learning by a property referred to as *improvement orientation*. It does not matter whether the choice of previous period resulted in a high or low payoff. What matters is the direction in which a better choice could have been found.

REASONING

Following Johnson-Laird (1983), I think of reasoning as being based on the inspection of mental models rather than something more akin to the use of a predicate calculus of formal logic. As we saw above, reasoning is a part of some basic modes of choice behavior, e.g., learning direction theory. Obviously it has a great influence on human decision making, even at a very basic level. In the following sections, some selected topics connected to reasoning will be examined, but admittedly not very closely.

Intuitive and Analytical Approaches to Decision Tasks

It is useful to distinguish between two kinds of approaches to a decision task. An *analytical approach* tries to base the decision on the structure of the problem, on the relationship between choice and outcome, and as far as possible on the use of numerical information for the calculation of a solution. In contrast, an *intuitive approach* is not based on an understanding of the task, but rather on its perceived similarity to other situations for which an appropriate behavior is known, which can be transferred to the problem. The term "appropriate" refers to what one does in such situations.

Analytical approaches are not necessarily superior to intuitive ones. They may be based on a false understanding of the situation or on faulty calculation. Intuitive approaches run the risk that the similarities, which seem to justify the transfer of behavior, are only superficial ones that hide crucial differences. However, in the case of a lack of understanding, an intuitive approach may be the only available one.

In some cases, the same experiment has been run with groups of students and with groups of professionals as subjects. The professionals had practical experience with similar tasks but their performance was worse than that of the students. This happened to professional wool buyers in sequential auctions (Burns 1985) and to dealers on financial markets (Abbink and Kuon 1998). In both cases there are reasons to suspect that the experimental situation did not really have the same structure as the real-life one and that the professionals wrongly transferred their practical behavior to the experiment. Since the students had no practical experience, they had to look more closely at the situation.

Undoubtedly, analytical approaches involve reasoning. Calculations must be based on some kind of mental model. This seems to be different for intuitive approaches. The perception of similarities may be a more basic process than reasoning.

Superficial Analysis

Somebody who wants to take an analytical approach to a new decision task must begin the analysis somewhere. At the beginning of the analysis, it is not yet clear which features of the problem are important and which are inessential. A judgment about this is not an input but at best an output of the analysis. Reasoning must begin at the surface, even though it may go deeper later. In this sense, the decision maker starts with a superficial analysis.

A study on face-to-face duopoly experiments provides an example (Selten and Berg 1970). Payoffs depended on final assets, composed of initial assets and total profits. Initial assets and profits were varied systematically in a way that did not change the relationship between behavior and final payoffs. Only the presentation of the game was varied, not its game theoretically essential features. However, this presentation influenced behavior.

One of two observed modes of cooperation was an agreement at a nearly pareto-optimal combination with equal profits. This equal profit solution depended on the presentation. How did this presentation effect arise?

Each subject had access to profit tables of both firms. The borders between the regions of positive and negative profits were a conspicuous feature of the situation, even if they were not essential from the point of view of game theory. The superficial analysis starts there. Both want positive profits. From there it is only a small step to the equal profit solution.

In the case of an agreement at the equal profit solution, the analysis stops before it is discovered that it is superficial. Boundedly rational analysis is a dynamic process. Initial conditions matter.

Superficial analysis explains the great importance of presentation or framing effects. I believe that such effects should not be dismissed as due to misleading instructions. It is important to understand in which way superficial analysis can be misled.

Human Problem Solving

The heading of this section refers to the title of a famous book by Newell and Simon (1972). They built up an experimentally well-supported theory about how people deal with sharply defined problems. An example is the puzzle about the three missionaries and the three cannibals who have to be brought from the left bank of a river to the right one by repeated trips of a boat carrying at most two people. This problem has to be solved under the constraints that at no time can there be more cannibals than missionaries on a river bank, including the persons just landing there.

The problem-solving process takes place in a *problem space*, a set of possible *problem states*. In the case of the example of the missionaries and the cannibals, a problem state is a vector (m, c, b) where m and c are the numbers of missionaries and cannibals, respectively, on the left bank and b is the position of the boat at one of the two banks. b may have the values L (left bank) or R (right bank). A problem state is *permissible* if it satisfies the constraints imposed by the task.

The description of the problem also specifies a set of operations by which a transition from one problem state to another is possible, in our case the transport of one or two persons from the bank where the boat is to the other one. A *solution* to the problem is a sequence of permissible states starting with the *initial state* to the *end state* in the example from $(3, 3, L)$ to $(3, 3, R)$. In this sequence, each state before the final one leads to the next one by one of the operations.

At each point of the search for the solution, the problem solver knows states that he can reach from the initial one (including the initial one) and others from which he can reach the end state (including the end state). He tries to narrow the gap between one of the former and one of the latter, i.e., he forms a subgoal of reducing the difference between them. The subgoal suggests the operation to be applied. In the search he may sometimes have to backtrack because he has met a dead end.

The problem space has to be constructed by the problem solver. Sometimes there are several possibilities. In our example, the problem space could also represent the situations with the boat on the middle of the river ($b = M$). However, this is a relatively minor variation. In other cases, the way in which the problem space is constructed by the problem solver can make a great difference for finding a solution. The presentation of the problem is important here.

Newell and Simon point out that tic-tac-toe is equivalent to a game in which the two players alternate in picking one of the numbers 1, ..., 9 not yet taken by the other; the first player with three numbers summing to 15 wins. The equivalence is due to the fact that the numbers 1, ..., 9 can be arranged in a magical square.

The problem-solving theory of Newell and Simon is a great contribution to the understanding of boundedly rational reasoning. However, the problems to which it applies are very special. Extensions are necessary to make the theory fruitful for modeling economic decision making. Consider the case of a tram company that has to work out a new time schedule. Various considerations (e.g., maximum waiting times, avoidance of overcrowding, and underuse) have to be met. One can think of such requirements as partial aspiration levels on goal variables.

Clearly, aspiration adaptation must enter the picture as an integrated part of the search for a solution. It must be decided whether an attempt to satisfy an aspiration should be continued or given up as hopeless. This may involve decision resource stocks as goal variables.

Qualitative Causal Reasoning

Qualitative statements about the causal influence of one variable on another concern the direction of the influence. The influence of x on y is *positive* if y is increasing in x and *negative* if y is decreasing in x. Qualitative reasoning is the derivation of qualitative conclusions from qualitative assumptions. The notion of a causal diagram, introduced for the purpose of explaining behavior in oligopoly experiments (Selten 1967), describes a mental model for the representation of qualitative causal relationships in a system.

A causal diagram is a directed signed graph whose nodes stand for the variables of a system and whose edges represent influences; the direction goes from the influencing to the influenced variable. A positive influence is indicated by a "+" at the edge and a negative one by a "–." The influences represented by edges are *direct* in contrast to *indirect* influences exerted along a *chain*, i.e., a sequence of variables such that each of them except the last one has a direct influence on the next one. An indirect influence along a chain is positive, if the number of negative influences on the chain is even. Otherwise it is negative. In Figure 2.1, we find three indirect influences of price on total profits:

1. price $\overset{+}{\rightarrow}$ unit profits $\overset{+}{\rightarrow}$ total profits,
2. price $\rightarrow$ sales $\rightarrow$ unit costs $\rightarrow$ unit profits $\overset{+}{\rightarrow}$ total profits,
3. price $\rightarrow$ sales $\overset{+}{\rightarrow}$ total profits.

The indirect influence of price on total profits is positive along the first chain and negative along the other two chains. The diagram is *unbalanced* in the sense that it does not yield unambiguous qualitative causal conclusions. A *balanced* diagram is defined by the requirement that for any two variables x and y with

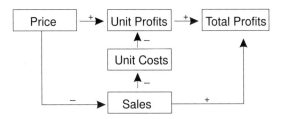

Figure 2.1   Causal diagram for a monopoly with decreasing unit costs.

indirect influences of x on y either all of them are positive or all of them are negative.

An unbalanced diagram can be changed to a balanced one by the removal of influences or variables. Experiments suggest that subjects tend to balance their qualitative beliefs in this way. Thus, in the example of Figure 2.1 the direct influence of price on unit profits may be removed on the basis of a judgment that it is relatively unimportant. Thereby a balanced diagram is obtained in which all direct influences of price on total profits are negative. Suppose that the management of the monopoly forms its beliefs in this way. Then it will come to the conclusion that price must be lowered in order to increase total profits.

The decision to decrease the price needs to be quantified, in the sense that the amount of the decrease has to be fixed. Since qualitative beliefs are insecure and may be only locally correct, management may decide to decrease price by a small percentage, say 5%, which seems to be great enough to have a nonnegligible effect but not greater. One can think of the quantification decision as reached by the process described earlier (see section on Prominence in the Decimal System).

Opinions about questions of economic policy expressed in journal articles seem to be based largely on qualitative reasoning. Quantitative information is used to argue that some influences are important and others unimportant, but only rarely are any arithmetic calculations made. I admit that this is an impression that has not yet been substantiated by systematic empirical research.

MOTIVATION

The human motivational system determines the goal pursued by boundedly rational decision making. Unfortunately we have no clear understanding of the interaction of different motivational forces. This is a serious difficulty for the development of a comprehensive theory of bounded rationality. Some decision problems are easy while others cause serious inner conflicts. What is an inner conflict? One approach to this question, going back to Freudian psychoanalytic theory, is the idea that the self is composed of several parts with different interests. Conflicts may arise among these components of self. This view of inner conflicts suggests modeling them as games. What are the rules of these games? How should we model them? The following two sections try to shed light on these questions.

Hyperbolic Discounting

In economic theory, the usual assumption about discounting streams of payoffs is that of a constant discount rate q with $0 < q < 1$. The payoffs are utilities u_t obtained in period $t = 1, 2, \ldots$.

This means that u_t enters the discounted sum of the payoff stream with the weight q^t. Experimental evidence shows that behavior is much better described by hyperbolic discounting with weights $1 / (A + t)$ for u_t, where A is a positive constant (Ainslie 1992). Thus a subject may prefer 95 money units now to 100 tomorrow, but 100 in a year and a day to 95 in a year. This involves a time inconsistency since after a year the second choice will look like the first one today.

Ainslie models decision making as a game among multiple selves, one for each time period. The self of time t decides what is done at time t with the aim of maximizing its own hyperbolically discounted utility, taking into account what later selves are expected to do. This means that a subgame perfect equilibrium is played. However, the game can have more than one such equilibrium, e.g., one in which the present self and all future selves continue to smoke and another one in which the present self stops smoking and all future selves follow this example. The second equilibrium may be better for all of them. Assume that this is the case.

The two equilibria have not yet been fully described. In the first, the *smoking equilibrium*, all selves smoke regardless of prior history. In the second, the *nonsmoking equilibrium*, the present self does not smoke and the later ones do not either, as long as none of them has deviated. If one of them smokes, all of the later ones will smoke under all circumstances.

To make these equilibria work, one has to assume that the sequence of future selves is infinite. Even if this is wrong, one may argue that an analysis based on this idea is nevertheless correct, since it is known that boundedly rational game players can show behavior akin to equilibria of infinite supergames in finite supergames (Selten and Stoecker 1986).

Suppose that the person is in the smoking equilibrium. It would be better to switch to the nonsmoking equilibrium. However, there may be many other subgame perfect equilibria, among them a *delayed nonsmoking equilibrium*, in which the present self smokes, but all future selves do not. Under plausible assumptions on payoffs, this is the case and the delayed nonsmoking equilibrium is better for the present self than the smoking equilibrium.

In this way, the inner conflict between stopping or continuing to smoke can be modeled as a problem of equilibrium selection. This is a very interesting modeling approach to the phenomenon of inner conflict, even if the game theoretic reasoning is not fully worked out by Ainslie. However, it is based on strong rationality assumptions. The multiple selves are modeled as fully rational game players. A more plausible picture of inner conflicts faced by boundedly rational players requires another kind of decision behavior. Perhaps one should try to modify Ainslie's theory in this direction.

The splitting of the person into muliple selves with conflicting goals is in itself a bound of rationality for the person as a whole, even if it is not cognitive but *motivational*. Not only cognitive but also motivational bounds of rationality must be taken into account by a comprehensive theory of bounded rationality.

Want Generator and Administrator

Otwin Becker (1967) has proposed a theory of household behavior that extends aspiration adaptation theory to this context. The household divides its monthly income into a number of funds for different kinds of expenditures, e.g., a fund for food, a fund for clothing, a fund for entertainment. The goal variables are the fund sizes and upper price limits for *wants*, like the desire for a pair of shoes seen in the window of a shop, or an excursion advertised by a travel agency. Such *wants* are produced by a *want generator*, modeled as a random mechanism.

When a want is generated by the want generator, another instance, the administrator, checks to see whether there is still enough money in the appropriate fund and whether the want remains under the price limit for such desires. If the price limit is violated, the want is rejected. If the want remains under the price limit but there is not enough money in the fund, then the want will still be granted if transfer rules permit the transfer of the missing amount from another fund. The structure of these transfer rules will not be explained here. If such a transfer is not permissible, then the want is rejected.

At the end of the spending period, a new aspiration level for the next one is formed by aspiration adaptation in light of recent experience. The details will not be explained here. If the household theory of Otwin Becker is applied to the spending behavior of a single person, then want generator and administrator are different personality components. Conflicts between them are not modeled by the theory but it may be possible to extend it in this direction. Everyday experience suggests that sometimes wants are realized against the will of the administrator.

The splitting of a person into a mechanistically responding want generator and a boundedly rational administrator seems to be a promising modeling approach, not only to household theory but also for other areas of decision making.

CONCLUDING REMARKS

I hope that I have been successful in conveying the essential features of bounded rationality as I understand it. In the introduction, I argued that rational decision making within the cognitive bounds of human beings must be nonoptimizing. The exposition of aspiration adaptation theory served the purpose of demonstrating the possibility of a coherent modeling approach to nonoptimizing but nevertheless systematic and reasonable boundedly rational behavior.

Some of the questions left open by aspiration adaptation theory are related to the topics discussed in the sections SOME BASIC MODES OF CHOICE BEHAVIOR, Prominence in the Decimal System, Expectation Formation (in the case of a univariate time series), Reinforcement Learning, and Learning Direction Theory. Of course, this is only a small sample of what can be found in the relevant literature. The remarks about reasoning in this essay do even less justice to important theoretical and empirical developments, such as Johnson-Laird's work on mental models (1983), the impressive book by Holland et al. (1989), and the illuminating analysis of analogy in "mental leaps" by Holyoak and Thagard (1995). Unfortunately these and other very interesting advances do not lend themselves to very short, condensed descriptions. The discussion of motivation was restricted to only one aspect of it: the idea that a person is subdivided into several components that may be in conflict with each other. A subject matter that was left out altogether is the strategic interaction of boundedly rational players in game situations, an area of research that I have discussed in a recent paper (Selten 1998b).

What is bounded rationality? A complete answer to this question cannot be given at the present state of the art. However, empirical findings put limits to the concept and indicate in which direction further inquiry should go.

REFERENCES

Abbink, K., and B. Kuon. 1998. An option pricing experiment with professional traders. SFB Discussion Paper B–426. Bonn: Univ. of Bonn.

Ainslie, G. 1992. Picoeconomics. Cambridge: Cambridge Univ. Press.

Albers, W., and G. Albers. 1983. On the prominence structure in the decimal system: In: Decision Making under Uncertainty, ed. R.W. Scholz, pp. 271–287. Amsterdam: Elsevier.

Aumann, R., and S. Sorin. 1989. Cooperation and bounded recall. *Games Econ. Behav.* **1**:5–39.

Becker, O. 1967. Die wirtschaftliche Entscheidungen des Haushalts. Berlin: Duncker und Humblot.

Becker, O., and U. Leopold. 1996. The bounds and likelihood procedure — A simulation study concerning the efficiency of visual forecasting techniques. *Cent. Eur. J. Oper. Res. Econ.* **4**:2–3.

Burns, P. 1985. Experience and decision making: A comparison of students and businessmen in a simulated progressive auction. In: Research in Experimental Economics, ed. V. Smith, vol. 3, pp. 139–157. Greenwich, CT: JAI Press.

Bush, R.R., and F. Mosteller. 1955. Stochastic Models of Learning. New York: Wiley.

Cyert, R., and J.G. March. 1963. (1992, 2d ed.). A Behavioral Theory of the Firm. Englewood Cliffs, NJ: Prentice Hall.

Erev, I., and A.E. Roth. 1998. On the role of reinforcement learning in experimental games: The cognitive game theoretic approach. In: Games and Human Behavior: Essays in Honor of Amnon Rapoport, ed. D. Budescu, I. Erev, and R. Zwick, pp. 53–78. Mahwah, NJ: Erlbaum.

Gigerenzer, G. 1997. Bounded rationality: Models of fast and frugal inference. *Swiss J. Econ. Stat.* **133**:201–218.

Gigerenzer, G., P.M. Todd, and the ABC Research Group. 1999. Simple Heuristics That Make Us Smart. New York: Oxford Univ. Press.

Hertwig, R., U. Hoffrage, and L. Martignon. 1999. Quick estimation: Letting the environment do some of the work. In: Simple Heuristics That Make Us Smart, G. Gigerenzer, P.M. Todd, and the ABC Research Group, pp. 209–234. New York: Oxford Univ. Press.

Reinhard Selten

Holland, J., K. Holyoak, R. Nisbett, and P. Thagard. 1986. Induction. Cambridge, MA: MIT Press.

Holyoak, K., and P. Thagard. 1995. Mental Leaps. Cambridge, MA: MIT Press.

Johnson-Laird, P. 1983. Mental Models. Cambridge, MA: Harvard Univ. Press.

Kahnemann, D., P. Slovic, and A. Tversky, eds. 1982. Judgment under Uncertainty, Heuristics and Biases. Cambridge: Cambridge Univ. Press.

Newell, A., and H. Simon. 1972. Human Problem Solving. Englewood Cliffs, NJ: Prentice Hall.

Roth, A., and I. Erev. 1995. Learning in extensive form games. *Games Econ. Behav.* **8**:164–212.

Sargent, T. 1993. Bounded Rationality in Macroeconomics. Oxford: Clarendon.

Sauermann, H., and R. Selten. 1962. Anspruchsanpassungstheorie der Unternehmung. *Z. ges. Staatswiss.* **118**:577–597.

Savage, L. 1954. The Foundation of Statistics. New York: Wiley.

Selten, R. 1967. Investitionsverhalten im Oligoexperiment. In: Beiträge zur experimentellen Wirtschaftsforschung, ed. H. Sauermann, vol. 1, pp. 60–102. Tübingen: J.C.B. Mohr.

Selten, R. 1991. Evolution, learning and economic behavior. *Games Econ. Behav.* **3**:3–24.

Selten, R. 1998a. Aspiration adaption theory. *J. Math. Psych.* **42**:191–214.

Selten, R. 1998b. Features of experimentally observed bounded rationality. *Eur. Econ. Rev.* **42**:413–436.

Selten, R., and C.C. Berg. 1970. Drei experimentelle Oligospielserien mit kontinuierlichem Zeitverlauf. In: Beiträge zur experimentellen Wirtschaftsforschung, ed. H. Sauermann, vol. 2, pp. 162–221. Tübingen: J.C.B. Mohr.

Selten, R., and J. Buchta. 1999. Experimental scaled bid first price auctions with directly observed bid functions. In: Games and Human Behavior, ed. D. Budescu, I. Erev, and R. Zwick, pp. 79–102. Hillsdale, NJ: Erlbaum.

Selten, R., and R. Stoecker. 1986. End behavior in sequences of finite prisoner's dilemma supergames. *J. Econ. Behav. Org.* **7**:47–70.

Simon, H.A. 1957. Models of Man. New York: Wiley.

Tietz, R. 1976. Anspruchsausgleich in experimentellen Zwei-Personenverhandlungen mit verbaler Kommunikation. Entscheidungsprozesse in Gruppen. *Z. Sozialpsych. Beih.* **2**:123–141.

Tietz, R., and H.J. Weber. 1972. On the nature of the bargaining process in the KRESKO-game. In: Contributions to Experimental Economics, ed. H. Sauermann, vol. 3, pp. 305–334. Tübingen: J.C.B. Mohr.

3

The Adaptive Toolbox

Gerd Gigerenzer

Center for Adaptive Behavior and Cognition, Max Planck Institute for Human
Development, Lentzeallee 94, 14195 Berlin, Germany

ABSTRACT

The notion of an adaptive toolbox provides a framework for nonoptimizing visions of
bounded rationality, emphasizing psychological plausibility, domain specificity, and
ecological rationality. Heuristics in the adaptive toolbox are modeled on the actual
cognitive abilities a species has rather than on the imaginary powers of omniscient
demons. They are designed for specific goals — domain specific rather than domain
general — which enable them to make fast, frugal, and computationally cheap decisions.
Heuristics are composed from building blocks that guide search, stop search, and make
decisions. Heuristics that are matched to particular environmental structures allow
agents to be ecologically rational. The study of ecological rationality involves analyzing
the structure of environments, the structure of heuristics, and the match between them.

INTRODUCTION

Humans and animals make inferences about unknown features of their world
under constraints of limited time, limited knowledge, and limited computational
capacities. Models of rational decision making in economics, cognitive science,
biology, and other fields, in contrast, tend to ignore these constraints and treat
the mind as a Laplacean superintelligence equipped with unlimited resources of
time, information, and computational might. Some forty years ago, Herbert
Simon challenged this view with his notion of "bounded rationality," but with
only limited success. Today, bounded rationality has become a diluted,
fashionable term, used by the proponents of quite disparate visions of
reasonableness: from optimization under constraints (e.g., Sargent 1993) to
judgmental errors and human irrationality (e.g., Jolls et al. 1998).

The notion of an adaptive toolbox promotes a specific vision of bounded rationality based on three premises (Gigerenzer et al. 1999):

1. *Psychological Plausibility.* The goal of the program is to understand how actual humans (or ants, bees, chimpanzees, etc.) make decisions, as opposed to heavenly beings equipped with practically unlimited time, knowledge, memory, and other infinite resources. The challenge is to base models of bounded rationality on the cognitive, emotional, social, and behavioral repertoire that a species actually has.

2. *Domain Specificity.* The adaptive toolbox offers a collection of heuristics that are specialized rather than domain general as would be the case in subjective expected utility (SEU). These heuristics are composed of cognitive and emotional building blocks that can be part of more than one heuristic and allow the composition of new heuristics. The building blocks are more general than the heuristics.

3. *Ecological Rationality.* The "rationality" of domain-specific heuristics is not in optimization, omniscience, or consistency. Their success (and failure) is in their degree of adaptation to the structure of environments, both physical and social. The study of the match between heuristics and environmental structures is the study of ecological rationality.

VISIONS OF REASONABLENESS

The first premise, psychological plausibility, sets our vision of bounded rationality apart from the two species of "demons" in Figure 3.1. *Unbounded rationality* encompasses decision-making strategies that have little or no regard for the constraints in time, knowledge, and computational capacities that real humans face. For example, models that seek to maximize expected utility or perform Bayesian calculations often must assume demonic strength to tackle real-world problems. Real decision makers (as opposed to participants in an experiment in which all information is already conveniently laid out in front of them) need, first of all, to search for information. This search cannot go on indefinitely; it is constrained by limited time, money, attention, or other finite resources. The key difference between models of unbounded rationality and models of *optimization under constraints* is that the latter model *limited information search* that was terminated by a *stopping rule*. The assumption behind optimization under constraints is that the optimal stopping point can be calculated — the point at which the costs for further search begin to exceed the benefits that a continued search could bring (Stigler 1961). However, the rule "stop search when costs outweigh benefits" can require even more time, knowledge, and computation to calculate than models of unbounded rationality (Vriend 1996; Winter 1975). This leads to the paradoxical consequence that "limited minds" are assumed to have the knowledge and computational ability of sophisticated econometricians equipped with statistical software packages.

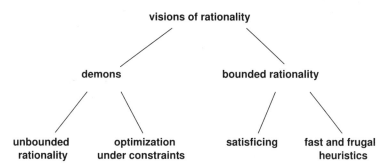

Figure 3.1 Models of bounded rationality consist of search for alternatives, such as houses and spouses (satisficing, Simon 1955; see also Selten, this volume) and search for cues, such as reasons for preferring one alternative to another (fast and frugal heuristics, Gigerenzer et al. 1999).

Unfortunately, optimization under constraints has often been labeled bounded rationality (e.g., Sargent 1993), which has (mis-)led many to conclude that there is, in the end, no difference between bounded and unbounded rationality.

The notion of ecological rationality puts models of bounded rationality — of which Figure 3.1 lists two general classes — in a functional, environmental perspective. In his 1956 article entitled "Rational Choice and the Structure of the Environment," Herbert Simon pointed out that there are two sides to bounded rationality: the "cognitive limitations" and the "structure of environments." His example was about an environment in which food is distributed randomly, and another environment in which cues for food distribution exist. An organism in the first environment can get away with very simple cognitive and behavioral strategies of search; an organism in an environment where cues exist, however, can benefit from cognitive abilities for learning cue–goal relations and planning search. The term environment, here, does not refer to a description of the total physical and biological environment, but only to that part important to an organism, given its needs and goals.

The notions of psychological plausibility and ecological rationality suggest two routes to the study of bounded rationality. The quest for psychological plausibility suggests looking into the mind, that is, taking account of what we know about cognition and emotion in order to understand decisions and behavior. Ecological rationality, in contrast, suggests looking outside the mind, at the structure of environments, to understand what is inside the mind. These research strategies are complementary, like digging a tunnel from two sides. However, the parties who dig from each side should meet at some point, and this has been a rare event, so far. On one hand, psychological plausibility has often been reduced to pointing out cognitive biases — typically by means of text problems, with little concern about environmental structures in which these purported biases could make sense (see Gigerenzer 1991; Gigerenzer and Murray 1987). On the other hand, the analysis of the structure of natural environments has often been paired with a behavioristic anxiety about opening the black box of the mind — from the psychologists Egon Brunswik and J.J. Gibson to ecologists and biologists. The neglect of one of the two sides of bounded rationality can even be traced in Simon's writings. For example, in his New Palgrave article, he explains that bounded rationality "takes into account the cognitive limitations of the decision maker — limitations of both knowledge and computational capacity" (Simon 1987, p. 266). The structure of environments he had emphasized repeatedly is not even mentioned.

I prefer to use the neutral term "cognitive abilities" over "cognitive limitations," since so-called limitations are relative to the fiction of optimizing demons, as in Figure 3.1. However, a serious program of bounded rationality needs to emancipate itself from the Christian ideal of an omniscient and omnipotent God, or its secularized version, Laplace's superintelligence. Bounded rationality in economics, cognitive science, and biology is about humans and animals, not about how they compare with demons and gods.

WHAT IS THE FUNCTION OF THE ADAPTIVE TOOLBOX?

The ultimate goal of organisms, according to evolutionary views, is reproduction, either of genes or some other units. The adaptive toolbox is designed to achieve proximal goals, such as finding prey, avoiding predators, finding a mate, and if a species is social or cultural, exchanging goods, making profits, and negotiating status. The tools are means to achieve proximal goals and include learning mechanisms that allow an adjustment of the tools when environments change. There can be a multitude of goals that attract the attention of an agent at any point in time, and these need not be compensatory, that is, a common psychological currency may not exist. Lack of a common currency is a psychological reality, and strategies of bounded rationality should be able to handle these situations in which no single goal variable exists that could be optimized. An example is aspiration adaptation theory (Selten, this volume).

Beyond Optimization

The strategies in the adaptive toolbox do not try to optimize, that is, they do not try to compute the maximum of some function, and for several good reasons. The general reason is that optimization is feasible in only a restricted set of problems, typically on the basis of simplifying assumptions. For example, even for well-defined games such as chess and go — where the rules and goals are simple, unambiguous, and not subject to change — no optimal strategy is known. Specific reasons are numerous, including (a) if multiple competing goals exist, optimization can become a heavy and unbearable computational burden, (b) if incommensurable goals exist, optimization can be impossible, (c) if incommensurable reasons (or cues) exist, optimization can be impossible, (d) if the alternatives are unknown and need to be generated in a lengthy process of search, optimization models assuming a finite, known choice set do not apply, (e) if the cues or reasons are unknown and need to be generated in a lengthy process of search, optimization models that assume a finite, known set of predictors do not apply, (f) if future consequences of actions and events are unknown, optimization models assuming a known, finite set of consequences do not apply, and (g) if optimization is attempted for the multitude of decisions an organism faces in real time, this can lead to paralysis by computational explosion (see Klein, this volume).

Note that optimization is always relative to a number of assumptions about the environment, social and physical, that are typically uncertain — except in textbook examples. The heuristics in the adaptive toolbox just "bet" on the environment on the basis of past experience or a little probing, without attempting a complete analysis and subsequent optimization (Gigerenzer and Todd 1999).

Beyond Consistency

The heuristics in the adaptive toolbox also do not take consistency as a *sine qua non* for rational behavior. In contrast, axioms and rules of internal consistency, such as property alpha, transitivity, and additivity of probabilities, are often seen as the cornerstones of human rationality, and of animal rationality as well (e.g., McGonigle and Chalmers 1992). Similarly, violations of consistency are typically seen as instances of irrationality, such as preference reversals (see, however, Sen's [1993] argument that consistency is an ill-defined concept unless the social goals and objectives of people are specified).

From a functional view, however, consistency in choice and judgment is not a general norm to follow blindly, but rather a tool for achieving certain proximal goals. For a given goal, consistent behavior can be an advantage, a disadvantage, or unimportant. For example, in cooperative relationships within families and businesses, some forms of consistent behaviors seem to be indispensable. They contribute to producing and maintaining a social climate of trust, fairness, and commitment. In competitive relationships, however, strategies with built-in inconsistencies can be an advantage. Protean behavior provides one such example: the erratic escape movements of prey, the "crazy dances" of predators, the sequential moves of two competitors who mutually try to make their future choices unpredictable, and the biochemistry of viruses (Driver and Humphries 1988). When unpredictability is adaptive, consistent preferences or behaviors may be deadly. There is also a class of situations in which neither consistency nor inconsistency seems functional, but other features of decision making are in the foreground: to make a fast decision, to make a frugal decision (with only meager information), or to make a decision at all — not to get it right, but to get a business or social interaction going.

Domain Specificity: Making Choices Fast and Frugal

Domain-specific heuristics allow faster reaction with less information than a general-purpose algorithm. A domain is a subset G' of the set G of goals. I consider two complementary ways to define domains: *cognitive tasks* and *adaptive problems*. Cognitive tasks include classification, estimation, and two-alternative choice. Here, the subset G' consists of tasks that afford the same type of result, such as classifying an object into one of several categories or estimating the value of an object on a criterion. Adaptive problems include mate choice, habitat choice, food choice, social exchange, and their modern equivalents such as dieting and stock markets. Adaptive problems are characterized by their common content rather than a common cognitive task. Cognitive psychology has almost exclusively focused on studying mechanisms for cognitive tasks rather than for adaptive problems. There is a large literature on classification, estimation, and choice — most of which ignores search and stopping and proposes demon-like models of decision, such as exemplar models of classification, multiple regression models of estimation, and SEU models of choice.

In our own work on fast and frugal heuristics (Gigerenzer et al. 1999), we decided on a complementary research strategy that studies both types of domain-specific heuristics for cognitive tasks and for adaptive problems. For example, the "QuickEst" heuristic (Hertwig et al. 1999) and the "Take The Best" heuristic (Gigerenzer and Goldstein 1996) are specific to certain cognitive tasks of estimation and two-alternative choice, respectively. Mate choice, in contrast, is an adaptive problem that demands boundedly rational heuristics designed for situations of mutual choice, sequential encounter of alternatives, and stopping rules that can include emotions such as love (Todd and Miller 1999). We found that studying heuristics for both types of domains has proved helpful. One might assume that the adaptive toolbox employs the same dual approach for handling new problems. Heuristics that are task specific can easily be generalized to new tasks of the same type, and strategies designed for specific adaptive problems can be generalized to new cultural versions of the strategy.

Emotions are prime examples of domain-specific tools for bounded rationality, in particular for solving adaptive problems. Emotions can help to limit the number of decisions to be made. Disgust, for example, limits the choice set of items to eat and serves the adaptive function of preventing food poisoning. However, disgust is of little help for other adaptive problems, such as social exchange, where anger and, conversely, feelings of guilt can keep people from cheating on contracts.

The Mind as a Backwoods Mechanic and Used Parts Dealer

Leibniz had a beautiful dream of discovering the universal logical language in which God had written the book of nature. This language, the Universal Characteristic, would replace all reasoning with one calculus (Leibniz 1677/1951). It would put an end to scholarly bickering and clamorous controversy — if there is a problem, just sit down and calculate. For some time, Enlightenment thinkers hoped that the calculus of probability would make Leibniz' dream a reality, but by the 1840s, most mathematicians had given up the task of reducing rational reasoning to a general calculus as a thankless and even antimathematical one (Daston 1988). However, the dream has survived in some quarters, where hearts still beat for a unified formula of rationality, be it some version of SEU or Bayesianism.

The notion of an adaptive toolbox full of specialized devices lacks the beauty of Leibniz' dream or that of SEU. It invokes the more modest abilities of a "backwoods mechanic and used part dealer," as Wimsatt (1999) describes nature. The backwoods mechanic has no general-purpose tool nor are all spare parts available to him. He must fiddle with various imperfect and short-range tools, a process known as vicarious functioning (Brunswik 1955). He will have to try one thing, and if it does not work, another one, and with step-by-step adjustments will produce serviceable solutions to almost any problem with just the things at hand.

The design of domain-specific mechanisms can be a viable alternative to building intelligent machines. Since its inception, artificial intelligence has relied upon perfect rationality — a complete representation of the world and some form of general optimization algorithm — as the desired property of intelligent systems, resulting in a wide gap between theory and practice hindering progress in the field (Russell and Subramanian 1995). This "Good Old Fashioned AI," or GOFAI, tends to produce robots that move a few feet and then sit there for a long time until they have computed the optimal direction in which to move the next few feet, and so on. In contrast, the argument has been made that smart robots need to be modeled after humans, equipped with special-purpose abilities without a centralized representation and computation control system, and an intelligence that emerges from their interactions with the environment (e.g., Brooks 1993).

The function of the adaptive toolbox is, thus, to provide strategies — cognitive, emotional, and social — that help to handle a multitude of goals by making decisions quickly, frugally, accurately, or, if possible, not at all. The function of the adaptive toolbox is not to guarantee consistency or solve differential equations to optimize some function. Clearly, I believe that the importance of optimization and consistency has been overestimated in theories of rational choice.

WHAT ARE THE TOOLS IN THE ADAPTIVE TOOLBOX?

The adaptive toolbox provides heuristics, and these are composed of building blocks. I describe three functions these building blocks have: they give search a direction, stop search, and make a decision.

Search Rules

One can think of search as an exploration of two dimensions: search for alternatives (the choice set) and cues (to evaluate the alternatives). On one hand, Simon's concept of satisficing involves search for alternatives, but not for cues

(Simon 1955). Cues can be thought of as implicit in his concept of an aspiration level. On the other hand, the fast and frugal heuristics studied by our research group (Gigerenzer et al. 1999) search for cues and are designed for situations in which the alternatives (such as job candidates or stocks) are already known. Thus, the division of bounded rationality into satisficing and fast and frugal heuristics, as shown in Figure 3.1, reflects the type of search: search for alternatives (satisificing) or search for cues (fast and frugal heuristics).

Building blocks for guiding search include random search, ordered search (e.g., looking up cues according to their validities), and search by imitation of conspecifics, such as stimulus enhancement, response facilitation, and priming. Imitation is an effective mechanism that allows humans (and the few other species that imitate behavior on some larger scale) to learn quickly where to look and what to look for.

When evaluating models of search, psychological plausibility should not be confused with irrationality. In noisy environments, search heuristics can be both psychologically plausible, simple, and successful. One reason is the robustness of simple search heuristics. For example, the Take The Best heuristic computes a simple order (of cue validities) to direct search for cues, which is suboptimal given the data it knows. Nevertheless, when it comes to making predictions about new data, Take The Best actually can make more accurate inferences using the simple order than the order that was optimal for the data available (Martignon and Hoffrage 1999).

The family of noncognitive tools for search has not been explored in depth. For example, emotions such as disgust can eliminate large numbers of alternatives from the search space. In general, emotions can narrow down choice sets more effectively and for a longer time than cognitive search tools.

Stopping Rules

Search for alternatives and cues must be stopped at some point. Strategies in the adaptive toolbox employ stopping rules that do not try to compute an optimal cost-benefit tradeoff as in optimization under constraints. Rather, building blocks for stopping involve simple criteria that are easily ascertained. In Simon's (1955) satisficing models, search is stopped when the first alternative is found that is as high as or better than the aspiration level; aspiration levels may go up or down depending on the time spent searching. Selten's (1998) aspiration adaptation theory provides a more general framework in which several goals, each with an aspiration level, exist, and the goals need not be commensurable. Simple rules for stopping search for cues are employed by Take The Best, Take The Last, and other heuristics, where search is stopped as soon as the first cue that favors one alternative is found (Gigerenzer and Goldstein 1996).

Building blocks for stopping need not be cognitive, as in these three examples. There are certain adaptive problems where cognitive stopping tools, such as comparison between an alternative and an adaptation level, are vulnerable to instability. The moment a more attractive alternative comes into sight, the chosen alternative might be discarded and search taken up again. For adaptive problems such as rearing children, dispensing with one's wife or husband every time a more attractive partner comes in sight might not be a successful strategy. In these situations, emotions can function as effective tools for stopping search. For example, love can stop search for partners more effectively and for a longer time than an aspiration level comparison, and, in addition, strengthen commitment to the loved one. Similarly, feelings of parental love, triggered by one's infant's presence or smile, can prevent cost-benefit computations as to whether it really pays to stay with one's child. The question of whether or not it is worthwhile to endure all the sleepless nights and physical constraints associated with infant care simply never arises once the emotion is triggered. Emotions illustrate domain-specific rather than domain-general mechanisms of stopping search.

Decision Rules

Once search has been stopped, a decision or inference must be made. Models of judgment and decision making have ignored search and stopping rules traditionally and have focused exclusively on the decision rule: Are cue values combined by multiple linear regression? By Bayes's rule? Or in some other fashion? There is no evidence that humans could perform the extensive computations demanded by multiple regression or Bayesian networks to make judgments and decisions in situations with large numbers of cues. However, this is not to say that fewer computations and less information imply significantly less accuracy, not to mention irrationality. For example, simple linear models that use only unit weights (+1 or –1), and forego the matrix computations linear multiple regression demands, can make predictions about as well as regression (e.g., Dawes 1979).

Models of rationality rely on weighting and summing. Simple linear models dispense with optimal weighting; heuristics that use *one-reason decision making* dispense with summing. For example, Take The Best and other lexicographic heuristics rely only on one cue to make the decision and ignore all others. An apparently paradoxical result is that Take The Best — which uses less information and fewer computations than multiple regression does — can make the *more* accurate predictions. This result has been obtained for two-alternative choice problems involving predictions about biological, demographic, economic, ecological, and psychological variables, including homelessness rates in U.S. cities, Chicago's inner city high-school dropout rates, fertility of individual charr fishes, professors' salaries, and sales prices of houses (Czerlinski et al. 1999).

Thus, simple, psychologically plausible decision tools need not be inferior to complex combination schemes; there are situations where there is no trade-off between simplicity and accuracy. The study of these conditions is part of the study of ecological rationality.

Incommensurability between goals is a psychological phenomenon that optimization models postulating a common currency cannot handle. Models of bounded rationality can (e.g., Selten 1998), as mentioned before. Incommensurability between cues or reasons is a second psychological phenomenon that prevents optimization. For example, when Darwin pondered whether to marry or not, the pro and contra reasons he wrote down on a piece of paper included having children and having conversations with clever friends. Children and conversations are not of a common currency for many of us. The question of how many conversations with clever friends equal having one child will be rejected, based on the invalid assumption that everything has a price tag. Moral institutions are built on the principle that some things have no price: doctorates, military honors, and love (Elster 1979). One-reason decision making accepts the possibility of incommensurable reasons and does not impose a summing-up of values. A heuristic such as Take The Best goes with the best reason and ignores the rest.

ECOLOGICAL RATIONALITY

Ecological rationality is possibly the most important idea for understanding why and when bounded rationality works. Consider two classes of strategies: simple lexicographic ordering and multiple regression. Traditional definitions of rationality are concerned with the internal order of beliefs and inference, such as consistency. By internal criteria, one might conclude that lexicographic strategies are poor strategies because, unlike multiple regression, they employ one-reason decision making, ignore much of the information available, and some lexicographic strategies even produce intransitive judgments. For example, when Keeney and Raiffa (1993) discuss lexicographic ordering, they declare that it "is more widely adopted in practice than it deserves to be" because "it is naively simple" and "will rarely pass a test of 'reasonableness' "(pp. 77–78).

Environmental Structure

The notion of ecological rationality, by contrast, is not concerned with internal criteria. The question of ecological rationality concerns the match between a strategy and an environment. A match concerns structural properties. For example, consider a lexicographic strategy and the task of inferring which of two alternatives scores higher on a criterion. Lexicographic strategies are *noncompensatory*, that is, the first cue on which two alternatives differ determines the choice, and no further cue or combination of cues can reverse this decision. Consider an environment consisting of M binary cues, $C_1, ..., C_M$. These cues are noncompensatory for a given strategy if every cue C_j outweighs any possible combination of cues after C_j, that is, C_{j+1} to C_M. In the special case of a weighted linear model with a set of weights, $W = \{w_1, w_2, w_3, ..., w_M\}$, a strategy is noncompensatory if for every $1 \leq j \leq M$ we have

$$w_j > \sum_{k>j} w_k .$$

(3.1)

An example is the set of weights $\{1, 1/2, 1/4, 1/8, 1/16\}$. For a lexicographic strategy called Take The Best, which uses the cue order $C_1, ..., C_M$, the following result can be proven: If an environment consists of cues that are noncompensatory for a given linear model, this model cannot be more accurate than the faster and more frugal Take The Best (Martignon and Hoffrage 1999).

This example illustrates a match between a strategy and an environment with respect to a property, noncompensatoriness. Heuristics that are matched to particular environments allow agents to be *ecologically rational*, making adaptive decisions that combine accuracy with speed and frugality. The degree to which a match exists (e.g., the cues in the environment may only be approximately noncompensatory) determines how accurate a heuristic is. In the present example, a match makes the simple Take The Best as accurate as multiple regression, that is, a judgment based on one reason is as good as one based on many reasons. Given that simple heuristics tend to be more robust when environments are noisy and information is scarce (see below), one-reason decision making can actually become more accurate than regression.

Robustness

Simple heuristics can be successful for two reasons: they can exploit *environmental structure*, as the example above illustrates, and they can be *robust*, that is, generalize well to new problems and environments. If there is uncertainty in an environment, in the sense of some degree of unpredictability and changing environments, robustness becomes an issue. A model with many free parameters can achieve a good fit to a given body of data but may not generalize well to new data if it *overfitted* the old data. Overfitting occurs when a model with more parameters fits a sample of data better than a model with fewer parameters but makes less-accurate predictions for a new data sample than the simpler model. Complex models with many free parameters, such as multiple regression or Bayesian methods, tend to overfit in environments where information is noisy or fluctuating, particularly when forced to make predictions from small samples.

Akaike (1973) discovered a way of estimating the degree of overfitting, which becomes larger as the number of parameters increases, resulting in higher rates of error and a larger sum of squares (see also Forster and Sober 1994). There are statistical techniques that expend considerable computational power and time trying to determine the point at which a model maximizes its predictive accuracy without overfitting. Fast and frugal heuristics sidestep this expenditure. Their simplicity helps them to avoid overfitting and to make robust predictions without doing these computations.

To summarize, the reasonableness of models of bounded rationality derives from their ecological rationality, not from coherence or an internal consistency of choices. A strategy is ecologically rational to the degree that it is adapted to the information in an environment, whether the environment is physical or social.

Social Rationality

The study of social rationality is a special case of ecological rationality when environments consist of other agents with which to interact. Humans are one of the few species that cooperate with genetically unrelated conspecifics for mutual benefit, and economic markets and educational institutions are products of this reciprocal altruism.

Social rationality adds a further class of goals to decision making: social goals that are important for creating and maintaining social structure and cooperation. These goals include transparency (i.e., making decisions that are understandable and predictable by the group with which one associates), fairness (i.e., making decisions that do not violate the expectations between people of equal social standing), and accountability (i.e., making decisions that can be justified and defended [Tetlock 1983]).

Social imitation can help make decisions with limited time and knowledge. Heuristics such as "eat what your peers eat" and "prefer mates picked by others" can speed up decision making by reducing the time spent on information search. Forms of social rationality can be found in the animal world, as well. For instance, female guppies tend to copy the mate choices of other female guppies — a tendency strong enough to reverse their prior preferences for one male over another (Dugatkin 1996). Female quail use a related form of mate copying (Galef and White 1998). In humans, mate copying is enhanced by the media; even academic hiring often seems to be under the spell of social imitation.

To summarize, the adaptive toolbox contains boundedly rational strategies that employ social norms, social imitation, and social emotions in addition to the cognitive building blocks outlined earlier. These additional heuristic tools are particularly important in the realm of social rationality.

REFERENCES

Akaike, H. 1973. Information theory and an extension of the maximum likelihood principle. In: Second International Symposium on Information Theory, ed. B.N. Petrov and F. Csaki, pp. 267–281. Budapest: Akademiai Kiado.
Brooks, R.A., and L.A. Stein. 1993. Building Brains for Bodies. A.I. Memo No. 1439, August. Cambridge, MA: MIT, Artificial Intelligence Lab.
Brunswik, E. 1955. Representative design and probabilistic theory in a functional psychology. *Psych. Rev.* **62**:193–217.

Czerlinski, J., G. Gigerenzer, and D.G. Goldstein. 1999. How good are simple heuristics? In: Simple Heuristics That Make Us Smart, G. Gigerenzer, P.M. Todd, and the ABC Research Group, pp. 97–118. New York: Oxford Univ. Press.

Daston, L.J. 1988. Classical Probability in the Enlightenment. Princeton, NJ: Princeton Univ. Press.

Dawes, R.M. 1979. The robust beauty of improper linear models in decision making. *Am. Psych.* **34**:571–582.

Driver, P.M., and D.A. Humphries. 1988. Protean Behavior: The Biology of Unpredictability. Oxford: Oxford Univ. Press.

Dugatkin, L.A. 1996. Interface between culturally based preferences and genetic preferences: Female mate choice in *Poecilia reticulata. Proc. Natl. Acad. Sci. USA* **93**:2770–2773.

Elster, J. 1979. Ulysses and the Sirens: Studies in Rationality and Irrationality. Cambridge: Cambridge Univ. Press.

Forster, M., and E. Sober. 1994. How to tell when simpler, more unified, or less ad hoc theories will provide more accurate predictions. *Brit. J. Phil. Sci.* **45**:1–35.

Galef, B.G., and D.J. White. 1998. Mate-choice copying in Japanese quail, *Coturnix coturnix japonica. Anim. Behav.* **55**:545–552.

Gigerenzer, G. 1991. How to make cognitive illusions disappear. Beyond heuristics and biases. *Eur. Rev. Soc. Psych.* **2**:83–115.

Gigerenzer, G., and D.G. Goldstein. 1996. Reasoning the fast and frugal way: Models of bounded rationality. *Psych. Rev.* **103**:650–669.

Gigerenzer, G., and D.J. Murray. 1987. Cognition as Intuitive Statistics. Hillsdale, NJ: Erlbaum.

Gigerenzer, G., and P.M. Todd. 1999. Fast and frugal heuristics: The adaptive toolbox. In: Simple Heuristics That Make Us Smart, G. Gigerenzer, P.M. Todd, and the ABC Research Group, pp. 3–34. New York: Oxford Univ. Press.

Gigerenzer, G., P.M. Todd, and the ABC Reasearch Group. 1999. Simple Heuristics That Make Us Smart. New York: Oxford Univ. Press.

Hertwig, R., U. Hoffrage, and L. Martignon. 1999. Quick estimation: Letting the environment do the work. In: Simple Heuristics That Make Us Smart, G. Gigerenzer, P.M. Todd, and the ABC Research Group, pp. 209–234. New York: Oxford Univ. Press.

Jolls, C., C.R. Sunstein, and R. Thaler. 1998. A behavioral approach to law and economics. *Stanford Law Rev.* **50**:1471–1550.

Keeney, R.L., and H. Raiffa. 1993. Decisions with Multiple Objectives. Cambridge: Cambridge Univ. Press.

Leibnitz, G.W. 1951. Preface to the universal science. In: Selections, ed. P.P. Wiener. New York: Charles Scribner's Sons. (Original published 1677).

Martignon, L., and U. Hoffrage. 1999. Why does one-reason decision making work? A case study in ecological rationality. In: Simple Heuristics That Make Us Smart, G. Gigerenzer, P.M. Todd, and the ABC Research Group, pp. 119–140. New York: Oxford Univ. Press.

McGonigle, B., and M. Chalmers. 1992. Monkeys are rational. *Qtly. J. Exp. Psych.* **45B**:189–228.

Russell, S.J., and D. Subramanian. 1995. Provably bounded-optimal agents. *J. Artif. Intel. Res.* **1**:1–36.

Sargent, T.J. 1993. Bounded Rationality in Macroeconomics. Oxford: Oxford Univ. Press.

Selten, R. 1998. Aspiration adaptation theory. *J. Math. Psych.* **42**:191–214.

Sen, A. 1993. Internal consistency of choice. *Econometrica* **61**:495–521.

Simon, H.A. 1955. A behavioral model of rational choice. *Qtly. J. Econ.* **69**:99–118.

Simon, H.A. 1956. Rational choice and the structure of environments. *Psych. Rev.* **63**:129–138.

Simon, H.A. 1987. Bounded rationality. In: The New Palgrave. A Dictionary of Economics, ed. J. Eatwell et al., pp. 266–268. London: Macmillan.

Stigler, G.J. 1961. The economics of information. *J. Pol. Econ.* **69**:213–225.

Tetlock, P.E. 1983. Accountability and complexity of thought. *J. Pers. Soc. Psych.* **45**:74–83.

Todd, P.M., and G.F. Miller. 1999. From pride and prejudice to persuasion: Satisficing in mate search. In: Simple Heuristics That Make Us Smart, G. Gigerenzer, P.M. Todd, and the ABC Research Group, pp. 287–308. New York: Oxford Univ. Press.

Vriend, N.J. 1996. Rational behavior and economic theory. *J. Econ. Behav. Org.* **29**:263–285.

Wimsatt, W.C. 1999. Re-engineering Philosophy for Limited Beings: Piecewise Approximations to Reality. Cambridge: Harvard Univ. Press.

Winter, S.G. 1975. Optimization and evolution in the theory of the firm. In: Adaptive Economic Models, ed. R.H. Day and T. Groves. New York: Academic.

4

Fast and Frugal Heuristics for Environmentally Bounded Minds

Peter M. Todd

Center for Adaptive Behavior and Cognition, Max Planck Institute for Human
Development, Lentzeallee 94, 14195 Berlin, Germany

ABSTRACT

Understanding what constraints put bounds on human rationality will help us understand
the nature of that rationality. Human decision making is unlikely to be adapted to fixed
cognitive constraints, because evolution could shift such limitations were benefits
sufficient. Instead, features of the external environment would have exerted strong
adaptive pressures, particularly the need to minimize time by minimizing the search for
information. In this chapter, I present evidence that human decision making is adaptive in
the face of time and information costs, through the use of fast and frugal decision
heuristics. These heuristics can be shown analytically to perform nearly as well as slower
and more information-greedy algorithms, and evidence that people use these simple
strategies has been found in experiments, developmental theories, and analysis of how
we restructure our own environments.

INTRODUCTION: THE SOURCE OF
RATIONALITY'S BOUNDS

Just what is it that bounds our rationality? A common argument is that, much as
the size of our brains is bounded by running up against the hard physical constraint of our skulls, human cognitive abilities are bounded by the hard mental
constraints of our limited memories and information-processing powers. We
would be smarter, if only we could. This argument may hold for some
evolutionarily novel situations, such as computing long division in our heads,

for which our minds were never selected to excel. But in more important, every-day decision tasks, such as deciding which of two objects is larger and thereby a greater threat or benefit, memory and processing power would not be constraints *within* which evolution had to work — these are the elements that evolution had to work *with*, to shape and extend as necessary to meet the selective demands at hand. The selective forces impinging on our cognitive evolution largely came instead from outside our heads, from our interactions with the world and the people and organisms in it. Thus, the most important bounds that shaped our evolving rationality were not internal, mental factors, but rather external, environmental ones.

This is, baldly and briefly stated, the thesis to be put forth in this chapter: that the human mind makes many decisions by drawing on an adaptive toolbox of simple heuristics, not because it is forced to by cognitive constraints, but rather because these fast and information-frugal heuristics are well matched to the challenges of the (past) environment. Not all of the necessary elements of this argument are fully in place, as will be seen, but there is enough converging evidence from several directions to make the thesis plausible and indicate where further support can be sought. The argument proceeds as follows: First, I will lay out the nature of the environmental selective forces that have shaped the evolution of simple heuristics, indicating that heuristics would have been selected for speed by minimizing the amount of information they use. Second, in the next section, I will examine whether or not simple heuristics that use minimal time and information can possibly perform adaptively in real environments — if not, then there is no point in arguing that people would be well adapted were we to use such heuristics. The evidence in this section comes primarily from simulations and mathematical analysis of proposed heuristics, in particular decision environments. Third, having found that fast and frugal heuristics can indeed perform well, I must still provide evidence that people do in fact employ them in making decisions. In the third section I indicate three sources of support for this proposal, from empirical studies, developmental considerations, and the ways that we structure our own environment. This step completes the argument that people behave adaptively by using simple fast and frugal decision heuristics. Finally, I will point out the holes and gaps that remain in this line of reasoning, and what should be done to fill them.

Few people would deny that we humans often employ simple shortcuts or heuristics to reach decisions and make judgments. The "heuristics and biases" research program established by Tversky and Kahneman (1974) has flourished for over two decades in psychology and economics, gathering evidence that this is so. However, the basic message of their research program, and the suspicion of many, is that this should not be so, that humans use heuristics at their peril, more often than not making errors of judgment and inaccurate decisions. According to this perspective on rationality, humans fall somewhat short of adaptive behavior. In contrast, the vision of ecological rationality (see Gigerenzer, this volume) emphasizes that humans use specific simple heuristics because they *enable* adaptive behavior, by exploiting the structure of information in natural decision environments. Simplicity is a virtue, rather than a curse.

This difference in world views on the nature of human rationality is reflected in underlying assumptions about the forces that shaped that rationality. From the heuristics and biases point of view, we are, and by extension have always been, stuck with our cognitive limitations — for example, in summarizing research on the effects of task complexity on decision behavior, Payne, Bettman, and Johnson state, "The general hypothesis has been that increased task complexity [e.g., a large number of alternatives] will increase cognitive workload, which will in turn lead to the increased use of heuristics in decision making" (1993, p. 147). This hypothesis can be applied both individually and evolutionarily. However, the causality is wrong in the latter, phylogenetic, case: Given sufficient adaptive pressure to succeed in complex tasks, evolution could build complex information-processing structures so that cognitive workload and use of simple, sometimes erroneous, heuristics are not increased. Cognitive limitations can be circumvented over the course of evolution — certainly at a price, such as the considerable costs involved in bearing a large-headed, long-dependent human baby, but at a price that clearly has been paid in the past. (This raises the question of why we do have such large brains if we are using simple decision heuristics; obviously we are also thinking a lot about rather involved issues, such as social scheming [see Whiten and Byrne 1997] and courtship [see Miller 1997].) For example, our ability to store and retrieve information from memory could be much greater, as the skills of mnemonists attest (Luria 1968). The amount of information that can be held and processed in working memory can be greatly increased through practice (Ericsson and Kintsch 1995). The processing of information itself could be more rapid and sophisticated, as evidenced both by the prodigious processing power that the visual system already possesses, and by the ability of some individuals to solve complex problems rapidly that most of us would find impossible (e.g., chess masters, or horse-race experts [see Ceci and Liker 1986]). Thus, our cognitive boundaries could have been extended, if they had been adaptive. What then *did* lead to our reliance on simple decision heuristics in so many situations?

As mentioned above, the most important factors shaping cognitive (and physical) evolution came from the external environment — and one of the most pressing concerns facing a variety of organisms in a variety of dynamic environmental situations is simply the passage of time. This pressure arises primarily through competition between organisms, in two main ways. First, time is short: Organisms have occasional speed-based encounters where the slower individual can end up at a serious disadvantage, for example, being slowly digested by the faster. Second, time is money, or at least energy: Beyond predator–prey or combative situations, the faster an individual can make decisions and act on them to accrue resources or reproductive opportunities, the greater adaptive advantage it will have over slower conspecifics. (Time and energy are two of the most important factors in cost-benefit analyses of the evolution of animal behavior, as explored at length in the field of behavioral ecology and particularly within optimal foraging theory.)

Consider an organism that must forage in an environment that contains edible and inedible objects, which are distinguishable on the basis of a number of cues. If two organisms explore this environment side by side, competing for each item encountered, then clearly the one that can make a decision more rapidly as to edibility or inedibility will be able to scoop up the edible objects first and thereby gain an adaptive advantage. However, even if the two organisms are not in direct competition — if one forages alone in one patch, while the other searches in a separate patch — the organism with the faster decision strategy will have a higher rate of energy intake, and thus will again be at an advantage, for example, being able to accrue enough energy to produce offspring sooner. If the patches overlap, this advantage is increased, as the faster individual not only has a higher intake but again also eats into the resources available to its competitor. Thus, adaptive advantages can accrue even when differences in decision speed are small and competition is indirect.

Closely connected with selective pressures related to time are those related to information. For decisions that must be made using cues obtained from the environment (rather than contained in memory), information is time, which is in turn again energy. That is, it takes time to find and assess cues, so there is pressure to base decisions on fewer cues (assuming cue perception and processing is not primarily performed in a parallel manner). However, even if the search for more cues could be accomplished quickly, it might not do the decision maker much good: Cues are often highly intercorrelated (Brunswik 1943), so that searching for additional cues provides rapidly diminishing returns in terms of useful information.

Thus, the proposal here is that many human decision heuristics (and those of other species) were selected to achieve speed by seeking and using as few cues from the environment as they could get away with. Of course, it still could be the case that such heuristics would simply very quickly end up making bad choices and inaccurate decisions, much as the heuristics and biases program has proposed, leaving us not behaving particularly adaptively after all. I will provide evidence that this is not the case in the next section. The basic reason is that even a few cues seem to provide enough information to guide adaptive behavior in a variety of situations — the tradeoff between time costs and decision accuracy benefits may well be best met by gathering very little information.

All this is not to say that the entirety of human thought can or should be characterized by simple heuristics — humans are uniquely able to set aside such mental shortcuts and engage in extensive cogitation, calculation, and planning — but that we spend much of our time *not* taking the time to think deeply. Nor do I mean to imply that humans have no appreciable limits to our cognitive abilities, no bounds to our computational power or memory. Of course we do. Simon's observation about the nature of our bounded rationality still holds: "Human rational behavior ... is shaped by a scissors whose two blades are the

structure of the task environments and the computational capabilities of the actor" (Simon 1990, p. 7). However, these are the scissors operating *today*; here we
are interested instead in what has shaped human behavior *over time*, including
forging the latter blade that currently affects us. The argument again is that the
historic shaping forces more closely resembled a single knife blade of environmental pressures, although we will see at the end of the third section that task environments and computational capabilities have probably always wielded
reciprocal coevolutionary shaping effects on each other.

EVIDENCE THAT FAST AND FRUGAL
COGNITION CAN BE ADAPTIVE

Humans are renowned for making decisions on the basis of little time, thought,
and knowledge. We make snap judgments and rash decisions; we jump to conclusions; we indulge in stereotypes. We infer "beyond the information given"
despite the fact that more information may be readily obtainable. Saad and
Russo (1996) found, for example, that people would make a choice between
apartments in an experimental setting after asking to see only a quarter of the
available pieces of information. Even when we take more time to make a choice,
we often do not appear to apply any more rigorous computation to the information we have: Judgments made after minutes of pondering are frequently identical to those made in an instant (J. Bargh, pers. comm.). (For a review of evidence
for bounded rationality in economic contexts, mostly focusing on negative behavioral implications as in the heuristics and biases tradition, see Conlisk
[1996].) All of these patterns of thought have at least slightly negative connota-
tions, at best seeming ill-advised, and at worst smacking of irrationality — but
are we really so wrong to think this way?

To find out, we need to examine the quality of the decisions made by strategies that use little information. Decision quality can be most easily measured in
terms of accuracy or percentage of correct inferences made (though other measures that take the importance of different decisions into account should be used
as well, as I will discuss below). However, raw decision accuracy is not by itself
a reasonable benchmark, because it implies a comparison with perfect accuracy,
which is typically an unachievable goal given the information available. Instead, we must compare the performance of simple fast and frugal heuristics
against the performance of other strategies that use all available information (or
at least more than the fast and frugal heuristics) across a variety of task environments. For more on the proper benchmarks with which to compare decision
mechanisms, see Martignon as well as Payne and Bettman (both this volume). In
this section, I review results of such comparisons for four classes of fast and frugal heuristics: (a) a heuristic that relies solely on recognition and ignorance; (b)
heuristics that make decisions based on the first encountered cue that indicates
an unambiguous choice; (c) heuristics that combine a small number of cues to

make a categorical decision; and (d) heuristics that stop a sequential search after encountering only a small number of alternatives.

Ignorance-based Decision Mechanisms

One of the simplest forms of decision that can be made is to select one option from two possibilities, according to some criterion on which the two can be compared. What simple cognitive mechanisms can be used to make this type of decision? This will depend on the amount and type of information that is available in the environment. If the only information available is whether or not each possibility has ever been encountered before, then the decision maker can do little better than rely on his or her own partial ignorance, choosing recognized options over unrecognized ones. This kind of "ignorance-based reasoning" is embodied in the *recognition heuristic* (Gigerenzer and Goldstein 1996; Goldstein and Gigerenzer 1999): When choosing between two objects (according to some criterion), if one is recognized and the other is not, then select the former. For example, Norway rats have evolved to behave according to a rule of this type, preferring to eat things they recognize through past experience with other rats (e.g., items they have smelled on the breath of others) over novel items (Galef 1987).

Following the recognition heuristic will yield correct responses more often than would random choice in those decision environments in which exposure to different possibilities is positively correlated with their ranking along the decision criterion being used. Thus, the rats' food preference copying presumably evolved because the things that other rats have eaten (i.e., recognized items) are more often palatable than are random (unrecognized) items sampled from the environment. Such usable correlations are likely to be present in species with social information exchange where important environmental objects are communicated and unimportant ones are ignored. But could an organism faced with a recognized and an unrecognized alternative use more than just recognition, for example, use what else it knows or can find out about the recognized object, to make a better choice between the two? In some cases yes; however, often extra knowledge and the time taken to access and process that information will not yield a much improved answer.

Goldstein and Gigerenzer (1999) investigated this question in an environment consisting of pairs of the 83 largest German cities, where the task was to decide which of the two cities in each pair was larger. Because we hear about large cities more often than small cities, using recognition to decide which of two cities is larger will often yield the correct answer (in those cases where one city is recognized and the other is not). If only recognition could be used to make this decision (with average recognition rates for each city assessed from a survey of American students, and around half of the cities assumed to be recognized), accuracy across all pairs could reach 65% — well above chance performance. When nine informative cues were added for the recognized cities and multiple regression was used over these cues to determine the larger city, accuracy only went up by about another 7%, and most of this increase was for more accurate choices in pairs where both cities were recognized. Thus in this case, extra time and knowledge provide little benefit over the recognition heuristic in those decisions where one alternative is recognized and the other is not.

In fact, adding more knowledge for the recognition heuristic to use, by increasing the proportion of recognized objects in an environment, can even decrease decision accuracy. This *less-is-more effect,* in which an intermediate amount of (recognition) knowledge about a set of objects can yield the highest proportion of correct answers, is straightforward from an information theory perspective, but surprising from a cognitive one. Knowing more is not usually thought to *decrease* decision-making performance, but when using simple heuristics that rely on little knowledge, this is exactly what is theoretically predicted and, as we will see later, what can be found experimentally as well (Goldstein and Gigerenzer 1999).

How widely these findings apply in other environments and tasks still remains to be determined. There is already some evidence that the recognition heuristic can outperform strategies relying on much more knowledge and computation in a very complex and dynamic environment: the stock market. When deciding which companies to invest in from among those trading in a particular exchange, the recognition heuristic would lead us to choose just those that we have heard of before. Such a choice can be profitable assuming that more-often-recognized companies will typically have better-performing stocks. This assumption has been tested (Borges et al. 1999): Several sets of people were asked to identify companies they recognized, and investment portfolios were put together based on this information. Nearly 500 people in the United States and Germany were asked which of 500 American and 298 German traded companies they recognized. To form portfolios based on very highly recognized companies, we used the American participants' responses to select their top 10 most-recognized German companies, and the German responses to choose the top 10 most-recognized American firms. In this trial performed during 1996–1997, the simple ignorance-driven recognition heuristic beat highly trained fund managers using all the information available to them, as well as randomly chosen portfolios (which fund managers themselves do not always outperform). This does not prove that people use the recognition heuristic when making such choices (though common investment advice suggests this is so), but it does show that heuristics designed to be fast and use as little information as possible can perform well even in a complex environment. Furthermore, here the measure of performance is not merely decision accuracy measured in terms of the correct choices, but rather the more realistic yardstick of resources accrued. Some "correct" stock choices could be worth much more than others, and it is important to compare decision heuristics where possible in a manner that takes the value or significance of their individual choices into account (Sober 1994).

One-reason Decision Mechanisms

How well can simple decision heuristics perform when multiple pieces of information are available, and recognition cannot be used? The fastest and simplest of such heuristics would rely on just a single cue to make a decision — but can this possibly work? The answer turns out to be yes, so long as the cue to use is itself chosen properly. Imagine that we again have two objects to compare on some criterion, and several cues that could be used to assess each object on the criterion. A one-reason heuristic that makes decisions on the basis of a single cue could then work as follows (see Figure 4.1): (1) select a cue dimension and look for the corresponding cue values of each option; (2) compare the two options with regard to their values for that cue dimension; (3) if they differ, then stop and choose the option with the cue value indicating a greater value on the choice criterion; (4) if the options do not differ, then return to the beginning of this loop (step 1) to look for another cue dimension. Such a heuristic will often have to

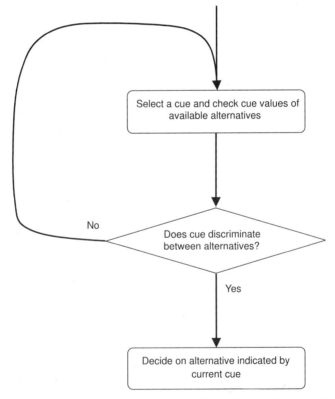

Figure 4.1   A flowchart of one-reason decision making: (1) a cue dimension is selected, and the corresponding cue values of each alternative are ascertained; (2) check whether the values for that cue dimension discriminate between the alternatives; (3) if so, then choose the indicated alternative; (4) if not, select another cue dimension and repeat this process. (Random choice can be used if no more cues are available.)

look up more than one cue before making a decision; however, the simple stopping rule (in step 3) ensures that as few cues as possible will be sought, minimizing the information-searching time taken. Furthermore, ultimately only a single cue will be used to determine the choice, minimizing the amount of computation that must be done.

This four-step loop incorporates two of the three important building blocks of simple heuristics (as described in Gigerenzer, this volume): a stopping rule (step 3) and a decision rule (also step 3 — deciding on the option to which the one cue points). To finish specifying a particular simple heuristic of this type, we must also determine just how cue dimensions are "looked for" in step 1, that is, we must pick a specific information search rule (the third building block). Two intuitive search rules can be incorporated in a pair of simple decision heuristics that we can then test in a variety of task environments (Gigerenzer and Goldstein 1996, 1999): the "Take The Best" heuristic searches for cues in the order of their (subjective) validity (i.e., their correlation with the decision criterion), while the "Minimalist" heuristic selects cues in a random order. Again, both stop their information search as soon as a cue is found that allows a decision to be made between the two options.

Despite (or often because of) their simplicity and disregard for most of the available information, these two fast and frugal heuristics can make very accurate choices. A set of twenty environments was collected to test the performance of these heuristics, varying in number of objects and number of available cues, and ranging in content from predicting population size as mentioned earlier to fish fertility to high-school dropout rates (Czerlinski et al. 1999). The decision accuracies of Take The Best and Minimalist were compared against those of two more traditional decision mechanisms that use all available information and combine it in more or less sophisticated ways: multiple regression, which weights and sums all cues in an optimal linear fashion, and Dawes's rule, which tallies the positive and negative cues and subtracts the latter from the former. The two fast and frugal heuristics always came close to, and often exceeded, the performance of the traditional algorithms when all were tested on the data they were trained on — the overall average performance across all twenty data sets is shown in Table 4.1 (under "Fitting"). This surprising performance on the part of Take The Best and Minimalist was achieved even though they only looked through a third of the cues on average (and only decided using one of them), while multiple regression and Dawes's rule used them all (see Table 4.1, "Frugality"). The advantages of simplicity grew in the more important test of generalization performance, where the decision mechanisms were tested on a portion of each data set that they had not seen during training. Here, Take The Best outperformed all three other algorithms by at least two percentage points (see Table 4.1, "Generalization").

Thus, making good decisions need not rely on the standard rational approach of collecting all available information and combining it according to the relative importance of each cue — simply betting on one good reason, even one selected

Table 4.1   Performance of two fast and frugal heuristics (Minimalist, Take The Best) and two linear strategies (Dawes's rule, multiple regression) across twenty data sets. The mean number of predictors available in the twenty data sets was 7.7. "Frugality" indicates the mean number of cues actually used by each strategy. "Fitting accuracy" indicates the percentage of correct answers achieved by the strategy when fitting data (test set = training set). "Generalization accuracy" indicates the percentage of correct answers achieved by the strategy when generalizing to new data (cross-validation, where test set ≠ training set). (Data from Czerlinski et al. 1999.)

Strategy	Frugality	Accuracy (% correct)	
		Fitting	Generalization
Minimalist	2.2	69	65
Take The Best	2.4	75	71
Dawes's rule	7.7	73	69
Multiple regression	7.7	77	68

at random, can provide a competitive level of accuracy in a variety of environments. The limited information search performed by fast and frugal heuristics is what gives them their main speed advantage over other less frugal algorithms, rather than a difference in the computations that each method involves. This is because the differences in time needed to perform a greater or lesser number of elementary information-processing operations (as discussed by Payne and Bettman, this volume; see also Payne et al. 1993) are typically likely to be dwarfed by differences in information search time, especially when information processing can be done in parallel in the brain and information search must be done sequentially in the environment.

An extensive set of tests of the performance of related simple decision strategies was conducted by Payne et al. (1993). These comparisons included two one-reason decision heuristics: LEX (like Take The Best with cue order determined by some measure of importance) and LEXSEMI (the same as LEX except for the requirement that cue values must differ by more than a specified amount before one alternative can be chosen over another; LEX merely requires any inequality in cue values). The heuristics were tested in a variety of environments consisting of risky choices between gambles with varying probabilities over a set of payoffs — there were two, five, or eight alternatives to choose between, each with two, five, or eight possible payoffs. Environments varied further in how the payoff probabilities were generated and in whether or not time pressure prevented heuristics from completing their calculations. Different heuristics performed best (in terms of accuracy compared against an expected utility maximizing weighted additive model) in different environments, supporting these researchers' argument that decision makers will choose among a set of alternative simple strategies depending on the particular task environment they face.

However, overall LEX and LEXSEMI performed very well in comparison with the weighted additive model, usually having the highest accuracy relative to their required effort (number of operations needed to reach a decision). When time pressure was severe, LEX performed particularly well, usually winning the accuracy competition because it could make a choice with fewer operations — as a consequence of looking for fewer cues — than the other heuristics. It is not clear the extent to which the risky gambles used in these studies meet our requirement of testing heuristic performance in realistic environments; however, these results nonetheless offer further support for the efficacy of one-reason decision mechanisms.

Simple Categorizing Mechanisms That Use More Than One Cue

These results on the efficacy of simple heuristics in structured environments are not restricted to decisions made between two objects. More generally, fast and frugal heuristics can also be found that use as few cues as possible to categorize objects. *Categorization by Elimination* (Berretty et al. 1997), similar to Tversky's (1972) *Elimination by Aspects* model of preference-based choices upon which it is based, uses one cue after another in a particular order to narrow down the set of remaining possible categories until only a single one remains. When cues are ordered in terms of their usefulness in predicting the environment, accurate categorization can be achieved using only the first few of the available cues. Payne et al. (1993) included a version of Elimination by Aspects in the comparisons described earlier and found it to be "the most robust procedure as task conditions grow more difficult" (p. 140), maintaining reasonable accuracy even in large problems with severe time constraints. Even more accurate performance can arise when categorization is based on only a single cue through the use of a fine-grained cue-value-to-category map (Holte 1993). However, there is a tradeoff here between memory usage and accuracy, and although it does not matter in terms of the argument presented in this chapter, it should be kept in mind when looking for experimental evidence of whether humans employ a few-cue/low-memory versus a single-cue/high-memory strategy.

Estimation can also be performed accurately by a simple algorithm that exploits environments with a particular structure. The *QuickEst* heuristic (Hertwig et al. 1999) is designed to estimate the values of objects along some criterion while using as little information as possible. To estimate the criterion value of a particular object, the heuristic looks through the available cues or features in a criterion-determined order, until it comes to the first one that the object does not possess. At this point QuickEst stops searching for any further information and produces an estimate based on criterion values associated with the absence of the last cue. QuickEst proves to be fast and frugal, as well as accurate, in environments characterized by a distribution of criterion values in which small values are common and big values are rare (a so-called "J-shaped" distribution).

Such distributions characterize a variety of naturally occurring phenomena in-cluding many formed by accretionary growth. This growth pattern applies to cities, and indeed big cities are much less common than small ones. As a consequence, when estimating population sizes of German cities, for example, QuickEst is able to estimate rapidly and accurately the small sizes that most of them have.

Simple Heuristics for Sequential Search through Alternatives

The simple heuristics described above all attempt to minimize decision time by nding the search for information about available alternatives as quickly as pos - sible. In situations where alternatives are not currently all available, but must themselves be sought, simple heuristics can still minimize decision time by terminating search for alternatives (rather than search for cues) quickly. Such sequential search problems are often posed with the goal of seeking an alternative with a good value on a single dimension (e.g., a low-priced cappuccino machine), where each alternative seen during search provides some information about the distribution of values on that dimension. Because alternative search usually takes considerably longer than cue search, the potential speed advantages of simple heuristics in these cases are great.

Economists have explored the efficacy of simple heuristics for search in shopping contexts where each alternative seen remains available to the searcher. Thus, if the lowest price is seen on the first alternative, the searcher can go back to that alternative later (after seeing others) and make the purchase at that price. In such situations, the general finding is that little search is needed: "It seems to be the case that most of the potential gains from search are obtained in the first few searches: whatever the distribution, the marginal gains from search thereafter are relatively small" (Hey 1981, p. 65). Thus, optimal rules dictate relatively little search when there are costs for viewing each alternative, and estimating a price distribution based on even a little less search can yield nearly the same performance because of the property of flat maxima (Hey 1981, p. 60). But how do simple heuristics that similarly use little search fare? Martin and Moon (1992) used simulation to assess the relative performance of different simple strategies in a consumer search setting and found that some rules can come within 3% of optimal performance.

Another search situation, perhaps more common outside of economic contexts, occurs when each alternative seen disappears if it is not chosen. Consider for instance the sequential search for a mate: often if a potential candidate is passed by at one point, he or she will be unavailable if the searcher attempts to re-kindle a romance at a later time. In such situations, the optimal search method dictates a rather lengthy search; however, here again a simple heuristic search can achieve similar performance much more rapidly (Todd and Miller 1999).

EVIDENCE THAT PEOPLE USE ADAPTIVELY SIMPLE COGNITION

Experimental Evidence

Based on the results summarized in the previous section, it appears that for many types of tasks in many environments, information is indeed structured in a way that simple algorithms can effectively exploit, reaching adaptive decisions using a minimum of time, computation, and data. (For more details about how simple algorithms can match environment structures, see Martignon, this volume.) We have already stated that humans, too, often seem to use little time and information in decision making — but are we also doing so in a sensibly fast and frugal manner, or is our information processing merely slapdash and stingy, and consequently often inaccurate? That is, do humans make use of appropriate simple heuristics matched to the structure of the particular environments they face? This is a rather more difficult question to address, because the ultimate answers lay hidden among the internal workings of the mind, and the external evidence we have to go on is typically indirect, tricky to obtain, and hence, so far, scant. If we perform an experiment in which human achievement falls well below that of a simple heuristic applied to the same task, we could take this as evidence that people are not behaving in an adaptive manner in this domain. More often (barring active attempts to trick people into making the wrong decisions), human performance levels are similar to those of simple heuristics. Then, because the accuracy of simple and complex heuristics is also often very close, as we saw earlier, we are faced with a new problem: How can we distinguish whether people are using a simple versus a more complex decision strategy?

Sometimes we can begin to answer this question. In testing whether or not people use the recognition heuristic, for example, Goldstein and Gigerenzer (1999) found that in more than 90% of the cases where individuals could use the recognition heuristic when comparing the sizes of two cities (i.e., when they recognized one city but not the other), their choices matched those made by the recognition heuristic. This does not prove that they were actually using the recognition heuristic to make their decisions, however — they could have been doing something more complex, such as using the information about the recognized city to estimate its size and compare it to the average size of unrecognized cities (though this seems unlikely). Additional evidence that the recognition heuristic *was* being followed, though, was obtained by giving participants extra information about recognized cities that contradicted the choices that the recognition heuristic would make, that is, participants were taught that some recognized cities had cues indicating small size. Despite this conflicting information (which could have been used in the more complex estimation-based strategy described above to yield different choices), 92% of the inferences made by participants still agreed with the recognition heuristic. Furthermore, participants typically showed the less-is-more effect predicted by the earlier theoretical analysis of the recognition heuristic, strengthening suspicions of this heuristic's presence.

More often, however, comparisons of decision performance — *outcome measures* — between humans and algorithms are insufficient to distinguish between simple and complex heuristics, and comparisons on only selected items chosen to accentuate the differences between algorithms can still lead to ambiguities or ungeneralizable findings (Rieskamp and Hoffrage 1999). Instead, *process measures* can reveal differences between algorithms that are reflected in human behavior. For example, noncompensatory algorithms, particularly those that make decisions on the basis of a single cue, would direct the decision maker to search for information about one cue at a time across all of the available alternatives. In contrast, compensatory algorithms that combine all information about a particular choice would direct search for all cues one alternative at a time.

Experiments using these process measures have produced evidence that people search for information in a way consistent with noncompensatory fast and frugal heuristics. Payne et al. (1993) found that decision makers are adaptive, in the sense that they use different strategies that provide better performance in different tasks. In particular, processing can be seen to shift from extensive, unselective, alternative-based information gathering consistent with compensatory mechanisms when accuracy is at a premium, to more focused, selective, cue-based information gathering consistent with noncompensatory heuristics such as Take The Best, LEX, and Elimination by Aspects when speed is weighted more highly than accuracy. Given the assumption that the latter type of situation is more representative of the environments that shaped our cognition, these studies provide support for the adaptive use of simple fast and frugal heuristics. Further evidence in this respect comes from the studies of Rieskamp and Hoffrage (1999), especially in situations where time pressure forces rapid decisions. Finally, in sequential search settings, Martin and Moon (1992) and Hey (1982) have found through process measures and protocol analysis that people do use simple rules that limit search while still yielding adaptive outcomes. However, there is considerable variability in the data of all of these studies, with many participants appearing to use more complex strategies or behaving in ways that cannot be easily categorized, so much more research effort is required in this area.

Developmental Evidence

In addition to providing accuracy and robustness in generalization, a brain designed to process only the minimum amount of information it can get away with may actually be necessary to enable the learning of more and more complex environmental patterns in the first place. For example, Turkewitz and Kenny (1982) have argued that infants are aided in learning a vital property of objects in the world — size constancy — by their nervous system's initial limitation on visual processing. By only being able to focus on very close objects for their first few months of life, infants can learn about relative object size without the added complication of size constancy. Once this environmental knowledge has been acquired, the gradually increasing depth of visual field allows the problem of size constancy to be learned in an independent, and therefore easier, manner.

Stronger arguments have been made for language learning. It has been put forth that the cognitive limitations of the developing brain are a necessary hindrance for a first language to be learned fluently. Newport (1990) has proposed another type of "less is more" phenomenon in this domain: Lesser ability to remember and process morphological and semantic components into form–meaning mappings in young children allows them to learn more rapidly and accurately those mappings that they do acquire, and then to build further upon these as language learning proceeds. Late language learners, in contrast, may falter when attempting to learn the full range of semantic mappings with their mature mental capacities all at once.

This situation has been studied concretely by Elman (1993) in a neural network model of language acquisition. When he tried to get a large, recurrent neural network with an extensive memory to learn the grammatical relationships in a set of several thousand sentences of varying length and complexity, the network faltered. It was unable to pick up such concepts as noun–verb agreement in embedded clauses, something that requires sufficient memory to keep embedded and nonembedded clauses disentangled. Instead of taking the obvious step of adding more memory to the model to attempt to solve this problem, though, Elman counterintuitively *restricted* its memory, making the network forget everything after every three or four words. He hoped in this way to mimic the memory restrictions of young children first learning language. This restricted-memory network could not possibly make sense of the long clause-filled sentences it encountered. Its limitations forced it to focus on the short, simple sentences in its environment, which it did learn correctly, mastering the small set of grammatical relationships inherent in this subset of its input. Elman then increased the network's effective memory by forcing it to forget everything after five or six words. It was now able to learn a greater proportion of the sentences to which it was exposed, building on the grammatical relationships it had already acquired. Further gradual enhancements of the network's memory allowed it ultimately to learn the entire corpus of sentences that the full network alone — without the benefit of starting small — had been unable to fathom.

Elman sees the restrictions of the developing mind as enabling accurate early learning about a small portion of the environment, which then provides a scaffold to guide learning and hypothesizing about the rest of the environment in fruitful, adaptive directions. Cognitive "constraints" are no longer a negative limitation of our (or our children's) ability to behave adaptively in our environment. Rather,

The early limitations on memory capacity assume a more positive character. One might have predicted that the more powerful the network, the greater its ability to learn a complex domain. However, this appears not always to be the case. If the domain is of sufficient complexity, and if there are abundant false solutions [e.g., local minima in a neural network's solution space], then the opportunities for failure are great. What is required is some way to artificially constrain the solution space to just that region which contains the true solution. The initial memory limitations fill this role; they act as a filter on the input, and focus learning on just that subset of facts which lay the foundation for future success.

(Elman 1993, pp. 84–85)

Thus, a smaller memory span should not be seen as a *constraint* on language learning, but rather as an *enabler* of learning. We should be careful not to extend these arguments automatically to every problem environment that humans face — language, after all, has evolved culturally to be something that our fast and frugal developing minds *can* readily learn. Yet, evidence for the idea that less is more developmentally will add further support to the argument that less computational time and knowledge are more adaptive for many of the tasks faced by our fully developed minds as well.

Environmental Evidence

Further evidence that people use simple fast and frugal heuristics adapted to a particular environmental structure comes from the observation that we frequently restructure our task environments where possible to allow faster, more accurate decisions to be made with less information. Kirsh (1996), for example, describes how people reorder objects in their environment (such as playing cards in game situations) so that the most salient cues can be obtained and used most readily, decreasing cue search and decision time. Norman (1993) describes how our physical and cognitive artifacts should be (and how the best ones are, from filing cabinets to hardware stores) designed in a hierarchically organized fashion so that the time spent searching for a particular function or aspect will be minimized. As a final example, in the apartment-hunting study mentioned at the beginning of this chapter, Saad and Russo (1996) found that people would use half as much information in making their choices if they could see the information in an order that they specified (rather than an order given by the experimenters).

We may have shaped our decision environments more than just in terms of the artifacts we build, however. The very animals and plants around us may reflect the influences of simple decision heuristics that determined the fates of their ancestors. For example, if our forebears used only a small number of cues to distinguish edible from inedible plants, then those plants that wanted to be seen and (partly) eaten (e.g., have their fruits ingested so that their seeds could be spread) would have evolved to display just those advertising cues preferentially. They would not waste energy growing and showing off a multitude of features that would never exert any sway on the behavior of the decision makers. In con-trast, if the fruit eaters had used a combination of all available cues to decide what to eat, then the plants may have evolved to display a wider range of enticing signals. Similarly, if choosy females used a simple evolved strategy to select be-tween displaying males on the basis of just their tail length and color, they would have exerted adaptive pressure on males to display only those two costly cues and not waste effort on a variety of other advertisements that would never influ-ence the female decisions. This coevolution between decision mechanisms, and the environment structures they operate within, may be most profitably studied in tasks involving choices that can be made on the basis of multiple sources of in-formation, such as the assessment of potential mates, potential food items, or po-tential combatants, because in these cases we can test whether a large or small number of cues is actually used by the organisms concerned. In addition to studying these behavioral ramifications of coevolution in the wild, we can simu-late interacting populations of organisms who decide each other's fates to see how coevolutionary processes could have unfolded and what cognitive out-comes were likely to emerge. We are just beginning to explore these coevolutionary ideas; however, this could be another useful avenue for uncover-ing where fast and frugal heuristics are employed.

WHAT REMAINS TO BE DONE

There are a few steps in the argument presented in this chapter that readers of a less charitable nature might instead deem jumps or leaps. In the spirit of honest disclosure, and in the hope of inviting further evidence to fill in those steps, I present some of the most worrisome current potholes. These issues must be ad-dressed to support the thesis that the environment is the main source of our cog-nitive bounds, but they cannot provide proof; indeed, this thesis may be most useful for organizing and guiding further research on fast and frugal heuristics, and less as an empirical goal in itself.

First, one person's "mere 7% increase in accuracy" is another person's "50% better accuracy relative to chance." How can we tell that the small differences in performance between ecologically rational fast and frugal heuristics and more traditionally rational full-information strategies are really small enough for the former to satisfy selective pressures for accuracy when combined with their time-saving benefits? This is a very difficult question to answer. Perhaps our best approach at present is to turn to behavioral ecology studies of other species where such tradeoffs can be more readily explored.

Earlier I questioned whether the risky gambles used to compare simple heuristics by Payne et al. (1993) represented realistic decision environments, specifically of the sort that would have exerted selective forces on the evolution of human decision mechanisms. We should be just as quick to question this sta-tus of the twenty "realistic" environments used to test the Take The Best and Minimalist heuristics (Czerlinski et al. 1999) or any of the other environments within which heuristic performance has so far been measured. The problem is that we do not yet have a good understanding of what the relevant features of realistic environments are, let alone what are the most important decision environments whose features we should begin to measure in the first place. There are some types of decisions that we must make several times a day, and others that may only confront us once in a lifetime. Which types will have provided sufficient selective pressure to shape our associated mental mechanisms in a particular consistent direction, and how? Which of these are amenable to fast and frugal heuristics? It is difficult to know where to turn for help with these types of questions, but again behavioral ecology (perhaps of primate species and their environments in particular) may provide some answers, coupled with paleoecology's insights into our ancestral environment.

How do we know which cues to use in a given situation and, just as importantly, which strategy to employ in processing them? In both cases, evolution could have given us tendencies (or certainties) to implement particular cues and strategies, if past decision environments were stable for long enough. In situations that are more evolutionarily novel or variable, our cue and strategy choices may be based on simple learning mechanisms that keep track of the frequency of co-occurrence of cues and outcomes, or that adjust our likelihood to use different strategies based on reinforcement received after past use (see Erev and Roth, this volume). Finally, when more than one decision strategy can be called on, we may employ a higher-level strategy-choice heuristic, which itself should be fast and frugal for the same reasons that apply to the individual strategies. All of these possibilities, and when they hold, must be explored further.

What are we to make of the observation that across individuals there appears to be a variety of simple heuristics employed for some problems (see, e.g., Rieskamp and Hoffrage 1999; Martin and Moon 1992)? This would seem to argue against the idea that the human mind has evolved to use particular simple heuristics in particular situations. Instead, the adaptive toolbox appears to have some drawers that are crammed with many alternative tools for the same task. This may be an indication that those particular tasks were not of evolutionary significance, and so we have no fixed method for dealing with them today. However, this hunch needs to be explored more systematically. If it does not turn out to be the case, we must search for another explanation or loosen our belief in strong selection for particular simple heuristics in particular situations.

Finally, we need more examples of individual heuristics that are supported by multiple forms of evidence simultaneously, including analytical, experimental, developmental, and environmental. Most of the heuristics presented here have been explored from only one or two of these perspectives so far. Nonetheless, the converging evidence for different heuristics from different sources all points to a happy confluence of features of our world: Simple strategies that use few cues can work well in real decision environments, and fast and frugal heuristics that exploit this feature can satisfy the true bounds — temporal, rather than cognitive — of our ecological rationality.

ACKNOWLEDGMENTS

Thanks to Geoffrey Miller for originally challenging my constrained thoughts on cognitive constraints, and to Anita Todd, Jason Noble, Jörg Rieskamp, and the other members of the Center for Adaptive Behavior and Cognition for comments and insights throughout.

REFERENCES

Berretty, P.M., P.M. Todd, and P.W. Blythe. 1997. Categorization by elimination: A fast and frugal approach to categorization. In: Proc. 19th Ann. Conf. of the Cognitive Science Society, ed. M.G. Shafto and P. Langley, pp. 43–48. Mahwah, NJ: Erlbaum.

Borges, B., D.G. Goldstein, A. Ortmann, and G. Gigerenzer. 1999. Can ignorance beat the stock market? In: Simple Heuristics That Make Us Smart, G. Gigerenzer, P.M. Todd, and the ABC Research Group, pp. 59–72. New York: Oxford Univ. Press.

Brunswik, E. 1943. Organismic achievement and environmental probability. *Psych. Rev.* **50**:255–272.

Ceci, S.J., and J.K. Liker. 1986. A day at the races: A study of IQ, expertise, and cognitive complexity. *J. Exp. Psych.: Gen.* **115**:255–266.

Conlisk, J. 1996. Why bounded rationality? *J. Econ. Lit.* **34**:669–700.

Czerlinski, J., G. Gigerenzer, and D.G. Goldstein. 1999. How good are simple heuristics? In: Simple Heuristics That Make Us Smart, G. Gigerenzer, P.M. Todd, and the ABC Research Group, pp. 97–118. New York: Oxford Univ. Press.

Elman, J.L. 1993. Learning and development in neural networks: The importance of starting small. *Cognition* **48**:71–99.

Ericsson, K.A., and W. Kintsch. 1995. Long-term working memory. *Psych. Rev.* **102**:211–245.

Galef, B.G., Jr. 1987. Social influences on the identification of toxic foods by Norway rats. *Anim. Learn. Behav.* **18**:199–205.

Gigerenzer, G., and D.G. Goldstein. 1996. Reasoning the fast and frugal way: Models of bounded rationality. *Psych. Rev.* **103**:650–669.

Gigerenzer, G., and D.G. Goldstein. 1999. Betting on one good reason: The Take The Best heuristic. In: Simple Heuristics That Make Us Smart, G. Gigerenzer, P.M. Todd, and the ABC Research Group, pp. 75–95. New York: Oxford Univ. Press.

Goldstein, D.G., and G. Gigerenzer. 1999. The recognition heuristic: How ignorance makes us smart. In: Simple Heuristics That Make Us Smart, G. Gigerenzer, P.M. Todd, and the ABC Research Group, pp. 37–58. New York: Oxford Univ. Press.

Hertwig, R., U. Hoffrage, and L. Martignon. 1999. Quick estimation: Letting the environment do the work. In: Simple Heuristics That Make Us Smart, G. Gigerenzer, P.M. Todd, and the ABC Research Group, pp. 209–234. New York: Oxford Univ. Press.

Hey, J.D. 1981. Are optimal search rules reasonable? And vice versa? (And does it matter anyway?) *J. Econ. Behav. Org.* **2**:47–70.

Hey, J.D. 1982. Search for rules for search. *J. Econ. Behav. Org.* **3**:65–81.

Holte, R.C. 1993. Very simple classification rules perform well on most commonly used data sets. *Mach. Learn.* **3(11)**:63–91.

Kirsh, D. 1996. Adapting the environment instead of oneself. *Adapt. Behav.* **4(3/4)**:415–452.

Luria, A.R. 1968. The Mind of a Mnemonist. Transl. L. Solotaroff. New York: Basic.

Martin, A., and P. Moon. 1992. Purchasing decisions, partial knowledge, and economic search: Experimental and simulation evidence. *J. Behav. Decis. Mak.* **5(4)**:253–266.

Miller, G.F. 1997. Protean primates: The evolution of adaptive unpredictability in competition and courtship. In: Machiavellian Intelligence II: Extensions and Evaluations, ed. A. Whiten and R.W. Byrne, pp. 312–340. Cambridge: Cambridge Univ. Press.

Newport, E.L. 1990. Maturational constraints on language learning. *Cog. Sci.* **14**:11–28.

Norman, D.A. 1993. Things That Make Us Smart: Defending Human Attributes in the Age of the Machine. Reading, MA: Addison-Wesley.

Payne, J.W., J.R. Bettman, and E.J. Johnson. 1993. The Adaptive Decision Maker. New York: Cambridge Univ. Press.

Rieskamp, J., and U. Hoffrage. 1999. When do people use simple heuristics, and how can we tell? In: Simple Heuristics That Make Us Smart, G. Gigerenzer, P.M. Todd, and the ABC Research Group, pp. 141–167. New York: Oxford Univ. Press.

Saad, G., and J.E. Russo. 1996. Stopping criteria in sequential choice. *Org. Behav. Human Decis. Proc.* **67(3)**:258–270.

Simon, H.A. 1990. Invariants of human behavior. *Ann. Rev. Psych.* **41**:1–19.

Sober, E. 1994. The adaptive advantage of learning and *a priori* prejudice. In: From a Biological Point of View, ed. E. Sober, pp. 50–70. Cambridge: Cambridge Univ. Press.

Todd, P.M., and G.F. Miller. 1999. From pride and prejudice to persuasion: Satisficing in mate search. In: Simple Heuristics That Make Us Smart, G. Gigerenzer, P.M. Todd, and the ABC Research Group, pp. 287–308. New York: Oxford Univ. Press.

Turkewitz, G., and P.A. Kenny. 1982. Limitations on input as a basis for neural organization and perceptual development: A preliminary theoretical statement. *Dev. Psychobiol.* **15(4)**:357–368.

Tversky, A. 1972. Elimination by aspects: A theory of choice. *Psych. Rev.* **79(4)**:281–299.

Tversky, A., and D. Kahneman. 1974. Judgment under uncertainty: Heuristics and biases. *Science* **185**:1124–1131.

Whiten, A., and R.W. Byrne, eds. 1997. Machiavellian Intelligence. II. Extensions and Evaluations. Cambridge: Cambridge Univ. Press.

5

Evolutionary Adaptation and the Economic Concept of Bounded Rationality — A Dialogue

Peter Hammerstein

Innovationskolleg Theoretische Biologie, Humboldt University,
Invalidenstr. 43, 10115 Berlin, Germany

Imagine a late night discussion between two scientists: one an economist, the other a biologist. Both have always been fascinated by each other's discipline and by the links between their disciplines. But tonight, as Fate would have it, after consuming a few too many drinks at the bar, they appear to have lost some of their intellectual self-restraint, not to mention inhibitions, and are eager to get each other's goat. As the conversation switches from family life to the more nitty-gritty subjects of rationality and Darwinian adaptation, they end up saying what has been on their minds all these years. Both are convinced that nobody is listening to their conversation, for such things would never be said for all to hear. But, of course, we do.

* * * * *

Economist: The edifice of thought in my field has for decades been built on the assumption that the business world consists of rational or almost rational decision makers. Much to our chagrin, however, empirical insights from psychology and experimental economics cast serious doubt on this assumption, and thus we economists have started to explore the bounds of rationality.

Have you experienced this too in your intellectual pursuits? Better yet, to what extent is bounded rationality an issue in the biological study of animal behavior?

Biologist: Let me give you a straight answer instead of beating around the bush. We biologists have never held much stock in your economic concept of full rationality. Quite frankly, it's a bit too strange for us. Think about it for a moment: under full rationality you have an organism that is supposed to be capable of correctly solving every mathematical problem — no matter how difficult — without any cognitive limitation, in zero time, and at no cost. That's some organism! Just imagine what kind of a "superbrain" it would have to possess, not to mention the fact that it wouldn't have to obey the laws of physics or the constraints of human physiology. Such an organism belongs in a science fiction novel.

In my opinion, full economic rationality resembles a straw man. First you economists build this straw man, and then you burn it! We biologists do not feel the urge to burn that which we haven't built in the first place. So you see, for us, "bounded rationality" is not very appealing.

Being scientists and not philosophers (*B straightens up a bit in his chair*), we have always strived to understand how animals, including humans, behave in *REALITY*. We can't help it if you've only just started to worry deeply about reality. We've been doing it for decades, if not centuries!

In the long history of empirical research on animal behavior (*note the extension of B's nose toward the heavens*), we have learned that organisms make excellent use of their mental resources, and thus our respect for the sophisticated evolutionary design of their minds is immense. If there is anything we would call rationality in biology, it is the "natural wisdom" that evolution has laid into our and other animals' minds.

Economist: Wait a minute now (*leaning forward, finger ready to point*), I don't quite buy your excessive, negative attitude toward the economic concept of rationality. You claim that this concept is of no importance to biology but it is evident to me that biologists frequently use ideas from traditional economics. Take the field of behavioral ecology, where animals are looked upon as if they were maximizing expected fitness. Now replace the term *fitness* with *utility* and you will most certainly see that you are dealing with individuals who are entirely rational in the sense of our traditional economic theory!

Biologist (*leaning back and stretching his legs*): Admittedly, it does make sense to talk about the quasi-rationality of animal behavior — and I have done so myself. The process of evolution has a tendency to create mental mechanisms that maximize fitness in the natural habitat. But be careful. Don't take this statement to mean that I agree with what you just said. First of all (*a light tap on the table for emphasis*), the maximization we are talking about in behavioral ecology does not take place in the animal's mind. The evolutionary process itself is conceived as the maximizing agent. Secondly, optimization is thought to happen in a constrained set of biologically realistic behavioral alternatives and is far from being global.

This is how we conceive of adaptation. So, clearly, one implication is that animals cannot be expected to be very good at handling situations that they have not repeatedly encountered in their evolutionary past.

Economist (*looking ever so sly*): How so? The human mind seems to be quite good at mastering new situations that have never existed in its evolutionary history. You've been driving a car for many years and are still alive! Some humans have even flown to the moon and returned safely. Certainly you would agree that to control a car or a spaceship is a difficult task and requires a long series of quick decisions in "real time." Consider now the notion of economic rationality as an idealization of this surprising capability of the human mind and not as something based on ignorance with regard to physics and physiology. Within this view, the notion of rationality does not look as odd as you suggest.

May I further remind you of the fact that biologists themselves are prone to base their thoughts on highly idealized pictures of the real world. For example, much if not most of the evolutionary thinking in behavioral ecology fails to be explicit about genetics and inheritance. It would be naive to dismiss all of this thinking simply because it ignores the basic mechanics of reproduction in sexually reproducing, diploid Mendelian populations.

Biologist: Wait a minute. First things first. Let's deal with my driving skills and leave the problem of genetics until later.

There is a difference between driving a car and directing a company. Our human ancestors often had to run at high speed and avoid hitting trees while doing so. This obviously means that preadaptions exist for the processing of visual information involved in car driving. But with business management, it is much harder to imagine the preadaptations for directing a large company. Furthermore, humans have adapted the automobile to our mental capacity. For example, instead of computing the car's speed ourselves, we rely on a speedometer; also, a signal tells us when we are running out of gasoline, etc. Cars are specifically designed to be manageable by the human mind. In contrast, the business world — with its markets and complicated interactions — is a product of self-organization. It wasn't designed by anybody, and nobody adapted it to the manager's mind.

Now, let's deal with the subject of idealization. Yes, indeed, we biologists make use of idealizations, just like everyone else in science. The question, however, is — what do we call a "good" idealization? Consider our brain. Its virtue lies not in the fact that it would beat a high-end computer when it comes to solving numerical problems in mathematics but, for example, that it has incredibly low energy consumption compared to a big computer. It runs on something like 7 watts, and yet is capable of governing an organism throughout its life. Now that's impressive! Even your personal computer on your desk consumes considerably far more energy than that and is not the all-purpose machine that runs your life.

Economist: Well, if so little energy goes into the brain, I fail to see why you admire its evolutionary design so much. Wouldn't it be reasonable to say that a creature with additional energy flow to the brain could do far better than current human beings?

Biologist: Come on. The 7-watt energy consumption of the brain may look negligible to you, but for our body, this is impressive. After all, when you think of it, we sacrifice 20 to 30 percent of our basic metabolic rate to brain activity, and this is quite a lot. We biologists view the animal brain, especially when one considers all of the various constraints under which it operates, as something close to a miracle!

Economist (*chuckling to himself*): A miracle? This makes you sound just like a creationist praising God's beautiful craftsmanship.

Biologist: If you're laughing now, wait 'til you hear the story about one of my international colleagues, who is currently living in Germany with his family. He has a young son in the third grade and, as you probably know, religion is taught as a subject in German schools. Well, recently, the son was asked by his schoolteacher what religion he had been taught at home. The boy pondered and thought, and had great difficulty answering the question, most likely because of the agnostic tendencies of his parents. But after awhile, he came to the conclusion that he probably belonged to the Darwinian religion that was so often discussed around the dinner table.

Economist: So, you admit to my criticism!

Biologist: Don't be ridiculous — of course I don't! Every strong theory runs the risk of slipping into the role of a religion. The fascination caused by a theory's explanatory power often leads one to overestimate this power. And the very act of overestimating demonstrates nicely the boundedness of human rationality. *This* is why I told you the story of my colleague's child.

Economist: Anything you say ... but you still owe me an explanation as to why the brain is so good at performing its tasks and is nevertheless a poor mathematician.

Biologist: No problem. Use your imagination. Pretend you are trying to program a robot to catch a ball that somebody is throwing at it. It won't be long before you will discover just what a formidable task this actually is. As a matter of fact, I saw you playing squash earlier — you do it quite well. So at least *your* brain is capable of accomplishing a very complicated task. The question is: How did your brain accomplish such a high level of performance?

We don't have enough time for me to go into that one, so let's look at what a smaller brain can do. Here it will be easier to discuss the mental mechanisms and their algorithmic structure. Take the desert ant *Cataglyphis*, found in the arid zones of Northern Africa. *Cataglyphis* has the morphological attributes of a very agile animal and resembles, to some extent, a racing horse.[1] To forage, individuals leave the nest and quickly move out of sight of the nest. They may easily need to travel more than 200 meters away from the nest. The formidable task to be performed by their little brains is a navigational one. After walking fast on a rather circuitous trajectory, they have to find their nest again. Usually they can be observed walking straight back home to the nest, although their habitat offers very few conspicuous landmarks. An engineer would maintain that by permanently measuring rotation and translation components of its movement, the ant could use path integration to keep track of the direction and distance at which the nest is to be expected. However, the brain of *Cataglyphis* has a very small number of nerve cells (about one millionth the number of nerve cells in the human brain). Thus it seems hard to believe that a very advanced "mathematical co-processor" could be found in this tiny information-processing machine.

Economist: Don't you want to claim a miracle again?

Biologist: Stop it! I would not have mentioned *Cataglyphis* had it not been studied very carefully, with success, I might add. Rüdiger Wehner[2] has conducted a series of experiments to find out just how this tiny brain actually achieves what seems so difficult a task. The following picture has emerged from his work: *Cataglyphis* has a skylight compass that utilizes the pattern of polarized light. The ant possesses an internal representation of the sky's polarization pattern for one particular position of the sun. The ant then compares this "template" with the external pattern and that is, roughly speaking, how the compass works. Wehner has also shown that this compass can make considerable errors, in particular because of the static internal representation of a changing external pattern. So much in terms of angle measurement. Distances can be measured by keeping track of leg movements. But how does the ant update the vector that points to the nest after walking for some time in a new direction? Does *Cataglyphis* perform anything like trigonometric calculations? From Wehner's experiments we learn that the ants seem to use a simpler procedure. Some of his empirical findings could be explained with the following procedural scheme:

Suppose that the ant's present estimate of the direction towards home is α, and the distance is d. Let the animal change its walking course by an angle δ and consider a unit step in the new direction. Calculate the updated value of α to be:

$$\alpha' = \alpha + \delta/(d+1) \, .$$

In other words, rescale the angle measuring the change of direction by the distance from home and calculate the new estimate of the home direction by adding the rescaled change of direction to the previous home direction.

In the experiments, the ants behave as if they did this kind of calculation, rather than using trigonometry, to solve their problems. I must admit, however, that we do not really know the complete information-processing sequence that is going on in their minds.

Economist: If the algorithm cannot be described fully in terms of neural circuitry, how did Wehner then come up with this picture of the algorithm?

Biologist: The method is to expose *Cataglyphis* to various situations in which its navigational system makes serious errors. From these errors one can learn about the way in which the ant processes information. To put it in your language, we should be happy that *Cataglyphis* is boundedly rational and makes mistakes. If it didn't make so many mistakes, it would probably be much harder to understand its navigational system.

Economist: Okay, but let's return to the major thread of our discussion. I can see that mistakes help to identify the ant's algorithms. However, the fact that serious mistakes are made does not exactly look to me like evidence in favor of the maximizing tendencies of the evolutionary process. I take it that these ants have been around for many generations and had a good chance, genetically speaking, to become perfect navigators.

Biologist: I don't like where you are going with this. You are pushing me into a position as if I had defended the idea of full rationality. Let us adopt the more down-to-earth view of an evolutionary biologist. There is, first of all, the problem of how the compass may have arisen. The compound eye of an insect can be seen as a preadaptation because it does, in some sense, represent the sky. After the compass had been invented, the new problem was how to deal with its errors. Instead of creating several internal templates of polarization patterns for various positions of the sun, evolution has maintained the simple compass but generated ways of coping with the error. Within a short time span, the error is systematic and can be corrected by some sort of initial calibration of the system. This is precisely what *Cataglyphis* seems to do.

Economist: Well, perhaps the ant is not quite as bad as I thought. But don't go too fast. The error correction by initial calibration is doomed to fail when the ant takes off on a long excursion and the sky pattern changes during the excursion. Thus, you still have failed to convince me of the power of evolutionary adaptation.

Biologist: Don't be in a hurry, we are almost there. You'll get the point of the desert ant example in a moment.

In this example, we are considering real organisms in their natural habitat. Anyone who has ever visited a desert, however, knows that physiological stress brought on directly or indirectly by solar radiation is a major threat to health and survival in this environment. Those who live in deserts have necessarily adapted their behavior to this threat. Unlike German tourists, Bedouins do not strip off their clothes for sun bathing in the desert and, in a similar spirit, *Cataglyphis* carefully avoids long excursions, where heat stress would represent real danger. Now, if the excursions have to be short anyway, then it does not matter to the ant's performance in life how poorly its compass works during a fictitious marathon run. The compass only has to work well in relation to how it is actually used by the organism. Single components of a living system do not have to be anything like close to perfection in order to create very good overall system performance in an organism. This is what we see again and again in our animal studies, and it does not at all invalidate the idea of evolutionary adaptation. Some of what is discussed in economics as bounded rationality may be caused by the imperfection of components of the behavior-generating system — components that work together synergistically in the natural habitat. In an atypical habitat, the interplay of the same components may turn into a disaster. Our ancestors probably did not suffer from being unable to do complicated mathematics, simply because other components of their behavior-generating apparatus would not have used the results anyway. However, in the modern world, we put ourselves into situations in which we make use of our computational potential. Not surprisingly, the effect can be very discouraging.

Suppose a member of the medical profession tests a person for an infection and the result is positive. Further, let us say that the prevalence of the disease in the population is 1/1000. Assume that the test is always positive if the tested person is infected, and that the probability of a false alarm is 0.05. What then is the probability that a person with a positive test result actually has the disease?

Economist (*groan*): I know what you are aiming at. It is the base rate fallacy. How boring! We have discussed this over and over again in psychology and economics!

Biologist: Yes, I know, but even still its importance has not diminished! If half the professional staff of a renowned medical school estimates this probability to be 0.95 instead of correctly saying "approximately 0.02," then I feel very insecure as to whether or not I should visit my physician at all!

Economist: Let's get off this subject and talk about fitness maximization. If the desert ant uses the algorithm that Wehner describes, does it really maximize fitness?

Biologist: Well, the ant is able to go straight back home. It solves this task very well, but like a golf ball that ends up a little to the left or right of the hole, the ant does not always hit its target exactly by merely relying on the procedure I outlined a few minutes ago. Instead, the ant deals with the imperfection of its basic navigation mechanism by using a second mechanism, which corrects the error of the first. It uses landmarks as soon as it is close to its target. I am not worried that the ant could do slightly better; in our theory, optimality is also an idealization. What really worries me is that one cannot design a model for the evolution of desert navigation systems, calculate the optima, and predict *Cataglyphis* in the end. The space of all potential navigation systems would be so immense that it seems impossible to ever delineate the optimization problem. A similar problem would arise in the study of the evolution of learning procedures.

Mind you, some biologists may have a different opinion and think that by knowing the properties of the primordial soup we can predict the elephant, solving a few optimization problems along the way. However, those who really participate in the mathematical modeling of evolutionary biology often feel like detectives trying to reconstruct a crime instead of predicting it. Perhaps the most frequent job of an evolutionary theorist is to reconstruct the selective forces that are likely to have shaped a trait under investigation. The reconstruction often involves construction of an optimization model or a game.

Economist: This sounds like curve fitting, except that you fit optimization models instead of simple curves to your data.

Biologist: I think you are right. Let me add that model fitting is what physicists have done throughout the history of their discipline. One has to do a lot of model fitting before new general principles are discovered.

Economist: One thing occurs like an indisputable law of nature in your picture of evolution: the principle of fitness maximization. Perhaps it blindfolds you in the same way that we have been blindfolded by assuming full rationality?

Biologist (*reflectively*): A blindfold? I would be as skeptical as you are if biologists had not succeeded in explaining so many traits of organisms by searching for optimality and the Nash equilibrium. But fitness maximization is far from being a law or first principle of evolutionary theory. We can write down models that idealize the evolutionary process in different ways. And in these models, optimality or Nash equilibria will occur if one characterizes equilibrium states with certain stability properties. Of course, this is only true if the appropriate assumptions are made.

Economist: Am I right in interpreting the look on your face that the list of assumptions under which optimality fails must be quite long, and that you are unwilling to go through all of this with me?

Biologist: Not exactly. I am not *unwilling* to do this, but it would be a rather comprehensive course in evolutionary theory, and I'm not sure that the bar stays open that long. Theoreticians have tortured their minds throughout this century trying to capture the spirit of Darwinian adaptation in the light of what we now know about the mechanics of reproduction. Repeatedly, it looked as if facts in genetics were blurring the Darwinian picture to such an extent that Darwin was said to be dead. And then we saw his resurrection.

Economist: Not bad for the founder of a religion!

Biologist: Stop teasing! Let me talk seriously about three major criticisms. The first stems from the idea that most replacements of genes in the genome are the result of selectively neutral chance events rather than Darwinian selection. This idea has created the controversy about neutral evolution. Let us play the devil's advocate and assume that indeed the majority of changes in the genome are due to random drift. Even then we would still have to explain why the male stickleback has a red spot on his belly. Believe me, any male stickleback without a red spot will have a hard time attracting females and will most certainly fail to reproduce. To mate or not to mate: this is what the spot is about!

We would contradict ourselves if we were to assume that the genes responsible for the spot undergo neutral evolution. Whenever we talk about fitness maximization, we are addressing a problem where nonneutral selective forces can be identified. These are the problems Darwin addressed in his work, just as these are the problems that have been overlooked by some advocates of the neutrality hypothesis.

Economist: And the other two criticisms?

Biologist: Well, the second one is that Mendelian genetics and recombination can impose constraints on phenotypic evolution, so that phenotypic optima and Nash equilibria may not be permitted by these constraints. One can argue, however, that evolution will successively remove these constraints and finally arrive at the phenotypic optimum if there is enough time before the environment changes. I like to compare this course of a population with a streetcar[3] that comes to a halt at various stops along its route before it reaches its final destination. Only the final stop has the optimality and Nash equilibria properties that we have discussed so far. The population will not stay forever at such a final stop: one reason being the changing environment; another being the possible occurrence of selfish genetic elements.

These are parts of the genome that have a positive effect on their own rates of reproduction but a negative effect on the organism's fitness.

One example of such an element is a little B-chromosome that occurs in a parasitic wasp called *Nasonia vitripennis*.[4] After fertilization of an egg, half the genome is destroyed by manipulation of the B-chromosome. This in turn induces a sex change from a female organism into a male. The reason why B-chromosomes benefit from this sex change is that they are better transmitted into the next generation by males than by females. To end the story about selfish elements, they can occur and may have strange effects. However, organisms defend themselves against selfish elements, and their scope seems to be fairly limited. Note, for example, that most populations of *Nasonia vitripennis* are not plagued by the selfish B-chromosome!

Economist: The two kinds of genetic problems you just mentioned do not seem to cause you nightmares. So, what would be your nightmares as a theoretician in evolutionary biology?

Biologist: The biggest problem in my field is to find a biologically meaningful set of phenotypes on which selection is assumed to operate, to identify trade-offs, constraints, and (last, but not least) the fitness effects. During a study it often turns out that one of these elements of the evolutionary model has been identified incorrectly.

Let me give you an example. Together with Susan Riechert, Peter Hammerstein analyzed territorial fights in the spider *Agelenopsis aperta*.[5] An interesting aspect of these fights is that two female opponents would initially use the web as a scale and assess their *relative* weight. This information plays a major role in determining who will start a physical attack, etc. Throughout their short lives the spiders have many fights with different opponents, each time measuring relative weight. By keeping track of these measurements, the spiders could also, in principle, have a good estimate of their own weight in relation to the local population. Two very small spiders should then have a tendency to fight fiercely against each other because most other potential opponents in the population will be larger and thus harder to defeat. In Hammerstein and Riechert's first model of the spider interactions, they assumed that the spiders knew how small or large they were in relation to the local population. This model made the true spiders look as if they were bad at maximizing fitness. But as soon as the assumption that spiders know their own weight compared to the population was dropped, the forces of Darwinian selection became very transparent.

Economist (*smiling*): I am pleased to hear that there is bounded rationality in a spider!

Biologist: Waiter ... could we have the bill?

ACKNOWLEDGMENT

I am grateful to Julia Lupp for being such a wonderful "bartender" and making sense of my "drunken raving."

NOTES

1 Wehner, R. 1994. Himmelsbild und Kompaßauge — Neurobiologie eines Navigationssystems. *Verh. Deut. Zool. Ges.* **87.2**:9–37.

2 Wehner, R. 1997. Sensory systems and behaviour. In: Behavioural Ecology: An Evolutionary Approach, ed. J.R. Krebs and N.B. Davies, pp. 9–41. Oxford: Blackwell Science.

3 Hammerstein, P. 1996. Darwinian adaptation, population genetics and the streetcar theory of evolution. *J. Math. Biol.* **34**:511–532.

4 Werren, J.H. 1991. The paternal sex ratio chromosome of *Nasonia. Am. Nat.* **137**:392–402.

5 Hammerstein, P., and S.E. Riechert. 1988. Payoffs and strategies in territorial contest: ESS analyses of two ecotypes of the spider *Agelenopsis aperta. Evol. Ecol.* **2**:115–138.

Seated, left to right: Bertrand Munier, Bettina Kuon, Abdolkarim Sadrieh
Standing, left to right: Massimo Warglien, Peter Hammerstein, Ulrich Hoffrage, Martin Weber, Stevan Harnad, Werner Güth, Peter Todd

6

Group Report: Is There Evidence for an Adaptive Toolbox?

Abdolkarim Sadrieh, Rapporteur
Werner Güth, Peter Hammerstein, Stevan Harnad,
Ulrich Hoffrage, Bettina Kuon, Bertrand R. Munier,
Peter M. Todd, Massimo Warglien, and Martin Weber

INTRODUCTION

There is ample evidence supporting Simon's (1955) observation that decision making often does not — and perhaps cannot — fully abide by the axioms of rationality (see chapters by Selten, Gigerenzer, Klein, and Payne and Bettmann, all this volume). However, establishing that the rationality of decision makers is bounded can only be the first step towards a better understanding of decision making. The second step should be the analysis of the structure of processes and outcomes. Many attempts have been made to identify and characterize the set of heuristics and rules that could play a fundamental role in boundedly rational decision making (see chapters by Selten, Gigerenzer, and Todd, all this volume). Yet, there is much left to learn about the "tools" in the "adaptive toolbox" that is used for decision making. In this chapter we provide a brief (and necessarily incomplete) assessment of commonly observed structures of boundedly rational decision making, in an attempt to spur future, more comprehensive explorations.

In a rather skeptical manner, we begin by scrutinizing: "What evidence do we have on the tools in the adaptive toolbox?" and then we provide the provisional answers that are currently available. In every answer we try to include and combine the knowledge from anthropology, biology, economics, and psychology. The goal is to gain deeper insight by crossing the conventional borders of the fields that study and model decision behavior.

In what follows, we often refer to "simple rules" or "simple heuristics." Obviously, the question of how to measure the complexity of rules is an important issue that should precede such discussions. However, we refrain from offering a general and rigorous definition of complexity, for two reasons. First, such a definition poses a challenge that is clearly out of the range of this paper. Second, in our view, the nature of complexity will be quite obvious in many of the applications we discuss (e.g., linear cost functions are much more easily understood than nonlinear ones, etc.). Usually it suffices to assume that simpler rules rely on fewer contingencies than more complex ones.

The rest of the chapter is organized as follows. We begin by asking why it is that the decision-making tools are simple rules, for animals as well as for humans. We will pay special attention to the role of evolution in this context. Next we examine the relation of the heuristics in the adaptive toolbox to the artifacts in the decision environment. We then ask how the hypotheses about the nature and significance of these rules and heuristics should be devised and validated. Finally, we try to find classifications for the decision situations by examining which of the rules can be most appropriately used to model decision making, in what types of situations. The final section is devoted to exploring the effect of social interaction on the modeling of the tools in the adaptive toolbox.

DID EVOLUTION PRODUCE SIMPLE RULES AND HEURISTICS?

To understand why evolution may support simple rules, two aspects of the matter must be examined. On one hand, tasks that seem difficult for human beings to perform may be easily performed by evolution. This is mainly due to the fact that the process of mutation and selection is quite different as a "problem-solving strategy" from cognitive problem solving by human beings. Experiments with human subjects, for example, have shown the "winner's curse" to persist even after many trials with complete information feedback (Ball et al. 1991; Bazerman and Samuelson 1983; Selten et al., in preparation). It seems extremely difficult to learn the relatively simple deliberation of conditional probabilities that leads to the resolution of this "adverse selection" problem. There are many examples in biology, however, showing that such an adverse selection would quickly lead to the extinction of the winner's curse in an evolutionary setting (see the example of the navigation of the *Cataglyphis* and other examples in Hammerstein, this volume.)

On the other hand, difficulties that seem easy to overcome by human standards may be left unresolved by evolution. Two major obstacles for the evolutionary process can be pointed out. First, evolution by mutation and selection can only go from one stage to the next gradually. The system cannot "jump" to any arbitrary better state. Thus, if the performance of a task can only be enhanced via a whole set of mutations that must come simultaneously, this enhancement is not likely to evolve. Second, effective selection only takes place if fitness differences are substantial. Finally, unlike human decision makers, natural selection has no "foresight." This particularly means that in cases in which human decision makers may "invest" some of their resources today for a better outcome tomorrow, natural selection cannot follow such a path.

There is plenty of evidence on animal behavior that can be explained best with models of simple rules and heuristics (see Hammerstein, Laland, and Seeley, all this volume). Testing for the relevance of such models is often relatively simple, because experiments with animals — especially insects — allow some manipulations which cannot be performed with human subjects.

Some objections, however, can be legitimately raised:

1. Humans were the most widely scattered species at the time the set of simple rules probably evolved. *Homo sapiens* could be found from the edge of the glacier to the center of the rain forest at the time. This "wide ecological range" may have caused a set of rules to evolve in human beings that was completely different from those in specific insects. Thus, some care should be taken in generalizing results from animal data, especially from insect data.
2. Insects have more stereotyped behaviors than mammals.
3. The functioning of the human brain is not fully understood, so it is hard to evaluate the physiological trade-offs that govern the activity of the brain. This in turn makes it very difficult to draw inferences on the evolutionary process leading to the creation of the brain.

Finally, it should be noted that in some organisms, simple important rules are "backed up" by other simple rules, either creating a redundant method for emergency cases or compensating the errors in the first rule. Experiments with pigeons, for example, have shown that if the magnetic navigation system usually used is manipulated, the pigeons are at first lost, but then switch to a back-up navigation system. The example of the *Cataglyphis* (see Hammerstein, this volume) shows that combining two simple rules guarantees that typical errors made by the first rule are compensated by the second instead of being summed up and leading to a catastrophic situation.

ARE COMPLICATED TASKS PERFORMED USING SIMPLE TOOLS?

Goldstein and Gigerenzer (1999) report an experiment in which both a North American (Chicago) and a German subject population were asked to judge which of the two cities, San Diego or San Antonio, was the larger. The surprising result of the experiment was that the right answer was given much more frequently by the subject population that had less background information about the question: in contrast to 100% of German subjects, only 62% of the American subjects gave the right answer. The result suggests that the German subjects were using a very simple, but successful heuristic: the recognition heuristic.

Using this heuristic the German subjects simply judged the city they had heard of to be the larger city.

Another experiment was conducted by Gigerenzer and Goldstein to test this hypothesis: a similar set of questions ("Which is the larger city?") was used; however, this time the subjects were also presented with a cue that contradicted the recognition heuristic. (Subjects were given specific information as to whether or not a particular city had a soccer team in the major league — a powerful cue for large population size. The information contained in this cue was selected so that subjects relying only on this information could infer that the city less likely to be recognized was the larger city.) Despite the supplemented information, about 90% of the subjects judged the city they recognized as being the larger. This seems to be evidence for the behavioral importance of the recognition heuristic.

A number of studies have put effort into discovering and/or testing heuristics that are actually used by decision makers (see Selten, Gigerenzer, and Payne and Bettmann, all this volume). The field is still quite far from presenting a complete and coherent picture. The basic problem is that, in most cases, decision heuristics for very specific tasks have been elicited or tested. Validating the discovered (or proposed) heuristics across broad classes of decision-making tasks remains an important open research question.

Next to the research concerned with the experimental elicitation or testing of heuristics, some theoretical work has been done with the aim of specifying sets of simple and frugal heuristics that are possible candidates for an adequate modeling of boundedly rational decision making (see Gigerenzer, Payne and Bettman, and Martignon, all this volume). The question arises as to what criteria should be used in judging the adequacy of these models. We defer this discussion to later (see section on HOW CAN WE DEVISE AND VALIDATE MODELS OF DECISION MAKING?). For now it is important to note that quite a bit of (partially anecdotal) evidence suggests that in some environments a number of different heuristics may be used by decision makers simultaneously. This point can be illustrated in the case of behavior in financial asset markets.

In an experiment reported by Borges et al. (1999), North American and German subjects were asked to indicate which companies they recognized from those listed on the New York and German stock exchanges. The portfolios containing only stocks of companies that were recognized by at least 90% of the subjects in each group performed better than the portfolios containing the stocks of those companies that were recognized by no more than 10%. The authors explain this in terms of a positive correlation between profitability and acclaim, concluding that a simple recognition heuristic can sometimes beat the market. However, they further suggest that the result should be interpreted with caution because of the short time span (6 months) it covered, especially as the experiment took place during a period of strong and rising stocks, a time when large, well-established firms are thought to perform better than average.

Long-term studies concerned with simple investment heuristics for asset markets have produced no clear evidence for the superiority of one heuristic over the other. Most of the research concerned with the question "Can an expert beat the market?" has concluded that the answer is: "In general, no." None of the many heuristics known to be used by traders (including anything from simple "technical" rules to astrology) results in long-term, above average performance. Several reasons have been put forward to explain why so many different heuristics coexist, i.e., are proposed, paid for, and actually used by traders on financial asset markets (see, e.g., Bromann et al. 1997).

One possible explanation is the difficulty in learning from feedback from a highly complicated decision situation. Making the right inferences from complex multicausal feedback is difficult. Diffuse reinforcement can quickly lead to the construction of inadequate and/or complicated heuristics. These heuristics might survive, in much the same way superstitions survive, through false correlation and biased attributions of success and failure (see, e.g., the phenomenon of "illusory correlation" described in Fiedler et al. 1993).

A second explanation of why inadequate heuristics sometimes govern the decisions of traders is that having a rule to follow makes traders "feel better" than having no systematic approach at all. This may also be the reason why gamblers often use a "system" for gambling. The demand for superstition-based decision support is huge and the number of publications on the topic is an indicator of the extent to which such heuristics are used.

A third conceivable reason why inadequate heuristics survive is that many of the technical analytic devices which provide asset market traders with decision support are closely related. The similarity between the devices in combination with widespread usage can cause substantial correlated action. These actions, i.e., simultaneous buy or sell offers on a certain cue, lead to self-induced market movements. Since the movements typically match the heuristics that produced them in the first place, a self-fulfilling cycle can be sustained.

That so many different heuristics coexist also supports the basic finding that none of the simple rules used in financial asset markets is truly superior to the others — at least not in the long run. Even though learning is difficult in the context of the diffuse feedback of such markets, it seems plausible to expect that a truly superior heuristic would quickly spread and evolve as the dominant rule in the environment. Since such domination is not observed, the hypothesis that no heuristic has clear performance advantages seems well founded.

The phenomenon of false correlation and attributions appears not only in the context of financial markets. It is much more general. It typically occurs in those situations in which the feedback on actions is multicausal, complex, and partially random. Anthropologists report that many superstitious beliefs have survived over multiple generations under such feedback circumstances. The example of the superstitious rituals followed before and during a sports competition by many athletes and onlookers suggests that this phenomenon is far from obsolete in modern human society.

Most imaginable and practicable heuristics will not produce superior results, but even those fast and frugal heuristics that have been shown experimentally and/or theoretically to be successful and robust (see Gigerenzer, Todd, and Martignon, all this volume) can sometimes perform quite poorly. The recognition heuristic, for example, can lead to suboptimal results when it is used to support private savings decisions. A decision maker following the rule typically ends up holding a portfolio that contains too many assets closely correlated with the current source of income. Instead of diversifying the joint risk of income and savings (i.e., buying assets from diverse countries and industries), investors using the recognition heuristic buy assets of their own home region or even of their own company. This type of investment behavior is often referred to as the "home bias" (see, e.g., Kilka and Weber 1997).

The question of the extent to which certain simple heuristics have been brought forth by the evolution of human beings is not yet well investigated. The "Follow the Expert" heuristic, for example, may have evolved from a "Follow the Leader" heuristic, which was adapted to hunting and gathering societies. Similarly, scenarios are conceivable that explain the evolution of the recognition heuristic, and thus, of the "home bias." However, at present, no coherent theory can account for the evolution of the heuristics used by human decision makers. This remains an important topic for future research.

Finally, it is still largely unknown whether individuals have methods for testing how well their heuristics toolbox is working. The conjecture is that the greater the distance between one's own payoff and the payoff of one's peers, the more likely it is that the quality of the heuristic is recognized. Notice, however, that in benevolent but heterogeneous environments, superstitious heuristics can be learned in this way. For example, an individual occupying a position with a more favorable environment than his peers may repeatedly experience relative successes that are only spuriously correlated to the heuristics used (see also the discussion on social learning by Mellers et al., this volume).

In summary, the evidence on the use of heuristics by human decision makers is quite impressive. The financial asset markets alone offer a multitude of examples about how decisions can be guided by heuristics. The evidence, however, on which heuristics are actually being used by decision makers in which situations is not yet very reliable.

HOW DO THE RULES IN THE ADAPTIVE TOOLBOX RELATE TO OUR ENVIRONMENTAL ARTIFACTS?

An artifact in the context of this section is taken to be a human-made object designed to help achieve a goal. Hence, artifacts are seen as entities devised to enhance human capabilities, including cognitive capabilities. This implies that artifacts enable human beings to use complicated decision processes. They can, in principle, help human decision makers use all available information in a theoretically optimal manner. A multidimensional decision problem with a host of cues, for example, could be solved using highly complex statistical methods provided by computer software. In this way, artifacts can replace simple heuristics with complex computational decision support systems.

In most cases, however, the user interface of an artifact in itself provides evidence that simple heuristics are used in decision making. When using complex decision support software, for example, users only need to know a few simple rules for inputting data and interpreting the software's output. In fact, the software industry puts much effort into designing decision support systems that fit the limited capabilities of users. This explains the design of the "nested menu structure" used by most software applications. These structures allow simple categorical search of the provided options and information. Although training enables individuals to deal with complicated artifacts, there are cost and competition incentives to design user interfaces that are adapted to limited human capabilities. Thus, it seems that while the usage of artifacts gives access to a much wider range of capabilities, the usage itself remains largely governed by simple heuristics.

Sometimes new simple heuristics are developed to overcome the shortcomings of the artifacts used. This, for example, can mean that a flaw in the software is circumvented by using a simple routine. Hence, the routine usage of most artifacts probably will be in place after some time, because it is either implemented through design or devised by users as a response to deficient design. This is supportive of a two-stage model of decision making: In the first stage, a relatively complex design process is used to devise an artifact or a routine to handle problems of the type under consideration. In the second stage, simple heuristics are used for operating the artifact or for initiating the routine.

This two-stage structure seems to be in line with Simon's assertion (1995) that, no matter what the choice procedure, it will exhibit two phases: a recognition phase and a phase of heuristic search. Depending upon the problem, the selected heuristic may be a routine (as in the case of lottery choice) or a convention (as in cases of social choices). In both cases, it may or may not be supported and/or influenced by artifacts. Munier (1998) presents some experimental results on choices between three outcome lotteries that also support the concept of a two-stage model of decision making. The lottery choices are shown to reveal patterns of preferences that quite robustly depend on the "type" of probability distribution faced by the individual, where a type defines a specific subset of the set of possible probability distributions. In the model, the decision maker first recognizes the type of probability distribution he is facing, before activating the corresponding heuristic.

In many cases, artifacts, heuristics, and conventions coevolve. A convention is a shared, arbitrary code. It has to be arbitrary, because otherwise it is not a convention. It is not a convention that we all eat when we are hungry; it is an instrumental act, based on biological needs we all share. The common meeting place of elephants, on the other hand, is conventional. It is a shared place, but an arbitrary one in that it could have been elsewhere and only became the meeting place as a result of some change in geographic and idiosyncratic experiential factors (but was then subsequently passed on from generation to generation as a shared set of habits and traditions). The chimpanzee's threat stare and fear grimace and the vervet's leopard and eagle calls are also shared sets of arbitrary habits. They differ, however, from the case of the elephants' meeting ground in that a specific code, in both sender and receiver, is encoded in the genome.

The evolutionary sequence is as follows: Something starts as an instrumental action, involving at least two organisms (in the case of the elephant meeting place, a leader and a follower). The instrumental act has some correlates (the leader treads the path to a meeting place) and hence can serve as a predictor (the follower can predict where the others are). When the instrumental function declines while the communicative function gains importance, the action is retained as an arbitrary communicative act.

Something similar happens in language, best illustrated in gestural language where the names of things are first instrumental or mimetic actions. For example, looking frightened and gesturing in fear to indicate fear eventually shrinks to a unique arbitrary facial and manual gesture that is just a fragment of the original one, and now names fear. This is the transition from the instrumental and iconic (iconic means mimetic, resembling, an analog of the thing the gesture names) to the arbitrary. The power of arbitrary names shared by convention lies not only in the fact that they are more economical (faster, more frugal) than the full instrumental or iconic act, but they are also open to combinatorics with other arbitrary conventions and, in principle, can lead to natural language with its power to express any and every proposition. It has been argued that the advent of natural language gave human beings the ability to perform all computations, given that time and resource constraints were not binding (Harnad 1996; Steklis and Harnad 1976).

Conventions can also be the result of deliberate design (Lewis 1969). Many conventions — and the related heuristics — pertain to artifacts and intentionally devised routines. The traffic light is a good example of an artifact that is linked to conventional usage and a simple heuristic: stop on red, go on green, and be cautious otherwise (in short: SORGOGABCO). It is important to notice that some other simple heuristics do not fare well when applied to the decision of which action to take at a traffic light. Imitation, for example, can lead to catastrophic outcomes when imitating a driver who crossed on yellow at the very last moment or who failed to stop on red.

Using SORGOGABCO not only solves the coordination problem, it does so at a very low cost. A market mechanism, for example, can also solve the problem by allocating the right to drive first to the highest bidder amongst the drivers who have arrived at the crossing. Trivially, the simple SORGOGABCO convention leads to much more efficient outcomes of the coordination problem than the auctioning method, because it saves time and effort by the drivers.

Other conventions have not been "invented" but have coevolved with the related simple heuristic. Many human settlements, for example, developed because the original choice to settle at that place was imitated by others. Thus, the simple rule of imitation enhanced the development of a focal point of cultural activity. At the same time, the focusing of cultural activity solved some important coordination problems, such as the problem of meeting new trading and mating partners. This in turn enhanced the success of the imitation heuristic.

There are several reasons why conventions can be useful from a boundedly rational point of view. First, as mentioned, they help to solve coordination problems. Second, conventions can simplify decision making by creating "default choices" and/or "default choice rules." The decision about which clothes to combine, for example, often follows a convention instead of being the outcome of an explicit aesthetic or practical deliberation. Third, conventions are of great importance in joint decision processes. Communication is not only facilitated through conventions because the coordination problem is solved, but also because it is easier to convey ideas about conventional things. This is especially true since forming expectations about the actions of others is simpler when only conventional behavior need be taken into account. It was further suggested that conventions can be used to divide the work load among the group members.

HOW CAN WE DEVISE AND VALIDATE MODELS OF DECISION MAKING?

Table 6.1 displays three levels at which human decision making can be modeled. At the lowest level, we have the observed outcomes. One requirement for a good model is that it be able to account for the observed outcomes. Unfortunately, even if we assume that a simple heuristic does a good job in describing the observed outcomes, this does not justify the inference that decision makers actually use this heuristic. The reason is that more complex strategies may end up

Table 6.1 Levels of modeling decision making.

Level of Model	Object of Model	Type of Model[a]	Environment of Model
1. Neural cognition	Biological equipment	Neural networks	Neurological
2. Procedural rationality process models[b]	Individual behavior	Rules and heuristics	Ecological, social
3. Substantive rationality outcome models[b]	Decision outcomes	Mathematical calculus	Symbolic, logical

[a] The type of model is only meant to be indicative for the class to which most models on a certain level belong.
[b] See Simon (1957).

with the same response as the simple heuristic and could thus account for the data as well. For example, in the paradigmatic "choose which is the larger German city" task, the proportion of items in which multiple regression and "Take The Best" make the same inference is greater than 90% (Rieskamp and Hoffrage 1999). Such a high overlap causes serious problems in uniquely identifying used heuristics, i.e., in validating the different hypotheses with observed response data.

One way to address this problem is to create item sets that reduce the overlap between the predictions of the heuristics (Camerer 1992; Hey and Orme 1994; Abdellaoui and Munier 1999). Another method is to gather data about the processes underlying individual behavior (the second level in Table 6.1). This can be attempted either by making use of the fact that different heuristics assume that information processing occurs in different ways (e.g., Hey and Carbone 1998) or by directly eliciting the decision heuristics experimentally.

Finally, we can go even deeper: we can collect data that relate to the first level in Table 6.1, for example, by using brain imaging. The aim here would be to identify the neural processes that correspond to a certain decision-making process. Ultimately, this information should be linked up to the heuristics used at the second level of Table 6.1.

For both theoretical and practical reasons, this approach may be premature. Theoretically, little is known about the relation between the symbolic representation and the processing of symbolic information, on one hand, and the neural processes uncovered by brain imaging on the other. Practically, it is clear that decisions which can be modeled by a simple heuristic can also be modeled by a more complex one. For example, a neural net can be tuned to behave so that outcomes and processes cannot be distinguished from Take The Best. There are proposals for cognitive architectures that are able to encompass all three levels presented in Table 6.1 (e.g., SOAR, proposed by Newell 1990).

Examining several outcome models, Rieskamp and Hoffrage (1999) find that under high time pressure, a variant of Take The Best most closely matches human behavior. Under low time pressure, they find that "Weighted Pros" (Huber 1979), a heuristic that demands slightly more effort than Take The Best, does best. The authors also analyzed variables that were assumed to correlate with the process of decision making, such as the order and duration of information accumulation. The results of the process analysis were consistent with those of the outcome analyses, e.g., as time pressure increased, participants spent relatively more time checking higher validity cues — a result that can be explained by a shift in strategy use (see also Payne and Bettman, this volume).

Direct elicitation of strategies and heuristics is another approach to gathering data on the process of decision making. The approach has been used by several authors who have conducted "strategy seminars" (Keser 1992; Kuon 1994; Selten et al. 1997). In strategies elicited with this method, success is often positively correlated with the simplicity of the strategy structure. These strategies are often noncompensatory and nonoptimizing.

When the direct elicitation of the heuristics used by individuals is not practicable, outcome level observations may indirectly provide valuable information. If for a class of such problems the choices made by the individuals can be retrieved through the maximization of some "stable" function, one could make a case for a strong rationality scheme within that class. Simon (1995) refers to the decisions in such classes of problems as "programmable" and sets these apart from the "nonprogrammable" decisions, which are not tractable by maximizing a "stable" function. It seems reasonable to conjecture that in the case of programmable decisions the heuristics used by individuals are quite standardized over the entire class of problems. In contrast, when nonprogrammable decisions are observed, the hypothesis seems plausible that the heuristics used are specially adapted to each specific problem.

Experimental observations (e.g., Munier 1998) show that even static choices among simple lotteries do not pass the programmability test, i.e., cannot be retrieved through the maximization of some "stable" function. Munier (1999), however, shows that the decisions in that class of problems can be traced by a single function, if we allow for a limited number of problem-specific coefficients. He suggests calling decisions with this property "quasi-programmable."

WHAT STRUCTURES CAN WE FIND THAT ARE BASIC TO THE TOOLBOX?

Reviewing the empirical and experimental evidence, three elements are identified as widely prevalent and especially important in the structure of boundedly rational decision making: simple heuristics, problem decomposition, and dominance relations.

Simple Heuristics

What is the structure of the simple heuristics in the adaptive toolbox? We can answer this at multiple levels, including the components that make up different decision-making tools, the tools themselves, and the larger groups into which the tools can be organized. Here we focus on the first and last levels of description, and on how the different components (building blocks) used in building tools can each define broad classes of those tools.

There are at least three important types of building blocks of which simple heuristics are composed (for details, see Gigerenzer, this volume): (a) there are building blocks to guide information search; (b) different heuristic building blocks determine how to stop search; (c) other building blocks are used to make a decision based on the information gathered. All of these building blocks can be influenced (or implemented) by processes involving emotions (e.g., for stopping information search or reducing the set of choice options; see Fessler, this volume), individual learning (e.g., for defining and ordering the cues which are searched through; see Erev and Roth, this volume), and social learning (e.g., for deciding which decision building block to use so as to communicate best and justify choices to others; see Laland, this volume).

The presence of different specific building blocks can define whole classes of heuristics. Ignorance-based heuristics, for example, search for identification information (see also Gigerenzer, Todd, and Payne and Bettman, all this volume). As soon as one of the objects is recognized, it is chosen. One-reason decision mechanisms, such as "Minimalist," Take The Best, or "LEX," search through cues in some arbitrary but prespecified order and stop the search as soon as a cue is encountered that differentiates between the options. The decision is then based on the single differentiating cue. Elimination heuristics also search for information in some arbitrary but prespecified order. At each stage, the current cue dimension is used to reduce the set of remaining options (e.g., to decide which restaurant to visit by eliminating those that are far, that are close but expensive, that are close and cheap but not Italian, and so on). Evidently, the search is stopped as soon as only a single option remains. Satisficing heuristics search through objects or choices rather than information or cues (usually in an order that is determined externally by the world). Here the search is stopped as soon as an object is encountered that exceeds some aspiration level (e.g., choose the first restaurant you walk by that is Italian and under $10 per meal). Other classes of simple heuristics can be similarly defined by what building blocks they use (e.g., social "do-what-others-do" heuristics that search for information by observing the actions of others; see Laland, this volume).

Problem Decomposition

Problem decomposition refers to the observation that in boundedly rational problem solving, the problem is frequently broken up into small subproblems that are solved one by one. This "divide and conquer" method is not only observed in satisficing for food and water by many animals, but also frequently in abstract problem solving by human subjects. Most organizations, for example, divide their total budget into sub-budgets, sub-sub-budgets, and so forth. This facilitates both accountability and controlling. Budgeting in this way may also reduce the potential for conflicts in an organization by reducing the necessity of coordination. Hence, the main advantage of problem decomposition seems to be that the total effort (and information and time) that is needed to solve all subproblems is less than what is needed to solve the problem as a whole.

The advantage of problem decomposition is well illustrated in examples of complex decision making by composite decision units. In such composite decision units (called "superorganisms" by Seeley, this volume), each individual (e.g., an individual bee, an engineer in an aircraft production line, a market trader) often solves just a small portion of the problem using a simple heuristic. The composition of these individual subproblem heuristics, however, induces a very sophisticated decision-making process that is applied to the complex problem. Hence, problem decomposition can be considered as a prerequisite to the division of labor.

Obviously, if the subproblems of the decomposed problem are correlated, the combined solutions of the subproblems that do not take this correlation into account can be inferior to the global solution. Indeed, the experimental and empirical observation that individuals have difficulties recognizing correlation (Weber and Camerer 1998) can be interpreted as evidence for problem decomposition.

In two experimental studies of investment behavior involving financial options, Kuon (1999a, b) shows that theories based on investment problem decomposition, known as mental accounting models, describe the observed behavior significantly better than the global solution of arbitrage-free option pricing, i.e., the system of prices in which no combination of trades exists that allows traders to realize risk-free profits at the cost of others. Mental accounting (Thaler 1985) refers to the tendency of subdividing financial assets and cost into separate decision units, thereby overlooking the correlations. Observed behavior is best explained by a model in which the two risky assets available in the experiment (the stock and the option) are associated with one mental account, while the riskless asset (the bond) is treated separately. Neglecting the correlations between the risky and riskless assets leads to substantial unexploited arbitrage possibilities, which would be exploited by rational decision makers who can derive the global solution as suggested by option pricing theory.

In a related empirical study, Warshawsky (1987) finds that individuals who were well aware that they could borrow money from their life insurance account at a much lower interest rate than was paid on treasury bonds (risk-free arbitrage) were reluctant to do so. This effect was associated with a "debt ethic," which advises individuals not to risk assets that have been saved for insurance purposes (e.g., pension fund accounts). This means that the general problem of managing financial assets is decomposed into at least two parts: a speculation and an insurance allotment.

Evidently, problem decomposition can simplify multi-goal tasks by reducing the number of goals in each subtask to one. This can lead to nonoptimal decisions, as the above examples show. However, if the multi-goal character of the task is eliminated in this way, how can boundedly rational decision making allow for compensatory trade-offs? The answer seems to lie in the hierarchical structure of the decision algorithm with which the partial solutions of the subtasks are combined to derive the final decision. The idea is that on each level of decomposition a simple heuristic (perhaps a "second level" or a "third level" heuristic) is used to make the decision about which subtask should be relevant for the decision. Thus, in decision making, each heuristic used is very simple and noncompensatory (probably single-goal). The final decisions observed on the outcome level, however, might exhibit compensatory trade-off properties. Some experimental evidence for the resolution of multi-goal trade-off problems with "second level" heuristics can be found in the literature, for example the "compromise effect" (Simonson 1989; Simonson and Tversky 1992).

Diverse decision-making methods might be used on the different levels of problem decomposition (or in different subtasks). In Simon's canonical model of decision making (Simon 1957), for example, some rules will be more appropriate to the "intelligence phase," some to the "design phase," and some to the "selection phase." Selten has suggested that the phase of "quantitative analysis" is often preceded by "qualitative analysis" (see Selten, this volume). Diverse types of analysis phases are also present in Kahneman and Tversky's prospect theory (1979).

Nonoptimizing compensatory trade-offs can also be accounted for by the relatively simple satisficing rules of Simon (1955) and the closely related aspiration adaptation theory of Sauermann and Selten (1962; reformulated by Selten 1998, see also this volume). In applying aspiration adaptation theory to a two-goal situation, for example, an implicit compensatory trade-off between the two goals can take place when the aspiration level for one goal has to be adjusted downwards, while the aspiration level for another goal can be adjusted upwards (Selten, this volume).

Dominance Relations

A fundamental regularity of behavior seems to be that dominance relations are respected. When alternative *A* "dominates" alternative *B*, i.e., when it is at least as good in every respect and even better in one, then the decision maker should choose *A* (or at least try to do so). If the decision situation is transparent and dominance is easily applicable, then the principle is agreed upon in most theories of boundedly rational behavior.

When the dominance relation is difficult to recognize, for example, because the decision problem is composite or multidimensional, then choice behavior often fails to comply with dominance. Tversky and Kahneman (1981) provide a classic example in which dominance as a choice criterion fails when dominance is opaque, but succeeds when dominance is transparent. In this example, subjects made pairs of simultaneous lottery choices. They chose dominated combinations most of the time, because typically each lottery was examined separately and not in combination with the others. However, after the experimenter made dominance transparent by presenting aggregate information on the two simultaneous choices, subjects invariably chose the dominant option.

WHAT IS THE RELATIONSHIP BETWEEN TOOLS AND TASK SPACE?

Classifying the decision situations in which boundedly rational heuristics are "particularly appropriate" has two aspects. First, we attempt to find classes of decision situations in which decision makers are or are not doing well enough by using one type of tool or another. Second, we attempt to find classes of decision situations in which one or the other heuristic is particularly adequate for model-ing the decision makers' behavior. The first typology may shed some light on the open (but recursive) question of what tool decision makers use to choose the tools that they will use. The second typology can help research assess the explanatory advantage of one decision model over another depending on the decision situation that is analyzed.

Several classifications of the decision situation are imaginable, depending on which environmental variables are examined. We restrict the discussion to three parameters: time pressure, information structure, and dynamics.

For purposes of illustration, Figure 6.1 gives examples of hypothetical decision situations, S_1 to S_m, and hypothetical decision-making tools, Tool 1 to Tool n.

In pure noise information situations, decision makers can make no inferences whatsoever about their environment. Trivially, all decision tools perform equally poorly in such situations (as S_m in Figure 6.1), and there is a reason neither for the decision maker to prefer one tool to the other nor for the researcher to prefer one outcome model of behavior to the other. Note, however, that on the level of process modeling, researchers should even in this case prefer the decision model that most closely describes decision makers' behavior.

In a case like S_1, in which all tools perform equally well, any of the tools can be used to derive the outcome model; on the level of process modeling, empirically validated decision tools should be preferred. It is plausible to assume that decision makers in these cases may prefer a fast and frugal heuristic to any cumbersome optimization since the performance differential is negligible.

Most of the interesting cases are somewhere between the two extremes. One dimension that can be used to classify decision situations is the amount of time a decision maker has for making the decision. Experimental evidence suggests that reducing decision time can systematically and significantly influence decisions (see Payne and Bettman, this volume; Rieskamp and Hoffrage 1999).

Figure 6.1   Examples of situations in which decision tools do or do not perform well (figure by John Payne).

Situations	S_1	S_2	S_3	S_4	...	S_m
Optimization	+	+	+	+		–
Tool 1	+	+	+	–		–
Tool 2	+	+	–	+		–
...	...	...	...	...		...
Tool n	+	–	+	+		–

+   In line i and column j, + means "using Tool i leads to better outcomes in situation S_j than can be expected by chance, with $i = 1...n$ and $j = 1...m$."

–   In line i and column j, – means "using Tool i does not lead to better outcomes in situation S_j than can be expected by chance, with $i = 1...n$ and $j = 1...m$."

Dichotomizing the time pressure variable leads to an interesting categorization of human decision modes, which can be called "online" and "offline" (Harnad, pers. comm.). The online or "real-time" mode is under time pressure, so that extended and explicit calculations are not possible. Instead, the decision-making process proceeds almost in parallel with new incoming information. In contrast, the offline mode is the relaxed mode of decision making in which explicit calculations and deliberations are possible. The straightforward implication of such a classification is that online decisions should be modeled as fast and frugal heuristics, while models of offline decision making can employ more complicated and exhaustive computations.

Another type of classification can be made that draws on the informational structure of the decision situation. In informationally unstable situations, in which cue validities fluctuate, more information-exhaustive heuristics perform better than frugal heuristics. A similar result holds for environments in which the cues are negatively correlated. Frugal heuristics, in contrast, can be useful in environments in which information is relatively scarce, but basically stable (Martignon and Hoffrage 1999). Some experimental evidence (Blackmond Laskey et al. 1999) can be found suggesting that more complicated outcome models (specifically, time-dependent models) are better suited for decision making in unstable environments (specifically, in a military setting).

There is little experimental evidence, however, on how the informational structure of the environment affects which decision heuristics are actually used. Thus, in terms of process level, no clear statement can be made concerning the validity of decision-making models with respect to the informational structure of the environment. Here much room is left for future research.

Considerable experimental evidence suggests that the heuristics used in dynamic decision situations often lead to low performance. Moxnes (1998), for example, finds that subjects are not capable of achieving sustainability in a hypothetical dynamic environment, even though they control all relevant parameters.

A different dynamic effect is demonstrated by Herrnstein (1970; Herrnstein and Prelec 1992) in his well-known "learning-trap" or "addiction" experiments. In these experiments, subjects tend to maximize myopically, thereby achieving a lower payoff compared to the long-run maximum. In these cases, although modeling decision making in terms of a myopic heuristic can be successful, decision makers would clearly be better off choosing a different heuristic from their toolbox.

A third example of the difficulty of coping with intertemporal decision making is the empirically validated "oversaving" paradox (Banks et al. 1998). Although the rate of saving should decrease with age, it is reported to remain constant (and even rise) after retirement. A large body of literature has tried to find economically valid reasons for this observation, but no completely satisfactory rational explanation has been proposed to date. The phenomenon can be fully explained, however, by assuming that the decision makers use a simple heuristic: "Save a certain part of the income." Since the heuristic works so well during the period of employment, many individuals see no reason to kick the "habit" when they retire.

HOW DOES SOCIAL INTERACTION INFLUENCE THE NATURE, DEVELOPMENT, AND EFFECTIVENESS OF THE USED HEURISTIC?

The issue of social interaction is closely related to topics discussed by other groups at the workshop. In addressing the rather fundamental nature of this section, we tried not to address their questions, but rather to examine the simple heuristics that are specially matched to cases of conflicting interests. These conflicting interests can occur in both intra- and interpersonal decision situations. Examples of the former are intertemporal decisions, such as the aforementioned savings and addiction problems (see, e.g., Frank 1996). In interpersonal decision making, myopic payoff maximization might conflict with social norms such as fairness, reciprocity, etc. The question concerns what mechanisms individuals use to solve these problems. A related topic is time structure in decision making, for example, playing an end effect in a repeated game. What mechanisms do people use to decide when to move from cooperation to defection?

In several experiments, both in psychology and economics, it has been observed that individuals' decisions differ depending on whether they were made within a group or a team of decision makers (for a survey, see Levine and Moreland 1990). An interesting example of how behavior can depend on the social environment is the phenomenon of "social loafing" (Williams et al. 1981). Social loafing refers to the tendency of subjects to choose a smaller effort level when acting within a group than they would when taking the same action alone. This often occurs unnoticed by the subject. The effect is reduced with an increase in identifiability of the individual effort levels. The interesting point is that the heuristic used to make the effort level choice obviously is contingent on the social setting.

A different aspect of social interaction emerges when individuals have to decide in groups. In such cases the rules and heuristics used by individuals must be combined with a group (or team) decision rule or heuristic. Kuon et al. (1999) found that lottery choice decisions made by groups of three are best described by a simple decision algorithm, called "excess-risk vetoing," which basically combines majority rule with the right to veto if the majority's proposal is to select an alternative that is dominated by another in the risk-value space. This simple rule accounts for the experimental observation that groups achieve significantly higher expected payoffs at a lower risk than individual decision makers.

Another question to address is how relation-specific tools emerge from the social norms pertaining to the framework of the decision situation. For example, a whole industry of bargaining experiments has shown that the simple heuristics implemented by equity theory can account for most outcomes (Güth 1995; Güth et al. 1982; Güth and Tietz 1990; Kuon and Uhlich 1993; Roth 1995; Selten 1978). In fact, videotaped bargaining experiments (Jacobsen and Sadrieh 1996) provide evidence that the equity model is not only valid at the outcome level but also at the process level of modeling. Similar experiments together with a number of strategy-eliciting experiments (Axelrod 1970; Selten et al. 1997) suggest that reciprocal strategies like tit-for-tat or measure-for-measure can also be adequate models on both the output and process levels.

These results, as many others presented in this volume, suggest that observed decision behavior often can be explained by assuming that decision makers use a set of simple tools — simple tools that are effective and efficient, if used in situations they are adapted to. The result that the heuristics used may depend on the social context, however, also indicates that further research on the features of the adaptive toolbox is necessary. The general observation is that the meta-rules used to choose an "adequate" tool from the toolbox may be contingent on a number of task and environment variables. Uncovering these dependencies is one of the great challenges of future research on boundedly rational decision making.

REFERENCES

Abdellaoui, M., and B. Munier. 1999. The risk-structure dependence effect: Experimenting with an eye to decision-aiding. *Ann. Oper. Res.*, in press.

Axelrod, R. 1970. Conflict of Interest — A Theory of Divergent Goals with Applications to Politics. Chicago: Markham.

Ball, S.B., M.H. Bazerman, and J.S. Caroll. 1991. An evaluation of learning in the bilateral winner's curse. *Org. Behav. Human Decis. Proc.* **48**:1–22.

Banks, J., R. Blundell, and S. Tanner. 1998. Is there a retirement-savings puzzle? *Am. Econ. Rev.* **88**:769–788.

Bazerman, M.H., and W.F. Samuelson. 1983. I won the auction but don't want the prize. *J. Confl. Res.* **27**:618–634.

Blackmond Laskey, K., B. D'Ambrosio, T. Levitt, and S. Mahoney. 1999. Limited rationality in action: Decision support for military situation assessment. *Minds and Machines*, in press.

Borges, B., D.G. Goldstein, A. Ortmann, and G. Gigerenzer. 1999. Can ignorance beat the stock market? In: Simple Heuristics That Make Us Smart, G. Gigerenzer, P.M. Todd, and the ABC Research Group, pp. 59–72. New York: Oxford Univ. Press.

Bromann, O., D. Schiereck, and M. Weber. 1997. Reichtum durch (anti-)zyklische Handelsstrategien am deutschen Aktienmarkt? *Z. betriebsw. For.* **7**:603–616.

Camerer, C. 1992. Recent test of generalizations of expected utility theory. In: Utility Theories, Measurements and Applications, ed. W. Edwards. Dordrecht: Kluwer.

Fiedler, K., S. Russer, and K. Gramm. 1993. Illusory correlations and memory performance. *J. Exp. Soc. Psych.* **29**:111–136.

Frank, B. 1996. The use of internal games: The case of addiction. *J. Econ. Psych.* **17**:651–660.

Goldstein, D.G., and G. Gigerenzer. 1999. The recognition heuristic: How ignorance makes us smart. In: Simple Heuristics That Make Us Smart, G. Gigerenzer, P.M. Todd, and the ABC Research Group, pp. 37–58. New York: Oxford Univ. Press.

Güth, W. 1995. On ultimatum bargaining experiments — A personal review. *J. Econ. Behav. Org.* **27**:329–344.

Güth, W., R. Schmittberger, and B. Schwarze. 1982. An experimental analysis of ultimatum bargaining. *J. Econ. Behav. Org.* **3**:367–388.

Güth, W., and R. Tietz. 1990. Ultimatum bargaining behaviour — A survey and comparison of experimental results. *J. Econ. Psych.* **11**:417–449.

Harnad, S. 1996. The origin of words: A psychophysical hypothesis. In: Communicating Meaning: Evolution and Development of Language, ed. B. Velichkovsky and D. Rumbaugh, pp. 27–44. Hillsdale, NJ: Erlbaum.

Herrnstein, R.J. 1970. On the law of effect. *J. Exp. Anal. Behav.* **13**:243–266.

Herrnstein, R.J., and D. Prelec. 1992. A theory of addiction. In: Choice over Time, ed. G. Loewenstein and J. Elster, pp. 331–361. New York: Russell Sage.

Hey, J., and E. Carbone. 1998. How do people tackle dynamic decision problems? EXEC Discussion Paper 9802, Univ. of York.

Hey, J., and C. Orme. 1994. Investigating generalizations of expected utility theory using experimental data. *Econometrica* **62**:1291–1326.

Huber, O. 1979. Nontransitive multidimensional preferences: Theoretical analysis of a model. *Theory Decis.* **10**:147–165.

Jacobsen, E., and A. Sadrieh. 1996. Experimental proof for the motivational importance of reciprocity. SFB 303 Discussion Paper No. B–386. Bonn: Univ. of Bonn.

Kahneman, D., and A. Tversky. 1979. Prospect theory: An analysis of decision under risk. *Econometrica* **47**:263–291.

Keser, C. 1992. Experimental Duopoly Markets with Demand Inertia. Lecture Notes in Economics and Mathematical Systems, vol. 391. Berlin: Springer.

Kilka, M., and M. Weber. 1997. Home bias in international stock return expectations. SFB 504 Discussion Paper No. 97–14. Mannheim: Univ. of Mannheim.

Kuon, B. 1994. Two-person Bargaining Experiments with Incomplete Information. Lecture Notes in Economics and Mathematical Systems, vol. 412. Berlin: Springer.

Kuon, B. 1999a. Arbitrage and mental accounting in behavioral models of option pricing. Univ. of Bonn. Mimeo.

Kuon, B. 1999b. Information aggregation, speculation, and arbitrage in an option market experiment. Univ. of Bonn. Mimeo.

Kuon, B., B. Mathauschek, and A. Sadrieh. 1999. Teams take the better risks. SFB 303 Discussion Paper No. B. Bonn: Univ. of Bonn.

Kuon, B., and G.R. Uhlich. 1993. The Negotiation Agreement Area: An Experimental Analysis of Two-Person Characteristic Function Games. *Group Decis. Negot.* **2**:323–345.

Levine, J.M., and R.L. Moreland. 1990. Progress in small group research. *Ann. Rev. Psych.* **41**:585–634.

Lewis, D. 1969. Convention: A Philosophical Study. Cambridge, MA: Harvard Univ. Press.

Martignon, L., and U. Hoffrage. 1999. Why does one-reason decision making work? A case study in ecological rationality. In: Simple Heuristics That Make Us Smart, G. Gigerenzer, P.M. Todd, and the ABC Research Group, pp. 119–140. New York: Oxford Univ. Press.

102 *Abdolkarim Sadrieh et al.*

Moxnes, E. 1998. Overexploitation of renewable resources: The role of misperceptions. *J. Econ. Behav. Org.* **37**:107–127.

Munier, B. 1998. Two stage rationality under risk: Experimental results and perspectives. *Riv. Mat. Sci. Econ. Soc.* **21**:3–23.

Munier, B. 1999. Les décisions en avenir risqué sont-elles programmables? Enseignements récents de la recherche expérimentale. In: Entre systémique et complexité, Mélanges offerts au Pr. Jean-Louis Le Moigne, GRASCE, pp. 211–232. Paris: P.U.F.

Newell, A. 1990. Unified Theories of Cognition. Cambridge, MA: Harvard Univ. Press.

Rieskamp, J., and U. Hoffrage. 1999. When do people use simple heuristics, and how can we tell? In: Simple Heuristics That Make Us Smart, G. Gigerenzer, P.M. Todd, and the ABC Research Group, pp. 141–167. New York: Oxford Univ. Press.

Roth, A.E. 1995. Bargaining experiments. In: The Handbook of Experimental Economics, ed. J.H. Kagel and A.E. Roth, pp. 253–348. Princeton, NJ: Princeton Univ. Press.

Sauermann, H., and R. Selten. 1962. Anspruchsanpassungstheorie der Unternehmung. *Z. ges. Staatswiss.* **118**:577–597.

Selten, R. 1978. The equity principle in economic behavior. In: Decision Theory, Social Ethics, Issues in Social Choice, ed. H. Gottinger and W. Leinfellner, pp. 289–301. Dordrecht: Reidel.

Selten, R. 1998. Aspiration adaptation theory. *J. Math. Psych.* **42**:191–214.

Selten, R., M. Mitzkewitz, and G.R. Uhlich. 1997. Duopoly strategies programmed by experienced players. *Econometrica* **65**:517–555.

Simon, H.A. 1955. A behavioral model of rational choice. *Qtly. J. Econ.* **61**:495–521.

Simon, H.A. 1957. Models of Man. New York: Wiley.

Simon, H.A. 1995. The information-processing theory of mind. *Am. Psych.* **50**:507–508.

Simonson, I. 1989. Choice based on reasons: The case of attraction and compromise effects. *J. Consumer Res.* **16**:158–174.

Simonson, I., and A. Tversky. 1992. Choice in context: Tradeoff contrast and extremeness aversion. *J. Marketing Res.* **29**:281–295.

Steklis, H.D., and S. Harnad. 1976. From hand to mouth: Some critical stages in the evolution of language. In: Origins and Evolution of Language and Speech, ed. H.D. Steklis and J.B. Lancaster. *Ann. NY Acad. Sci.* **280**:445–455.

Thaler, R. 1985. Mental accounting and consumer choice. *Marketing Sci.* **4**:199–214.

Tversky, A., and D. Kahneman. 1981. The framing of decisions and the psychology of choice. *Science* **211**:453–458.

Warshawsky, M. 1987. Sensitivity to market incentives: The case of policy loans. *Rev. Econ. Stat.* **LXIX**:286–295.

Weber, M., and C.F. Camerer. 1998. The disposition effect in securities trading: An experimental analysis. *J. Econ. Behav. Org.* **33**:167–184.

Williams, K., S. Harkins, and B. Latane. 1981. Identifiability as a deterrent to social loafing: Two cheering experiments. *J. Pers. Soc. Psych.* **40**:303–311.

7

The Fiction of Optimization

Gary Klein

Klein Associates Inc., 1750 Commerce Center Blvd. North,
Fairborn, OH 45324, U.S.A.

ABSTRACT

One of the definitions of optimizing a decision choice is to be able to maximize expected utility. Several analytical procedures have been developed to help people pursue this goal, even though researchers and practitioners realize that in field settings, it will not be possible to maximize expected utility. This chapter lists a number of barriers to selecting an optimal course of action and further asserts that optimization should not be used as a gold standard for decision making. An alternative approach, based on the strategies of chess grandmasters, is proposed as a substitute.

INTRODUCTION

Optimization refers to the attempt to find the best option out of a set of potential courses of action. Simon (1955, 1972) contrasted optimization with satisficing. He defined optimization as the selection of best choice, the one with the highest expected utility. (A more technically accurate term would be "maximizing," as in maximizing expected utility, rather than "optimizing.") Unfortunately, according to Simon, the computational requirements for optimizing are usually too high for decision makers. Therefore, people will satisfice, which means selecting the first course of action that appears to be successful, even if it is not the best. Satisficing is a heuristic that allows decision makers to overcome their limited information-processing capacities.

The concept of optimization relies on a number of assumptions. These assumptions are very restrictive. I have not identified any decision researcher or analyst who believes that these assumptions will be met in any setting, with the possible exception of the laboratory or the casino. In the majority of field settings, there is no way to determine if a decision choice is optimal owing to time pressure, uncertainty, ill-defined goals, and so forth. Some of these problems stem from limited computational capacities, as Simon (1955, 1972) argued, while others are due to the nature of the situation. Some decision analysts merely use the concept of optimization as a shorthand for encouraging people to carry out more thoughtful analyses of a situation and do not hold to the requirements for maximization in the strict sense. Nevertheless, for many decision analysts and researchers, the dream of optimization lingers as a gold standard. Even if we cannot optimize, we often feel regret, as if we should have tried harder.

Why do decision researchers and practitioners cling so tenaciously to the gold standard of optimization? One reason is that the concept of maximization rests on faith in mathematics. Once the mathematical formulation for expected utility theory was obtained (Bernoulli 1738/1954; Coombs et al. 1970; Edwards 1954; von Neumann and Morgenstern 1947), the agenda for researchers and practitioners seemed clear: to find ways to translate decisions into the appropriate formalism. Within this framework, deviations from maximization, such as satisficing, are viewed as defective decision making, perhaps required because of limits of time or computational ability, but defects nonetheless. Because maximization is based on mathematical proofs, these theorems act as a bedrock. Few areas in behavioral science can boast such a solid basis for investigation.

After several decades of vigorous research, however, we may find it useful to question the value of expected utility theory for understanding decision making. Simon (1983), Frisch and Clemen (1994), and many others have pointed out that subjective expected utility theory does not describe what people do and is not capable of being employed because of the limited processing capacity of human decision makers. March (1978) has taken this further to a critique of the mathematical principles of calculated rationality. In other words, casting the limited information-processing capacity aside, there is more to the story than calculating probabilities and utilities. Herein lies the primary reason for this chapter: to argue that optimization cannot and should not be a gold standard for decision making.

DEFINING OPTIMIZATION

Most researchers agree that "maximizing" refers to the attempt to select the option with the highest expected utility (Elster 1977; Fischhoff 1991; Neumann and Politser 1992; Vos 1990). I have maximized expected utility when I select a course of action with the highest payoff. If I am considering several options, then I need to identify the option that probabilistically offers me the highest gains and the fewest risks, compared to any of the others. If I can do that, and appreciate it, then I sleep well at night, untroubled by doubts. This is the temptation of maximization, to know that I have chosen wisely.

The term "optimizing," however, can be used in several different ways, as will be evident in reading the other chapters in this book. A courageous author would attempt to provide clarity by presenting a definition of optimizing. Unfortunately, this chapter was not written by such an author. Instead, I will describe some of the different ways that the concept of optimization can be used. It can be used to describe the outcome of the choice or the process. A researcher may be concerned with the quality of the option selected, or with the way in which the choice was made, or both. Another distinction is the level of the discourse: cognitive, behavioral, cultural, or evolutionary. At the cognitive level, if I have gone through all of the processes required to maximize expected utility, then I will believe I have optimized. This is both a desire to optimize outcome and an attempt to optimize process. At the behavioral level, we are more concerned about outcome: is the option selected really going to improve my condition, or have I been deceiving myself or suffering from diminished capacity? At the cultural level, we may focus on the outcome to the group, not the individual. For example, the risks of entrepreneurship are so great that anyone who chooses to become an entrepreneur is probably guilty of poor decision making. (As an entrepreneur myself, I would have to concur.) Yet the benefit to the group of having entrepreneurs is fairly high, so these choices are optimizing the group's success, even though the individuals within the group may not always benefit. At the evolutionary level, we would focus on the outcome to the species. Biologists would examine whether an inherited behavior conferred a competitive advantage, increasing the chances of finding food, reproducing, and so forth.

These different levels make it hard to enter into constructive dialogue and posed a difficulty at the Dahlem Workshop. The opportunity to consider new perspectives, and to learn about new mechanisms, more than offset the difficulty, in my opinion. Nevertheless, we must be careful to identify what each author in this volume means by the term "optimization."

In this chapter, I will concentrate on the first level, the cognitive level, and I will view optimization as synonymous with maximizing expected utility. However, even here, the definition is not easy to resolve. Does optimization refer only to the outcome, selecting the best, or also to the methods used? Does optimization refer to selecting the absolute best course of action that exists, or only the best that I can determine, given the information at hand? Does optimization refer to the best way of achieving a goal, or also to the additional factors that must be taken into account in a situation?

Does Optimization Refer Only to the Outcome, Selecting the Best, or Also to the Methods Used?

Some researchers (e.g., Elster 1977) take optimization to mean only the outcome, the ability to maximize expected utility, whereas others (Fischhoff 1991; Janis and Mann 1977) include the methods used. Beyth-Marom et al. (1991) state that:

> ...According to the most general normative model, a person facing a decision should (a) list relevant action alternatives, (b) identify possible consequences of those actions, (c) assess the probability of each consequence occurring (if each

action were undertaken), (d) establish the relative importance (value or utility) of each consequence, and (e) integrate these values and probabilities to identify the most attractive course of action, following a defensive decision rule. People who follow these steps are said to behave in a *rational* way. People who do so effectively (e.g., they have accurate probability estimates, they get good courses of action into their list of possibilities) are said to behave *optimally*. Thus, if one does not execute these steps optimally, one can be rational without being very effective at getting what one wants. (p. 21)

This is saying that in order to optimize, it is not enough to find the option with the best rating; one must also follow the steps of decision analysis, and follow those steps effectively in order to provide accurate and reliable inputs into the analysis.

Therefore, the definition of optimization in terms of *outcome* is not sufficient. Decision researchers are vitally concerned with *process*. Although the outcome is clear enough to maximize expected utility, the steps are implied, even demanded, by the words used: "expected" and "utility." The tenets of expected utility theory presuppose the steps of decision analysis and also of methods such as multiattribute utility analysis (Pitz 1992). The methods are the ways of maximizing expected utility. Any departure from the methods is a departure from optimization. Thus, optimization may lack a clear meaning outside of this methodology, and the question of how to optimize is moot — we would optimize by following the steps listed by Beyth-Marom et al. (1991). For this chapter, I will be concerned with optimizing the process as well as the outcome.

A difficulty arises because it may not be sufficient to follow the steps of decision analysis. They must be followed well. If a decision maker does not do a good job of following the steps, then he/she is not behaving optimally, according to Beyth-Marom et al. (1991). If it is impossible to follow these steps (as in many field settings), then optimization carries no meaning. In that case, it cannot be used as a gold standard.

The problem gets worse when we ask what it takes to follow the steps of decision analysis optimally. There are no criteria for what it means to follow those steps optimally. To know that I have listed the relevant action alternatives, I need to know all the alternatives and have a prior criterion for relevance. To identify possible consequences of those actions, I have to be able to turn to an exhaustive procedure for generating consequences for future states. To assess the probabilities of each consequence, I must have some validating criteria to determine if my estimates are reasonably accurate, and this will be difficult to come by unless I actually examine all the different courses of action sequences. To establish the relative importance (value or utility) of each consequence, I again need some validation criteria. The point here is that a decision maker is unlikely to be able to determine if the steps of decision analysis have been carried out optimally. If that is the case, then the concept of optimization may suffer from inherent incompleteness. These concerns are further developed below (see section on BOUNDARY CONDITIONS OF OPTIMAL CHOICE).

Does Optimization Refer to Selecting the Absolute Best Course of Action That Exists, or Only the Best That I Can Determine, Given the Information at Hand?

The difficulties in applying a strict definition of optimization have given rise to different forms of constrained optimization. One way to constrain optimization is to restrict the investigation to the way a person uses the available data, rather than getting into the problem of information gathering. It may be impossible to select the absolutely best option in most settings, owing to lack of complete knowledge along with the resources to process that knowledge. To overcome that barrier, we can define optimization as selecting the best option that we can determine, given the information at hand.

This position, however, raises other problems. This is a restrictive and artificial paradigm, in which an intelligent decision maker is not permitted to ask questions in order to obtain information. The task is simply to rearrange data, such as probability estimates and value judgments, in order to find a procedure that leads to an unambiguous differentiation between pathways.

On the other hand, a decision process that is open to inquiry and data gathering raises different problems with regard to optimization. Elster (1977) and Gigerenzer et al. (1999) have each described the infinite regress that must occur when information gathering is brought into the picture. Now, in addition to trying to identify the best course of action, I also have to estimate the marginal value of the information that I have not yet gathered, in order to judge whether to try to obtain it. However, the act of deliberating about the marginal value of information is itself time consuming and effortful, so I need to consider the marginal value of the cognitive resources I expend trying to figure out whether to gather information, and so on. Gigerenzer and Todd (1999) describe this problem as the lack of a stopping rule. We can say that the information search would be stopped when the effort to obtain the information becomes greater than the expected value of the information. Clearly, some sort of subjective judgment along these lines is made by decision makers, but it does not fold neatly into an optimization strategy without running into the problem of infinite regress.

None of these alternatives appears acceptable: picking the absolute best course of action, picking the best course of action given the data provided, or picking the best course of action given the data that can be obtained. Thus the concept of optimization may suffer from internal inconsistencies.

Does Optimization Refer to the Best Way of Achieving a Goal, or Also to the Additional Factors That Must Be Taken into Account in a Situation?

Another approach to constrained optimization is to narrow the focus to achieving the primary goal in the situation. For instance, Elster (1977) defines optimization as finding the best means for accomplishing the agent's goal. This would make the research on optimization more tractable.

In field settings, however, we also need to consider global issues such as opportunity costs for the resources that might be used. The trouble with a global examination of factors is that we usually do not have an optimal stopping rule to tell us when we can stop considering additional factors, and if we try to consider every relevant factor, we may not finish the analysis in a finite amount of time.

In the engineering community, suboptimizing strategies are usually preferred to optimizing strategies because suboptimizing strategies are usually more robust under a wider range of conditions, even if they are not as successful in handling the target task. Engineers prefer to trade a small loss in performance at the central conditions for a much larger overall gain using solutions that will work fairly well under a wide range of circumstances. This robustness is analogous to widening the perspective from a local to a global consideration of conditions, goals, and values. The dilemma is that the effort to optimize may become intractable if decision makers have to consider the full range of issues, but the task of optimizing may be trivial and irrelevant if decision makers only consider the primary goal. Thus, the concept of optimization may lack required constraints.

These problems do not arise if we restrict the concept of optimization to the task of arranging evidence. As Fischhoff (1986) describes optimization: "Given that this is what you want and believe, here are the procedures that you must follow in deciding what option to choose (if you want to be considered rational)" (p. 155). Such a view is internally consistent, but, as Fischhoff notes, it is mute about the content of the decision-making process. Fischhoff goes on to argue that psychologists try to control the inputs in an experiment so that there is little ambiguity about what the subjects believe, and the focus can be on "*how* their subjects combine these facts and values. In doing so, such investigators sacrifice the opportunity to explore how their subjects interpret situations (identifying the relevant facts and values) in order to get a better look at how people exploit them."(p. 157) This difficulty is the same as the one discussed earlier. The concept of optimization is viable only as long as we restrict the phenomenon of decision making to the analysis of data and exclude the information-gathering activities needed to populate the decision equations.

BOUNDARY CONDITIONS OF OPTIMAL CHOICE

The thesis that decision makers can make optimal choices depends on a number of assumptions. Decision researchers have compiled these assumptions and have described their limitations. Table 7.1 presents a set of the boundary conditions discussed in the literature. With regard to the distinction between optimizing the outcome and optimizing the process, the criteria listed in Table 7.1 refer primarily to optimizing the *process* of decision making.

Table 7.1 Boundary conditions for optimizing decisions.

1. The goals must be well defined, in quantitative terms (Koopman and Pool 1991).
2. The decision maker's values must be stable (Fischhoff 1991; Slovic 1995; March 1978).
3. The situation must be stable (Pitz 1992).
4. The task is restricted to selection between options (Berkeley and Humphreys 1982).
5. The number of alternatives generated must be exhaustive (Janis and Mann 1977; Koopman and Pool 1991).
6. The optimal choice can be selected without disproportional time and effort (Gigerenzer and Todd 1999; Minsky 1986; von Winterfeldt and Edwards 1986).
7. The options must be thoroughly compared to each other (Janis and Mann 1977).
8. The decision maker must use a compensatory strategy (Janis and Mann 1977).
9. The probability estimates must be coherent and accurate (Beyth-Marom et al. 1991).
10. The scenarios used to predict failures must be exhaustive and realistic (Pitz 1992).
11. The evaluation of each scenario must be exhaustive (Pitz 1992).

To be fair, a violation of some of the assumptions in Table 7.1 will also cause a problem for models of bounded rationality. For instance, aspiration adaptation theory does not apply if the goals are ill defined, and fast and frugal heuristics, as discussed by Gigerenzer and Todd (1999), certainly suffer if the situation is not stable. On the other hand, they suffer less than more complex algorithms.

We can view the boundary conditions in Table 7.1 as barriers to optimization, but in another sense they may be the design features for boundedly rational models of decision making. Some of the mechanisms for bounded rationality (e.g., the imitation heuristic, and also recognition-primed decision making) are derived for domains in which goals are not well defined and are only expressed in qualitative terms, the decision maker's values are not stable, the situation is not stable, and options cannot be thoroughly compared to each other. The processes in these models would be carried out more easily with well-defined goals, and so forth. They are intended, however, for use in natural settings.

1. *The goals must be well defined, in quantitative terms.* Koopman and Pool (1991) presented this criterion. If a goal is ill defined, researchers cannot make unambiguous judgments of whether a course of action was effective in achieving the goal. If the goals cannot be readily measured, then there are no metrics for use in comparing courses of action, and no way to ever verify that a course of action was optimal. Inasmuch as most goals are ill defined, this requirement limits the concept of optimization to a very small proportion of decisions.

This requirement restricts optimal choice to tasks where the best answer can be calculated. Thus, tasks involving mathematics and logic seem to permit optimization. There is, however, little sense in solving a mathematics problem to a reasonable level. The point is to find the right answer. The concept of optimization may not be meaningful for mathematics or logic, where the solution is either correct or incorrect, not optimal versus nonoptimal. Questions of fact do permit optimization (e.g., the third longest river in the world, the empty weight of a Boeing 757 aircraft) because the accuracy of the answer can be scaled.

Questions of value do not permit optimization. If I have three job offers and need to select one, I cannot optimize because there is no way to demonstrate whether I have made the optimal choice. I can use some form of decision analysis to compare the options. However, methods such as multiattribute utility analysis do not address the difficulty of generating options (perhaps I should continue to seek more job offers rather than settling for these three). They do not help me find accurate values for the evaluation dimensions I select or the ratings I assign.

2. *The decision maker's values must be stable.* For researchers such as Fischhoff (1991), Slovic (1995), and March (1978), this is a troubling requirement. If values are not stable, then the exercise of decision analysis loses much of its force. The choice made at time A (e.g., which of three job offers to accept) will not necessarily match the choice at time A plus one hour. Fischhoff's reading of the data is that values are labile, rather than stable. If that is true, then one's choice will vary depending on one's mood, and, in the worst case, one's values at the end of a long session of decision analysis may depart from one's values at the beginning, calling the whole analysis into question. We might try to salvage things by suggesting that the session was successful in helping the person clarify values, but, whether or not this was true, it is not the same thing as helping the person make the optimal choice.

March goes further. He is concerned about the need to generate accurate predictions of future states but is even more concerned about the stability of future tastes. Optimization assumes that tastes and values are absolute, relevant, stable, consistent, and precise. Experience suggests that these assumptions are unrealistic. The difficulty may be in the concept of "values" as decomposable elements of a decision analysis equation.

Further, if we do not trust decision makers to select an option directly, without decomposition, because we do not trust these judgments, why would the smaller judgments of value for each option on each evaluation dimension be any more reliable? The advantage gained by decomposing the problem into smaller units is to reduce the cognitive complexity of the task, but this advantage may be canceled because the task of rating options on evaluation dimensions is less practiced.

3. *The situation must be stable.* Pitz (1992) has noted that decision analysis is not suited for decisions that dynamically adapt, such as the hedge clipping described by Connolly (1988). Connolly contrasted hedge clipping, in which we make each cut on the basis of the results of the previous cut, to tree felling, in which we decide in advance how to cut down the entire tree. In practice, if

feedback from the outcome of the decision sequentially affects the implementation, this moves the task outside the boundary conditions for decision analysis. Techniques such as dynamic programming have been developed to try to help people handle changing situations, but they still require stability of the assumptions outside of the small set of variables that can be programmed.

4. *The task is restricted to selection between options.* In field settings, decision making and problem solving are usually blended. The process of hedge clipping captures part of this blend. Typically, I am not just trying to select between courses of action; I am also learning about the situation, finding gaps in all the options, discovering ways to combine courses of action, and inventing new courses of action. This process of problem solving complicates the task of selecting the optimal course of action. Therefore, optimization requires that we restrict the task to what Berkeley and Humphreys (1982) have referred to as "the moment of choice."

5. *The number of alternatives generated must be exhaustive.* Janis and Mann (1977) and Koopman and Pool (1991) stipulated this condition. Unless we have carefully considered all of the reasonable options available, we cannot be sure that we have selected the best.

Some definitions constrain the concept of optimization to the task of considering only the information presented, rather than selecting the absolute best course of action in a situation. If we are trying to maximize expected utility, given a set of options, then we need not worry if there are better options out there that are never considered.

Our dilemma is that if we accept this requirement for exhaustive option generation, the task of optimization becomes impractical in most settings. If we ignore it, then the task of decision making becomes artificial, and we can wind up in a paradoxical situation in which we have optimized but have little confidence in the option selected.

A more reasonable criterion is to require that the candidate options be of high quality. Instead of worrying about collecting an exhaustive set of options, we need only try to assemble a high-quality set. The only trouble here is that the requirement is circular. We cannot know that the options are high quality prior to doing the evaluation.

6. *The optimal choice can be selected without disproportional time and effort.* At a theoretical level, it should not matter how much time and effort is expended, because the issue is just whether someone can make an optimal choice. However, in most settings it matters very much. If the optimal choice is barely superior to the closest alternatives, and it takes weeks to differentiate them and many hours of effort, then the optimality is a fraud. The costs of obtaining it offset the advantages it provides. This requirement was discussed earlier.

Minsky (1986) has raised a similar concern in presenting Fredkin's paradox. The paradox is that as the different options become closer and closer together in value, the effort needed to select the best one will increase, but the benefit of selecting the best one will decrease. (A similar issue was raised by von Winterfeldt and Edwards [1986] in their discussion of the flat maximum.) Thus, the comparisons that mean the least (for options that are microscopically differ- ent in value) will call forth the greatest effort. This argues that optimization may exist primarily for local tasks and may be unworkable when more global consid- erations such as effort are taken into consideration. To the extent that this is true, it then diminishes the relevance of optimization for field settings and raises other difficulties, such as the self-referential problem of calculating the cost of calcu- lating. Thus, if I want to optimize, I must also determine the effort it will take me to optimize; however, the subtask of determining this effort will itself take ef- fort, and so forth into the tangle that self-referential activities create.

7. *The options must be thoroughly compared to each other.* This entails comparing each option to every other option and making the comparisons on a full set of dimensions. Janis and Mann (1977) contrasted optimizing with satisficing and noted that satisficing permits minimal comparisons. The deci- sion maker does not have to compare every option to every other option. Opti- mizing requires that all the reasonable options be compared on all dimensions, in carrying out a multiattribute utility analysis.

Janis and Mann (1977) further stated that a satisficing strategy is attractive because it can be conducted using a limited set of requirements. They point out that an optimizing strategy contains an unrealistically large number of evalua- tion criteria and factors that have to be taken into account. Thus, the compari- sons must be conducted over a wide range of considerations. This was discussed earlier in terms of the need to look at global issues. Hill-climbing algorithms rep- resent a middle ground between satisficing (e.g., selecting the first option that works) and exhaustive comparisons (all options on each dimension), but they re- quire a well-structured problem space and do not constitute optimizing.

8. *The decision maker must use a compensatory strategy.* In critiquing the feasibility of an optimization strategy, Janis and Mann (1977) note that the com- parison needs to take into account the degree of advantage and disadvantage that each option carries, on each evaluation dimension, rather than merely noting whether or not a difference exists. A problem arises when we consider findings such as Erev et al. (1993), who found that the decomposition needed to conduct formal analyses seemed to result in lower quality decisions than an overall pref- erence would yield. If the implementation of optimization procedures interferes with expertise, then the methodology may have a serious disadvantage.

9. *The probability estimates must be coherent and accurate.* It makes little sense to use the appropriate methods if those methods are not carried out well. Beyth-Marom et al. (1991) noted that in carrying out a decision analysis, the probability estimates for different outcomes must be reasonably accurate. This requirement makes sense. Yet how should a decision maker determine if the re- quirement is satisfied? Unless the different outcomes are systematically tested, the requirement is more an admonition to try hard to be accurate. Sometimes,

baseline data may be available as a guide. However, in most cases, these data will be missing, and attempts to generalize from related data sets will be questionable. Furthermore, the probability that I will successfully accomplish an enabling task will depend in part on my workload, experience status, and confidence.

10. *The scenarios used to predict failures must be exhaustive and realistic.* Pitz (1992) was concerned about the branches of the decision tree, and how different sequences of events needed to be examined. If the sequels are shallow, the analysis cannot be very good. Pitz worried about future events that had never been experienced, and how these could be incorporated into a decision analysis.

11. *The evaluation of each scenario must be exhaustive.* This requirement, stated by Pitz (1992), follows from the previous one. Once the scenario has been generated, the examination of each option must also be rigorous. Pitz also argues that all possible outcomes must be considered. In field settings, this would be unrealistic.

The review of assumptions suggests that decision makers might never encounter the conditions that permit optimization. Decision analysts and decision researchers understand this and have been candid in describing the problems — most of the references cited above are from decision researchers identifying the difficulties of optimizing. Their candor has been based on scientific integrity, not wanting to make stronger claims for methods than is warranted. Their candor is also fueled by a desire to lay out the problems that future research in optimization must address.

Despite these difficulties, the concept of optimization as a gold standard persists for several reasons. One is that the criteria for optimization are useful as guides, in showing us what we need to do to improve decision quality. A second reason is that we do not have any other standards for effective decision making. My argument with the first reason is that much of the guidance that stems from trying to maximize expected utility is counterproductive in field settings. My argument with the second reason is that I believe we can find more useful standards.

THE CRITERIA FOR A "GOOD" DECISION

The concept of optimization serves as a gold standard for the field of decision making. Once we are able to determine that one course of action dominates the others, and maximizes expected utility, then we are free to accept it. Prior to that point, a good decision maker must be reluctant and must wonder if it might be better to gather more data.

While there is some benefit in having a gold standard as a yardstick for assessing the adequacy of our deliberations, there are drawbacks as well. The review of assumptions listed in Table 7.1 makes it clear that very few decision problems will permit optimization, outside of the limited-context problems presented in laboratory studies. Long ago, Simon (1955, 1972) cautioned about the limited computational ability of humans. For that reason, Simon described the heuristics, satisficing strategies, and bounded rationality that would be necessary to substitute for maximization.

The "heuristics and biases" approach (Kahneman and Tversky 1982) in part grew out of this view. Their studies showed how people used heuristics even when the heuristics generated erroneous responses. At this juncture, the field of decision research was poised between two directions. One possible direction was to examine more fully how the heuristics arose, how they were used, and how they enabled people to use prior experience. Such an approach would have moved decision researchers into greater connection with the fields of expertise and cognitive science. However, this path was not traveled until decades later, when the naturalistic decision-making framework coalesced (Klein et al. 1993). This framework examines the way people use their experience, and their heuristics, to make decisions in field settings that are characterized by conditions such as time pressure, uncertainty, ill-defined goals, and shifting conditions.

My own research on recognitional decision making (Klein 1998) has resulted in a model that essentially blends three of the heuristics described by Kahneman and Tversky (1982): availability, representativeness, and the simulation heuristic. Instead of seeing these as biases, I have found it more useful to see them as strengths that permit skillful decision making in field settings. Experienced decision makers are able to categorize situations rapidly as typical of various prototypes, using representativeness and availability heuristics, and are able to evaluate the courses of action suggested by these prototypes by conducting mental simulations, using the simulation heuristic, without having to compare options.

Rather than taking the path of studying how heuristics are developed and used, the field of decision research took the direction of compiling heuristics that might, under controlled conditions, degrade decision performance. I suspect that one of the reasons for taking this path was the mindset that any departure from the gold standard of optimization was a departure from rationality. In this view, even though optimization does not usually apply, an analytic approach with a thorough consideration of options is rational, and a heuristic approach is not.

How can we apply the findings of the heuristics and biases approach? One of the current strategies is to recommend debiasing methods (e.g., Hammond et al. 1998; Plous 1993; Russo and Shoemaker 1989). These are methods to overcome the decision biases such as anchoring and adjustment, availability, and representativeness. I find two disturbing features in this attempt. One is that while the debiasing methods have been demonstrated in the laboratory (e.g., Arkes et al. 1987; Lichtenstein and Fischhoff 1980), the methods have not been shown to improve decision making in field settings. In fact, data suggest that decision biases have a minimal impact in field settings (Fraser et al. 1992). Second, the strategy of debiasing seems inconsistent with the original concept of heuristics, which was to find and use quick and dirty methods to overcome information-processing limits. If we "debias" people, then we force them to give up their heuristics, and this would plunge them into computational overload. The promotion of debiasing illustrates the strength of optimization as a gold standard.

If we dismiss optimization as a standard for decision making, with what can we replace it? Perhaps we can gain some insights by studying skilled decision makers in action. Chess is a domain that appears relevant. Chess players actively try to find the best course of action at each move. Chess has many features of naturalistic decision making: time pressure, shifting conditions, and highly experienced practitioners. It lacks other features such as uncertainty. The positions of all the pieces are known; the only unknown is the opponent's response to a move. Chess has fairly well-defined goals; observers cannot define a "right" answer, but they will usually agree about good and poor moves.

de Groot (1946/1978) asked chess grandmasters to provide think-aloud protocols while solving chess problems. This exercise did not involve time pressure, and the task was removed from the context of playing a game. Therefore, we would expect that his findings would show more careful analysis than usual.

One of the most striking findings of de Groot's study was that the chess grandmasters did not use anything resembling decision analysis in selecting moves. In reviewing the protocols for the five grandmasters (de Groot 1946/1978), I estimated that for board position A, approximately forty moves were considered (each grandmaster examined about eight moves), but only five of these moves were evaluated by contrasting it to another move to specify the relative strengths and weaknesses of each. The comparisons were made at a global level, based on the promise of each alternative.

The grandmasters sought to find the best move, but they did not compare options on a common set of decomposed criteria. Instead, they used a strategy that de Groot (1946/1978) termed "progressive deepening" to play the move out in their minds, to see how it would work. Progressive deepening is an example of the simulation heuristic. The grandmasters did not use multiattribute utility analysis because they did not evaluate moves on common evaluation dimensions (e.g., gains in center control, protection of the king). They evaluated each move separately, imagining what might transpire if it were played, to see the opportunities and vulnerabilities that opened up. The grandmasters did not use decision analysis because they did not care about probabilities at each juncture (or "ply"). They tried to see the overall lines of play that were created or blocked. They tried to understand the causal dynamics of the position, in an attempt to discover the affordances that they might exploit. Causal reasoning replaced probabilistic reasoning.

The grandmasters also compared options because they wanted to select the best one. The comparison was generally based on an overall judgment of the opportunities and risks associated with each move. Some moves were immediately seen as defective and were eliminated from consideration. Others were seen as adequate but not exciting. Some were seen as superior. Sometimes, only a single move fit into this category and it was selected. Sometimes a few moves fit this category, and the grandmasters appeared to savor the possibilities opened up by each, much the same way a restaurant diner mentally "tries out" different items on a menu to see which will taste better. The comparisons in several cases were pair-wise, in that two were compared at a global level, the winner was compared to another, until a clear favorite emerged. In some sense, this was a judgment of expected utility. Any form of decision strategy must involve preferences and expectations. However, I do not believe this fits the definition of maximizing expected utility that is linked to decision analysis or multiattribute utility analysis, for reasons presented above.

The evaluation of different options is also shaped by the status of the game. If a player is behind, then a sense of "creative desperation" may take over, favoring riskier moves that might have serious flaws but also open up more possibilities. One of the criticisms of the IBM computer program Deep Blue was that it lacked this sense of creative desperation and would only choose the move that was calculated to be the best, regardless of whether it was ahead or behind.

In a game situation, the grandmasters would have the additional constraint of working against a clock. Deliberations have a cost. Chess players would have to estimate the time needed to find a good continuation, compared to the time they had available. de Groot (1946/1978) notes that the judgments of "promisingness" and "urgency" are needed to make these metacognitive decisions. Moreover, the decision about how much time to spend studying a position will change dynamically as a function of what is learned during the progressive deepening of a move.

In light of the interest in emotion at this Dahlem Workshop, it might be worth questioning whether these judgments achieve their impact through emotional reactions as well as through cognitive appraisal. The emotional reaction of enthusiasm for a strong move may be what helps sustain it while the progressive deepening is occurring. The judgments of promisingness and urgency may also carry emotional force, particularly under time pressure. Whereas anxiety can be studied as a state or a trait, we might also consider it a useful emotional reaction in alerting someone to a weakness in a plan.

There are ways in which the strategy of progressive deepening is an improvement over maximizing expected utility. A chess grandmaster tries to identify all of the most promising moves, either by immediately recognizing them or by discovering them during the progressive deepening. The grandmaster also tries to learn whether any of the moves has serious flaws, and whether any of the moves stands out as superior to the others. At the end of an analysis, a chess grandmaster understands the opportunities and limitations of the move selected, the leverage points to press forward with, and the vulnerabilities to protect. The grandmaster has also learned a great deal about the dynamics of the position. In contrast, at the end of a decision analysis, a decision maker would not have this type of understanding of situational dynamics. Progressive deepening is a vehicle for learning, whereas decision analysis is a vehicle for calculating.

The progressive deepening strategy depends on expertise. The expertise in chess covers the ability to size up situations quickly, to detect leverage points, vulnerabilities, urgency, and so forth. In contrast, decision analysis and multiattribute utility analysis make only a limited use of expertise. Skill is needed to identify all the leading courses of action, and skill is needed in estimating probabilities and utilities. Situational understanding may be necessary for generating good options; however, with a few exceptions (e.g., Gettys 1983), option generation has not been studied. Instead, the requirement to generate a complete set of options largely eliminates the need to rely on skill in generating effective options. Moreover, the skills needed to estimate probabilities and utilities do not appear to correspond to the expertise people gain with experience in a domain.

If we move away from optimizing as a criterion for evaluating good and poor decisions, an alternate criterion might be: to select a course of action that is not clearly inferior to any other option, given a reasonable examination of the situation. This standard is higher than satisficing (merely picking the first option that seems workable). The standard reflects the possibility that several options will be clustered together, so that it avoids Fredkin's paradox (spending enormous amounts of energy on the smallest differences in preference). If the time and energy needed to determine which of two options is clearly inferior are estimated to be sizeable, then that is the indicator that the difference is not sufficiently great to be worth examining further. It allows for the potential to pick an option that may stand out from the others, if such is the case. It appeals to a "reasonable" examination of the situation, based on the estimated effort versus expected benefit of further information gathering.

How many options should a decision maker consider before selecting one that is not clearly inferior to any other? Once we move away from issues of optimization, we do not have to prescribe rules but instead can make this the topic of research, to explore the stopping rules used in different settings by decision makers at different levels of skill. The evaluation criterion suggested (selecting an option that is not clearly inferior to any other, given a reasonable examination of the situation) leads us to a descriptive program of research. Such a research program could tie into bounded rationality by investigating how decision makers actually make the judgment of ceasing to identify new options, and how they organize mental simulations without exceeding cognitive limitations.

The decision criterion proposed would rely on the judgment of Subject Matter Experts (SMEs) with regard to the courses of action worth considering, the relative merits of these, and the amount of time that is reasonable to spend in situation assessment. The program for using proficient decision makers to evaluate option quality needs to be worked out further. Even for a domain as constrained as chess, grandmasters have difficulty in judging the courses of action of mediocre players. This is because a course of action may be high quality yet the grandmaster may suspect that the player does not see the implications of the move. Therefore, some indication of rationale may need to accompany the stated move selection. These and other considerations would have to be examined in greater depth.

By relying on the judgments of SMEs, subjectivity is introduced, and this is unfortunate from the point of view of experimentation. Moreover, terms such as "not clearly inferior" and "reasonable examination of the situation" are vague and would be unacceptable to many decision researchers. The problem here runs deeper than terminology. Once subjective criteria are introduced to replace quantitative criteria, the rigor of the research will be compromised. This can be seen as an unacceptable step backwards, or it may be seen as an opportunity for new lines of research.

CONCLUSIONS

In reviewing the requirements for optimization, it is clear that decision makers will be unable to optimize in field settings. Simon (1955, 1972) voiced this concern decades ago. Once we move out of the laboratory, the requirements listed in Table 7.1 are too restrictive.

However, the situation is worse than that. The concept of optimization seems to have internal inconsistencies. First, optimization may refer to the selection of the best option or also to the methods used. Yet the concept of optimization only makes sense in the context of the methods used. It is not enough to follow the prescribed methods. They must be followed well. Decision makers, however, rarely have guidance to determine if they are following the steps well. Second, optimization may refer to selecting the best possible option, or the best option given the data available, but neither of these paths is workable. If it refers to the best possible option, that will be impossible to determine, and an infinite regress of estimating the effort to be expended in trying to gather additional information will result. If it refers to the best option given the data available, then it is more suited to the laboratory than to a natural setting. Third, optimization is easiest to achieve in pursuing a single goal; however, this may lead to poor choices unless the decision maker examines all relevant goals, and this becomes a daunting task.

There is worse news yet. The activity of optimizing expected utility may be insufficient because it does not guide the decision maker in learning about the dynamics of the situation. A decision maker who faithfully follows the rules for estimating expected utilities will not necessarily understand the affordances of a situation and will be less prepared than a decision maker who is studying the opportunities and constraints in the situation.

One might argue that optimization is useful as a standard to encourage more thoughtful decision making. The counterargument is that we are better served with a standard that will improve decision quality, rather than one that is unrealistic and, under some circumstances, counterproductive. We can identify other standards, using the example of the chess grandmaster who relies on causal reasoning and progressive deepening. For novices, we can even suggest the use of a relaxed version of decision analysis (e.g., Janis and Mann 1977) as a vehicle to foster clear thinking, articulate options, identify evaluation categories, and communicate ideas to others, as long as they do not trust the numbers, and as long as they do not become fixated on optimizing.

Once we abandon optimization as a goal, the issue of training takes on new possibilities. Previously, training was seen as instruction in the processes of optimization. Instead of teaching analytical strategies, we may be more effective in building up the expertise needed to handle resource-intensive processes such as progressive deepening (Klein 1997). Will this yield more productive results than the decision analytical strategies advocated by researchers such as Hammond et al. (1998)? This could be treated as an empirical question, to allow researchers to clarify the boundary conditions of the normative and the naturalistic decision research frameworks.

ACKNOWLEDGMENTS

Michael Doherty provided a thorough critique of an earlier draft, and his criticisms helped to strengthen this manuscript. I would also like to thank Baruch Fischhoff for his help in identifying different approaches to the question of optimization, and Rebecca Pliske for reviewing an earlier draft and bringing to my attention many shortcomings of the manuscript.

I would also like to thank all of the anonymous reviewers from the Dahlem Workshop who provided me with useful reactions and suggestions.

REFERENCES

Arkes, H.R., C. Christensen, C. Lai, and C. Blumer. 1987. Two methods of reducing overconfidence. *Org. Behav. Human Decis. Proc.* **39**:133–144.

Berkeley, D., and P. Humphreys. 1982. Structuring decision problems and the "bias heuristic." *Acta Psych.* **50**:201–252.

Bernoulli, D. 1738/1954. Specimen theoriae novae de mensura sortis. *Commentarii academiae scientarum imperialis Petropolitanae* **5**:175–192. (Engl. transl. by L. Sommer, Exposition of a new theory on the measurement of risk. *Econometrica* **22**:23–26.)

Beyth-Marom, R., B. Fischhoff, M.J. Quadrel, and L. Furby. 1991. Teaching decision making to adolescents: A critical review. In: Teaching Decision Making to Adolescents, ed. J. Baron and R.V. Brown, pp. 19–60. Mahwah, NJ: Erlbaum.

Connolly, T. 1988. Hedge-clipping, tree-felling, and the management of ambiguity: The need for new images of decision-making. In: Managing the Challenge of Ambiguity and Change, ed. L.R. Pondy, R.J. Boland, Jr., and H. Thomas, Jr., pp. 37–50. New York: Wiley.

Coombs, C.H., R.M. Dawes, and A. Tversky. 1970. Mathematical Psychology. Englewood Cliffs, NJ: Prentice Hall.

de Groot, A.D. 1946/1978. Thought and Choice in Chess. New York: Mouton.

Edwards, W. 1954. The theory of decision making. *Psych. Rev.* **51**:380–417.

Elster, J. 1977. Ulysses and the Sirens: Studies in Rationality and Irrationality. Cambridge: Cambridge Univ. Press.

Erev, I., G. Bornstein, and T.S. Wallsten. 1993. The negative effect of probability assessments on decision quality. *Org. Behav. Human Decis. Proc.* **55(1)**:79–94.

Fischhoff, B. 1986. Judgment and decision making. In: The Psychology of Human Thought, ed. R.J. Sternberg and E.E. Smith, pp. 153–187. New York: Cambridge Univ. Press.

Fischhoff, B. 1991. Value elicitation: Is there anything in there?*Am. Psych.* **46**:835–847.

Fraser, J.M., P.J. Smith, and J.W. Smith. 1992. A catalog of errors. *Intl. J. Man-Machine St.* **37**:265–307.

Frisch, D., and R.T. Clemen. 1994. Beyond expected utility: Rethinking behavioral decision research. *Psych. Bull.* **116**:46–54.

Gettys, C.F. 1983. Research and theory on predecision processes. Publ. No. TR 11–30–83. Norman, OK: Univ. of Oklahoma, Decision Processes Lab.

Gigerenzer, G., and P.M. Todd. 1999. Fast and frugal heuristics: The adaptive toolbox. In: Simple Heuristics That Make Us Smart, G. Gigerenzer, P.M. Todd, and the ABC Research Group, pp. 3–34. New York: Oxford Univ. Press.

Gigerenzer, G., P.M. Todd, and the ABC Research Group. 1999. Simple Heuristics That Make Us Smart. New York: Oxford Univ. Press.

Hammond, J.S., R.L. Keeney, and H. Raiffa. 1998. Even swaps: A rational method for making trade-offs. *Harvard Bus. Rev.* **76(2)**:137–150.

Janis, I.L., and L. Mann. 1977. Decision making: A psychological analysis of conflict, choice, and commitment. New York: Free Press.

Kahneman, D., and A. Tversky. 1982. The simulation heuristic. In: Judgment under Uncertainty: Heuristics and Biases, ed. D. Kahneman, P. Slovic, and A. Tversky, pp. 201–208. Cambridge: Cambridge Univ. Press.

Klein, G. 1997. Developing expertise in decision making. *Thinking and Reasoning* **3(4)**:337–352.

Klein, G. 1998. Sources of Power: How People Make Decisions. Cambridge: MIT Press.

Klein, G.A., J. Orasanu, R. Calderwood, and C.E. Zsambok. 1993. Decision Making in Action: Models and Methods. Norwood, NJ: Ablex Publ.

Koopman, P., and J. Pool. 1991. Organizational decision making: Models, contingencies and strategies. In: Distributed Decision Making: Cognitive Models for Cooperative Work, ed. J. Rasmussen, B. Brehmer, and J. Leplat, pp. 19–46. Chichester: Wiley.

Lichtenstein, S., and B. Fischhoff. 1980. Training for calibration. *Org. Behav. Human Perf.* **26**:149–171.

March, J.G. 1978. Bounded rationality, ambiguity, and the engineering choice. *Bell J. Econ.* **9**:587–608.

Minsky, M. 1986. The Society of Mind. New York: Simon and Schuster.

Neumann, P.J., and P.E. Politser. 1992. Risk and optimality. In: Risk-taking Behavior, ed. J.F. Yates, pp. 27–47. New York: Wiley.

Pitz, G.F. 1992. Risk taking, design, and training. In: Risk-taking Behavior, ed. J.F. Yates, pp. 283–320. New York: Wiley.

Plous, S. 1993. The Psychology of Judgment and Decision Making. Philadelphia: Temple Univ. Press.

Russo, J.E., and P.J.H. Shoemaker. 1989. Decision Traps: Ten Barriers to Brilliant Decision Making. Garden City, NY: Doubleday.

Simon, H.A. 1955. A behavioral model of rational choice. *Qtly. J. Econ.* **69**:99–118.

Simon, H.A. 1972. Theories of bounded rationality. In: Decision and Organization, ed. C.B. Radner and R. Radner, pp. 161–176. Amsterdam: North Holland Publ.

Simon, H.A. 1983. Reason in human affairs. Palo Alto: Stanford Univ. Press.

Slovic, P. 1995. The construction of preference. *Am. Psych.* **50**:364–371.

von Neumann, J., and O. Morgenstern. 1947. Theory of Games and Economic Behavior. Princeton: Princeton Univ. Press.

von Winterfeldt, D., and W. Edwards. 1986. Decision Analysis and Behavioral Research. New York: Cambridge Univ. Press.

Vos, H.J. 1990. Simultaneous optimization of decisions using a linear utility function. *J. Educ. Stat.* **15(4)**:309–340.

8

Preferential Choice and Adaptive Strategy Use

John W. Payne and James R. Bettman

Fuqua School of Business, Duke University, Durham, NC 27708, U.S.A.

ABSTRACT

How do people evaluate and choose among a set of multiattribute alternatives? Research makes clear that a given individual utilizes a variety of information-processing strategies to solve preferential choice problems contingent upon task demands. Often the information-processing strategies that are used are heuristics in that only a subset of the potentially relevant information is processed, and the processing of that information may not involve the making of trade-offs. This paper argues that the use of a variety of choice heuristics by an individual is an intelligent response of a decision maker characterized by limited cognitive capacity and goals for a decision that extend beyond accuracy to include effort minimization, ease of justification, and avoidance of negative emotions. For instance, certain heuristics are shown to provide high levels of accuracy with substantial savings in effort; such heuristics are also shown to vary in accuracy and effort savings across task environments. Certain heuristics also provide easier-to-justify decisions and allow a person to avoid emotionally difficult trade-offs. A review of the research suggests that people are generally adaptive in their use of various decision strategies, i.e., how they solve decision problems varies in ways that are consistent with how variations in tasks impact accuracy, effort, and other important process considerations. However, it is also clear from research that the use of heuristic processes can, and does, lead to systematic errors such as intransitive preferences. People are not perfectly adaptive in the use of alternative decision strategies. Errors in decision making occur not only because a heuristic is used but also because the wrong decision strategy is sometimes used.

INTRODUCTION

One of the oldest areas of decision research concerns how people evaluate and choose among a set of multiattribute alternatives. A prototypical decision

Table 8.1   An example of a consumer decision task.

Car	Reliability	Price	Safety	Horsepower
A	Worst	Best	Good	Very poor
B	Best	Worst	Worst	Good
C	Poor	Very good	Average	Average
D	Average	Poor	Best	Worst
E	Worst	Very poor	Good	Best

Note: Attributes are scored on seven-point scales ranging from best to worst, with best indicating the most desirable value for the attribute and worst indicating the least desirable value.

problem of this type is the simplified automobile choice task illustrated in Table 8.1. Each choice option *i* (cars *A* − *E*) can be thought of as a vector of attribute values $(x_{i1}, x_{i2}, \ldots, x_{in})$ that reflect the extent to which each option meets the objectives (goals) of the decision maker. The set of alternatives can vary in size from one choice problem to the next, with some choices involving as few as two options and others potentially involving many more (in some cases the two options may be simply to either accept or reject an alternative). The attributes may vary in their desirability to the decision maker, in the decision maker's willingness to trade off less of one attribute for more of another, and in the certainty with which the potential consequences associated with an attribute value will be experienced.

A key feature of most preferential choice problems is the presence of conflict brought on by the fact that no single alternative is best (most preferred) on all the attributes. Conflict has long been recognized as a major source of decision difficulty, including the negative emotions that can arise as a result of the need to accept less of one valued attribute in order to achieve more of another valued attribute (Shepard 1964; Hogarth 1987; Luce et al. 1999). The presence of conflict and the fact that a rule for resolving the conflict often cannot readily be drawn from memory are also reasons why preferential decision making, even in the simplest laboratory tasks, can be characterized by tentativeness and the use of relatively weak problem-solving methods (heuristics). The use of such "weak methods" (heuristics) is often associated with more novice-like problem solving rather than the kind of recognize-and-calculate processes associated with expertise (Chi et al. 1988).

How do people make preferential decisions of the type described above? Research over the past thirty years makes clear that a given individual uses a variety of different decision strategies (heuristics) when making a preferential choice. That is, the same person will make different decisions in different ways *and* will make the same decision in different ways at different points in time. Thus, there is both within-subject variability in strategy use across tasks and within the same task over time. For a recent review of research showing contingent strategy use in decisions, see Bettman et al. (1998).

An obvious, and very important, question arising from the observed variability in strategy use is how, and why, do people select among different strategies when faced with a given preferential choice problem? In this chapter, we review research relevant to that question. Many of the ideas expressed herein, and much more extensive reviews of the relevant research, can be found in Payne et al. (1993) and Bettman et al. (1998). As will become apparent, our approach to understanding strategy selection shares many features with the "fast and frugal" heuristics approach of Gigerenzer et al. (1999).

Much of the research to be reviewed derives from the assumption that decision behavior is shaped by the interaction between the properties of the decision task and the properties of the human information-processing system. We, and many other researchers, believe that two properties of the human information-processing system are crucial for understanding decision behavior. First, the limited capacity people have for processing information means that people generally cannot process all of the available information in a particular situation. Even when the amount of available information is within the bounds of processing capacity, limited cognitive capacity means that the processing of that information imposes cognitive costs. Thus, selective processing of information (i.e., the use of a heuristic) is generally necessary, and which information is selected for processing will have a major impact on choice. Put another way, it is critical to understand the determinants of the focus of attention in decision making because many variations in choice behavior are brought about by making salient different aspects of the decision environment.

Second, people can, and do, bring multiple, potentially conflicting processing goals to a decision problem. Examples of such goals are (a) maximizing accuracy, (b) minimizing cognitive effort, (c) minimizing negative decision-related emotions, and (d) maximizing the ease of justification of a decision to others (see Bettman et al. 1998).[1] Obviously, an approach to understanding strategy selection based on goals for choice is compromised if too many goals are postulated, such as a different goal for each decision. However, we believe that the limited set of goals mentioned above captures many of the most important motivational aspects relevant to decision making.

Clearly, different subsets of choice goals will be relevant to different situations. Strategies for processing information when making a decision will also differ to the extent to which the strategies allow one to achieve each of these goals. Further, how well a strategy allows each goal to be achieved is likely to vary across task environments. Consequently, an intelligent, if not optimal, decision maker will need to adapt his or her decision processes in systematic ways to task demands. Thus, we believe that strategy selection can usefully be

---

[1] For a different but related discussion of how preferences are sensitive to the different goals evoked by choice processes, see Sen (1997) .

modeled in terms of adaptive behavior in light of the multiple goals that a limited capacity information processor brings to preferential choice problems.

The rest of this chapter is organized as follows: First, we briefly describe some of the many decision strategies that have been identified. Second, we identify some of the important task variables that have been shown to influence when different strategies are more likely to be used. Third, we present a choice goals framework for predicting when different strategies will be used. Fourth, evidence supporting that framework and the idea of adaptive strategy selection is reviewed. Finally, we raise some issues concerning when adaptivity in strategy use might fail.

DECISION STRATEGIES

There are many different decision strategies. One classic decision strategy is the weighted adding strategy (WADD), which embodies the additive composition notion that the utility of a multiattribute option equals the sum of the utilities of its components.[2] The additive composition idea implies that the decision maker is both willing and able to make trade-offs. More specifically, a WADD process consists of considering one alternative at a time, examining each of the attributes for that option, determining the subjective value of the attribute values, multiplying each attribute's subjective value times its importance weight (e.g., multiplying the subjective value of average reliability in a car times the importance of a car's reliability), and summing these products across all of the attributes to obtain an overall value for each option. Then the alternative with the highest value would be chosen, i.e., the decision maker maximizes over the calculated values.

The WADD strategy assumes that the decision maker either knows or can assess the relative importance of each attribute and can assign a subjective value to each possible attribute level. More generally, the WADD strategy is characterized by extensive processing of information, consistent (not selective) processing across alternatives and attributes, processing that is alternative based (i.e., focused on one alternative at a time), and processing that is compensatory in that a good value on one attribute can compensate for a poor value on another. The making of trade-offs means that the conflict among objectives is directly

---

[2] Over thirty years ago, Ward Edwards and Amos Tversky (1967) wrote that the idea that the utility of a multiattribute option equals the sum of the utilities of components "so dominates the literature on riskless choice that is has no competitors" (p. 255). The additive composition idea continues to play the major role in studies of multiattribute choice. For example, Meyer and Kahn (1991), in a review of models of consumer choice behavior, note that most applications of choice theory assume that the value of an option A to decision maker i is given by the following linear composition of the attribute values a_{ik}, $V_i(A) = b_i + \Sigma_k w_k\, a_{ik}$, where w_k is a scaling constant that is often interpreted as the "weight" given to attribute k, and b_i is a constant for the particular decision maker.

confronted (Hogarth 1987) with a WADD strategy. Because WADD involves complete (extensive) processing and making explicit trade-offs, it is also considered to be normatively appropriate as a decision strategy (Frisch and Clemen 1994). Weighted adding is the decision model that underlies many of the techniques used by economists, market researchers, and others to assess preferences. The WADD strategy is closely related to expectation models of risky choice, both in terms of processing behavior and in the making of trade-offs, e.g., accepting a lesser amount to win for a greater probability of winning.

The equal weight strategy (EQW) also considers all of the alternatives and all of the attribute values for each alternative. However, processing is simplified by ignoring information about attribute weights. A value is obtained for each alternative by summing all of the attribute values for that option, and the alternative with the highest value is selected. The EQW strategy is thus a special case of WADD if unit weights are assumed. The EQW strategy has often been advocated as a simplified form of compensatory decision making (Dawes 1979). Processing with the EQW strategy is extensive, consistent across alternatives and attributes, and alternative based.

The lexicographic strategy (LEX) provides a good contrast to additive composition strategies: the alternative with the best value on the most important attribute is simply selected (assuming that there are no ties on this attribute). For example, if a decision maker, faced with the car choice problem in Table 8.1, thought that reliability was the most important attribute for cars, he or she could use a LEX strategy, examine reliability (and no other information) for all five cars, and choose car *B*. If two alternatives have tied values, the second most important attribute is considered, and so on, until the tie is broken. The LEX strategy involves a much more limited amount of processing that is selective across attributes and consistent across alternatives, and it is clearly noncompensatory. In other words, the LEX strategy is a *choice heuristic*. It is a good example of a conflict-avoiding decision strategy. For preferential choice, it is also a form of the "one-reason" decision making emphasized by Gigerenzer et al. (1999).

Sometimes the LEX strategy includes the notion of a just-noticeable difference (JND). If several alternatives are within a JND of the best alternative on the most important attribute (or any attributes considered subsequently), they are considered tied. An important consequence of using a LEX strategy with a JND mechanism is that a person may exhibit intransitive preferences in which $A > B$, $B > C$, and $C > A$, which is generally considered a decision error (Tversky 1969).

Satisficing (SAT) is a classic strategy in the decision-making literature (Simon 1955). Alternatives are considered sequentially, in the order in which they occur in the choice set. The value of each attribute for the option currently under consideration is considered to see whether it meets a predetermined cutoff level for that attribute. If any attribute fails to meet the cutoff level, processing is terminated for that option, the option is rejected, and the next option is considered.

For example, car *A* might be eliminated very rapidly because it has the worst level of reliability. The first option passing the cutoffs for all attributes is selected. If no option passes all the cutoffs, the levels can be relaxed and the process repeated. The SAT strategy is alternative based, selective, and noncompensatory. The extent of processing will vary depending upon the exact values of the cutoffs and attribute levels.

One implication of the SAT strategy is that whichever option is chosen can be a function of the order in which the options are processed. More generally, the preferences expressed when using choice heuristics are subject to potentially "irrelevant" task variables such as the order in which options and/or attributes are considered.

Elimination-by-aspects (EBA) combines elements of both the LEX and SAT strategies. EBA eliminates options that do not meet a minimum cutoff value for the most important attribute. This elimination process is repeated for the second most important attribute, with processing continuing until a single option remains (Tversky 1972). In our car example, suppose that the decision maker's two most important attributes were reliability and safety, in that order, and that the cutoff for each was an average value. This individual would first process reliability, eliminating any car with a below-average value (cars *A*, *C*, and *E*). Then the person would consider safety for cars *B* and *D*, eliminating car *B*. Hence, car *D* would be selected. EBA focuses on the attributes as the basis for processing information and is noncompensatory. The extensiveness and selectivity of processing with the EBA strategy will vary depending upon the exact pattern of elimination of options. EBA is a commonly used choice heuristic.

Decision makers also use combinations of strategies. A typical combined strategy has an initial phase, in which some alternatives are eliminated, and a second phase, where the remaining options are analyzed in more detail (Payne 1976; see also Beach's [1990] image theory for further analysis of the role of elimination or screening processes in decision making). One frequently observed strategy combination is an initial use of EBA to reduce the choice set to two or three options followed by a compensatory strategy such as WADD to select among those. An important implication of the use of combined strategies is that the "properties" of the choice task itself may change as the result of using a particular strategy first. For example, the use of a process for eliminating dominated alternatives from a choice set, an often advocated procedure, will make the conflict among attribute values more extreme, perhaps then triggering the application of a new strategy.

CONTINGENT STRATEGY USE

Research demonstrates that the use of a particular decision strategy is contingent on many task and context variables. Some of the most compelling and earliest demonstrations of contingent strategy use concerned how people adapted their decision processes to deal with task complexity. For example, when faced with a decision problem involving only two or three alternatives, people use compensatory types of decision strategies. When faced with more complex (multialternative) decision tasks, people tend to use noncompensatory strategies such as EBA and SAT (Payne 1976; Johnson et al. 1989). Related work shows that contingent strategy use is found in children as well as adults (Klayman 1985; Gregan-Paxton and John 1997).

Another example of contingent processing is in response to variations in information display. Stone and Schkade (1991), for example, found that using words to represent attribute values led to less compensatory processing than numerical representation of the values. Bettman and Kakkar (1977) showed that individuals acquired information in a fashion consistent with the format of the display. Jarvenpaa (1989) extended those results by showing that information was processed consistent with the manner in which graphic displays were organized, i.e., by alternative or by attribute. In a finding that is worrisome for the adaptivity of decision making, MacGregor and Slovic (1986) showed that people will use a less important cue simply because it is more salient in the display. Much of the work on information display effects is consistent with a "concreteness" principle (Slovic 1972), which states that decision makers tend to use information in the form it is displayed, without transforming it, as a way to conserve cognitive effort.

Number of alternatives and information display represent task variables that are associated with general characteristics of the decision problem and are not dependent on the particular values of the alternatives. Context variables, on the other hand, are associated with the particular values of the alternatives and the relationships among those values (Payne 1982). Context variables also have been shown to impact strategy use. For example, an important context variable is interattribute correlation. The more negative the correlation among the attributes, the more one has to give up something on one attribute in order to get more of another attribute, a notion clearly related to the concept of conflict among attributes. Bettman et al. (1993) found that people used more extensive processing strategies characterized by less selective and more alternative-based processing under negative correlation. Widing and Talarzyk (1993) report related results showing that a decision aid that provided weighted average scores using importance weights provided by the user was highly evaluated by users and resulted in the best decision accuracy in a negative correlation environment.

Given the substantial evidence for contingent decision behavior (for more detailed reviews, see Payne et al. 1993 or Bettman et al. 1998), a natural question is why a decision maker, given a particular task, selects one particular decision strategy instead of another. Below we propose a choice goals framework for answering that question.

A CHOICE GOALS FRAMEWORK FOR
STRATEGY SELECTION

Contingent strategy selection has most frequently been explained within a cost-benefit framework that sees the strategy selected as a compromise among the multiple goals a decision maker brings to a problem.[3] For choice problems where there is relatively little emotional involvement or need to justify, we and others argue that the primary benefit associated with a decision process is making an "accurate" choice and the primary cost is the amount of cognitive effort involved in reaching a decision (e.g., Beach and Mitchell 1978; Hogarth 1987; Johnson and Payne 1985). Thus, it should not be surprising to see increased use of choice heuristics like the EBA strategy as decision tasks become more complex, i.e., there is more information available that needs to be processed (Payne 1976). For the moment we focus on situations where accuracy and effort are the two most important goals; in later sections we will briefly consider scenarios where minimizing negative emotion or maximizing ease of justification are relevant.

Issues for a Choice Goals Framework

Measuring Goals

There are a number of issues related to a multiple goals framework for strategy selection. A choice goals framework is most useful if we have conceptually appropriate and easily calculable measures of the various goals and can hence readily determine the extent to which different decision strategies accomplish these goals in different task environments. As indicated below, much progress has been made in developing useful measures of cognitive effort and decision accuracy. Less progress has been made in developing such measures for ease of justification and the degree of negative emotion invoked by a decision.

Strategy Selection

Another issue has to do with the process by which strategy selection occurs. Inherent in the ideas that people possess a "toolbox" of different decision heuristics and that these heuristics perform differentially across task environments is the question of how one decides how to decide. If no single decision strategy works equally well in every task environment, how does an individual choose the appropriate heuristic (tool) for a given situation? Much of the debate in trying to answer this question concerns the extent to which strategy selection is a conscious, top-down process or a more unconscious, bottom-up process.

---

[3] The decision on how to decide can itself be viewed as a multiattribute decision problem (Einhorn and Hogarth 1981).

One view of strategy selection is that when faced with a decision task, a decision maker evaluates the available tools in her toolbox in terms of her multiple goals and her beliefs about how well various tools are suited to the task and then selects the strategy which is best fitted for solving the given decision problem. Empirical evidence and introspection make clear that strategy selection is sometimes such a conscious, top-down process. For example, the following two excerpts from verbal (think aloud) protocols of two decision makers illustrate this point:

1. "Well, with these many apartments (six) to choose from, I'm not going to work through all the characteristics. Start eliminating them as soon as possible." (Payne 1976)
2. "With just two (gambles) to choose from, I'm going to go after all the information. It won't be that much trouble." (Payne and Braunstein 1978)

More generally, it is clear that people sometimes plan how to solve various types of problems (Anderson 1983). For instance, there is evidence that a crucial difference among students in terms of reading skill is the ability to adjust reading approaches (strategies) to different reading tasks (Garner 1987). As Gagne (1984) argues, good problem-solving behavior often requires knowledge of when and how to use procedural (tool) and declarative (fact) knowledge when solving a problem.

A major concern that has been expressed about a top-down view of strategy (tool) selection is the issue of infinite regress, i.e., one decides on the basis of costs and benefits how to decide how to decide ... This infinite regress problem in decision strategy selection is similar to the problem in game theory regarding the use of one's beliefs about the beliefs of others, who have beliefs about one's beliefs about the beliefs of others ... (Lipman 1991). Clearly, the potential for infinite regress in the strategy selection process is a serious issue. However, there are both theoretical reasons and empirical evidence to suggest that the sequence of decisions on deciding how to decide may quickly converge to some fixed point (Lipman 1991; Nagel 1995). In her work on experimental games, for example, Nagel (1995) reports that the depth of reasoning about what others are thinking about what you are thinking typically does not extend beyond one or two levels deep. Thus, a top-down view of strategy selection seems both warranted and feasible for some situations.

A different view of strategy (tool) selection views the decision of how to decide as a much more bottom-up process. Instead of a conscious decision on how to decide, the selection of a tool from the toolbox simply reflects a learned response that has related various task factors to the effectiveness and efficiency of various strategies (for a related view, see Rieskamp and Hoffrage 1999). For instance, people may have learned that the "Take The Best" rule works very well for certain tasks, and that rule is then typically evoked whenever those situations are encountered. This bottom-up view of strategy selection avoids the infinite regress problem but faces the problem of deciding how to decide when faced with more novel situations.

Our view is that the strategy selection problem is sometimes solved in a top-down way while at other times it proceeds in a much more bottom-up fashion. Specifically, we believe that the top-down approach to strategy selection will be more prevalent when people are faced with complex problems and have the time to decide how to decide. It is also possible that people may start with a top-down approach to a decision problem and then constructively adjust their processing during the course of making the decision as they learn more about the problem structure. Processing, in other words, can change on the spot to exploit the task structure in an "opportunistic" fashion (Hayes-Roth and Hayes-Roth 1979). For many other situations, however, we believe that people have simply learned which rule works best for certain classes of decision problems and will use that rule when such tasks are recognized. (For more discussion of the processes of strategy selection, see Chapters 3 and 5 of Payne et al. 1993.)

Anticipated versus Experienced Effort and Accuracy

A third issue concerns the distinction between anticipated and experienced levels of effort and accuracy. We believe that it is the anticipated effort and accuracy of different decision strategies in a particular environment that guides strategy use. However, anticipations of effort and accuracy need not be veridical. That is, people may be overconfident in the ability of a strategy to produce an accurate decision or overly sensitive to immediate feedback on the effort involved in implementing a strategy. This issue is explored in greater detail below, when we discuss possible sources of failure in adaptive decision making. We now consider the measurement of strategy effort and accuracy in more detail.

Assessing Cognitive Effort

The concept of cognitive or mental effort has a long and venerable history as a theoretical construct in psychology (Kahneman 1973; Navon and Gopher 1979). It has also long been assumed that different decision strategies require different amounts of computational effort (e.g., Simon 1955). However, as mentioned above, the usefulness of a choice goals framework for strategy selection is greatly enhanced by the development of more precise metrics for concepts like cognitive effort.

Based on the work of Newell and Simon (1972), O. Huber (1980) and E. Johnson (unpublished) suggested that the cognitive effort involved in making a decision could be measured in terms of the number of elementary information-processing operations needed to complete a decision task, given a specified decision strategy. The basic idea was that any decision strategy can be decomposed into more elementary information processes (EIPs), such as reading an item of information, comparing two items of information, multiplying or adding items of information, eliminating items of information, and so on (for a general discussion on the use of EIPs to analyze information processing, see Chase 1978). A LEX strategy, for example, could be conceptualized as reading the value for each attribute weight, comparing the weight just read with the largest weight found previously until the most important attribute has been found, and then reading the values for the options on that attribute and comparing them until the largest value is found. A WADD strategy could be thought of as reading weights and values, multiplying the two, moving on to the next weight and value and multiplying them, adding the products, and so on. Thus, for any given strategy, a representation in terms of EIPs can be developed. When the given strategy is applied to make a selection in a given situation, how many EIPs of each type were required to make that selection can be determined. The number of EIPs used will be a function of the specific rule, the size and other characteristics of the problem, and the specific values of the data (for detailed examples, see Payne et al. 1993, Chapter 3). Cognitive effort can then be defined as a function of the number and types of EIPs needed to complete a task. When modeled as production rules, IF–THEN statements and the number of EIPs needed to complete a task can easily be simulated with a computer.

The EIP approach to measuring cognitive effort has been validated by showing that the time to make a decision using a specified strategy and individuals' self-reports of the effort required are predicted quite well by weighted counts of the EIPs characterizing that strategy (Bettman et al. 1990). Importantly, such research also makes clear that predicting cognitive effort in choice requires not only concern for the amount of information processed, but also a concern for *how* the information is processed (i.e., some EIPs require more effort than others). Further, there are individual differences in how effortful various EIP operations are to perform (e.g., some individuals may find arithmetic computations more difficult to perform than do other individuals).

Assessing Decision Accuracy

At least three bases for judging the quality of a decision have been suggested in the literature: "correspondence," "coherence," and "process." Hammond (1996) discusses the relationships between correspondence and coherence approaches to decision quality. A correspondence theory of truth argues that truth ultimately resides in judgmental accuracy, e.g., was the investment with the greatest return selected? In contrast, a coherence theory of truth emphasizes relationships among observations, e.g., are preferences transitive or was a dominated option selected? Coherence approaches also relate observations to some theoretical standard of what is a "good" or "rational" response (e.g., the additive utility model for riskless choice and the expected utility model for risky choice). Such "rational" models are themselves derived from assumptions about preferences, e.g., transitivity, and are frequently motivated by reference to good or bad outcomes, e.g., avoiding the possibility of becoming a "money pump."

The third measure of judgmental quality argues that "truth ultimately resides in the process rather than the outcome" of the decision (Slovic 1995, p. 369). Although researchers differ on the details, there seems to be general agreement that a good decision process involves thorough (requisite) processing, logical thinking, and careful trade-offs (see Baron 1988; Frisch and Clemen 1994; Janis and Mann 1977; Slovic 1995). A good decision-making process is expected (on average) to lead to more desirable outcomes than a poor decision-making process (Frisch and Clemen 1994).

The process and coherence approaches to measuring decision quality provide a standard of accuracy for preference tasks where a correspondence standard is more difficult to apply. For example, it is hard to evaluate a particular individual's preference for one (nondominated) option over another in a specific decision as either good or bad using a correspondence approach. It is also difficult to argue that a decision to accept a unique gamble that may yield a poor outcome due to the occurrence of an unfavorable event is necessarily a "bad" or inaccurate decision. Consequently, we believe that accuracy for preferential choice tasks is best defined using a WADD-type model, which is normative in that it specifies how individuals can best reflect their preferences if certain assumptions about those preferences are met. Also, as noted above, a model like WADD that uses all relevant information and allows for trade-offs can be considered normative from a "process" perspective (Frisch and Clemen 1994). Thus, in the simulation work described below, we use a weighted additive rule or the similar expected value (EV) rule for risky choice problems. The main advantage of EV as an accuracy measure is that utility values from individual decision makers are not required to operationalize the rule. We also compare the performance of more normative strategies like EV and various choice heuristics like EBA against the baseline rule of random choice. Random choice uses none of the relevant choice information and is therefore the simplest process. While we concentrate in this chapter on these measures of accuracy, we have used other measures with similar results (e.g., Johnson and Payne 1985).

EVIDENCE SUPPORTING THE CHOICE
GOALS FRAMEWORK

Here we outline how measures of cognitive effort and accuracy can be used in simulations to develop predictions about contingent use of decision strategies and describe empirical tests of such predictions.

Using Effort and Accuracy Assessments to Make Predictions

We can characterize the accuracy and effort of various strategies in particular environments by running a computer simulation of each strategy in each environment and keeping track of the number of EIPs used for each choice and the

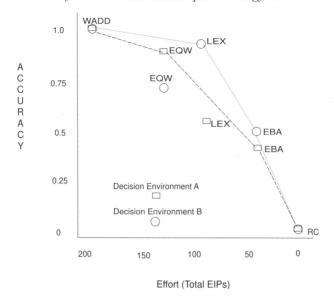

Effort (Total EIPs)

Figure 8.1 Accuracy (measured in terms of the percentage obtained of the weighted additive value) and the average effort (in total EIPs) for five decision strategies (WADD: weighted adding; EQW: equal weighting; LEX: lexicographic; RC: random choice; EBA: elimination-by-aspects) as determined through computer simulations. A line is used to connect the "pure" strategies for each environment that offer nondominated combinations of accuracy and effort.

option chosen. Examples of such simulation work can be found in Johnson and Payne (1985), Payne et al. (1988), Bettman et al. (1993), and Payne et al. (1996).

Figure 8.1 illustrates typical results from those simulations for five "pure" strategies: WADD, LEX, EBA, EQW, and random choice (RC). This figure shows the accuracy (measured in terms of the percentage attained of the WADD value) and the effort (in total EIPs) for the five strategies. The accuracy and effort values for the decision strategies are plotted for two distinct decision environments. There are a number of important conclusions about various decision strategies that can be drawn from our simulations.

First, as illustrated in Figure 8.1, there are decision environments in which heuristic choice rules provide excellent accuracy and substantial savings in cognitive effort. For instance, the LEX rule achieves roughly 90% of the accuracy of the WADD rule with only about 40% of the effort in environment *B*. Thus, the use of a heuristic to solve a preferential choice problem makes sense in that environment for a decision maker concerned with the two goals of accuracy and effort minimization.

Second, also illustrated in Figure 8.1, the most efficient heuristics in terms of accuracy and effort *vary* across task environments. For example, the LEX rule is better in environment *B* and less effective in environment *A* than alternative heuristics. Thus, a decision maker who wanted to achieve both a reasonably high level of accuracy and low effort would need to use a repertoire of strategies, with selection contingent upon situational demands.

Third, although not shown in Figure 8.1, the simulation results make clear that the effort required to use heuristics increases more slowly than the effort required to use the WADD strategy as tasks become more complex. The accuracy of heuristics, on the other hand, is fairly robust over increases in the number of alternatives. Some heuristics are also fairly robust over changes in the number of attributes, although LEX does decrease in accuracy as the number of relevant attributes is increased. Thus, the accuracy–effort ratio seems to favor increasingly the multiple use of heuristics as tasks become more complex. More generally, the relative effort of a strategy is impacted more by task variables such as the number of available alternatives. The relative accuracy of a decision strategy, on the other hand, tends to be impacted more by context variables such as amount of conflict between attribute values (for details, see Payne et al. 1993, Chapter 4).

Fourth, there are task environments, e.g., time-constrained situations, in which the WADD strategy is less accurate than some choice heuristics because processing is truncated. For example, the EBA rule is remarkably robust to variations in time pressure, and it is actually the most accurate rule in some time-pressured environments. Generally, it seems that strategies like EBA and LEX, which involve an initial processing of all alternatives using a limited set of attributes, do well under severe time pressure (Payne et al. 1988).

Fifth, except for such time-pressured environments, the WADD strategy is robust in terms of accuracy across a variety of decision environments. One of the greatest strengths of normative strategies like WADD is that they generalize across tasks and contexts. There are also some environments, such as those characterized by negative correlations (increased conflict) among the attributes, in which the accuracy of the WADD rule is substantially greater than that of heuristics. Also, as would be expected, the greater the number of relevant attributes of value, the relatively better the WADD strategy. Thus, to obtain high levels of accuracy in some environments, one may need to devote the additional effort necessary for a WADD strategy.

Several of the points made above are relevant for the debate about whether or not compensatory rules like WADD should be considered to be generally the most accurate decision rules (see, e.g., Gigerenzer and Goldstein 1996; Martignon and Hoffrage 1999). As noted above, it is clear that for some task environments simple heuristics, like LEX (a version of the Take The Best rule), can be very accurate, i.e., the cost in accuracy of using such heuristics is small. Put another way, there are some environments in which such heuristic strategies and more normative rules such as WADD will work equally well. Simple examples of such environments include cases where there is no signal in the task environment, i.e., zero cue validities, or where all the cues are redundant. There are also some situations in which errors in estimating the weights or values necessary to properly operationalize a rule like WADD can produce poorer performance than using a simple rule.

Nevertheless, we believe that there are many situations where more elaborate rules will outperform heuristics like Take The Best in terms of accuracy. That is, for many tasks, a more elaborate rule that uses more information than a rule like Take The Best will lead to greater performance. For example, simulation work reported in Payne et al. (1993, Chapter 4) shows cases where WADD clearly outperforms Take The Best. Task environments for which WADD is likely to be more accurate than Take The Best include those that have multiple, nonredundant, multivalued cues (dimensions) that are relevant to the decision; we believe that many multiattribute preference problems have such characteristics. Of course, the more elaborate rules will generally not be as "frugal" nor as fast as the simple heuristics in the toolbox.

To summarize, a series of simulation studies indicate that choice heuristics are an efficient way to solve preferential choice problems. However, a decision maker who wanted to achieve high levels of accuracy and save cognitive effort would need to be prepared to use a variety of decision strategies, contingent upon task demands. In the next section we briefly review evidence supporting contingent strategy use and the proposed multiple goals framework as applied to strategy selection in preferential choice.

Empirical Validation of the Simulation Results

First, people generally change strategies in ways that the simulation results indicate are appropriate, given changes in the features of the decision problem. For example, people shift decision strategies as a function of task complexity in ways consistent with a concern for conserving cognitive effort (for a review of the many studies demonstrating this effect, see Ford et al. 1989). People also become less extensive processors of information, more selective processors, and more attribute-based processors under time pressure. More specifically, people appear to use a hierarchy of responses to time pressure: acceleration of processing, then increased selectivity, and finally change from depth-first (alternative-based) to breadth-first (attribute-based) strategies (Payne et al. 1988; Payne et al. 1996). People are also sensitive to changes in context variables. For example, the use of extensive, less selective, and alternative-based strategies increases as the interattribute correlations become more negative (Bettman et al. 1993). However, people seem to be less sensitive to context variables than to task variables. This latter fact is probably due to the increased difficulty people have in assessing context variables.

Second, people are sensitive to the trade-offs between accuracy and effort. As more emphasis is placed on the goal of maximizing accuracy relative to the goal of minimizing effort, people do shift processing. In particular, under a greater accuracy goal, people process more, show less selective processing, are more alternative based, and select the option that maximizes EV more often (Creyer et al. 1990; Payne et al. 1996). However, increased incentives frequently serve merely to increase the amount of effort people devote to a selected strategy (for more on incentive effects and strategy selection, see Payne et al. 1993, Chapters 3 and 6).

Third, people who are more adaptive decision makers also appeared to be more efficient in terms of relative payoffs received and effort conserved (Bettman et al. 1993; Payne et al. 1996). Thus, people who shift strategies appropriately (are more adaptive) can earn higher payoffs while still saving effort.

Fourth, people are not perfectly adaptive. For instance, people sometimes do not change strategies as quickly as tasks may change. People also sometimes fail to adapt appropriately; e.g., adapting to the goal of maximizing accuracy can interfere with the need to adapt to certain forms of time pressure (e.g., Payne et al. 1996). More generally, people may have trouble adapting to multiple, conflicting decision task properties.

To summarize, although not perfect, people do appropriately use a variety of decision strategies contingent upon task and context factors. People are sensitive to both accuracy and effort concerns when deciding how to decide. In that regard, people are generally adaptive in that they make intelligent, if not necessarily optimal, responses to decision task demands. For further evidence in support of this adaptive decision maker hypothesis, see Senter and Wedell (1999).

ANALYZING SITUATIONS WHERE MAXIMIZING EASE OF JUSTIFICATION AND MINIMIZING NEGATIVE EMOTION ARE RELEVANT

In this section we briefly discuss evidence indicating that the hypothesized goals driving adaptive strategy selection must be extended to include ease of justifying a decision and the avoidance of the negative emotions sometimes generated by a decision problem.

Accountability and Ease of Justification

Decisions are often evaluated, either by others to whom one is accountable or by oneself. Hence, people often must be able to justify or provide reasons for a decision (Shafir et al. 1993). Tetlock (1992) has proposed a contingency approach that allows for both effort-minimizing and accuracy-maximizing responses to increased accountability. In particular, Tetlock argues that people will cope with accountability in some situations by simply deferring to the preferences of the person(s) to whom they are accountable, an effort-minimizing strategy. If the preferences of those to whom one is accountable are not known, Tetlock proposes that individuals may process more thoroughly.

The EBA strategy discussed throughout this article was originally proposed not only as an effort-minimizing heuristic but also as a process for decision making that could lead to easier-to-justify decisions (Tversky 1972). The idea is that the choice of option *A* over option *B* because option *B* failed to have an important aspect is easier to justify than a choice that depends on a trade-off as a justification.

At a more general level, choice heuristics that depend on the relationships among the values of different options rather than absolute values seem to be more justifiable. For example, Simonson (1989) found that the relationship of asymmetric dominance in a choice set (i.e., option *C* is dominated by option *A* but not by option *B*) increases the likelihood of choosing *A* to a greater extent when justification is required.[4] While relationships like asymmetric dominance can provide good reasons for a choice, the difficulty of assessing such relationships is likely to increase with problem complexity. However, we do not have good measures of the effort involved in using relationships. It is also not clear how using such relationships affects accuracy; this probably depends on the exact structure of the choice sets. Nevertheless, there is a growing amount of research suggesting that *how* people decide depends on the extent to which a need to justify a decision exists. For a review of the effects of accountability on judgment, see Lerner and Tetlock (1999).

The Role of Negative Emotions

People sometimes face emotion-laden choices. Such choices arise when there are choice conflicts between goals that are very important to the individual (e.g., one cannot attain all goals given the set of available options and must give up something on one important goal to attain more of another important goal). More generally, the degree of emotion often depends upon the values of the options (e.g., the degree of conflict and which specific attributes are involved in the conflict). An example of such an emotion-laden decision in the consumer domain might be trading off the safety of an automobile against environmental concerns (if larger vehicles fare better in crashes but worse in gas mileage). The nature of emotion-laden choices is that the ensuing negative emotion is associated with the *decision itself*, not some unrelated ambient affect such as negative mood attributable to background noise at the site where the decision must be made (for a discussion of affect and decision making, see Isen 1997).

When faced with more emotion-laden trade-offs, people seem to vary their processing and choice behavior. For example, Luce et al. (1997) showed that increased negative emotion due to more difficult trade-offs or more serious consequences led to more extensive, more selective, and more attribute-based processing (consistent with the notion that consumers try to avoid emotion-laden, difficult trade-offs). Luce et al. (1999) showed that consumers more

---

4 The "asymmetric dominance" effect (Huber et al. 1982; Simonson and Tversky 1992) is a clear violation of the assumption of "menu-independence" (Sen 1997) in rational choice theory. It is one of the strongest pieces of evidence demonstrating that preferences are often constructed (see Payne et al. 1992; Slovic 1995).

often chose an option that was better on a quality attribute rather than an option better on price when that quality attribute was rated as inherently more emotion-laden, or involved losses rather than gains. These effects were in addition to any effects of the consumers' importance weights for quality relative to price. Luce (1998) showed that increases in negative emotion led to increased avoidance of choice; in particular, increased trade-off difficulty led to increased choice of a status quo option, increased choice of an asymmetrically dominating alternative, and a greater tendency to prolong search. In addition, she demonstrated that choosing an avoidant option resulted in less negative retrospective emotion. Finally, Kahn and Baron (1995) found that consumers were likely to use a noncompensatory lexicographic rule when making their own high-stakes decisions, but that consumers wanted advisors to make decisions for them using compensatory rules.

Overall, the results summarized above, and other research, suggest that negative emotions cannot simply be treated as another form of decision cost; negative emotions associated with a decision task tend to lead to avoidant processing and choices. Strategy selection is impacted by more than just accuracy and effort considerations.

FAILURES OF ADAPTIVITY

Much of the discussion above has focused on how individuals adapt to different choice situations by contingent use of various strategies. However, it is important to emphasize that such adaptivity need not occur. Indeed, there are many reasons why adaptivity may fail. Clearly people do not always use the right strategy to solve a particular decision problem or do not use that strategy appropriately.

Two major classes of factors associated with potential failure in adaptivity exist. First, being adaptive requires various types of knowledge, and decision makers' knowledge may be deficient. Deficits in knowledge can include difficulties in assessing the task and context factors characterizing the decision environment, lack of knowledge of appropriate strategies, not being able to assess veridically the effort and/or the accuracy of a strategy in a particular situation, and not knowing one's desired trade-offs between various process goals like accuracy and effort. Second, being adaptive requires the ability to execute strategies appropriately. The inability to execute a strategy might be due to memory or computational difficulties caused by the complexity of the task and/or by various environmental stressors.

A common source of maladaptivity due to lack of knowledge is difficulty in assessing decision accuracy. Individuals, for instance, may overestimate what they will achieve with particular decision heuristics. This overestimation may be due to a hindsight bias and/or a general overconfidence bias. Brehmer (1990) has also suggested that the knowledge of one's own suboptimality in solving a complex and dynamic decision problem is not a primary perceptual datum. Instead, "it is an inference based on a normative model of the task, and, if the decision maker does not have a well-developed model of the task, the possibility of doing better will not be detected" (Brehmer 1990, p. 267). A related problem is that the difficulty one has in knowing how well one is doing compared to the relative ease of assessing the degree of effort being extended may lead to an overweighting of effort minimization relative to accuracy maximization in strategy selection.

As noted above, individuals may fail to adapt even when they have selected the appropriate strategy if they are unable to execute that strategy. The ability to execute a strategy, for example, may be impaired if the required computations are too difficult. Interestingly, work by Kotovsky et al. (1985) suggests that alternative (but isomorphic) representations of a problem can impose different levels of working memory demands on a problem-solving strategy, making certain operations more difficult.

Finally, one of the most likely sources of failures in adaptivity is overreliance on the most salient surface features of a decision task, e.g., a salient anchor value. If such properties capture the decision maker's attention but are not related to the individual's underlying values, choices will likely not be adaptive.

In summary, there are many ways in which decision makers may fail to be adaptive; see Payne et al. (1993, Chapter 6) for more examples. Therefore, techniques like decision analysis, man–machine decision systems, and the design of better information environments for decision making can all help improve the decisions even of a generally adaptive decision maker.

CONCLUSION

People use a variety of information-processing strategies to solve preferential choice problems. A given individual will often make different decisions using different strategies and will make the same decision with different processes at different points in time. Often the information-processing strategies that are used are heuristics in that only a subset of the potentially relevant information is processed, and the processing of that information may not be very involved, e.g., may not utilize trade-offs. In this chapter, we have argued that an individual's use of a variety of choice heuristics contingent on task demands is an intelligent response for a decision maker characterized by limited cognitive capacity and goals that extend beyond accuracy to include effort minimization, ease of justification, and avoidance of negative emotions. The heuristics that are used by people often provide high levels of accuracy with substantial savings in effort. Certain choice heuristics also provide easier-to-justify decisions and allow a person to avoid emotionally difficult trade-offs. People generally seem adaptive in their use of various decision strategies in that they vary how they solve decision problems in ways that are consistent with how variations in tasks impact accuracy, effort, and other important process considerations.

Of course, the use of heuristics is not cost free. People do make systematic, and predictable, errors when faced with preferential choice problems, e.g., intransitive patterns of preference. People also are not perfectly adaptive in their use of alternative decision strategies. Errors in decision making occur not only because a heuristic is used but also because the wrong decision strategy is sometimes used.

Overall, we argue that the flexibility with which individuals respond to a wide variety of task conditions is one of the most fascinating aspects of human decision behavior. We propose that a multi-goal approach to understanding how people decide to decide is a powerful one for exploring the contingent nature of decision making.

ACKNOWLEDGMENT

Much of the work described was carried out in collaboration with our colleagues. We particularly wish to acknowledge the fundamental contributions made to both the conceptual and empirical aspects of our work by Eric Johnson and Mary Frances Luce.

REFERENCES

Anderson, J.R. 1983. The Architecture of Cognition. Cambridge, MA: Harvard Univ. Press.

Baron, J. 1988. Thinking and Deciding. Cambridge: Cambridge Univ. Press.

Beach, L.R. 1990. Image Theory: Decision Making in Personal and Organizational Contexts. Chichester: Wiley.

Beach, L.R., and T.R. Mitchell. 1978. A contingency model for the selection of decision strategies. *Acad. Manag. Rev.* **3**:439–449.

Bettman, J.R., E.J. Johnson, M.F. Luce, and J.W. Payne. 1993. Correlation, conflict, and choice. *J. Exp. Psych.: Learn. Mem. Cogn.* **19**:931–951.

Bettman, J.R., E.J. Johnson, and J.W. Payne. 1990. A componential analysis of cognitive effort in choice. *Org. Behav. Human Decis. Proc.* **45**:111–139.

Bettman, J.R., and P. Kakkar. 1977. Effects of information presentation format on consumer information acquisition strategies. *J. Consumer Res.* **3**:233–240.

Bettman, J.R., M.F. Luce, and J.W. Payne. 1998. Constructive consumer choice processes. *J. Consumer Res.* **25**:187–217.

Brehmer, B. 1990. Strategies in real-time dynamic decision making. In: Insights in Decision Making: A Tribute to Hillel J. Einhorn, ed. R.M. Hogarth, pp. 262–279. Chicago: Univ. of Chicago Press.

Chase, W.G. 1978. Elementary information processes. In: Handbook of Learning and Cognitive Processes, ed. W.K. Estes, vol. 5, pp. 19–90. Hillsdale, NJ: Erlbaum.

Chi, M.T.H., R. Glaser, and M.J. Farr, eds. 1988. The Nature of Expertise. Hillsdale, NJ: Erlbaum.

Creyer, E.H., J.R. Bettman, and J.W. Payne. 1990. The impact of accuracy and effort feedback and goals on adaptive decision behavior. *J. Behav. Decis. Mak.* **3**:1–16.

Dawes, R.M. 1979. The robust beauty of improper linear models in decision making. *Am. Psych.* **34**:571–582.

Edwards, W., and A. Tversky, eds. 1967. Decision Making. Baltimore: Penguin.

Einhorn, H.J., and R.M. Hogarth. 1981. Behavioral decision theory. *Ann. Rev. Psych.* **32**:53–88.

Ford, J.K., N. Schmitt, S.L. Schechtman, B.M. Hults, and M.L. Doherty. 1989. Process tracing methods: Contributions, problems, and neglected research questions. *Org. Behav. Human Decis. Proc.* **43**:75–117.

Frisch, D., and R.T. Clemen. 1994. Beyond expected utility: Rethinking behavioral decision research. *Psych. Bull.* **116**:46–54.

Gagne, R.M. 1984. Learning outcomes and their effects: Useful categories of human performance. *Am. Psych.* **39**:377–385.

Garner, R. 1987. Metacognition and Reading Comprehension. Norwood, NJ: Ablex.

Gigerenzer, G., and D.G. Goldstein. 1996. Reasoning the fast and frugal way: Models of bounded rationality. *Psych. Rev.* **103**:650–669.

Gigerenzer, G., P.M. Todd, and the ABC Research Group. 1999. Simple Heuristics That Make Us Smart. New York: Oxford Univ. Press.

Gregan-Paxton, J., and D.R. John. 1997. The emergence of adaptive decision making in children. *J. Consumer Res.* **24**:43–56.

Hammond, K.R. 1996. Human Judgment and Social Policy: Irreducible Uncertainty, Inevitable Error, Unavoidable Injustice. New York: Oxford Univ. Press.

Hayes-Roth, B., and F. Hayes-Roth. 1979. A cognitive model of planning. *Cog. Sci.* **3**:275–310.

Hogarth, R.M. 1987. Judgement and Choice, 2nd ed. New York: Wiley.

Huber, J., J.W. Payne, and C.P. Puto. 1982. Adding asymmetrically dominated alternatives: Violations of regularity and the similarity hypothesis. *J. Consumer Res.* **9**:90–98.

Huber, O. 1980. The influence of some task variables on cognitive operations in an information-processing decision model. *Acta Psych.* **45**:187–196.

Isen, A. 1997. Positive affect and decision making. In: Research on Judgment and Decision Making: Currents, Connections, and Controversies, ed. W.M. Goldstein and R.M. Hogarth, pp. 509–534. Cambridge: Cambridge Univ. Press.

Janis, I.L., and L. Mann. 1977. Decision Making. New York: Free Press.

Jarvenpaa, S.L. 1989. The effect of task demands and graphical format on information processing strategies. *Manag. Sci.* **35**:285–303.

Johnson, E.J., R.J. Meyer, and S. Ghose. 1989. When choice models fail: Compensatory representations in negatively correlated environments. *J. Marketing Res.* **26**:255–270.

Johnson, E.J., and J.W. Payne. 1985. Effort and accuracy in choice. *Manag. Sci.* **31**:394–414.

Kahn, B., and J. Baron. 1995. An exploratory study of choice rules favored for high-stakes decisions. *J. Consumer Psych.* **4**:305–328.

Kahneman, D. 1973. Attention and Effort. Englewood Cliffs, NJ: Prentice-Hall.

Klayman, J. 1985. Children's decision strategies and their adaptation to task characteristics. *Org. Behav. Human Decis. Proc.* **35**:179–201.

Kotovsky, K., J.R. Hayes, and H.A. Simon. 1985. Why are some problems hard: Evidence from Tower of Hanoi. *Cog. Psych.* **17**:248–294.

Lerner, J.S., and P.E. Tetlock. 1999. Accounting for the effects of accountability. *Psych. Bull.* **125**:255–275.

Lipman, B.L. 1991. How to decide how to decide how to ... Modeling limited rationality. *Econometrica* **59**:1105–1125.

Luce, M.F. 1998. Choosing to avoid: Coping with negatively emotion-laden consumer decisions. *J. Consumer Res.* **24**:409–433.

Luce, M.F., J.R. Bettman, and J.W. Payne. 1997. Choice processing in emotionally difficult decisions. *J. Exp. Psych.: Learn. Mem. Cogn.* **23**:384–405.

Luce, M.F., J.W. Payne, and J.R. Bettman. 1999. Emotional trade-off difficulty and choice. *J. Marketing Res.* **36**:143–159.

MacGregor, D.G., and P. Slovic. 1986. Graphical representation of judgmental information. *Human-Computer Inter.* **2**:179–200.

Martignon, L., and U. Hoffrage. 1999. Why does one-reason decision making work? A case study in ecological rationality. In: Simple Heuristics That Make Us Smart, G. Gigerenzer, P.M. Todd, and the ABC Research Group, pp. 119–140. New York: Oxford Univ. Press.

Meyer, R.J., and B.E. Kahn. 1991. Probabilistic models of consumer choice behavior. In: Handbook of Consumer Behavior, ed. H.H. Kassarjian and T.S. Robertson, pp. 85–123. Englewood Cliffs, NJ: Prentice-Hall.

Nagel, R. 1995. Unraveling in guessing games: An experimental study. *Am. Econ. Rev.* **85**:1313–1326.

Navon, D., and D. Gopher. 1979. On the economy of the human information processing system. *Psych. Rev.* **86**:214–255.

Newell, A., and H.A. Simon. 1972. Human Problem Solving. Englewood Cliffs, NJ: Prentice-Hall.

Payne, J.W. 1976. Task complexity and contingent processing in decision making: An information search and protocol analysis. *Org. Behav. Human Perf.* **16**:366–387.

Payne, J.W. 1982. Contingent decision behavior. *Psych. Bull.* **92**:382–402.

Payne, J.W., J.R. Bettman, and E.J. Johnson. 1988. Adaptive strategy selection in decision making. *J. Exp. Psych.: Learn. Mem. Cogn.* **14**:534–552.

Payne, J.W., J.R. Bettman, and E.J. Johnson. 1992. Behavioral decision research: A constructive processing perspective. *Ann. Rev. Psych.* **43**:87–131.

Payne, J.W., J.R. Bettman, and E.J. Johnson. 1993. The Adaptive Decision Maker. Cambridge: Cambridge Univ. Press.

Payne, J.W., J.R. Bettman, and M.F. Luce. 1996. When time is money: Decision behavior under opportunity-cost time pressure. *Org. Behav. Human Decis. Proc.* **66**:131–152.

Payne, J.W., and M.L. Braunstein. 1978. Risky choice: An examination of information acquisition behavior. *Memory Cogn.* **6**:554–561.

Rieskamp, J., and U. Hoffrage.1999. When do people use simple heuristics, and how can we tell? In: Simple Heuristics That Make Us Smart, G. Gigerenzer, P.M.Todd, and the ABC Research Group, pp. 141–167. New York: Oxford Univ. Press.

Sen, A. 1997. Maximization and the act of choice. *Econometrica* **65**:745–779.

Senter, S.M., and D.H. Wedell. 1999. Information presentation constraints and the adaptive decision maker hypothesis. *J. Exp. Psych.: Learn. Mem. Cogn.* **25**:428–446.

Shafir, E.B., I. Simonson, and A. Tversky. 1993. Reason-based choice. *Cognition* **49**:11–36.

Shepard, R.N. 1964. On subjectively optimum selection among multiattribute alternatives. In: Human Judgments and Optimality, ed. M.W. Shelley and G.L. Bryan, pp. 257–281. New York: Wiley.

Simon, H.A. 1955. A behavioral model of rational choice. *Qtly. J. Econ.* **69**:99–118.

Simonson, I. 1989. Choice based on reasons: The case of attraction and compromise effects. *J. Consumer Res.* **16**:158–174.

Simonson, I., and A. Tversky. 1992. Choice in context: Tradeoff contrast and extremeness aversion. *J. Marketing Res.* **29**:281–295.

Slovic, P. 1972. From Shakespeare to Simon: Speculations — and some evidence — about man's ability to process information. *Oregon Res. Inst. Bull.* **12**.

Slovic, P. 1995. The construction of preference. *Am. Psych.* **50**:364–371.

Stone, D.N., and D.A. Schkade. 1991. Numeric and linguistic information representation in multiattribute choice. *Org. Behav. Human Decis. Proc.* **49**:42–59.

Tetlock, P.E. 1992. The impact of accountability on judgment and choice: Toward a social contingency model. In: Advances in Experimental Social Psychology, ed. M.P. Zanna, vol. 25, pp. 331–376. San Diego: Academic.

Tversky, A. 1969. Intransitivity of preferences. *Psych. Rev.* **76**:31–48.

Tversky, A. 1972. Elimination by aspects: A theory of choice. *Psych. Rev.* **79**:281–299.

Widing, R.E., III, and W.W. Talarzyk. 1993. Electronic information systems for consumers: An evaluation of computer-assisted formats in multiple decision environments. *J. Marketing Res.* **30**:125–141.

9

Comparing Fast and Frugal Heuristics and Optimal Models

Laura Martignon

Center for Adaptive Behavior and Cognition, Max Planck Institute for Human
Development, Lentzeallee 94, 14195 Berlin, Germany

ABSTRACT

Gigerenzer, Todd, and the ABC Research Group (1999) have used the term *adaptive toolbox* as a metaphor to communicate their beliefs on how humans make inferences. On evolutionary grounds, an essential part in the architecture of the human mind is seen as consisting of a collection of fast and frugal heuristics, each of which is well designed for solving a specified class of inference tasks. This adaptive toolbox contains strategies for estimation, comparison, and categorization, to name a few. One important step in the analysis of these simple heuristics is to evaluate their predictive accuracy. The natural approach to evaluating the performance of a heuristic is to compare it with that of an adequate benchmark. Science has developed candidate benchmarks in what can be viewed as the normative toolbox: a set of normative, optimizing models for decision and inference problems. This chapter evaluates the performance of some of the fast and frugal heuristics in the adaptive toolbox, by means of a systematic comparison with optimizing models. The standards for comparison will be both predictive performance and complexity. The heuristics are remarkably accurate, often outperforming multiple regression, the normative benchmark in the class of linear models. Even compared to Bayesian models, the differences in accuracy are seldom large. The surprising accuracy of the heuristics is due to what Gigerenzer, Todd, and the ABC Research Group have called their ecological rationality, i.e., the way in which they exploit the structure of their task environment.

INTRODUCTION

Traditional models of rational decision making tend to ignore the fact that the human mind has to make inferences on aspects of the world under constraints of limited time, knowledge, and computational capacity. They treat the mind as a Laplacean Demon (cf. Gigerenzer, this volume) equipped with unlimited resources. Bounded rationality, as proposed by Simon in the 1950s, challenges this view and provides a new key for understanding how actual people make decisions. The adaptive toolbox of Gigerenzer, Todd et al. (1999) is a metaphor illustrating how bounded rationality can actually be implemented in the human mind. The essential features of the heuristics in the toolbox are their psychological plausibility (they are conditioned on the cognitive limitations that species exhibit), their domain specificity (they are strategies that are specialized rather than domain general), and their ecological rationality (their success lies in their degree of adaptation to the structure of environments).

In this chapter I evaluate a few representative heuristics in the adaptive toolbox. The heuristics investigated are algorithms composed of elementary building blocks of extremely low computational complexity, which, in environments exhibiting the structure to which they are adapted, provide near-optimal solutions with little computational effort. The tasks investigated require inferring which of two objects has a higher score on a criterion. The objects can be characterized by profiles of binary (0 and 1) cue values. I present empirical evidence as well as analytical proof of when and why simple heuristics perform well relative to normative models proposed in the literature, where the criteria for comparison are predictive accuracy and complexity.

Further, I discuss the general problem of model selection and how Occam's Razor has recently been implemented, both in machine learning and statistics, by means of criteria such as the Akaike Information Criterion (Akaike 1973; Forster 1999) or the Bayes Information Criterion (Kass and Raftery 1995), which penalize unnecessary model parameters. These criteria guarantee a gain in predictive accuracy not *in spite* of the simplicity they enforce, but *because* of it. They provide a theoretically grounded approach to identify models that are subtle enough to represent the inherent structure in a data set, yet simple enough to avoid "fitting the noise." It can, of course, be argued that the simplicity introduced by these formalizations of Occam's Razor is of complex nature since it is based on extensive search through model spaces and thus has nothing to do with the innocent simplicity of our fast and frugal toolbox. The adaptive toolbox, as Gigerenzer, Todd et al. (1999) claim, has implemented Occam's Razor by means of its ecological rationality, i.e., by the adaptive coevolution with the environment.

I will focus on two heuristics that embody one-reason decision making, "Take The Best" and "Minimalist" (Gigerenzer, Czerlinski et al. 1999; Gigerenzer and Goldstein 1996), which are members of the fast and frugal heuristics toolbox (Gigerenzer, Todd et al. 1999). We will consider a comparison task, such as which of two German cities has a larger population, which of two American cities has a higher homelessness rate, or which of two stocks will yield a higher return. In general terms, the task is to predict which object, A or B, has the higher value on a criterion. This inference is to be made on the basis of *n* binary cues, valued either 1 or 0. From a formal point of view this task is a categorization task. Here a pair (*A*, *B*) is to be categorized as $X_A > X_B$ or $X_B > X_A$ (where *X* denotes the criterion), based on cue information.

TWO HEURISTICS FOR CHOICE FROM THE ADAPTIVE TOOLBOX

When searching for a word in a dictionary, we know which word comes first by comparing letters in lexicographic fashion. The lexicographic ordering of digits in numbers also makes their choice easy. For example, to establish that 110 is larger than 101, we check the value of the first digits on the left and, since they coincide, move to the second digits, which differ. At this moment we make the decision that the number containing 1 as a second digit is larger than the number containing a 0.

This is exactly how Take The Best and Minimalist operate. In their most general form, these heuristics operate even if some of the objects are unknown to us. Being unfamiliar with a city, for example, may be a hint that the city is small. Thus, when comparing city populations, having heard of one city and not the other is in itself useful information. When recognition is correlated with the criterion, it is the very first building block of both Take The Best and Minimalist (Goldstein and Gigerenzer 1999). For the purpose of this chapter I will analyze these two heuristics as operating on sets of known objects to be compared on a criterion based on binary cues, all of whose values are known and encoded by 0's and 1's. If object *A* has a 1 on a cue and object *B* has a 0, we expect to have $X_A > X_B$, at least most of the time. Take The Best can be described as follows:

Learning phase. Compute the cue validities defined by:

$$v_i = \frac{R_i}{R_i + W_i}, \tag{9.1}$$

where R_i is the number of right (correct) inferences and W_i the number of wrong (incorrect) inferences based on cue *i* alone, when one object has the value 1 and the other has the value 0. For convenience, I define $0.5 < v_i < 1$, which can always be obtained by inverting a cue that shows validity of less than 0.5, i.e., change each 1 into a 0 and each 0 into a 1. Rank the cues according to their validity.

Step 1. Ordered search: Pick the cue with the highest validity and look up the cue values of the two objects.

Step 2. Stopping rule: If one object has a cue value of one ("1") and the other has a value of zero ("0"), then stop search. Otherwise go back to Step 1 and pick the cue with the highest validity among the remaining ones. If no cues are left, guess.

Step 3. Decision rule: If one object has a cue value of one ("1") and the other has a value of zero ("0"), predict that the object with the cue value of one ("1") has the higher value on the criterion.

Minimalist is quite similar to Take The Best. The only difference is in Step 1, which now reads:

Step 1. Random search: Pick a cue randomly (without replacement) and look up the cue values of the two objects.

Observe that for both heuristics, search for information is stopped when the first cue is found on which the two alternatives differ. This simple stopping rule demands no cost-benefit considerations. Its motto is, "Take the best and ignore the rest," in one case and, "Take any reason and ignore the rest," in the other.

Below let us consider the following questions:

- What are the optimizing alternative models when the task is judging which criterion value of a pair is larger, given a set of binary cues?
- What are the characteristics of the environment in which different strategies perform well or poorly for this type of task?

Two different situations must be envisaged when talking about algorithm performance.

- *Fitting known data*: The task is fitting a model to make inferences on known data.
- *Generalization to new data*: The task is to fix the parameters of the model in a set of known data to make predictions on new data.

Let us also define what we mean by environment: An environment consists of a set of objects, where each object is characterized by a criterion value and a cue profile. Table 9.1 is an example of an environment consisting of eight objects listed in criterion order, i.e., *A* scores highest on the criterion value, *B* next

Table 9.1 An environment consisting of eight objects listed in criterion order where *A* scores highest. Each object is characterized by a profile of three cues. This is a perfect environment for Take The Best, because in a complete paired-comparison it achieves 100% performance when using the cues to infer which object scores higher.

Object	Cue 1	Cue 2	Cue 3
A	1	1	1
B	1	1	0
C	1	0	1
D	1	0	0
E	0	1	1
F	0	1	0
G	0	0	1
H	0	0	0

highest, and so on. Each object is characterized by a *cue profile* of three cues, where the cues have been ranked according to their validity from left to right. The first cue makes only right inferences and thus has validity 1. To compute validities easily, one counts how many times 1 is on top of 0 (= right inferences) and how many times 0 is on top of 1 (= wrong inferences) and then divides the number of right inferences by the sum of right and wrong inferences. With the words "structure of the environment," I refer to the structure of information that is known about an environment.

This environment is abstract. Here. Take The Best achieves 100% correct inferences. Each cue is perfectly tuned to the preceding one, and objects are encoded by cue profiles of length 3. The real world does not provide such perfect information. As a concrete, real-world example, let us recall the classic task originally investigated by Gigerenzer and Goldstein (1996), where pairs of German cities with more than 100,000 inhabitants were compared to determine which one had a larger population. There were nine cues:

1. Is the city the national capital? (*NC*)
2. Is the city a state capital? (*SC*)
3. Does the city have a soccer team in the major national league? (*SO*)
4. Was the city once an exposition site? (*EX*)
5. Is the city on the intercity train line? (*IT*)
6. Is the abbreviation of the city on license plates only one letter long? (*LP*)
7. Is the city home to a university? (*UN*)
8. Is the city in the industrial belt? (*IB*)
9. Is the city in former West Germany? (*WG*)

The *NC* cue has validity 1, because Berlin, which is Germany's national capital, has a larger population than any other German city. Cues with validity 1 provide sure knowledge and trivialize the inference problem. If the environment provides us with many such cues, we can eliminate a large number of the pairs to be compared, namely all of those for which these perfect cues make inferences. The problem of inference is nontrivial only for those cues that have validity less than 1. The *SO* cue is such an *uncertain* yet valid cue: Düsseldorf does not have a soccer team in the national league although it is larger than Leverkusen, whose soccer team Bayer Leverkusen has been in the national league for decades. The *WG* cue is the *inverse* of the cue "Is the city in former East Germany?" which I denote by *EG*.

Optimal Ranking for Lexicographic Choice

Take The Best and Minimalist are computationally simple because their basic step is the comparison of two binary values. They are fast because the number of comparisons is linear as a function of the number of available cues. Their rules for ranking cues are also simple: Take The Best ranks cues in its learning phase and orders them according to their validities, v_i, (Equation 9.1), while Minimalist takes them in any order.

What is the optimal ranking for lexicographic choice? If training and test set coincide, i.e., if we are fitting known data, then optimal ranking is well defined. It can be obtained, for example, by exhaustively searching through all possible permutations of the given cues (and their inverses) and by computing the performance obtained for each ranking. This is an extremely laborious task. Is there a simpler way to find the optimal ranking? By *simpler,* I mean shorter, involving less steps. To answer this question, we must first define simplicity/complexity of an algorithm rigorously. In theoretical computer science, the complexity of an algorithm is defined in terms of the time required to perform all necessary operations. One possibility is to count the number of operational steps in an algorithm, express this number as a function of the parameters involved in the algorithm, and determine the *order of complexity* of this function. One popular criterion for order of complexity is denoted by $O(\ )$ (called the Landau symbol) and is defined as follows: given two functions $F(n)$ and $G(n)$ defined for all natural numbers, we say that F is *of the order of* G, and write $F = O(G)$, if there exists a constant K such that:

$$\frac{F(n)}{G(n)} < K, \tag{9.2}$$

for all natural numbers n, when $n \neq 0$. Thus, for example, the function $F(n) = 3n + 1$ is of the order of $G(n) = n$. However, n^3 is not of the order of n^2, whereas, by this definition, n^2 is of the order of n^3. Every polynomial in n, i.e., every linear combination of powers of n, is of the order of its highest power of n. Because what is being counted is the number of steps in a sequential process, it is common to view the resulting $O(\ )$ criterion as the "time complexity" of the algorithm. $O(1)$ means constant time. There are algorithms with a complexity of order larger than any power of n. They are clearly of an order larger than any polynomial in n (because, as noted above, a polynomial is of the order of its highest power of n) and are therefore called *NP-complete,* which means "not (to be) complete(d) in polynomial time." In practice, these NP-complete algorithms are intractable for large n's. Searching across all permutations of n objects requires $n!$ steps, and $n!$ is of an order larger than any fixed power of n. It has recently been proven (Martignon and Schmitt 1999) that there are no essentially simpler strategies to find the optimal ranking of n cues.

Theorem 1: Intractability of optimal order search.   The problem of finding the optimal ranking of binary cues for lexicographic choice is NP-complete.

Finding the optimal ordering of cues for the German city environment across all permutations of the nine cues requires comparing the performance of 9! = 362,880 possible rankings. Martignon and Hoffrage (1999) found it, and this task took a UNIX machine four days to complete! Lexicographic choice with the optimal ranking achieved 76% correct inferences, while Take The Best, in all its simplicity, reached 74%. Was this 2% accuracy worth the effort? As we shall see below (section on THE ROBUSTNESS OF TAKE THE BEST: GENERALIZING AKAIKE'S THEOREM), optimal ordering is not only computationally expensive, it fits noise in the data and is less robust than Take The Best under cross validation.

Performance Ratio of Take The Best and Minimalist

Is there a general way to measure the goodness of a ranking? Or, more generally, are there formal rules for evaluating the accuracy of an algorithm? Theoretical computer science deals with this type of question in all sorts of contexts and for all sorts of tasks. One of the simplest concepts used to measure the goodness of an algorithm is the *performance ratio*, defined as the number of correct inferences obtained by the optimal algorithm divided by the number of correct inferences obtained by the algorithm considered. In the context of lexicographic choice, the performance ratio of a given ranking R is given by:

$$\text{Performance ratio} = \frac{\text{number of correct inferences by } O}{\text{number of correct inferences by } R}, \qquad (9.3)$$

where O is the optimal ranking. The performance ratio of a ranking can range from 1 to infinity. Of special interest are algorithms that have constant bounds for their performance ratio, across all possible data sets. Clearly, the closer the performance ratio is to 1, the more accurate the algorithm is. For Take The Best in the German city environment, the performance ratio is almost 1. However, it is possible to construct environments where this ratio is larger than or equal to 2 (Martignon and Schmitt 1999). This is because new cues are not necessarily good cues on the set of pairs left for inference. A slight modification of Take The Best's building blocks can ensure that the performance ratio is less than 2 in all possible environments. Instead of inverting bad cues only at the very beginning, i.e., in the learning phase, one introduces a rule for conditional cue inversion: Invert each cue that has a validity of less than 0.5 on the pairs of objects left undiscriminated by preceding cues. If we make sure that we invert cues conditionally, we can actually pick them in any prescribed order and still have a performance ratio of less than 2. This heuristic can be called *Sophisticated Minimalist*. In situations where time is limited, it may be more advisable to rely on any arbitrary ordering of cues (i.e., to take them as they come) and to make the best of it.

Theorem 2: Performance ratio of Sophisticated Minimalist. If cues are picked in any order, and each cue with conditional validity less than 0.5 is inverted, then the performance ratio of the resulting algorithm is always less than two.

The argument of the proof is simple: The total number of (right or wrong) inferences made by lexicographic choice does not depend upon the ordering of cues. If one makes sure that each cue is taken in the *positive* direction, then more than half of the possible inferences made by the cue are correct. Thus at least half of the total number of inferences made by the algorithm will be correct. Optimal ordering can achieve a total number of correct inferences that is at most equal to the total number of inferences made by the set of cues.

One can see that Take The Best has a performance ratio of at least two (Martignon and Schmitt 1999). Another interesting variant of Take The Best incorporates the idea of conditional validity, which we have termed *Take The Very Best*. Given a set of cues, one proceeds to choose the best one by comparing validities (of cues and their inverses) on the given set of objects. The second cue in the ranking will be the one (chosen from the remaining cues and their inverses) with the best performance on the objects left undiscriminated by the first cue. The third one is again the best one on the remaining set of pairs. The following theorem has a straightforward proof.

Theorem 3: Conditional validity.   Take The Very Best is more accurate in fitting than Take The Best. Its performance ratio is always less than two.

Figure 9.1 shows the performance of lexicographic strategies based on three types of ranking—Take The Best, conditional validity, and optimal ordering—and shows two important results. First, in a real-world, noisy environment, Take The Best actually comes close to optimal ordering when the task is to fit given data (training set). Second, and most important, when the task is to predict new data, the simple ordering used by Take The Best is actually more robust and

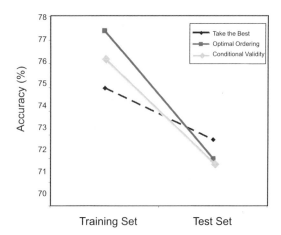

Figure 9.1   Accuracy of lexicographic choice for different rankings under cross validation with a training sample size of 50% objects and 1000 runs (Martignon and Hoffrage 1999).

makes more accurate predictions (on the test set) than the ordering that was optimal on the test set and the ordering that is obtained by means of conditional validity. These results are also a consequence of the variant of Akaike's Theorem: lexicographic strategies can all be identified with subfamilies of the linear models.

Are unaided humans aware of the conditional value of information? This may be hard to test empirically. Not being aware of how the value of information changes along an inference process leads to serious mistakes when we are making inferences on known data. It should be noted, however, that the role of conditional validity is crucial mainly when dealing with known data, i.e., when training and test set coincide. When making predictions on new objects, being too subtle may cause losses. As we will see below (section on THE ROBUSTNESS OF TAKE THE BEST: GENERALIZING AKAIKE'S THEOREM), subtlety can be an enemy of robustness. Ranking by conditional cue validity is not robust.

OPTIMAL MODELS FOR CHOICE FROM
THE LINEAR TOOLBOX

There is another, more traditional way of tackling the choice problem: by using linear models. Objects can be scored by adequately weighting and adding cue values so that the resulting linear scores can be compared. The inference will then be made that the object with the larger score has the higher criterion value. Linear models, which have historically been used as models for inference, are not part of the fast and frugal toolbox. One could argue that they are fast if implemented in parallel machines: one neuron computes a linear combination of cue values in one single shot. However, if the mind processes information sequentially, in procedural, step-by-step fashion, then linear models are not fast. They are obviously not frugal, since their decisions are based on all available information. What I want to establish here is how the performance of linear models can be compared with that of fast and frugal lexicographic strategies. One optimizing model in the linear toolbox is *multiple regression.* As Einhorn and Hogarth (1975) and Dawes (1979) remarked, regression (i.e., regression on all available cues, without estimates of significant or "true" regressors) does not make more accurate predictions than much simpler linear models (see below).

Take The Best can also be seen as a linear model that uses cues in a noncompensatory way. Let us define, in general terms, what a noncompensatory strategy is. Consider an ordered set of M binary cues, $C_1, ..., C_M$. These cues are noncompensatory for a given strategy if every cue C_j outweighs any possible combination of cues after C_j, i.e., C_{j+1} to C. In the case of a weighted linear model with a set of weights, $W = \{w_1, ..., w_M\}$ is noncompensatory if for every $1 \leq j \leq M$ we have:

$$w_j > \sum_{k > j} w_k \ , \tag{9.4}$$

i.e., each weight is larger than the sum of all weights to come. A simple example is the set {1, 1/2, 1/4, 1/8, 1/16}. A linear model with a noncompensatory set of weights ends up making exactly the same inferences as Take The Best.

Theorem 4: Noncompensatory information.   In the fitting situation, the performance of Take The Best is equivalent to that of a linear model with a noncompensatory set of weights. If an environment consists of cues that, for a specified order, are noncompensatory for a given weighted linear strategy, this strategy cannot outperform the faster and more frugal Take The Best if that order coincides with the decreasing order of validities.

Loosely speaking, Take The Best bets on a noncompensatory structure, and if the environment has this type of structure, then there is a fit. The degree to which this fit exists contributes to the ecological rationality of Take The Best. Four of the twenty data sets that Czerlinski et al. (1999) investigated have noncompensatory regression weights, decreasing in the same order as do the validities of the cues; and, as predicted by Theorem 4, the performance of regression and Take The Best coincide (see Table 9.3 in the section on THE ROBUSTNESS OF TAKE THE BEST: GENERALIZING AKAIKE'S THEOREM). If the fit is not perfect but approximate, then Take The Best will still be about as accurate as the corresponding linear model. If regression has noncompensatory weights decreasing in an order that differs from the validity order it can even happen that Take The Best beats regression. Note that Theorem 4 holds only in the fitting situation. When generalizing to new data, Take The Best beats Regression quite often, as plain regression tends to overfit the data (see Table 9.3).

If objects A and B have as cue profiles (001001101) and (100100100) respectively, Take The Best makes the inference that B has a larger value on the criterion. However, a strategy that tallies the number of 1's in each cue profile predicts that A has the larger value. *Tallying* is the term that Gigerenzer and Goldstein (1996) used to denote this very simple linear model. This model is related with important concepts in information theory. If we view a cue profile as a codeword for an object, then the number of 1's in this codeword divided by the length of the codeword represents the information content, or the *Hamming weight* of the encoded object (Cover and Thomas 1991). Since the length of cue profiles is constant and equal to the number of cues, tallying is equivalent to comparing the information contents of objects. Dawes's rule (see Todd, this volume), which compares scores of cue profiles obtained by subtracting the number of 0's from the number of 1's, is equivalent to tallying, in the sense that it makes exactly the same inferences (unless some of the cue values are unknown). This is because twice the score of tallying minus the number of cues is equal to the score of Dawes's rule (Gigerenzer and Goldstein 1996). Both are simple, linear models that are not frugal but compensatory. Being compensatory has its advantages in the long run. Looking for more and more valid cues and comparing the information contents of cue profiles can lead to perfection, as can be shown analytically. An environment provides *abundant information* when all uncertain, yet valid cues are present. In an environment with N objects and binary cues, the number of possible cues is the number of different 1–0 sequences of length N. Note that the expression "all possible uncertain, yet valid cues" does not refer to all possible real-world cues but to the different 1–0 sequences. Whereas the number of real-world cues could be infinite (because different real-world cues may have the same value on each object), the number of different 1–0 sequences is finite. As an example of abundant information, consider five objects $\{A, B, C, D, E\}$ where, as usual, A scores highest on the criterion, B next highest, and so on. Table 9.2 shows the eight uncertain and valid, binary cues (i.e., with validity larger than 0.5 but less than 1) that exist for five objects.

Dawes's rule and tallying achieve a performance of 100% correct inferences in this environment. Eight uncertain cues are sufficient for guaranteeing perfect inferences on five objects. (In an environment consisting only of the first seven cues, Dawes's rule would have to make one guess, for pair (B, C), and give a performance of 95%.) Franklin's rule (Gigerenzer and Goldstein 1999), which multiplies each cue value by its validity, adds these numbers and infers that the object with the larger sum ranks higher on the criterion; it also achieves a performance of 100% in this environment.

The following is true for environments with five or more objects (Hoffrage and Martignon 1999).

Theorem 5: Abundant information. When information in an environment with five or more objects is abundant, tallying, Dawes's rule, and Franklin's rule are optimal in the fitting situation. They make a correct inference for any possible pair of objects.

This theorem is mainly of theoretical interest. It states that the information contained in uncertain but valid cues is enough to solve the choice problem without errors. It also states that the concept of validity (Equation 9.1) is well chosen from an information theoretical point of view: when all uncertain but valid

Table 9.2 An environment with five objects ordered according to criterion and with abundant information, i.e., with all nonredundant binary cues which have a validity of more than 0.5 and less than 1. Dawes's rule is perfect in this environment. The same holds for Franklin's rule.

Object	Cue 1	Cue 2	Cue 3	Cue 4	Cue 5	Cue 6	Cue 7	Cue 8	Score
A	1	1	1	0	1	1	0	1	6
B	0	1	1	1	0	0	1	1	5
C	1	0	1	0	1	0	1	0	4
D	0	1	0	0	1	1	0	0	3
E	0	0	1	0	0	0	0	1	2
$v =$	5/6	5/6	3/4	3/4	4/6	4/6	4/6	4/6	

information is present, cue profiles are perfect codewords for the comparison problem. Unfortunately, in real-world situations, we have to face scarceness of information, not abundance. From information theory, it is a simple fact that we need at least $\log_2 N$ binary cues in order to discriminate between N objects, i.e., different objects are to have different codewords. Furthermore, $\log_2 N$ cues will suffice only if they are perfectly tuned to each other as in the environment described in Table 9.1. If they are not, there will necessarily be repeated profiles. We say that an environment provides *scarce* information if the number of cues in it is less than $\log_2 N$, where N is the number of objects. Scarce information favors Take The Best. For environments with less than 500 objects which we call *small,* a computer-aided proof can be found for the following theorem (Hoffrage and Martignon 1999).

Theorem 6: Scarce information. In the class of small environments with scarce information, for every fixed environment size (i.e., fixed numbers of objects and cues) there is a larger number of environments where Take The Best is more accurate than Dawes's rule.

Estimating Criterion Values and Comparing Them

An alternative solution to the choice task is to estimate the criterion value of each object in the pair and then to compare these estimates. When comparing the populations of two cities in Germany, some may tend first to estimate their populations and then to compare the results. When we use the regression model for the choice task (using the criterion as the dependent variable), we are comparing linear scores of the objects, which are estimates of their criterion values. The estimation task and the choice task are closely related, but there are important differences. Ranking the German cities according to their population size is one thing; estimating the distribution of their populations is another. The former is simple, the latter quite sophisticated. Ranking is readily obtained from the estimate distribution. The adaptive toolbox contains a simple heuristic for the estimation task, which deserves to be introduced.

The *QuickEst* heuristic (Hertwig et al. 1999) is designed to estimate the values of objects along some criterion while using as little information as possible. The estimates are constrained to map onto the kind of round numbers typically used by humans, which Albers (1997) called spontaneous numbers. Spontaneous numbers are powers of 10 multiplied by 1, 1.5, 2, 3, 5, and 7, such as 300 and 1,500.

QuickEst uses binary cues, with values 0 and 1. The rule for establishing the ranking of a cue looks at the average criterion value of the objects, which have a zero on the cue. In the environment of German cities described above, the soccer cue (*SO*) is a very valid cue because most small cities in Germany do not have a soccer team in the national league. To estimate the criterion value of a particular object, the heuristic looks through the cues or features in order of validity, until it comes to the first one that the object does not possess; here it stops searching for any further information (e.g., if a city has the first several features in order but lacks an exposition site, search will stop on that cue). QuickEst then gives the spontaneous mean criterion value associated with the absence of that cue as its final estimate (e.g., the mean size of all cities without an exposition site). Thus, in effect, QuickEst uses features that are present to eliminate all smaller criterion categories and features that are absent to eliminate all larger criterion categories, so that only one criterion estimate remains. No cue combination is necessary, and no adjustment from further cues is possible. QuickEst proves to be fast and frugal, as well as accurate, in environments characterized by a distribution of criterion values in which small values are common and big values are rare (a so-called J-shaped distribution, where the J is seen on its side). Such distributions are quite common in natural phenomena. Estimating by means of QuickEst and then comparing estimates is not only an accurate but also a very robust strategy (Hertwig et al. 1999). In fact, the performance of this comparison strategy is comparable to that of Take The Best or regression in the German city environment. Even a back propagation network with one hidden layer is less robust than QuickEst for small sizes of training sets.

THE BAYESIAN TOOLBOX AND THE CHOICE TASK

Modern experimental psychology opened up a front in the war against the view of rational man as probabilist, in a flurry of work documenting the ways in which actual human reasoning differs from the probabilistic norm. These deviations were regarded by many as cognitive illusions, as proof that unaided human reasoning is riddled with fallacies (e.g., Tversky and Kahneman 1974). However, it has turned out that ordinary people's Bayesian reasoning can be improved and cognitive illusions eliminated when information is presented in frequency formats (Gigerenzer and Hoffrage 1995). This fundamental finding proves that "being or not being a Bayesian" is a consequence of how information is presented for a given task. If a categorization task is to be solved (a patient has or does not have breast cancer) given the information provided by one binary cue value (positive mammography), participants easily find the Bayesian solution if information is presented in *natural* frequencies, while they have difficulties if information is presented in probabilities. Even if the task involves two cues (positive mammography and positive ultrasound test), applying the Bayesian norm does not pose problems if information is presented in natural frequencies, as has been demonstrated for the following problem (Krauss et al. 2000):

- 100 out of every 10,000 women at age 40, who participate in routine screening, have breast cancer.

- 80 of every 100 women with breast cancer will get a positive mammography.
- 950 out of every 9900 women without breast cancer will also get a positive mammography.
- 76 out of 80 women who had a positive mammography and have cancer also have a positive ultrasound test.
- 38 out of 950 women who had a positive mammography, although they do not have cancer, also have a positive ultrasound test.
- How many of the women who get a positive mammography and a positive ultrasound test do you expect to have breast cancer?

Observe that if a doctor keeps a record of all her patients' histories, these frequencies are the natural format in which she stores information. Thus, we might argue, if the doctor retrieved this type of information from memory or from her index files, she would reason the Bayesian way because she would simply have stored the numbers that express the proportion of women with both positive tests that actually had cancer (say, "7" out of "88"). Note that there is nothing unnatural in the Bayesian approach, when natural frequencies (for the nested sets corresponding to cue configurations) are first stored and then retrieved. In fact, the Bayesian approach is the most natural and the correct one. What makes the straightforward Bayesian approach cumbersome is the representation of information in probabilities.

Harries and Dhami (submitted) recently investigated how a group of English doctors from the British National Health System categorized patients, according to whether they should be prescribed a drug or not, under the constraint of limited time (seven minutes per categorization). The categorization task "should take the drug or should not take the drug," based on binary symptoms, is similar to the "cancer or no cancer" task described above and might have been treated in a Bayesian fashion. The requirement would have been that the doctors had kept records of the relevant nested subsets of treated patients, where the nested subsets would correspond to the relevant configurations of symptom values. Yet the English doctors investigated by Harries and Dhami did not choose a Bayesian strategy. Their inference procedure, as Harries and Dhami proved, can be modeled by a fast and frugal heuristic. They checked cue values in the order determined by a validity criterion and stopped the moment a cue reached a so-called critical value. The work of Harries and Dhami (submitted), the empirical findings of Gigerenzer and Hoffrage (1995), and those of Krauss et al. (2000) provide empirical proof of the fact that being a Bayesian or being fast and frugal is determined by the representation of information and, therefore, by the storage and retrieval constraints of human memory. As we shall see, the differences in accuracy between the fast and frugal heuristics used by humans and the Bayesian solutions to the same problems are not dramatic. Humans, we might argue, are approximate Bayesians who employ fast and frugal approximations of Bayesian approaches.

For realistic problems, simply storing the probability distribution over all possible configurations often becomes impossible, even for computers. Reducing the complexity of the probability distribution over all possible configurations requires using a model (see below for a Bayesian treatment of the choice task in the German city environment). This model can again be selected with a Bayesian paradigm. Recently, smart implementations of Occam's Razor have been used to tackle the problem of model selection for complexity reduction. This development has created the vigorous renaissance of the Bayesian approach.

How does the Bayesian face the choice task discussed in the above sections? She begins by expressing the comparison probabilistically: What are the chances that an object A with cue profile, say, equal to (100101010), will score higher than an object B with cue profile, say equal to (011000011), on the established criterion? In symbols:

$$\text{Prob}\left(X_A > X_B \,|\, A \cong (100101010), B \cong (011000011)\right) = ? \qquad (9.5)$$

Here the symbol $\cong$ is used to signify "has the cue profile."

The question can be expressed as: What is the probability that the pair (A, B) is categorized as $X_A > X_B$ or $X_B > X_A$ (where X denotes the criterion), given that the first cue takes the value $(1, 0)$ on the pair, the second cue takes the value $(0, 1)$ on the pair, and so on? Observe that there are no essential differences between this task and the task of categorizing a patient as having or not having a disease, based on a set of symptoms. Here again, the ideal solution would be to have an excellent memory and to be able to retrieve the necessary natural frequencies. Thus, when training set and test set coincide, the Bayesian with perfect memory knows what to do: She has memorized all pairs of cue profiles with the corresponding criterion values. For each profile in a pair, she will compute the proportion of cases in which it scores higher than the other cue profile in the pair. This proportion will be the probability that the corresponding object scores higher on the criterion. Forced to make a deterministic answer, she will choose the profile with the higher proportion. In case of a tie she will throw a coin. This memory-based strategy can be called the *profile memorization method*. It is the Bayesian/frequentist method that corresponds to using the natural frequency format of information stored/retrieved, precisely as in the cancer task described above. Assuming that this type of question has to be answered again and again by our Bayesian, there is no other strategy that would lead to a better performance over time.

If the Bayesian has a limited memory and retrieval capacity, she has to construct a good model of the data. The same is, of course, true if she has a generalization task where new, unknown profiles may appear. The Bayesian can start with a prior distribution for the relationship between cues and criterion, use the training sample to update the prior distribution, and obtain a posterior distribution. The posterior distribution is then used to evaluate the test set. At this point we can imagine an unboundedly rational approach to finding the adequate model. The unbounded Bayesian demon is not sure which class of models — regression, logistic regression, classification tree, Bayesian network, or other — applies to a problem. (For an explanation of the term *demon*, see Chapter 3 by Gigerenzer, this volume.) Anything this demon is uncertain about is assigned a prior distribution, so each class of models is assigned a prior distribution. The next level of uncertainty applies to structural assumptions within a class of models, which regressors to include in the regression equation, where to make the splits in the classification tree, and what arcs belong in the Bayesian network. Again, the demon assigns a prior distribution to these uncertainties. Finally, it assigns a prior distribution to the parameters for a given structure, regression weights, criterion probabilities at the leaf nodes of the classification tree, and local conditional probability tables in the Bayesian network. Thus, this demon carries a staggering number of possible models. Each is assigned a prior probability, and each is updated to obtain a posterior probability. The final judgment is based on a weighted average of the conclusion of each of the models, where each model is weighted by its posterior probability. Clearly, the task faced by such a demon is far too daunting for even the fastest computers.

The bounded Bayesian will restrict her model selection problem to a more specific class of models, based on experience or experts' advice. For the choice task she may tend to choose from the flexible family of Bayesian networks. Another possibility is a Bayesian classification tree. Yet a third possibility is a mixture of these two. As a concrete example, let us go back to the pairs of German cities that were compared according to population size (Martignon and Laskey 1999).

A network for our type of task (Figure 9.2) considers pairs of objects (A, B) and the possible states of the cues, which are the four pairs of binary values (0, 0), (0, 1), (1, 0), (1, 1) on pairs of objects. The rudimentary Bayesian network of Figure 9.2 neglects all interdependencies between cues: A way of simplifying the computation of Equation 9.5 is to perform a computation à la Naive Bayes. If Naive Bayes has no specific prior distribution but simply assumes that the chances of an object scoring higher than another are uniformly distributed (Prob $(X_A > X_B)$ = Prob $(X_B > X_A)$), then the posterior odds are:

$$\frac{\text{Prob}\left[X_A > X_B \,|A \cong (100101010), B \cong (011000011)\right]}{\text{Prob}\left[X_B > X_A \,|A \cong (100101010), B \cong (011000011)\right]} = \quad (9.6)$$

$$\frac{\text{Prob}\left[(C_1)(A)=1, C_1(B)=0\,|X_A > X_B\right] \times \ldots \times \text{Prob}\left[(C_9)(A)=0, C_9(B)=1\,|X_A > X_B\right]}{\text{Prob}\left[(C_1)(A)=1, C_1(B)=0\,|X_B > X_A\right] \times \ldots \times \text{Prob}\left[(C_9)(A)=0, C_9(B)=1\,|X_B > X_A\right]}$$

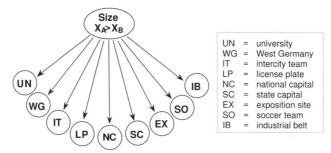

Figure 9.2   Naive Bayes network for the German city data. All cues are independent given the criterion (Martignon and Laskey 1999).

and will depend on factors, each of which is either the validity of a cue or the inverse of the validity of a cue. When both values in a pair coincide, the corresponding factors are 0.5 in both the numerator and denominator, and can therefore be omitted. The posterior odds for the pair (A, B) above are given by:

$$\frac{v_1 \times (1 - v_2) \times (1 - v_3) \times v_4 \times v_6 \times (1 - v_9)}{(1 - v_1) \times v_2 \times v_3 (1 - v_4) \times (1 - v_6) \times v_9}. \tag{9.7}$$

This is, all in all, a relatively simple formula of the validities that can automatically be determined by checking corresponding cue values in the profiles. Forced to make a deterministic answer, Naive Bayes will predict that A scores higher than B on the criterion, if the odds are larger than 1. Due to its simplicity, Naive Bayes is the fast but not frugal strategy used by Bayesians in a hurry.

The other extreme in the family of Bayesian networks is the fully connected network, where each pair of nodes is connected both ways. This corresponds to storing the original distribution as it is, without decomposing it into simpler factors. Computing Equation 9.5 in terms of this fully connected network amounts to using the profile memorization method. Assuming no dependencies between cues given criterion is a radical attitude. To assume that cues are all interdependent is at least as radical. The Bayesian would like to strike a balance. She would like to detect those links between cues that are relevant and robust. In other words, she would like to find a good Bayesian network for cue interdependencies.

In a Bayesian network, the nodes (i.e., the vertices of the graph representing the network) with arrows pointing to a fixed node are called the parents of that node. The node itself is called a child of its parents. What follows is a fundamental rule for operating with Bayesian networks.

Theorem 7: The Markov Blanket.   The conditional probability of a node i being in a certain state, given knowledge on the state of all other nodes in the network, is proportional to the product of the conditional probability of the node given its parents times the conditional probability of each one of its children given its parents.

In symbols:

$$\text{Prob}\left(\text{node } j \,|\, \text{all other nodes}\right) =$$
$$K \times \text{Prob}\left(\text{node } j \,|\, \text{parents of } j\right) \times \prod \text{Prob}\left(\text{child } k \text{ of } j \,|\, \text{parents of } k\right). \quad (9.8)$$

The set consisting of a node, its parents, its children, and the other parents of its children is called the Markov Blanket of that node. K is the normalizing constant.

What Theorem 7 states is that the Markov Blanket of a node determines the state of the node regardless of the state of all other nodes not in the Blanket (Pearl 1988). The theorem, based essentially on Bayes's rule, represents an enormous computational reduction for the storage and computations of probability distributions. It is precisely due to this type of reduction of computational complexity that Bayesian networks have become a popular tool both in statistics and in artificial intelligence over the last decade. Given a specific inference task and a set of data, the decision maker will search for a network that fits the data, without fitting noise in the data, and based on that network she will make inferences.

A more accurate Bayesian network (than the one depicted in Figure 9.2) has to take into account the conditional dependencies between cues and the dependencies from hypothesis to cues. Of course, some dependencies are more relevant than others. Some may be so weak that we may choose to neglect them to avoid overfitting. Thus the Bayesian needs a Bayesian strategy for deciding which are the relevant links that should remain and which are prune irrelevant links that will only produce overfitting and should therefore be pruned. She should find a feasible way for searching through the possible networks and should evaluate each network in terms of its performance. This search is infeasible without some heuristic that reduces the search space (the general problem of Bayesian inference is NP-complete [Cooper 1990]). A heuristic that is justified by Bayesian theory, which can be thought of as an instantiation of Occam's Razor, is to score Bayesian networks based on their posterior probability given the training set. If the posterior probability cannot be computed analytically, various estimators are available, such as the Bayes Information Criterion (Kass and Raftery 1995). A number of algorithms have been developed that combine heuristic search over network structures with scoring based on actual or approximate posterior probabilities. These algorithms find a Bayesian network that is among the most probable given the training set. The one we used here was put forward by Nir Friedman (see, e.g., Friedman and Goldszmit 1996).

Figure 9.3 illustrates the Markov Blanket of the node size, which represents the hypothesis "City *A* has more inhabitants than city *B*" and can obviously be in two states (the other state is "City *B* has more inhabitants than city *A*"). According to the theorem:

$$\text{Prob}\left(\text{Size} \,|\, UN, NC, IB, SO, EX, SC, IT\right) =$$
$$K \times \text{Prob}(\text{Size} \,|\, SO, EX, SC) \times \text{Prob}\left(IB \,|\, \text{Size}, UN, NC\right) \times \text{Prob}\left(IT \,|\, SO, EX, \text{Size}\right), \quad (9.9)$$

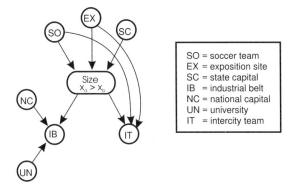

Figure 9.3   The Markov Blanket of size in our Bayesian network (obtained by Friedman's search method) for predicting city population includes all nodes with the exception of *LP* and *WG*, which become irrelevant to size, given the other cues (Martignon and Laskey 1999).

where K is the normalizing constant.

The number of probabilities to be estimated is still exponential in the number of parents per node, because each node stores a probability distribution for each combination of values for its parents. Again, the complexity of the problem may be further reduced by making structural assumptions constraining the probabilities. The algorithm applied uses a simple classification tree to estimate the local probability tables. The classification tree greatly reduces the number of computations. Here the problem of finding a good tree was solved with the same type of approach used to determine the network describing dependencies between cues, described above.

Figure 9.4 illustrates the tree produced by the program for Prob (Size | *SO*, *EX, SC*). The probability distribution for the size variable is obtained by tracing the arcs of this tree. From Figure 9.4 we see that the first step is to check the exposition (*EX*) cue. If neither city is an exposition site, the probability is determined by whether the city has a soccer team (*SO*), and the state capital (*SC*) cue is irrelevant. Conversely, when one or both cities are exposition sites, then the probability distribution is determined by the state capital (*SC*) cue, and the soccer team (*SO*) cue is irrelevant. Thus, instead of requiring $2^7 = 128$ probabilities for the size node given *EX*, *SO*, and *SC*, the tree representation of Figure 9.4 requires only $2^4 = 16$ probabilities. This is an important reduction of complexity.

To summarize, the method used to find a probability model for the relationship between cue and criterion involves:

1. Searching over a large space of directed graphs representing Bayesian networks on cue and criterion variables.
2. Searching over decision tree models for quick estimation of local probabilities factoring the distribution of criterion given cues.
3. Estimating the local probabilities.

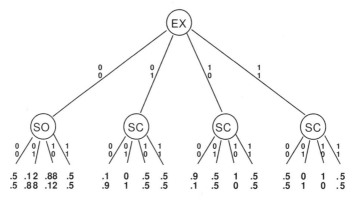

Figure 9.4 Tree for computing local probability table for size node of Figure 9.3. If, for example, neither of the two cities, *A* and *B*, is an exposition site (*EX*) (symbolized by the two zeros in the left branch), then the only relevant cue is *SO* (soccer team), i.e., whether a city has a soccer team in the major league (*SC*, state capital) is irrelevant. If *A* has a soccer team but *B* does not ("1" for *A* and "0" for *B*) then Prob $(X_A > X_B \mid SO, EX, SC) = 0.88$ (Martignon and Laskey 1999).

4. Computing the posterior distribution of the criterion variable given cue values using Equation 9.9.

To evaluate the performance of Take The Best (TTB) we compared it with that of profile memorization (PM), plain regression (Reg), Naive Bayes (NB), and the savvier Bayesian network (BN) described above, both in the fitting situation and under cross validation. The size of the randomly chosen training set for cross validation was 50% and there were 10,000 runs. Table 9.3 illustrates the results. The Bayesian network found by means of Friedman and Goldszmit's method was handicapped by the small size of some of the data sets. In larger data sets (1000 objects or more), this type of Bayesian network becomes more robust (Friedman and Goldszmit 1996). Both TTB and NB are robust on small sample sizes.

THE ROBUSTNESS OF TAKE THE BEST: GENERALIZING AKAIKE'S THEOREM

One use of models is to fit known data. This becomes necessary for agents with limited memory and limited retrieval capacity. Another use of models is to summarize the regularities found in known data in a form that can be used to predict new data. Prediction is subject to the well-known danger of overfitting the training set. A model overfits the training set if an alternative model exists that, even though it does not perform as well on the training set, nonetheless is more accurate when it generalizes to observations it has not yet seen. To understand why overfitting occurs, it helps to appreciate that the training set usually has both

Table 9.3 Performance of different algorithms in 20 data sets. In the generalization task, 50% of the objects in the data set were chosen at random 10,000 times and the model obtained on the training set was then tested on the remaining 50%. PM = profile memorization, TTB = Take The Best, Reg = regression, NB = Naive Bayes, BN = Bayesian network (Martignon and Laskey 1999).

Environment	# Objects	# Cues	Fitting					Generalization			
			PM	TTB	Reg	NB	BN	TTB	Reg	NB	BN
Ozone in San Francisco	11	3	85	84	85	84	84	79	77	80	78
Cow manure	14	6	83	79	79	79	80	76	72	78	79
Oxidant	17	4	93	84	84	84	84	80	76	81	82
Mortality	20	15	100	77	83	78	79	62	54	66	67
House price	22	10	96	86	86	87	87	84	68	86	86
Rainfall	24	6	71	67	71	68	68	53	56	57	59
Biodiversity	26	6	88	84	80	83	83	80	72	80	82
Attractiveness of women	30	3	80	71	71	71	71	66	67	68	59
Attractiveness of men	32	3	75	73	73	73	73	71	69	72	70
Mammals' sleep	35	9	95	78	79	77	83	75	65	76	80
Car accidents	37	13	93	71	79	75	75	64	64	71	71
Obesity at age 18	46	10	70	74	74	77	79	71	63	71	69
Fuel consumption	48	6	87	78	79	78	80	73	74	76	76
Homelessness	50	6	82	69	70	68	77	63	62	64	65
Professors' salaries	51	5	87	80	83	80	84	80	80	80	81
High school dropout rates	57	18	90	65	72	65	65	60	54	61	60
Land rent	58	4	82	80	81	80	81	77	80	77	78
City population	83	9	80	74	74	74	76	72	71	72	74
Body fat	218	14	87	59	61	80	82	56	55	79	80
Fish fertility	395	3	75	73	75	73	75	73	75	74	75
Average over the 20 data sets			85	75	77	77	79	71	68	73	74

inherent structure and noise. It is the inherent structure that generalizes beyond the training set, and this is what a model should capture. When a model is too flexible, it will go beyond the inherent structure to fit the noise in the training set. This can cause significant degradation in performance when it is generalized. We analyzed the robustness of Take The Best compared with that of regression and the Bayesian models in Table 9.3.

The results of Table 9.3 show how robust Take The Best is under generalization (cross validation), at least for small sample sizes. On average, Take The Best comes within 3 percentage points close to the savvier Bayesian network. Recall that Occam's Razor is a heuristic evolved by scientists to favor simple models, and that simple models tend to be more robust in their ability to generalize. Akaike (1973) proved a theorem that provides a natural implementation of Occam's Razor. Assume we have a nested family of models (polynomials, e.g., represent one such family of models, since polynomials of degree n form a subset of polynomials of degree $n + 1$) and two subfamilies. If one of the subfamilies has more adjustable parameters than the other and both make basically the same number of correct predictions on the training set, then the simpler one overfits less, i.e., it is better at predicting new data. Dawes's rule, tallying, Take The Best (in its linear model version) and regression are linear models with the same number of adjustable parameters (namely the number of cues), and thus this type of theorem does not apply in its original form. However, it is possible to prove a variant of Akaike's Theorem, which holds under quite general conditions (Martignon and Schmitt 1999), stating that rigid coefficients overfit less than adjusted coefficients. The coefficients in the linear model version of Take The Best are rigid (more precisely, they are adjustable only in the ordering determined by the relative cue validities, and therefore are more rigid than the regression coefficients). The coefficients of tallying and Dawes's rule are also rigid, while regression's coefficients are flexible. The variant of Akaike's Theorem by Martignon and Schmitt (1999) shows that one expects regression to overfit more than Take The Best. The fact that simple linear models tend to be more accurate than the more subtle regression was discovered in the early 1970s (Einhorn and Hogarth 1975; Hogarth 1978).

CONCLUDING REMARKS

A number of authors have suggested learning strategies for categorizing tasks that involve search over a large space of models, with selection based on a formal simplicity metric appropriately balanced against a metric of fit to empirical observations (e.g., Geman et al. 1992). In this chapter I have shown how a Bayesian approach to the choice task (a special form of categorization task) ends up searching for very simple trees (Figure 9.4) that ultimately categorize pairs (A, B) in $X_A > X_B$ or $X_B > X_A$, where X is the criterion. Trees are among the

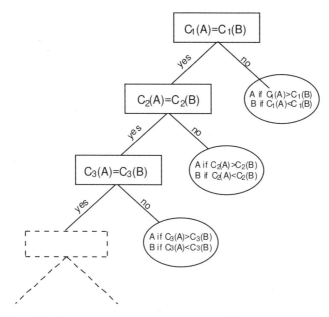

Figure 9.5   Take The Best as a classification tree (Martignon and Hoffrage 1999).

simplest inference procedures one can imagine. It is no exaggeration to say that classification trees have been used by humans for millennia. As early as the third century, the Greek philosopher Porphyrius Malchus classified species by the method called "per genus et differentiam" (collecting items of the same genus and separating them according to specific differences), which corresponds to using a simple classification tree. One of the many ways to look at Take The Best is as the simple tree illustrated in Figure 9.5. A classification tree is a tree-structured graph. Each path from root to leaf consists of a possible combination of cue values, and the leaf node indicates the decision to be made (e.g., $X_A > X_B$ or $X_A < X_B$). In the Take The Best tree, the root node is the cue with the highest validity.

Take The Best's construction is exceedingly simple. The branches are constructed one from the other, in the order established by the validity of the cues. In general, constructing the adequate classification tree for a given data set can be difficult. What is amazing is that, as shown in Table 9.3, this simple lexicographic tree is extremely robust under cross validation and comes close to much more complex Bayesian networks. In the last twenty years, deriving classification trees from data has become an important research topic, both in statistics and machine learning. Much interest has focused on the development and evaluation of efficient heuristics for constructing classification trees that perform and generalize well to new data sets. CARTs (classification and regression trees, introduced by Breiman et al. 1993) have been extremely successful as tree construction mechanisms that guarantee high accuracy. The Bayesian paradigm discussed in this chapter provides efficient search methods for good classification trees.

It is amazing to note that both the Bayesian toolbox and adaptive toolbox meet in the end, adopting, at least in the final steps (see Figure 9.3), very similar inference machines, namely trees. As I have pointed out, being or not being a Bayesian is a matter not only of information formats but of memory and retrieval capacity. Nothing is more psychologically plausible than the Bayesian approach, when natural frequencies (of the correct cue configurations) are either provided or retrieved from memory. All other models are surrogates for the profile memorization method, not just when training and test set differ, but also when fitting known data. Once being a natural Bayesian becomes impossible, models make their entrance. They can be fast and frugal models (e.g., the Take The Best tree) or amount to simple trees searched by means of laborious implementations of Occam's Razor.

The normative and the adaptive toolboxes came to exist because of our limited memory, limited retrieval capacity, and the need to make predictions on unknown data. Both toolboxes have a bias toward simplicity. The normative toolbox uses complex computations to become simple while the adaptive toolbox became simple by adaptively exploiting the structures of environments through the millennia.

ACKNOWLEDGMENT

I am very grateful to Robin Hogarth for his helpful comments and advice.

REFERENCES

Akaike, H. 1973. Information theory and an extension of the maximum likelihood principle. In: Second International Symposium on Information Theory, ed. B.N. Petrov and F. Csaki, pp. 267–281. Budapest: Akademiai Kiado.

Albers, W. 1997. Foundations of a theory of prominence in the decimal system. Working Papers Nos. 265–271. Institute of Mathematical Economics. Bielefeld, Germany: Univ. of Bielefeld.

Breiman, L., J.H. Friedman, R.A. Olshen, and C.J. Stone. 1993. Classification and Regression Trees. New York: Chapman and Hall.

Cooper, G. 1990. The computational complexity of probabilistic inferences. *Artif. Intel.* **42**:393–405.

Cover, T.M., and J.A. Thomas. 1991. Elements of Information Theory. New York: Wiley.

Czerlinski, J., G. Gigerenzer, and D.G. Goldstein. 1999. How good are simple heuristics? In: Simple Heuristics That Make Us Smart, G. Gigerenzer, P.M. Todd, and the ABC Research Group, pp. 97–118. New York: Oxford Univ. Press.

Dawes, R.M. 1979. The robust beauty of improper linear models in decision making. *Am. Psych.* **34**:571–582.

Einhorn, H.J., and R.M. Hogarth. 1975. Unit weighting schemes for decision making. *Org. Behav. Human Perf.* **13**:171–192.

Forster, M.R. 1999. Key concepts in model selection: Performance and generalizablity. *J. Math. Psych.*, in press.

Friedman, N., and M. Goldszmit. 1996. Learning Bayesian networks with local structure. In: Proc. 12th Conf. on Uncertainty in Artificial Intelligence (UAI), Portland, OR, vol. 12, pp. 252–262. San Mateo, CA: Morgan Kaufmann.

Geman, S., E. Bienenstock, and R. Doursat. 1992. Neural networks and the bias/variance dilemma. *Neur. Comp.* **4**:1–58.

Gigerenzer, G., J. Czerlinski, and L. Martignon. 1999. How good are Fast and Frugal Heuristics? In: Decision Research from Bayesian Approaches to Normative Systems: Reflections on the Contributions of Ward Edwards, ed. J. Shanteau, B. Mellers, and D. Schum, pp. 81–104. Norwell, MA: Kluwer Academic.

Gigerenzer, G., and D.G. Goldstein. 1996. Reasoning the fast and frugal way: Models of bounded rationality. *Psych. Rev.* **103**:650–669.

Gigerenzer, G., and U. Hoffrage. 1995. How to improve Bayesian reasoning without instruction: Frequency formats. *Psych. Rev.* **102**:684–704.

Gigerenzer, G., P.M. Todd, and the ABC Research Group. 1999. Simple Heuristics That Make Us Smart. New York: Oxford Univ. Press.

Goldstein, D.G., and G. Gigerenzer. 1999. The recognition heuristic: How ignorance makes us smart. In: Simple Heuristics That Make Us Smart, G. Gigerenzer, P.M. Todd, and the ABC Research Group, pp. 37–58. New York: Oxford Univ. Press.

Hertwig, R., U. Hoffrage, and L. Martignon. 1999. Quick estimation: Letting the environment do the work. In: Simple Heuristics That Make Us Smart, ed. G. Gigerenzer, P.M. Todd, and the ABC Research Group, pp. 209–234. New York: Oxford Univ. Press.

Hoffrage, U., and L. Martignon. 1999. Fast, frugal, and fit: Lexicographic heuristics for paired comparison. *Theory and Decision*, in press.

Hogarth, R.M. 1978. A note on aggregating opinions. *Org. Behav. Human Perf.* **21**:40–46.

Kass, R., and A. Raftery. 1995. Bayes factors. *J. Am. Stat. Assn.* **90**:430.

Krauss, S., L. Martignon, and U. Hoffrage. 2000. Simplifying Bayesian inference. In: Model-Based Reasoning in Scientific Discovery, ed. L. Magnani, N. Nersessian, and N. Thagard. New York: Plenum, in press.

Martignon, L., and U. Hoffrage. 1999. Why does one-reason decision making work? A case study in ecological rationality. In: Simple Heuristics That Make Us Smart, G. Gigerenzer, P.M. Todd, and the ABC Research Group, pp. 119–140. New York: Oxford Univ. Press.

Martignon, L., and K.B. Laskey. 1999. Bayesian benchmarks for fast and frugal heuristics. In: Simple Heuristics That Make Us Smart, G. Gigerenzer, P.M. Todd, and the ABC Research Group, pp. 169–188. New York: Oxford Univ. Press.

Martignon, L., and M. Schmitt. 1999. Simplicity and robustness of fast and frugal heuristics. *Minds Machines*, in press.

Pearl, J. 1988. Probabilistic Reasoning in Intelligent Systems. San Francisco: Morgan Kaufmann.

Tversky, A., and D. Kahneman. 1974. Judgment under uncertainty: Heuristics and biases. *Science* **185**:1124–1131.

Standing, left to right: Karl Schlag, John Payne, Gary Klein, Alex Kacelnik, Yaakov Kareev
Seated, left to right: Dan Goldstein, Robin Hogarth, Gerd Gigerenzer, Laura Martignon

10

Group Report: Why and When Do Simple Heuristics Work?

Daniel G. Goldstein, Rapporteur
Gerd Gigerenzer, Robin M. Hogarth, Alex Kacelnik,
Yaakov Kareev, Gary Klein, Laura Martignon,
John W. Payne, and Karl H. Schlag

In a remote stream in Alaska, a rainbow trout spies a colorful dimple on the undersurface of the water with an insect resting atop it. Darting over with mouth agape, the fish bites down and turns in search of its next victim. It does not get far, however, before the "insect" strikes back. The trout is yanked from the quiet stream by the whiplike pull of a fly fisherman's rod. In a world without fishermen, striking at all that glitters is adaptive; it increases chances for survival. In a world with predators, however, this once-adaptive strategy can turn a feeding fish into a fisherman's food.

Herbert Simon provided the metaphor of a pair of scissors for thinking about rational behavior: one blade has to do with the psychology of the organism and the other with the structure of the environment. In this chapter, we think of the two blades as the simple heuristics used by organisms and the structures of environments that govern their performance. As the case of the poor trout illustrates, a strategy cannot be evaluated without taking into account the environment in which it operates. Attempts to model just one blade of the scissors simply will not cut it. We provide several examples of simple heuristics at work in the world and discuss how the environment determines their success or failure. To do this, however, we are led to ask what counts as success or failure for a strategy. Focusing on the capabilities of the organism and the structure of the environment, we explore the question of how organisms may choose among the heuristics available to them. In conclusion, we generalize about the properties of environments that allow heuristics to work and speculate about the psychological building blocks of decision strategies.

SIMPLE HEURISTICS AT WORK IN THE WORLD

Strategies in the adaptive toolbox are fast and frugal. Fast refers to the relative ease of computation the strategies entail, which has been measured as order of complexity or with elementary information-processing steps (Payne et al. 1993; Czerlinski et al. 1999). Frugal refers to the very limited amount of information these strategies need. Each strategy is described along with a discussion of how the structure of the environment can cause it to succeed or fail.

Imitation

Imitation is a fast and frugal strategy that saves an organism from having to extract information from the environment anew, or from calculating from scratch. For instance, New Caledonian crows use imitation to make tools from Pandanus tree leaves to extract grubs from trees (Hunt 1996). Evidence of imitation is seen in the local similarity of the tools — birds of a particular region tend to make tools of a similar shape (such as facing left or right, for instance). Humans embrace imitation as well and have been observed to imitate those who are compatible with themselves. Hogarth et al. (1980) studied industrial plant relocation decisions of small firms in a town in southern France. The owners of these firms had great difficulty in making these decisions and did not want to commit themselves even though they could see large foreign firms taking advantage of conditions offered by local government. However, when they observed the move made by a local mid-sized firm with a high reputation and whose "values" were compatible with theirs, they quickly adopted the same strategy and moved. A couple of years after these decisions, the small business owners were glad they had relocated. Imitation certainly has its advantages; however, it may not lead to desirable outcomes in all situations, as we shall soon see.

What makes it work? To answer this question, it is perhaps most illuminating to think about when imitation will *not* work. If the environment is changing rapidly, imitation will fail because a successful strategy at the time of observation may no longer be effective, or even executable, at a later time. If the environment masks or obscures what individuals are doing, imitation will be impossible or unwise. The environment also includes other organisms, and the available choice of whom to imitate matters as well. Sometimes, this is a Hobson's choice, and the results can be costly if the sole alternative is not the ideal one. The Mapuche Indians of the high country of Chile have grown wheat for several generations, but before the emergence of a crop disease long ago, they grew barley. Today, barley would be a more profitable crop for them, and modern-day pesticides have solved the disease problem (Henrich 1999). However, attempts by developers to reintroduce the crop have been met with the Mapuche's response that barley farming "is not the present custom" and that they would rather stay with their "traditional" crop. In a world without pesticides, there is no need to pass down knowledge of how to grow crops that are prone to diseases. In a world with access to new ideas and technologies from other cultures, lack of willingness to try the new can hinder progress.

One cannot get specific about how the environment affects the success of imitation without getting specific about the exact kind of imitation at hand, as Schlag (1998) has proven. One rule considered, called "Imitate If Better," assumes that individuals imitate all others who are more successful than themselves, and stick with their current strategies otherwise. Surprisingly, in risky environments this can lead the entire population to choose the alternative with the lowest expected payoff. On the other hand, another quite simple rule called "Proportional Imitation" — which dictates imitating those who are more successful than oneself with a probability that is proportional to the difference between the observed and current degrees of success — always leads the population to the expected payoff-maximizing action. Imitation is promising as one of the simplest and most effective heuristics an organism can employ. As Schlag and others have shown, the success of imitation depends upon the environment, its inhabitants, and the exact kind of imitation being applied. For a discussion of how imitation compares with individual learning, see also Boyd and Richerson (this volume).

Equal Weighting

Multiple regression and Bayesian networks are exemplary of complex models that capture desired properties of classical rationality: they consider all information, and they integrate this information in a compensatory way. Additionally, they apply complicated routines to find the optimal set of weights (the beta weights in regression, or the internode weights in Bayesian networks) that the model will use. Some thinkers (Dawes 1979; Einhorn and Hogarth 1975) have considered a simpler class of model that replaces real-valued weights with simple unit weights (such as +1 and −1). Though one might expect performance to drop appreciably, in some situations these simple models can outperform multiple regression (see also Gigerenzer and Goldstein 1996).

What makes it work? As an example, imagine ranking applicants to a graduate program where candidates' profiles are measured on a number of variables such as test scores, quality of previous education, letters of recommendation, and so on. If you believe that these variables are compensatory or trade-off, then simply give all variables equal weight in the evaluation. The advantage of this procedure is that you cannot make the error of reversing the size of weights attached to two variables. In other words, if — unknown to you — one variable is more important than another but, because of sampling fluctuations, estimation by regression reverses the "true" relative sizes of the weights, regression will make inferior predictions. Equal weighting insures you against making this kind of error. More generally, Einhorn and Hogarth (1975) showed that equal weighting makes better predictions than regression as (1) the number of predictor (or independent) variables increase, (2) average inter-correlation between predictors increases, (3) the ratio of predictors to data points (on which regression weights are estimated) increases, and (4) the R^2 of the regression model decreases. To see how equal weighting can help you pick the "all star" basketball team or decide how many and which forecasters you should consult in making a "consensus" forecast, see Einhorn and McCoach (1977) and Hogarth (1978).

Take The Best

Take The Best is a heuristic from the adaptive toolbox (Gigerenzer and Goldstein 1996) that neither looks up nor integrates all available information. It is a lexicographic procedure (similar to the LEX model tested by Payne and colleagues) that uses a rank ordering of cues to make inferences and predictions (Martignon and Hoffrage 1999). Cues are searched through one at a time, until a cue that satisfies a stopping rule is found. The decision is made on the basis of the cue that stopped search, and all other cues are ignored. In empirical tests, Take The Best used less than a third of all information available to it. Remarkably, despite its simplicity, Take The Best can make predictions that are more accurate than those made by multiple regression and approximates the accuracy of Bayesian networks (Martignon and Laskey 1999; Czerlinski et al. 1999).

What makes it work? In Take The Best, the decision made by a higher-ranked cue cannot be overruled by the integration of lower-ranked cues. Its predictions are equivalent to those of linear models with noncompensatory families of weights (Martignon and Hoffrage 1999), e.g., consider the linear model:

$$y = 8x_1 + 4x_2 + 2x_3 + 1x_4 \qquad (10.1)$$

where x_i is a binary (1 or 0) cue for $i = 1, 2, 3, 4$. Each term on the right-hand side cannot be equaled or exceeded by the sum of all the terms with lesser weights. If cues are not binary but have positive real values, which become neither infinitely small nor infinitely large (i.e., bounded from below and from above by strictly positive real numbers), it is always possible to find weights that determine such a noncompensatory linear model equivalent to Take The Best in performance. If the "true" weights of the cues (i.e., those of an optimal model like regression) are noncompensatory, then Take The Best cannot be beaten by any other linear model when fitting data.

When making predictions on new data, the frugality and simplicity of Take The Best are responsible for its robustness. Here the predictive accuracy of Take The Best is comparable to that of subtle Bayesian models, often surpassing optimal linear models (which tend to overfit). A variant of Akaike's Theorem

(Forster and Sober 1994; Martignon, this volume) explains when and why Take The Best makes more accurate predictions than models that base their decisions on larger sets of adjusted parameters.

Take The First

Experts, such as pilots, firefighters, and chess players, have a simple strategy at their disposal: when faced with a problem to solve, often the best course of action to take is the first (or only) one that comes to mind. The strategy of evaluating solutions as they come to mind, and stopping with the first one that satisfies an aspiration level, is called Take The First. (Actually, this strategy has been described as the recognition-primed decision [RPD] model [Klein 1998], but for purposes of this volume, we use a language that better conforms with the heuristics described by the ABC Research Group [Gigerenzer et al. 1999].) Experiments have been carried out to test the quality of solutions that come to the minds of experienced chess players (Klein et al. 1995). When experts were asked to rate all possible moves from given board situations, they rated only one in six as worthy of consideration. However, when looking at the set of first moves that came to the minds of seasoned players, the experts evaluated four out of six of these moves worthwhile. Furthermore, even if the first move considered was not playable, the flaws were usually discovered quickly, so the cost of rejection was low in terms of time and effort.

What makes it work? Take The First is argued to be effective because, for an expert, part of recognizing or categorizing a situation as typical is to recall what to do in that situation. Options generated are not random but may come to mind in order of quality. Take The First is less successful in domains where the decision maker is not an expert or in completely novel situations within a domain of expertise. (Prescriptive decision analysis methods also struggle under these conditions.) It has limited effectiveness in domains where learning is difficult, such as domains with noisy feedback, or where there are low costs for making errors.

Small-sample Inferences

We all detect meaningful covariation fairly rapidly, seemingly despite the fact that we have only small samples to draw upon. Kareev (1995) has shown that, for correlations, the limitation in sample size imposed upon us by working-memory capacity actually acts as an amplifier of correlations. This allows organisms to detect relationships in the environment because of, not despite, their limited working-memory capacity. With the degree of amplification negatively related to sample size, this effect is more pronounced for children, who both have a smaller capacity and are more in need of detecting correlations.

What makes it work? This model of correlation detection gets its power from a mathematical truth, namely, that small samples tend to overestimate Pearson correlations. It benefits an organism in tasks and domains where the costs of missing a relationship in the world is high.

The Recognition Heuristic

When German and American subjects were asked which of San Diego or San Antonio had a greater population (Goldstein and Gigerenzer 1999), all of the Germans correctly answered that San Diego was larger. Only two-thirds of the Americans got the right answer. Many of the Germans had only heard of San Diego, and not of San Antonio, and chose on the basis of what is called the recognition heuristic. In one formulation, the recognition heuristic dictates that when choosing between two objects, if only one of them is recognized, then choose the recognized object. As it did with the Germans and Americans, this heuristic can lead to a counterintuitive state of affairs in which those who know more perform worse than those who know less, the so-called *less-is-more effect*. The adaptive advantage of this strategy is that it exploits a resource most organisms have in abundance: missing knowledge.

What makes it work? The recognition heuristic depends foremost on missing knowledge—only when some objects are not recognized can the heuristic come into play. However, not any kind of missing knowledge will do when being correct is crucial. Only when ignorance is systematically, rather than randomly, distributed can it be used to make accurate inferences. If the cities people did *not* recognize were not particularly small ones, this missing information could not be used to increase accuracy. It could even hurt it. Luckily, in a wide array of domains (such as the deadliness of diseases, the length of rivers, or the success of sporting teams), the objects people recognize stand out on dimensions they find important. Indeed, it is because people find these objects important that they talk about them, and in so doing assure them a place in the recognition memory of others.

MEASURING SUCCESS

We have looked at a short list of simple strategies thought to be used by human decision makers and discussed structures of the environment that affect their chances of success or failure. A large question remains, however: What does it mean for a strategy to succeed, to fail, or to be optimal?

Optimality

Optimality can refer to outcomes or processes. Optimal outcomes are considered to be the best behavioral consequences an organism can achieve given the information it has available. Any means may be used by scientists to compute optimal outcomes, from analytic proof, to simulation methods, to mechanized optimization routines. Similarly, many processes can lead an organism to achieve these outcomes. For instance, a seedling may achieve optimal orientation towards a light source by differential growth of the two sides of its stem. Optimizing processes, on the other hand, are considered to be those that satisfy various criteria of rationality, for instance, that all available information is considered, or that information is weighted in an optimal (for instance, in a least-squares minimizing) way. Optimality models of animal behavior utilize the assumption of optimality at the level of outcomes, but not at the level of processes. Indeed, in many cases, identification of the process used by the organism can explain why an optimal outcome is *not* achieved under specific circumstances, such as those created in the laboratory. If the process used by the organism was selected in an environment different from that in which it is being tested, this result is not surprising.

The more accurate the specification of the optimal outcome, the more helpful it will be in guiding research into the processes controlling behavior. In the following example, the contrast between a predicted optimum and observed behavior serves to guide research into behavioral mechanisms.

Consider an animal choosing between two foraging sites that differ in prey distribution. In habitat *A*, prey are found regularly at intervals of *F* seconds. In habitat *B*, prey are found in pairs, so that they take intervals of either *S* (for short interval) or *L* (for long interval) seconds between prey.

We may ask how long *F* should be so that the two environments will be equally desirable to an organism. The scientist first interprets the problem faced by the organism as that of maximizing the overall rate of gain. Equalizing rates (Rate *A* = Rate *B*), an animal should be indifferent between the sites when:

$$\frac{1}{F} = \frac{2}{S+L}, \text{ or } F = \frac{1}{2}(S+L). \tag{10.2}$$

With this normative solution, or "optimum," worked out, the matter can be tested empirically. Bateson and Kacelnik (1996, 1997) conducted a series of experiments with starlings, where the birds had to choose between two colored keys that delivered food according to schedules as shown in Figure 10.1, with *S* and *L* equal to 3 seconds and 18 seconds, respectively. In a typical experiment, they used a titration procedure: when the subject chose "*A*," *F* grew by 1 second, but when it chose "*B*," *F* became 1 second shorter. They found that birds were indifferent when $F \cong 5.14$ seconds. This result differs from the expected $F = 10.5$

A ..... x ..... x ..... x ..... x ..... x ..... x ..... x ..... x x
B ... x .... x ... x .... x ... x .... x ... x

Figure 10.1 The occurrence of food at different time intervals in various environments. Each dot represents one second of search time and each x represents a prey capture.

seconds predicted by Equation 10.2. This proves puzzling in light of the fact that the birds would be getting more food per time unit by acting otherwise. For instance, if they faced a habitat *A* where *F* = 8 seconds, they would choose *B*, even though they would be getting one prey every 8 seconds in *A* and only one prey every 10.5 seconds in *B*.

Since there was a gulf between the computed optimum and what was observed in the data, it was appropriate to go back to the blackboard to make another attempt at specifying an algorithm that may be a better predictor. The empirical data turned out to match the equation:

$$\frac{1}{F} = \frac{1}{2}\left(\frac{1}{S} + \frac{1}{L}\right), \tag{10.3}$$

which describes F as the harmonic mean of S and L, rather than the arithmetic mean described by Equation 10.2. Similar results have been reported in other species and with other experimental protocols, and the cost of employing such policies is well known (Gilliam et al. 1982; Mazur 1984; Gibbon et al. 1988). Why would birds use such a policy? The answer may lie in the process of choice.

The birds chose between colored keys which had no intrinsic value, other than that acquired by association with food. The process by which these associations are acquired can be modeled as shown in Figure 10.2.

To use this model in the context of choice between the two sites, it is assumed that choices are controlled by the subjective value of the stimulus (colored key) signaling each place. V_i indicates the value of option *i*.

Figure 10.2 shows that when

$$F = \frac{1}{2}(S + L), \quad V_F < \frac{1}{2}(V_S + V_L). \tag{10.4}$$

Actually, if

$$m(t) \cong \frac{1}{t}, \ V_F = \frac{1}{2}(V_S + V_L) \ \text{when} \ \frac{1}{F} = \frac{1}{2}\left(\frac{1}{S} + \frac{1}{L}\right), \tag{10.5}$$

as found experimentally. In this approach, the researchers "explain" why the subject fails to optimize (namely, maximize rate of gain over time) by the mechanisms that it uses to choose. This finding leads to another target for research, namely the adaptive significance of the process by which stimuli acquire value. Biologically, what needs to be explained is why natural selection has not eliminated this mechanism. One answer is that associative learning is a tool that has a much wider domain than the problem posed by the foraging task. Associative learning is a rather general tool to predict events by temporal contiguity (this is a deliberate simplification of the laws of learning). In terms of the blades of Simon's scissors, one could say that the organism has evolved in environments where the advantages of employing such an associative learning process for predicting relations between events outweigh the losses due to the occasional foraging costs the mechanism may entail. In Figure 10.3, we summarize the research path.

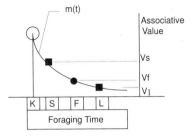

Figure 10.2   A simple hypothetical model for the acquisition of value by arbitrary stimuli (colored keys) while foraging in an environment as depicted in Figure 10.1. The open circle marks the time in which the key lights up with a color and the solid symbols the times at which food is delivered. The solid circle indicates the typical time of delivery in site *A* and the solid squares the two possible times in site *A*. *m(t)* shows the "memory trace" of the onset of the key light. We assume that the key gains associative strength in proportion to the value of *m(t)* when food occurs.

In this and many other foraging examples, "optimality" is assumed and defended at the evolutionary level, but is not proposed as the mechanism of choice used by the subject. When faced with a gulf between hypothetical optimum and outcome, the model was revised to take account of the psychological properties of the organism. In the end, it was posited that the deviation from optimality was

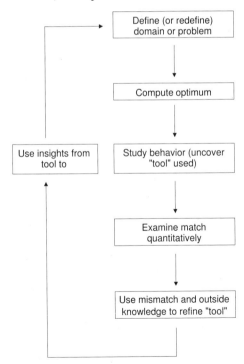

Figure 10.3   A research path.

due to the fact that a more general associative learning mechanism, not evolved to handle this particular task, was being used, and thus the individual is found performing at a less than optimal level. This explanation is reminiscent of Campbell's (1959) hypothesis, i.e., when one observes biases in behavior, it is important to check whether this is not due to a competing response function of the same mechanism. Organisms are less complex than their environments and thus certain responses must be able to handle multiple tasks. Depending on environmental payoffs, trade-offs should be expected.

Other ways for a researcher to explain deviations from predicted optima have to do with changing the level of analysis. Many decisions that are considered nonoptimal for the individual could make sense when one considers that the individual exists within a group. Most small businesses fail, so it arguably does not make sense for an individual to open one. A collection of overoptimistic entrepreneurs, however, each perhaps making the "wrong" move by attempting to open a small business, could, under certain assumptions, lead to an economy in which they are on average wealthier than if they had all made the "right" decision, not been enterprising, and stagnated the economy. Clearly some apparent "irrational" decisions appear more rational upon further considerations of a decision maker's goals for a task, or for instance, when looking at equilibria instead of simple optima. In evolutionary biology, the computation of optima is by no means the only or preferred research tool. The analysis of evolutionary stability is often more useful, as the complexity of frequency-dependent problems tends to make analytical identification of optima impossible. The vast literature on the evolution of cooperation is dominated by the identification (mostly through simulation) of putative evolutionarily stable interaction rules, such as Tit-for-Tat, Pavlov, or image scoring (Nowak and Sigmund 1998a, b). The example of how self-motivated businessmen may be led to equilibria where all players overestimate their individual chances may require this form of treatment, as might the coexistence of sellers and buyers for each share in the market. We should add, however, that all attempts to "rationalize" behavior are disputed by some who believe that ample evidence of nonoptimal decisions and nonoptimal equilibria can be seen in both the laboratory and in the "real world" (e.g., Thaler 1991; Tversky 1996).

Coherence

Many psychological and economic research programs concern themselves not just with an organism's behavior compared to an optimum, but also with how several instances of behavior form patterns. Coherence is the degree to which an organism's patterns of behavior satisfy various criteria of rationality, such as transitivity, consistency over time, and so on.

Incoherence, like deviations from optimality, can also be explained away. Consider the example of the child who hates fish and refuses to eat it, but who can be tricked into eating and liking it through the use of food coloring. When the parent accuses her of being inconsistent, she replies that she has been consistent in her true objective: to nonplus the parent.

Some scholars address incoherence by observing that although a strategy may in principle admit some flaws from the standpoint of classical rationality, the structure of the environment is such that these deviations will have little or no consequence in practice (Fraser et al. 1992). For instance, a heuristic called Minimalist studied by Gigerenzer and Goldstein (1996) admits intransitivities; however, when tested in a real-world environment, it was nearly as accurate, or better, than some linear models that never make intransitive choices. Contrasting such views, many researchers feel that coherence is a major concern for human decision makers, since we live in a constructed economic world, rigged with traps set by those who wish to exploit vulnerable, incoherent decision strategies. Thus, unless people are consistent in their assessment of probabilities, others may exploit their behavior so that they become, in effect, "Dutch books" (Savage 1954). In other words, whatever bets they place, they will always lose. Similar fates await those who would consistently use intransitive choice rules because they could be turned into "money pumps" (Tversky 1969).

CHOOSING AMONG STRATEGIES

A review on strategy selection by Payne and Bettman (this volume) shows how various structures of the environment (such as the number of alternatives, correlational structure, or the presence of time pressure) and the concerns of the decision maker (such as accuracy, effort, or ease of justification) affect which decision strategies human decision makers choose. We look now at the meta-decision problem and then suggest some ways in which the capabilities (perceptual and cognitive) of the actor and the structure of the environment may do much of the work in strategy selection.

Deciding How to Decide

The deciding-how-to-decide problem is inherent in the idea that there is an adaptive toolbox for the solving of decision problems; that is, individuals are postulated to have a toolbox of different heuristics, and these different heuristics perform differentially across task environments. If no single heuristic works well in every environment, this suggests that an individual must choose the appropriate heuristic for a given situation, i.e., decide how to decide. The question of how people decide how to decide is an ongoing research question subject to debate. In this section we briefly review some of the issues and evidence relating to how people select a tool or tools from the toolbox of decision strategies.

One view of strategy selection is that a decision maker, when faced with a judgment or choice task, evaluates the available tools in his or her toolbox in terms of relative benefits and costs and selects the one that is best fitted for solving the decision problem. This "top-down" view of strategy (tool) selection is consistent with the evidence that people do plan how to solve problems (Anderson 1983) in a variety of cognitive tasks. For example, as discussed by Payne and Bettman (this volume), there is evidence of such planning in solving decision problems as well. There is also evidence that a crucial difference among students in terms of reading skill is the ability to adjust different reading processes (e.g., reading approaches) to different reading tasks (Garner 1987). More generally, Gagné (1984) argues that good problem solving requires strategic knowledge of when and how to use procedural (tool) and declarative (fact) knowledge.

The top-down view of tool (or strategy) selection has the potential for infinite regress. On the basis of benefits and costs, one decides how to decide, how to choose, ... The infinite regress problem in deciding how to decide is similar to the problem in game theory regarding one's beliefs about the beliefs of others, who have beliefs about one's beliefs about the beliefs of others (Lipman 1991). The potential for infinite regress in strategy selection is a serious issue. However, there are both theoretical reasons and empirical evidence to suggest that the sequence of decisions on deciding how to decide may quickly converge to some fixed point (Lipman 1991; Nagel 1995). In her work on games, for example, Nagel (1995) reports that the depth of reasoning about what others are thinking about what you are thinking does not extend much beyond one or two levels.

A different view of strategy selection sees the issue of deciding how to decide as involving a much more bottom-up process. Instead of a conscious decision on how to decide, the selection of a tool from the toolbox may reflect a learned response that has related various task factors to the effectiveness and efficiency of various strategies (for a related view, see Rieskamp and Hoffrage 1999). For instance, people may have learned that the Take The Best rule works very well for certain tasks, and that rule is then typically evoked whenever those situations are encountered. This bottom-up view of strategy selection avoids the infinite regress problem. However, the learned response approach does raise the problem of deciding how to decide when faced with a novel situation.

Of course, it is quite likely that the strategy selection problem is sometimes solved in a top-down way and at other times in a much more bottom-up fashion. One possibility is that the top-down approach to strategy selection will be seen more often when people are faced with complex problems and have the time to decide how to decide. It is also possible that people may start with an approach to a decision problem and then constructively adjust their processing during the course of making the decision as they learn more about the problem structure. Processing, in other words, can change on the spot in an "opportunistic" fashion (Hayes-Roth and Hayes-Roth 1979). In any event, asking the question of "when do simple heuristics work?" clearly raises important issues, such as when and how heuristics that work differentially in different situations are more or less likely to be selected. Below, we explore the strategy selection question as it is affected by the interplay between the capacities of the organism (both perceptual and cognitive) as well as the structure of the environment.

Perceptual Specialization as a Strategy Selector

The particular perceptual system of an organism might cause it to choose among strategies in a way an onlooker will not suspect. Heyes and colleagues (Heyes 1993; Heyes and Dawson 1992) studied imitation by placing two rats face to face in adjoining cages. One rat, the demonstrator, learned to push a joystick to the left to be rewarded with food, while another rat, an observer, looked on. From the observer's head-on perspective, the joystick appeared to move to the right, not left, to trigger the release of food. Later, the observer was later placed in the demonstrator's cage. Which way would it push the joystick? It correctly pushed the joystick to the left. What perceptual strategy did the rat use to compute the direction? The scientists wondered if rats could map observed actions onto their own bodies when undertaking imitative behavior. However, in later experiments, the experimenters learned that by giving the joystick a twist, they could make the observer push the joystick in the opposite direction (Heyes, pers. comm.). The observed behavior was caused by sniffing at the side of the joystick where it detected the scent of the demonstrator. The tendency to show olfactory interest in places where there were signs of conspecific activity was capable of reaping the benefits of imitation, but by another means than the human observers originally suspected. The specialization of a perceptual system can keep classes of strategies out of the choice set (and thereby reduce the meta-decision problem without any utility computations) and favor the selection of strategies other organisms might not have at their disposal.

Cognitive and Knowledge Limitations as Strategy Selectors

In addition to perceptual capacities, cognitive capacities vary between species and individuals. Humans differ in their working memory capacity, and experiments performed by Kareev and his associates (Kareev et al. 1997), on the detection of correlations, show how these differences in cognitive capacity lead to different outcomes in the detection of correlation. The larger a person's working-memory capacity, the larger the sample they were assumed to consider in assessing correlations. Individuals with smaller working memories were actually more effective at detecting correlations. This is a surprising result, but predicted by the simple mechanism Kareev proposes: people with small working memories consider small samples, which in turn amplify correlations to a larger degree than do the larger samples likely to be considered by people with larger capacity. Another little-studied dimension on which individuals differ is their degree of ignorance (lack of recognition) in certain domains. The recognition heuristic depends on a lack of knowledge to be applicable, and can become less and less effective as recognition knowledge is gained. Here again, a deficit on the part of the organism (missing knowledge) enables a strategy which can lead to better performance in specific environments than can be achieved without the deficit (for an explanation of why this happens, see Goldstein and Gigerenzer 1999).

Domain Specificity as a Strategy Selector

The research program that has come to be known as evolutionary psychology has emphasized the existence of modules of the mind that are domain specific, that is, are concerned with solving specific tasks (see, e.g., Cosmides and Tooby 1997). These modules are assumed to have evolved in the so-called Environment of Evolutionary Adaptation (EEA) and are hence capable of quite inappropriate performance in different circumstances. Domain-specific strategies are advantageous because they circumvent the meta-decision problem: they restrict the set of strategies. Furthermore, heuristics from the adaptive toolbox may be specialized for solving particular tasks. For instance, Take The Best is designed for choosing between two alternatives—the question would not arise whether it should be applied to an estimation or categorization problem.

When Will Strategies Be Learned?

Any discussion of strategy selection would be incomplete without mentioning how new strategies may enter an organism's vocabulary through learning. A conception of Hogarth (unpublished) helps us think about which environments will lead to the learning of strategies. There are situations in which the consequences of errors are large or small, and there are situations in which the quality of feedback one gets from the environment is perfect or noisy, as shown in Figure 10.4.

Common sense tells us that learning should occur most rapidly on the left side as opposed to the right, and in the upper half as opposed to the bottom. One question we found quite provocative is to speculate about what types of

		Quality of Feedback	
		Perfect	*Noisy*
Consequences of Errors	*Large*	Pressure for valid strategies – good strategies can emerge	Difficult for valid strategies to emerge
	Small	Little pressure for valid strategies – good and bad strategies can coexist	Superstitious learning quite likely

Figure 10.4 Quality of feedback and the consequences of errors.

strategies would be learned in environments denoted by the various quadrants. For example, in which quadrant would one expect complex strategies to be learned, and in which would one expect fast and frugal heuristics to be learned? One view is that complex strategies would be essential in the top half, because being correct counts a great deal in this region. An alternative view would suggest that fast and frugal heuristics would be learned in the top half, because some issues are so grave that only stubborn, inflexible strategies can be trusted to address them. Consider the strategies "learned" through natural selection. A complex, compensatory strategy—in which, for instance, a prey animal would learn through trial and error the optimal escape distance from a predator, as opposed to simply always reacting in an overcautious way—might cost a creature its life. A useful model of the relative advantage of learning and nonlearning strategies according to environmental parameters has been discussed by Stephens (1991).

WHAT MAKES SIMPLE HEURISTICS WORK?

The general point that has been introduced with Simon's metaphor of the two blades of the pair of scissors is that the success and failure of heuristics depends on their match with the structure of environments. We summarize here, without claim for completeness, some heuristics, some structures of environments, and their match. Note that the term "structure of environment" is shorthand for the information a person, animal, or institution knows about a physical or social environment.

Systematic lack of knowledge. The recognition heuristic is a mechanism that exploits lack of knowledge. In the simplest case, the task is to predict which of two alternatives scores higher on a criterion X. The heuristic will perform above chance if the lack of recognition of alternatives is not random, but systematically correlated with X. The precise proportion of correct inferences is a function of the recognition validity and the number of objects recognized among all alternatives (see Goldstein and Gigerenzer 1999).

Presence of others to imitate. In noisy but stable environments, imitation can allow one to find the best action among those currently being employed. Imitation reduces decision costs by leaving to others the task of discovering new choices. A necessary condition for the good performance of imitation is the existence of observable individuals in similar situations to the observer.

Noncompensatory information. Take The Best is a heuristic that exploits situations in which the cues (predictors) are noncompensatory (or approximately so). For instance, in an environment where binary cues have the weights 1, 1/2, 1/4, 1/8, ..., the simple Take The Best achieves the same predictions as multiple regression (Martignon, this volume; Martignon and Hoffrage 1999).

Scarce information. Information is scarce when the number of cues is small compared to the number of objects one has to make predictions about. Specifically, if the number of cues is less than $\log_2 N$, Take The Best outperforms on average a class of linear models including unit-weighting strategies (Martignon and Hoffrage 1999).

Abundant information. Simple unit-weighting tends to outpredict linear regression as the number of cues increases (Einhorn and Hogarth 1975).

Redundant information. Unit-weighting tends to outpredict linear regression as the average intercorrelation between the predictors increases (Einhorn and Hogarth 1975).

Noisy information. The larger the noise in a set of training data, the better the accuracy of a simple strategy relative to a complex strategy (where simpler means fewer free parameters) when making predictions about new data (Akaike 1973; Forster and Sober 1994).

J-shaped Distributions. Many distributions are not normal, but J-shaped, that is, most objects have small values and only a few have large values (consider the population of cities, or number of publications per person). If the distribution of objects is J-shaped on a criterion, a simple heuristic, QuickEst, can exploit this structure to make fast and frugal quantitative estimates of individual objects on the criterion that are highly accurate (Hertwig et al. 1999).

This is an incomplete catalogue of when and why simple heuristics work. We agree that their secret is in the environment.

WHAT WE DO NOT YET UNDERSTAND

As the various examples in this chapter show, simple strategies can be quite effective in the right environments. However, there is work to be done. We still need a conceptual language to measure and communicate the structure of environments. We still need precise models of heuristics built with respect to the cognitive architecture of organisms. We still need to understand how the two blades of the scissors fit together, i.e., which heuristics are suited to which environments. Finally, there is the large question which kept us arguing days and nights, lunches and dinners, coffees and teas: which homunculus selects among heuristics, or is there none?

REFERENCES

Akaike, H. 1973. Information theory and an extension of the maximum likelihood principle. In: Second International Symposium on Information Theory, ed. B.N. Petrov and F. Csaki, pp. 267–281. Budapest: Akademiai Kiado.

Anderson, J.R. 1983. The Architecture of Cognition. Cambridge, MA: Harvard Univ. Press.

Bateson, M. 1993. Currencies for Decision Making: The Foraging Starling as a Model Animal. Ph.D. diss., Oxford Univ.

Bateson, M., and A. Kacelnik. 1996. Rate currencies and the foraging starling: The fallacy of the averages revisited. *Behav. Ecol.* 7:341–352.

Bateson, M., and A. Kacelnik. 1997. Starlings' preferences for predictable and unpredictable delays to food. *Anim. Behav.* **53(6)**:1129–1142.

Campbell, D.T. 1959. Systematic error on the part of human links in communication systems. *Inf. Cont.* **1**:334–369.

Cosmides, L., and J. Tooby. 1997. Dissecting the computational architecture of social inference mechanisms. In: Characterizing Human Psychological Adaptations, ed. G. Bock and G. Cardew, vol. 208, pp. 132–158. Chichester: Wiley.

Czerlinski, J., G. Gigerenzer, and D.G. Goldstein. 1999. How good are simple heuristics? In: Simple Heuristics That Make Us Smart, G. Gigerenzer, P.M. Todd, and the ABC Research Group, pp. 97–118. New York: Oxford Univ. Press.

Dawes, R.M. 1979. The robust beauty of improper linear models. *Am. Psych.* **34**:571–582.

Einhorn, H.J., and R.M. Hogarth. 1975. Unit weighting schemes for decision making. *Org. Behav. Human Perf.* **13**:171–192.

Einhorn, H.J., and W. McCoach. 1977. A simple multiattribute procedure for evaluation. *Behav. Sci.* **22**:270–282.

Forster, M., and E. Sober. 1994. How to tell when simpler, more unified, or less ad hoc theories will provide more accurate predictions. *Brit. J. Phil. Sci.* **45**:1–35.

Fraser, J.M., P.J. Smith, and J.W. Smith. 1992. A catalog of errors. *Intl. J. Man-Machine St.* **37**:265–307.

Gagné, R.M. 1984. Learning outcomes and their effects: Useful categories of human performance. *Am. Psych.* **39**:377–385.

Garner, R. 1987. Metacognition and Reading Comprehension. Norwood, NJ: Ablex.

Gibbon, J., R.M. Church, et al. 1988. Scalar expectancy theory and choice between delayed rewards. *Psych. Rev.* **95**:102–114.

Gigerenzer, G., and D.G. Goldstein. 1996. Reasoning the fast and frugal way: Models of bounded rationality. *Psych. Rev.* **103**:650–669.

Gigerenzer, G., P.M. Todd, and the ABC Research Group. 1999. Simple Heuristics That Make Us Smart. New York: Oxford Univ. Press.

Gilliam, J.F., R.F. Green, et al. 1982. The fallacy of the traffic policeman: A response to Templeton and Lawlor. *Am. Nat.* **119**:875–878.

Goldstein, D.G., and G. Gigerenzer. 1999. The recognition heuristic: How ignorance makes us smart. In: Simple Heuristics That Make Us Smart, G. Gigerenzer, P.M. Todd, and the ABC Research Group, pp. 75–96. New York: Oxford Univ. Press.

Hayes-Roth, B., and F. Hayes-Roth. 1979. A cognitive model of planning. *Cog. Sci.* **3**:275–310.

Henrich, J. 1999. Rationality, Cultural Transmission, and Adaptation: The problem of culture and decision-making in anthropology. Univ. of California, *www.bol.ucla.edu/~henrich/*.

Hertwig, R., U. Hoffrage, and L. Martignon. 1999. Quick estimation: Letting the environment do some of the work. In: Simple Heuristics That Make Us Smart, G. Gigerenzer, P.M. Todd, and the ABC Research Group, pp. 209–234. New York: Oxford Univ. Press.

Heyes, C.M. 1993. Imitation, culture and cognition. *Anim. Behav.* **46**:999–1010.

Heyes, C.M., G.R. Dawson, et al. 1992. Imitation in rats: Initial responding and transfer evidence. *Qtly. J. Exp. Psych.* **45B**:229–240.

Hogarth, R.M. 1978. A note on aggregating opinions. *Org. Behav. Human Perf.* **21**:40–46.

190   *Daniel G. Goldstein et al.*

Hogarth, R.M., C. Michaud, and J.-L. Mery. 1980. Decision behavior in urban development: A methodological approach and substantive considerations. *Acta Psych.* **45**:95–117.

Hunt, G.R. 1996. Manufacture and use of hook-tools by New Caledonian crows. *Nature* **379**:249–251.

Kareev, Y. 1995. Through a narrow window: Working memory capacity and the detection of covariation. *Cognition* **56**:263–269.

Kareev, Y., I. Lieberman, and M. Lev. 1997. Through a narrow window: Sample size and the detection of correlation. *J. Exp. Psych.: Gen.* **126**:278–287.

Klein, G. 1998. Sources of Power: How People Make Decisions. Cambridge, MA: MIT Press.

Klein, G., S. Wolf, L. Militello, and C. Zsambok. 1995. Characteristics of skilled option generation in chess. *Org. Behav. Human Decis. Proc.* **62**:63–69.

Lipman, B.L. 1991. How to decide how to decide how to … Modeling limited rationality. *Econometrica* **59**:1105–1125.

Martignon, L., and U. Hoffrage. 1999. Why does one-reason decision making work? A case study in ecological rationality. In: Simple Heuristics That Make Us Smart, G. Gigerenzer, P.M. Todd, and the ABC Research Group, pp. 119–140. New York: Oxford Univ. Press.

Martignon, L., and K.B. Laskey. 1999. Bayesian benchmarks for fast and frugal heuristics. In: Simple Heuristics That Make Us Smart, G. Gigerenzer, P.M. Todd, and the ABC Research Group, pp. 169–188. New York: Oxford Univ. Press.

Mazur, J.E. 1984. Tests of an equivalence rule for fixed and variable reinforcer delays. *J. Exp. Psych.: Anim. Behav. Proc.* **10**:426–436.

Nagel, R. 1995. Unraveling in guessing games: An experimental study. *Am. Econ. Rev.* **85**:1313–1326.

Nowak, M.A., and K. Sigmund. 1998a. The dynamics of indirect reciprocity. *J. Theor. Biol.* **194**:561–574.

Nowak, M.A., and K. Sigmund. 1998b. Evolution of indirect reciprocity by image scoring. *Nature* **393**:573–577.

Payne, J.W., J.R. Bettman, and E.J. Johnson. 1993. The Adaptive Decision Maker. New York: Cambridge Univ. Press.

Rieskamp, J., and U. Hoffrage. 1999. When do people use simple heuristics, and how can we tell? In: Simple Heuristics That Make Us Smart, G. Gigerenzer, P.M. Todd, and the ABC Research Group, pp. 141–167. New York: Oxford Univ. Press.

Savage, L.J. 1954. The Foundations of Statistics. New York: Wiley.

Schlag, K.H. 1998. Why imitate, and if so, how? A boundedly rational approach to multi-armed bandits. *J. Econ. Theory* **78**:130–156.

Stephens, D.W. 1991. Change, regularity and value in the evolution of animal learning. *Behav. Ecol.* **2**:77–89.

Thaler, R.H. 1991. Quasi Rational Economics. New York: Russell Sage.

Tversky, A. 1969. Intransitivity of preferences. *Psych. Rev.* **76**:31–48.

Tversky, A. 1996. Contrasting rational and psychological principles of choice. In: Wise Choices: Decisions, Games, and Negotiations, ed. R.J. Zeckhauser, R.L. Keeney, and J.K. Sebenius, pp. 5–21. Boston: Harvard Business School Press.

11

Emotions and Cost-benefit Assessment

The Role of Shame and Self-esteem in Risk Taking

Daniel M.T. Fessler

Dept. of Anthropology, University of California at Los Angeles,
Los Angeles, CA 90095–1553, U.S.A.

ABSTRACT

Ethnographic and experimental findings indicate that emotions influence decision making in a number of ways, including the weighting of cost-benefit assessments. One pair of emotions, shame and pride, biases such assessments in the service of both rank-striving and approval-seeking behaviors. The frequency with which these emotions influence decision making is determined by self-esteem, a mechanism that sums events to date. This allows for the adjustment of risk-taking choices in light of future prospects. Studies of humans and nonhuman primates suggest that serotonin, a neurotransmitter, plays a key role in such a system. In the environment in which humans evolved, this patterned attunement of cost-benefit assessments would have optimized fitness.

INTRODUCTION

The world is not intrinsically divided into options. Instead, an organism must parse stimuli in such a way as to define events, and thus to define choices. Because decision making is logically prior to action, we can expect that natural and sexual selection will have acted to create in organisms the capacity to divide up the world in this manner in order to facilitate adaptive behavior (Tooby and Cosmides 1990). Finer parsing of the environment produces greater flexibility and complexity of behavior: Whereas a single-celled organism may chunk the world along only a few axes (warm versus cold, edible versus toxic, etc.), and may possess only a few responses (approach versus avoid, etc.), creatures as complex as mammals divide the world into many more categories and possess a much wider range of responses. Such complexity introduces still more complexity, as meta-decisions must then be addressed, i.e., it becomes necessary to prioritize decisions to be made. Humans, and probably other mammals (and perhaps other vertebrates), seem to manage these various demands not through brute information-processing power, but rather through discrete decision-making apparatuses that shape and constrain the tasks at hand. Specifically, it appears that emotions are integral parts of decision-making mechanisms that parse the world into decisions, prioritize some decisions over others, and weight particular options within decisions (Tooby and Cosmides 1990).[1]

Any decision embodies an assessment of the future, for the value of a given option is contingent on what the organism's circumstances are likely to be the next moment, day, year, or decade. Organisms thus require a means of prognostication. The most reliable way of predicting the future is to extrapolate from the past. Organisms therefore probably possess mechanisms that aggregate experience and, in so doing, influence the proximate mechanisms of decision making. In this chapter I argue that a pair of emotions, shame and pride, importantly influence decision making. These emotions, in turn, are linked to self-esteem, a mechanism that sums experience to date (where the nature of that experience is itself defined in emotional terms). The result is a decision-making system which adjusts risk-taking behavior in accord with probable future opportunities, where such opportunities are predicted on the basis of past events.

DRIVES AND EMOTIONS

Observing patterned, species-typical behavior that appears strongly goal-oriented, investigators have often posited the existence of discrete drives. However, "drive" is simply a label for a black box — the mechanism is defined wholly in terms of its output. Moreover, when we examine actual human behavior, we find that informants often explain actions largely in terms of emotions. Individual emotion events, while importantly shaped by both idiosyncratic past experience and the cultural context, are nonetheless constructed upon panhuman capacities and proclivities to experience particular reactions to particular classes of events. Presumably, such marked and pervasive features evolved because they provided adaptive advantages to those who possessed them (Tooby and Cosmides 1990).

How might emotions be advantageous? First, emotions inform the individual about how she currently stands in relation to the world. Each emotion is an integral part of a system which parses the world into decision categories by "telling" the individual about particular types of relationships with the world (Tooby and Cosmides 1990). Fear, for example, is a way of "knowing" that the environment is threatening to the individual — the emotion, elicited by particular stimuli in the environment, tags a particular type of event in the world, causing it to be salient. Second, emotions heighten and prolong monitoring of stimuli relevant to the given type of event, probably at the expense of other stimuli — fear maintains the attention directed at potentially threatening stimuli (reviewed in Mineka and Sutton 1992). Third, emotions influence the recall of stored information, as memories relevant to the given type of event become more accessible, while other information is more difficult to recall — during an exam, a fearful student may be able to remember how one can escape from frightening situations, but he may be unable to recall the course material.[2] Fourth, emotions proportionately influence meta-decision making (Tooby and Cosmides 1990) — the experience of intense fear prioritizes decisions concerning the eliciting threat ahead of any other decisions, such as what to have for dinner. Fifth, emotions help to constrain the available choices to those which will address the eliciting event (Tooby and Cosmides 1990) — fear may or may not assist an individual in deciding which way to flee (see endnote), but it clearly inclines the individual to flee, rather than to engage in any of an infinite variety of other possible behaviors.[3] Sixth, because they are distinctly rewarding or aversive, emotions direct decision making in a number of ways. In the simplest case, individuals experience an emotion and then act either to terminate or to extend the circumstances that elicited it, depending upon the emotion's hedonic value. More complexly, as a consequence of past experience, individuals actively seek either to create or to avoid the circumstances that elicit a given emotion. Furthermore, emotions are sometimes paired such that situation X elicits a rewarding emotion, while situation NOT-X elicits an aversive emotion. This redundancy increases the likelihood that an actor will seek out or avoid particular types of situations, i.e., it lends robustness to the ordered nature of decisions. Seventh, as will be discussed at length below, emotions may influence decision making by affecting the relative salience or weight of costs versus benefits. Finally, because multiple emotions may be elicited simultaneously, emotions' influence on decision making is sometimes the product of the interaction among emotions. When two emotions having antithetical features, such as fear and love, are elicited simultaneously, indecision may occur (until such time as one emotion is more strongly elicited). Conversely, when two emotions having complementary features, such as fear and disgust, are elicited simultaneously, the result may be an additive influence on decision making. In sum, evolution appears to have patterned decision making, and hence behavior, by shaping the eliciting conditions, cognitive consequences, action tendencies, hedonic values, and biasing effects of specific emotions (see also Mellers et al., this volume). We can therefore think of "drives" as consisting of evolved sets of emotions that work together to produce particular outcomes in particular circumstances.

SHAME AND RISK

All decisions involve a weighing up of the relative costs and benefits of different courses of action. As noted above, emotions influence decision making in part by biasing some outcomes over others. Sometimes, such biasing is in keeping with a commonsensical understanding of the "sensible" choice in the given situation — the benefits of running away from a large predator obviously far outweigh the costs, and hence we are content to describe the decision to flee as "sensible" even if, in fact, it was the product of an emotional reaction rather than a conscious calculation. Often, however, commonsensical assessments view emotional decisions as "senseless," particularly when the potential costs, or risks (the costs considered in light of the likelihood that they will be incurred) seem to outweigh the potential benefits. Nowhere is this more true than in instances of spontaneous violence. Below is a case drawn from my anthropological fieldwork in Bengkulu, southwestern Sumatra:

> Rustam and his girlfriend left the party around 11:30 p.m. They found a minibus and, after bargaining with the driver and his assistant, they set off. As they neared Rustam's village, a disagreement arose over the fare. The discrepancy was 50 rupiah, the price of a single cracker at a village shop. Words were passed. A fight began. The two young men stabbed Rustam 14 times and dumped him by the side of the highway. He died as his girlfriend knelt wailing at his side.
>
> The next day, after the killers had been arrested, the body had been buried, and the stain by the highway had been washed away, people gathered in the shops. "They must've been possessed by the Devil!" several old men said. "Imagine, killing somebody over 50 rupiah. Only a madman would do such a thing!" But the young men knew that possession and insanity were only metaphors. "It was all because of *malu*," one said, and others nodded. "No one wants to be *malu* in front of a girl."

Viewed cross-culturally, Rustam's death was a prototypical murder. Violent interactions frequently involve young men and frequently begin as altercations over trivial points, often with an audience looking on (Daly and Wilson 1988). From a commonsensical position, such events seem notably senseless, as the contested point appears insignificant relative to the potential costs. However, as Daly and Wilson have compellingly argued, it is likely that young men possess the propensity to make such choices because, in our evolutionary past, such reactions would have allowed a maturing male with little status or influence to rapidly establish a reputation as someone to be taken seriously in the highly competitive male social arena. Hence, if utility is defined in terms of inclusive fitness, while such a choice may or may not be rational now, it was rational in the evolutionary context in which it arose (cf. Hammerstein, this volume) — given high variance in male reproductive success, risk taking made sense for young males with uncertain futures.

Note that the above explanation operates at the ultimate level — we have an account of why a predisposition exists, but not of how it operates. To gain insight into the proximate workings of the system, we return to informants' analyses of events. In explaining the combatants' behavior, villagers made frequent reference to *malu*, an aversive, shame-like emotion. Apparently, the experience of this emotion (combined with the prospect of its intensification) colored the participants' assessments of the costs and benefits of escalation. To understand why *malu* had this effect, we must explicate this emotion more fully.

It is possible to describe an emotion in terms of what I call its "logic," i.e., the abstracted set of conditions wherein it is experienced. The Bengkulu emotion *malu*, like the English emotion *shame*, is characterized by the following six-point logic:

1. Ego^4 violates a norm.
2. Ego is aware of his failure.
3. An Other is also aware of Ego's failure.
4. Ego is aware of the Other's knowledge.
5. The Other displays hostility and revulsion towards Ego, or Ego assumes that Other experiences hostility and revulsion towards Ego.
6. As a consequence of the above, Ego experiences an aversive emotion.

Conversely, *bangga*, the opposite of *malu*, is characterized by the same logic as the English emotion *pride*, the opposite of *shame*:

1. Ego successfully fulfills a norm.
2. Ego is aware of her success.
3. An Other is also aware of Ego's success.
4. Ego is aware of the Other's knowledge.
5. Other displays towards Ego either (a) a positive appraisal and affection or (b) a positive appraisal and hostility, *or* Ego assumes that Other experiences (a) or (b) towards Ego.
6. As a consequence of the above, Ego experiences a pleasurable emotion.

At first glance it thus appears that *malu* and *shame* are isomorphic, as are *bangga* and *pride*. Moreover, cross-cultural comparison (see Fessler 1999) reveals that disparate cultures possess the same pair of opposing six-point logic emotions, suggesting that a shame-like emotion and a pride-like emotion are probable human universals. However, this observation does not in itself shed light on how a shame-like emotion could have led to Rustam's murder, since the fight did not revolve around any clear violation of a norm. To understand the connection between *malu* and violence, we must explore this emotion still further.

In addition to being characterized by the six-point logics, *malu* and its opposite, *bangga*, are also characterized by simpler three-point logics, as follows:

1. Ego assesses an Other as significantly more important than Ego.
2. Ego must interact with the Other in a situation in which the discrepancy between Ego and the Other is salient for Ego.

3. As a consequence of the above, Ego experiences an aversive emotion.

and

1. Ego assesses an Other as significantly less important than Ego.
2. Ego must interact with the Other in a situation in which the discrepancy between Ego and the Other is salient for Ego.
3. As a consequence of the above, Ego experiences a pleasurable emotion.

Moreover, it is clear that these are not cases of simple polysemy, as the same display and outcome behaviors, familiar to English speakers, are associated with each term whether it is in regard to the six- or three-point logic:

malu:
1. averted gaze
2. face turned down and away from others
3. stooped shoulders
4. shrinking posture
5. bent-kneed, shuffling gait
6. reddening of the face and neck
7. attempts to avoid being seen, culminating in flight

bangga:
1. eye contact sought
2. face slightly elevated and turned towards others
3. squared shoulders
4. erect posture
5. stiff-legged gait
6. seeks out opportunities for exhibition

Cross-cultural comparison (see Fessler 1999) indicates that English is unusual in its failure to recognize these three-point logics — around the world, diverse cultures concur that each of these emotions is characterized by both a six- and a three-point logic. Moreover, there is evidence that English speakers are capable of experiencing shame- and pride-like reactions under the three-point conditions despite the absence of a cultural label (see Fessler 1999). It therefore appears that the universal emotions, which we can label Shame and Pride, are each characterized by both a six- and a three-point logic. Importantly, unlike the six-point logics with their focus on norm violation, the three-point logics revolve primarily around questions of dominance and subordinance. It is this latter facet of Shame to which the Bengkulu villagers were referring when they cited *malu* as the cause of Rustam's death, for physical combat is the most elementary form of the struggle for dominance. Still, understanding that subordinance elicits an aversive emotion does not explain why the altercation on the minibus continued to escalate even after violence became a foreseeable outcome — surely being hurt or killed is more aversive than being ashamed?

Before exploring further the nature of Shame and Pride, consider the following: In a series of experiments involving real-world consequences of demonstrated personal significance, Baumeister, Heatherton, and Tice found that a class of North American subjects exposed to "ego threat" (negative feedback on ability, i.e., conditions meeting the six-point logic of Shame) adopted "a high-risk, high-payoff strategy that offered the individual a chance at a glorious success — but that increased the danger of costly failure" (1993, p. 153). Using different methods, Leith and Baumeister (1996) then examined the effects on decision making of "embarrassment" (produced by demonstrating the subject's inadequacy, i.e., what I would again term shame) and "anger" (produced by having the subject vehemently act out a hostile response to someone who had angered the subject). Subjects who were experiencing either of these emotions followed high-risk, high-gain strategies when making choices which (the subjects believed) would have real-world impact on them. In contrast, such strategies were avoided by other subjects who were experiencing happiness, sadness, or an emotionally neutral condition at the time of decision making. Subjects who were experiencing shame and anger "seem[ed] merely to seek out the best possible outcome and grab for it, without being deterred by rational [sic] cost-benefit calculations or even by the prospect of possible unpleasant consequences" (1996, p. 1264). Relatedly, an increasing body of clinical literature ties shame to aggression in Western settings, and ethological investigations of dyadic interactions that end in aggression reveal a sequence of display behaviors in which rage is preceded by shame (Retzinger 1991).[5]

It appears that when people feel either intense Shame or intense anger, they disregard both the likelihood that a given goal will be achieved and the potential costs entailed if failure occurs, and instead choose a course of action solely designed to maximize benefits. This finding is consistent with Bengkulu accounts of conflicts among young men, as increasingly intense Shame and anger eventually lead participants to expose themselves willingly to enormous risks. To see why Shame has this effect, and why it is often linked to anger, we must explore the evolutionary history of Shame and Pride, as an understanding of the factors that led to the development of these emotions will shed light on how and why they influence decision making today.

THE PHYLOGENETIC DEVELOPMENT OF
SHAME AND PRIDE

To begin, consider the differing cognitive demands entailed by the six- and three-point logics. Six-point logics are premised on the ability to manipulate a "theory of mind" (Ego must know what it is that the Other knows about Ego, etc.). In contrast, three-point logics have no such requirements — the Other is viewed not as a target for intersubjectivity, but merely as a feature of the social world. Next, consider this distinction in light of the display behaviors of Shame and Pride, which we can summarize as follows:

	Shame	Pride
Eye contact	avoided	sought
Manipulation of apparent body size[6]	smaller than baseline state	larger than baseline state
Visibility and social interaction	avoided	sought

In many primates and other animals, staring is an important part of threat behavior, while gaze avoidance is a component of appeasement behavior. In many, perhaps most vertebrates, increasing apparent body size is a component of threat behavior, while decreasing it is a component of appeasement behavior. Seeking visibility is a central part of many primate threat displays, while avoiding interaction with others or attracting attention to oneself is often a form of submission (for discussion and citations, see Fessler 1999).[7]

We can summarize the above by stating that the displays associated with the postulated universal emotions Shame and Pride are composed of components used for the negotiation or reaffirmation of relative rank. Note therefore that the three-point logics of Shame and Pride, which focus on dyadic interactions and revolve around issues of rank, are more congruent with the associated display behaviors than are the six-point logics. It thus appears that the three-point versions of Shame and Pride developed initially to shape rank-related behavior. The six-point logics, with their reliance on a theory of mind, apparently only appeared much later in the course of human evolution, after hominid cognitive capacities had increased significantly. It is plausible that initially the six-point logics served the same purpose as the three-point logics, focusing on rivalry — a defeated contestant in an agonistic interaction feels Shame before his rival in part because he knows that his rival knows that he has failed. Although this facet of the emotion persists to the present, it has been importantly overlaid by a focus on interaction with an audience rather than with a rival. This focus is most likely an evolutionarily recent addition, selected for as increases in cognitive sophistication made complex cooperation possible, thereby creating benefits for those who sought group approval (see Fessler 1999).

The two opposing configurations of the three-point logics, subjective experiences, and display behaviors of Shame and Pride, are thematically integrated. We can label these integrated configurations Protoshame and Protopride to distinguish these emotions from the more complex forms that involve both the three- and six-point logics. Focusing on the consequences of the hedonic values of Protoshame and Protopride offers an explanation of why humans (and probably other creatures) possess emotions centering on issues of rank. In general, rank is positively correlated with reproductive success. Because Protoshame, an aversive emotion, is elicited by subordinance, while Protopride, a rewarding emotion, is elicited by dominance, individuals capable of experiencing these emotions would have been motivated to seek out higher rank. Hence, individuals who possessed the capacity and proclivity to feel these emotions would have had greater reproductive success than those who lacked these traits. Relatedly, the existence of the respective displays is a consequence of simple economics: It is always "cheaper" to signal superiority or inferiority than to demonstrate it in a contest, and hence selection favored individuals who experienced both the motivational and the communicative aspects of these emotions.[8]

PROTOSHAME, RANK, AND DECISION MAKING

The decision-making functions of Protoshame can be summarized as follows: First, Protoshame calls Ego's attention to a particular facet of his relationship with his surroundings by informing him that he is in an inferior position relative to an Other, i.e., it tags a decision domain. Second, Protoshame directs increased attention to cues indicative of relative social standing. Third, Protoshame makes it extremely aversive for Ego to be in the subordinate position. This can affect action in two ways: (a) Ego may regularly seek to avoid being subordinate so as to preclude an aversive emotional experience, i.e., the emotion may bias anticipatory decisions; or (b) if Ego finds himself in a subordinate position, he may seek to get out of it as soon as possible so as to end the aversive emotional experience, i.e., the emotion may bias reactive decisions. Both (a) and (b) are reinforced by Protopride, as Ego will both regularly seek to be dominant and regularly seek to invert a relationship in which he is subordinate so as to attain the rewarding experience of Protopride.

We can express the above account in terms of Protoshame's influence on cost-benefit assessments as follows: If utility is defined in terms of fitness, then, because subordination is inversely correlated with reproductive success, the more that Ego is subordinate, the more he should discount costs and focus on benefits when considering actions which may improve his social standing. The individual at the bottom of the dominance hierarchy, facing a high probability of leaving no descendants, should be willing to take large risks to improve his situation, while the individual at the top of the hierarchy, being very likely to leave many descendants, should be relatively conservative about risk. Emotions are calibrated to the intensity of the situation that arouses them; hence mild subordination elicits mild Protoshame, while intense subordination elicits intense Protoshame. As a result, the influence of Protoshame on the relative salience of cost and benefit is proportional to, and reflective of, the degree to which the eliciting event indicates a decline in Ego's probable future fitness.

Before going on to consider the analogous influence of Shame, we must pause to consider why the experience of Protoshame leads to flight in some situations and aggression in others. We can distinguish two types of subordination events. In one, Ego is subordinate purely by virtue of his own inadequacy (think of missing easy shots in a tennis match). In the other, a condition commonly labeled humiliation, Ego is subordinate because the Other has actively revealed Ego's inadequacy (think of the tennis player who toys with his opponent, then resoundingly defeats him). When Ego feels Protoshame in the first type of situation, he is made aware that, by virtue of features of himself, he now occupies a lower position in the hierarchy. Unlike a dispassionate recognition of this fact, the subjective experience of Protoshame forces Ego to attend to this change in status and to take appropriate action: Since his subordination is a result of his own failings, the best tactic is to withdraw from interaction in a headlong fashion (i.e., "blind" to obstacles or other costs) before his position worsens. In contrast, when Ego feels Protoshame in the second type of situation, he is forced to recognize that an Other has used features of Ego to lower his position in the hierarchy. Once again, emotions function to make these events highly salient and motivationally significant. When Ego feels Protoshame in such a situation, the possibility exists that, since his subordination is only partly due to his own failings, and partly due to the actions of the Other, attacking the individual who dominates him may invert the dominance relationship. Moreover, in this situation, Protoshame, acting as a proxy for the damage done to Ego through a reduction in his future fitness prospects, is experienced as harm. Recognizing that an Other is responsible for that harm elicits a second emotion, one attuned to transgressions against Ego, namely anger.[9]

The principal action tendency associated with anger is the attempt to inflict harm on a transgressor. In addition, as noted earlier, like Shame, anger leads to an indifference to risk. As a consequence of these two features, individuals who experience anger are likely to inflict significant harm on a transgressor, even at great cost to themselves. By increasing the costs incurred by the transgressor, Ego's anger makes such transgressions less attractive for the Other, and thus generally helps to protect Ego against further transgressions. Moreover, the more intense the reaction, and the lower the threshold for elicitation, the greater this prophylactic effect, and the more likely it is that minor transgressions will provide a learning opportunity for Others, whereafter they will refrain from transgressing against Ego (Frank 1989; cf. Daly and Wilson 1988). Rivalrous interactions that elicit both Protoshame and anger are likely to produce particularly dramatic responses, as the two emotions have a compound effect in decreasing the salience of potential costs. Note that because the antidote to subordinance is dominance, Ego may seek to exploit the Other's failings to assert his own superiority, a tactic that is likely to elicit both Protoshame and anger in the Other. As a consequence of these two effects, Ego's actions will produce a similar indifference to cost in the Other, and will prompt similar reactive aggression from the Other. Furthermore, because anger and Protoshame increase the salience of the eliciting stimuli, both Ego and Other become acutely sensitive to the possibility that one another's actions constitute further transgressions and attempts at subordination. This heightened sensitivity causes an increase in both the disproportionate nature and the certainty of the two actors' reactions to one another. The net result is often a runaway escalation of aggressive interaction such as that which claimed Rustam's life (cf. Retzinger 1991).

SHAME, CONFORMITY, AND DECISION MAKING

Although Protoshame and anger can explain why participants in trivial altercations may come to disregard the risks of escalating conflict, they cannot account for the significance of an audience in exacerbating such confrontations.

Likewise, these emotions cannot explain the indifference to risk that is charac-teristic of a wide variety of behaviors that we might label "showing off" (think of teenagers in a fast car). Rather, these situations pertain to the phylogenetically more recent facet of Shame, the six-point logic. Importantly, the six-point logic revolves around Ego's assessment of an Other's assessment of Ego. As noted earlier, I believe that this logic arose in response to fitness advantages offered by participation in cooperative endeavors. Sensitivity to Others' expectations, and motivation to conform to them, leads Ego to adhere to standards for behavior. In turn, this makes Ego a reliable and thus desirable member of cooperative groups. Hence, an existing mechanism, initially designed to promote rank-striving, was, through the addition of another cognitive level, co-opted to promote conformity. Note, however, that while the intrinsic goals of this newer aspect of Shame differ from those of Protoshame, the implications for decision making are similar: By highlighting stimuli indicative of negative social evaluation, and thus marking potential group rejection resulting from Ego's failure to live up to standards, the six-point logic of Shame is also marking a drop in Ego's probable future fitness, since exclusion from cooperative ventures is costly. Accordingly, if Ego be-lieves that Others think poorly of her, it is adaptive to adopt desperate measures to try to improve her standing. At still higher levels of intensity, the individual may flee as soon as possible to decrease the social prominence of her failure, then search ardently for an opportunity to redeem herself before the group. In ex-treme instances the individual may emigrate, seeking a new group that knows nothing of her past failure. In all cases, as is true of Protoshame, the intensity of the emotion, a marker of the severity of the threat to future fitness, corresponds to the degree of indifference to risk and focus on benefit.

Note that the above position implies that the larger the audience, the more significant any failures or successes will be, since such events will have a greater impact on Ego's opportunities to participate in cooperative activities. In accord with this prediction, both introspection and ethnographic observations from Bengkulu (Fessler, unpublished data) suggest that the intensity of Shame or Pride experienced is in part contingent on the size of the audience present. We can therefore expect that the degree to which failures result in indifference to risk will be in part dependent on the number of witnesses. Likewise, because the strength of the Shame response elicited by being subordinated by a rival is partly a product of the number of witnesses, humiliation before a larger audience will elicit more intense anger, with correspondingly greater indifference to risk and motivation to harm the transgressor. Finally, this perspective can also explain why the composition of the audience affects the intensity of emotions elicited by failure or success: If the proclivity to attend to the judgments of an audience is an adaptation selected for by the benefits of inclusion in cooperative endeavors, then it follows that the influence of the audience on the intensity of emotions elicited will in part be a function of (a) the degree to which the audience is com-posed of potential collaborators, and/or (b) the value of those potential collaborators. Hence, both peers, who are likely collaborators, and superiors, who are valuable potential collaborators, can constitute highly evocative audiences. Conversely, individuals who belong to a disparate social group (i.e., different culture, ethnicity, etc.), or with whom Ego is unlikely to have future interactions (i.e., inhabitants of an area that Ego is visiting only temporarily), constitute far less evocative audiences. In sum, via the intensity of the emotions elicited, both the size and the composition of an audience can influence decision making in the wake of public events.

PREDICTION, SELF-ESTEEM, AND THE INTERPRETATION OF EVENTS

I have argued that the various facets of Shame adjust the salience of risk and benefit in response to events that indicate probable changes in future prospects. However, this explanation ignores the problem of the interpretation of the meaning of any given event. How do individuals gauge the severity of events, i.e., how are they able to calibrate the appropriate intensity of emotional response, along with the concomitant biasing of cost-benefit assessments? Importantly, the significance of any given event is in large part a product of the probable future in which its consequences will play out. Just as any given expense will loom larger for an individual with meager resources than for an individual with abundant resources, so too will any current setback loom larger for an individual with poor prospects than for an individual with excellent prospects. Accordingly, to gauge the meaning of an event, individuals must be able to predict their probable future prospects independent of that event. Such a forecast must then be updated with each passing event, and yet this updating must be buffered, as long-term prospects are best determined on the basis of long-term experience.

An organism's local environment often remains relatively stable over the course of its lifetime. The task of predicting the future can thus be seen as derived from the larger task of learning what sort of a world it is that one inhabits.[10] The optimal way to identify the principal stable characteristics of one's environment, those that will best predict the future, is to sum past experience. The longer and more inclusive this summation, the more likely it is that dominant trends or features of the local environment will be distinguished from uncharacteristic chance events, and hence the more accurate any resulting forecast is likely to be. We can thus expect decision-making organisms to possess some means of tallying experiences in order to learn what sort of world they inhabit. This process establishes a baseline from which the meaning of any ongoing event is derived. In turn, as immediate events pass into past experiences, they are incorporated into the continuing construction of the portrait of the local world.

Earlier, I described Shame as the subjective marker of social failure. The above discussion suggests that the degree to which individuals identify an event as constituting such a failure should be contingent on past experience.

Consistent with this perspective, clinical evidence indicates that interindividual differences in the ease with which Shame is elicited are largely the product of differing life histories (Lewis 1987). Significantly, successes and failures seem to have a cumulative effect — repeated (and early) failures lower the Shame threshold (Miller 1985). Moreover, both clinical and experimental results indicate that the propensity to experience Shame is negatively correlated with *self-esteem* (Retzinger 1991; Miller 1985). Self-esteem can be conceptualized as the generalized assessment of self as relatively successful or unsuccessful, a summation of the events that constitute Ego's self-perceived successes and failures to date.[11] Self-esteem influences whether events are seen as constituting relatively greater or lesser successes or failures, and it is this which determines the ease of elicitation of Shame. In turn, because Shame affects the salience of risk and benefit during decision making, by setting the threshold for experiencing Shame, self-esteem indirectly determines the likelihood that benefit will be maximized or risk will be avoided. Self-esteem thus operates to create a consistent situation-sensitive strategy, linking life experience to immediate decisions. For illustrative purposes we can represent two polar cases as follows:

poor performance to date → low self-esteem → low Shame threshold →
more frequent Shame experiences → more frequent use of benefit maximizing strategy
VERSUS
good performance to date → high self-esteem → high Shame threshold →
less frequent Shame experiences → more frequent use of risk avoiding strategy

Because both social position and social acceptance are determinative of fitness, the motivational system that regulates risk-taking decision making in light of future prospects should be sensitive to each of these factors. We have already seen that Shame, the most proximate component of the system, can be elicited by either subordination or audience disapproval. Correspondingly, self-esteem, the modulator of Shame, is determined both by one's relative social standing over time (Barkow 1989) and by one's history of social inclusion or exclusion (Leary and Downs 1995).[12] In broad evolutionary terms, a proclivity for risk taking can be understood as an adaptive preference for immediate resources and reproductive opportunities, a preference that is itself the product of early life experiences which conveyed the message that the local environment is unfavorable and/or unpredictable (Hill et al. 1997).[13] I suggest that, together, self-esteem and the Shame/Pride constellation constitute the evolved psychological mechanism whereby such adaptive preferences are determined and instantiated in humans.

In contradiction to the pattern proposed above, a large body of research indicates that individuals with low self-esteem tend to be conservative, avoiding situations that might expose them to negative feedback, while those with high self-esteem are more adventurous, seeking out opportunities to exercise their talents. Note, however, that such strategies involve choices that are made far in advance of action — when it is possible to make decisions in anticipation of particular emotions rather than under their influence, risk avoidance is adopted by the very same individuals who are most prone to experience Shame, the emotion that creates an indifference to risk. The influence of self-esteem is thus paradoxical — low self-esteem leads to both advance risk avoidance and spontaneous risk taking. This paradox may be indicative of the imperfect nature of the system. Because each adaptation is a response to particular selective pressures, there is no intrinsic reason why adaptations will be completely complementary with one another. Instead of viewing organisms as perfectly integrated wholes, it is best to see any given adaptation as functioning within an environment which is in part composed of the other features of the organism. Hence, while selection will preclude adaptations that consistently interfere with one another, compromises may occur in cases where different adaptations are each sufficiently valuable, and sufficiently disparate from one another, so that the costs incurred (when they occasionally interfere with one another) are outweighed by the benefits accrued (when they are able to function independently). In the present case, on the one hand, it is often adaptive to be able to plan actions using complex multistage extrapolations into the future. On the other hand, it is also adaptive for failure to be experienced as aversive, and for failure to lead to a devaluation of future prospects and a discounting of risk. However, these two types of adaptations may sometimes interfere with one another — the human ability to play out scenarios far in advance can undermine the adaptive influence of emotions. From the perspective of maximizing fitness, individuals with a history of failure should seek out, and seize, every opportunity for advancement. However, humans, able to see far down the road, and having learned how painful failure can be, may cautiously avoid such opportunities long before they arise. Note, however, that this evolutionarily counterproductive approach operates only when behavior is influenced by the anticipation of emotion, rather than by emotion itself — when dramatic, future-altering events occur, actual emotions are elicited, and these are often able to override the strategies developed through cognitively complex anticipatory planning. Hence, the interference of long-range extrapolation with the adaptive functioning of self-esteem fades when critical turning points arise.[14]

PATTERNED DIFFERENCES IN RISK TAKING

Earlier, I noted that Daly and Wilson have argued that impulsive aggression should be most likely to occur among young males, as, in the environment in which humans evolved, young males had the most to gain, and the least to lose, from such behavior. Indeed, this reasoning pertains to all forms of risk taking, a prediction supported by insurance statistics on young males' involvement in accidents (Gardner 1993). We can account for this pattern in terms of the proximate mechanisms described above, as follows: Sexual maturation is accompanied by a profound change in Ego's position in the social structure. Unlike the child, the adolescent is evaluated according to many of the same standards of skill, attractiveness, and social facility that are applied to adults. Given the adolescent's lack of experience in the larger adult arena, it is inevitable that even a relatively successful adolescent will experience more failures than was true earlier in life. Hence, we can expect that adolescents as a category should suffer reduced self-esteem, and should experience Shame more often than either children or adults, and there are some indications that this is the case (Reimer 1996). As time passes, a social sorting out occurs such that an individual's life trajectory is likely to stabilize, with a corresponding stabilization in self-esteem and a decrease in emotional oscillations. As a consequence, for all but the least successful individuals, risk taking declines. This change is also adaptive, as accumulating successes decrease the uncertainty of the future, with the result that risk taking becomes increasingly unattractive (Gardner 1993).

Gambling with one's life is largely the domain of young males. This is in keeping with the higher variance in reproductive success among males than among females, and hence the higher stakes to be won or lost in social competition — in our evolutionary past, for males, the issue was whether or not it would be possible to mate; for females, the issue was whether or not it would be possible to mate well. Accordingly, the same developmental logic that makes increased risk taking rational for adolescent males applies to adolescent females as well, but females should gamble with their reproductive resources, rather than with their lives. Consistent with this perspective, we see an increase in female risk-taking behavior at adolescence, with many of the actions taken involving sexual or other adventurous behaviors which, while potentially putting future social and reproductive progress in jeopardy, do not carry the same risk of death as many male pursuits. Furthermore, like males, females are subject to the life history logic which, in the past, made dramatically increased risk taking rational for those individuals who, having a troubled background, were likely to possess poor future prospects as well. Consistent with this view, girls who have a history of victimization and deprivation suffer from low self-esteem and, upon reaching adolescence, become sexually active sooner, and become markedly more promiscuous, than girls with a history of stable, caring family relationships (reviewed in Belsky et al. 1991). Hence, the same Shame/self-esteem system seems to influence the salience of risk and benefit in both males and females, although sexually dimorphic mechanisms which are beyond the scope of this paper regulate the content, rather than the relative degree, of risk taking.

THE NEUROCHEMICAL BASIS OF SELF-ESTEEM

If the system posited above is an evolved adaptation, we can expect to find an underlying species-typical physiological correlate. Recalling that the roots of this system predate human cognitive complexity, we begin first with nonhuman primate models. Experimental manipulations in primates reveal that adverse early experiences result in subnormal levels of brain serotonin, a neurotransmitter (Rosenblum et al. 1994). In rhesus monkeys, low serotonin levels predict early death or disappearance (Higley et al. 1996). Young males with low serotonin are more likely to "initiate . . . aggression, often at inappropriate targets such as high-ranking subjects or much larger adult males, and once aggression has started, it is more likely to escalate to injurious intensity" (Higley et al. 1996, p. 542). Such males are also more likely to risk their lives in other ways, such as repeatedly entering baited traps (Higley et al. 1996, p. 542). In keeping with the position that (a) risk taking should be inversely proportional to future prospects and (b) rank is a principal determinant of future fitness, dominant adult male vervet monkeys have nearly double the concentration of blood serotonin of subordinate adult males, and changes in rank are accompanied by corresponding changes in serotonin levels (Raleigh et al. 1984).

In humans, there is an inverse correlation between adverse early experience and the density of serotonin receptors (Pine et al. 1996). A sizable body of clinical evidence supports a strong connection between subnormal serotonergic activity and impulsivity, including impulsive aggression (Coccaro 1989). Relatedly, consider the subjective and physiological correlates of depression: Depression is associated with an assessment of the self as worthless, and Shame appears to play a central role in the disorder (Lewis 1987). Contrary to conventional portraits of depressives as passive, depression can be associated with significant anger (Fava et al. 1993) and even homicide (Malmquist 1995), and is notably linked with pathological gambling, sexual compulsions, and other impulse control disorders (Hollander and Wong 1995) — behaviors that exemplify the risk indifferent/benefit maximizing bias that Shame induces. Likewise, depression is a precursor to suicide, a behavior that can be viewed as a maladaptive extreme outgrowth of insensitivity to risk: Suicidal individuals are generally blind to the fear of suffering and death that others feel, and instead focus solely on how their deaths will solve a multitude of problems.[15] Depression in general and suicidality in particular, are associated with inadequate serotonergic activity, and pharmacological interventions that effectively increase such activity are the principal means of treatment.[16] These same therapies mitigate both associated anger attacks (Fava et al. 1993) and the impulse control disorders noted earlier (Hollander and Wong 1995). Taken together, the above findings suggest that serotonergic activity is involved in the tracking of experience, the adjustment of risk-taking behavior, and the generation of affectively laden assessments of self. At present it is unclear exactly how serotonergic activity maps onto subjective experience. However, since significant changes in serotonin levels apparently occur over a period of hours, days, or weeks, rather than seconds, it is likely that serotonergic activity is more closely linked to the experience of self-esteem than to the experience of those emotions that both contribute to and are modulated by self-esteem.

While the nuanced subjective manifestations of human serotonergic activity are doubtlessly related to our neural complexity, it is worth noting that serotonin levels appear to be linked with dominance in a variety of vertebrates.[17] Furthermore, because evolutionary processes generally operate through modification rather than innovation, it is likely that this system predates even the relatively unsophisticated social behavior characteristic of dominance relations in these animals. In all creatures, social or not, a prerequisite for reproduction is survival, and a prerequisite for survival is food. Serotonin is endogenously constructed using tryptophan, an amino acid derived from dietary sources. Accordingly, reduction in food consumption (indirectly) causes decreases in levels of available serotonin. Consistent with the role described above for serotonin, in humans, birds, and, I suspect, all vertebrates, food deprivation results in increases in impulsivity in general, and in impulsive risk taking in particular (cf. Keys et al. 1950; Fachinelli et al. 1989). Hence, it appears that a primitive decision-making function of the serotonergic system is the calibration of risk taking in light of future prospects calculated on the basis of recent food availability. Apparently, as sociality evolved, social position was added to food availability as an index of future prospects. Thus, the evolution of hominid cooperative behavior probably involved the addition of a third layer, the regulation of risk taking in light of social acceptance, to an already ancient system.

IMPLICATIONS

Like the villagers in Bengkulu who sought to explain Rustam's murder, observers the world over are quick to note the correlation between an actor's emotional state and the action taken. Moreover, such explication is not limited to others' behavior, for individuals often retrospectively explain their own conduct with reference to the emotions experienced at the time ("I did it because I was mad," etc.). Although it is likely that such analyses are often ultimately correct, they nonetheless dichotomize decision making as either influenced by emotion, or not. However, given emotion's central role as the motivator of action (recall the discussion of "drives"), it is unlikely that normal individuals are ever completely free of the influence of emotion: Victims of brain injuries that interfere with emotional experience become catatonically apathetic. They make no decisions, in part because no option appears any better than any other option (cf. Damasio and van Hoesen 1983). Nevertheless, it is important to distinguish between the more generalized motivational role of emotions as goals/anti-goals and those specific influences on decision making which particular emotions exercise when they are elicited.

The powerful influence of active emotions on decision making is often visible only to observers or in retrospect — during an emotional event, we do not experience some options as highlighted by the given emotion, rather we experience them simply as self-evidently better.[18] This is not an accident. For several reasons, the transparency of emotional biasing enormously augments emotions' power to shape behavior. First, by making some options appear obviously better, rather than merely better-in-light-of- how-you're-feeling-now, the transparency of emotions' influence facilitates decision making, since anything which introduces ambiguity at critical junctures delays the process and lessens the certainty of the outcome. Second, as we saw in the discussion of self-esteem, transparency is particularly important in a complex creature capable of both remembering distant suffering and planning far into the future. From an evolutionary perspective, the final objective in all decisions must be fitness, not the avoidance of suffering. Relatedly, many situations that maximize fitness may require forsaking short-term gains in favor of long-term benefits. If emotions were unable to dictate, both powerfully and transparently, the biasing of options, organisms might often make choices that were in their personal and/or short-term best interests, but not in their genetic and/or long-term best interests (cf. Frank 1989). An individual with poor prospects would be ill-served by an emotion that either (a) only weakly highlighted the benefits to be gained by risk taking, or (b) strongly highlighted those benefits, but did so in a fashion whereby the source of the highlighting was evident. Presumably, in the distant past, some young males, upon being humiliated by their rivals, were able to see beyond experiences of Shame and anger to the agony that conflict or other dramatic action might entail. These farsighted individuals did not take risks, did not gain glory, and did not pass on to us the genes for such attenuated emotions. Likewise, presumably, in the distant past some young males were tempted to take risks in such situations, but were able to recognize that their impulses arose from ephemeral emotional states, and hence they refrained from acting. These introspective individuals did not take risks, did not gain glory, and did not pass on to us the genes for subjectively opaque emotions. We are the descendants of those for whom emotionally induced biases were both compelling and transparent.

Our emotional inheritance shapes our decisions on a daily basis. Are our decisions more rational, in the economic sense of maximizing utility, or less as a consequence of this influence? The answer depends on several factors. First, as I have argued throughout this chapter, emotions are premised upon discrete utilities which include both the overarching ultimate goal of fitness maximization and a specific proximate goal, such as rank striving, whereby the former is served. Importantly, these utilities may differ from those which an individual consciously holds when not experiencing a given emotional state. It is this discrepancy that has led many philosophical traditions to view emotions as "irrational," since emotions may result in behavior that is counterproductive from the perspective of self-consciously formulated personal agendas. Hence, emotions may often be economically rational only in light of the change in utilities which they themselves entail. Second, even if we limit our evaluation of economic rationality to those utilities upon which emotions are premised, emotions may still result in irrational decisions as a consequence of the discrepancies between our current world and that in which the emotions were designed to operate. Shame and anger led Rustam and his rivals into violent conflict despite the fact that the "winners" of the confrontation gained only imprisonment. Had they been members of a small, acephalous band of foragers, rather than citizens of a nation-state possessing a designated police force and judiciary, their actions might have resulted in heightened social position and the preclusion of future transgressions.

ACKNOWLEDGMENTS

I thank the following individuals for their input: Jon Haidt, Roy D'Andrade, Jim Moore, Peter Biella, Paul Rozin, Joe Henrich, Alan Fiske, Rob Boyd, and Klaus Scherer.

NOTES

1   This paper presents my own speculations on shame and pride and, more broadly, on the relationship between emotion and decision making. Space constraints preclude extensive citation —for a review of the literature on emotion and decision making, see Lerner and Keltner (1999).

2   The influence of emotion on memory may operate via a labeling process wherein the emotions associated with events constitute tags that facilitate both storage and retrieval, a possibility supported by the key role the limbic system plays in learning (cf. LeDoux 1996).

3   In addition to constraining choices to a given category of outcomes, some emotions may also affect decision making by placing constraints on the search process that evaluates and/or generates choices. It seems likely that emotions such as fear and anger lead individuals to evaluate only a small number of options that address the given task, and to choose the first option evaluated that does better than previous options on the central criterion (cf. Todd, this volume). This effect would be consistent with the time urgency associated with these emotions. In contrast, however, some emotions seem to lead to the extensive review of a wide range of options that could address the given task. For example, although Gigerenzer (this volume) and others have noted that romantic love leads to a cessation of the search for a mate, at another level of analysis, a hallmark of romantic love is obsessive evaluation of a wide variety of means whereby the individual might attract and retain the prospective partner. A similar preoccupation with the evaluation of multiple possibilities also seems to characterize grief. In both cases, the particular relationship with the world marked by the emotion is such as to demand efficacy rather than rapidity in the response (in the case of grief, efficacy can be defined in terms of the prevention of future losses of the same type, i.e., the review of possible pasts is a learning process which benefits future action). Hence, it appears that to understand the effect of an emotion on the evaluation of options within the given domain, we must first consider the type of situation that the emotion is designed to address.

Daniel M.T. Fessler

4   Throughout this chapter, the term "Ego" is used in the anthropological sense (i.e.,
        the focal actor in the given discussion), not in the psychological sense (i.e., a com-
        ponent of the mind).

5   J. Lerner and associates have recently demonstrated that, relative to others, indi-
        viduals who are prone to anger tend to discount the likelihood of negative out-
        comes (J. Lerner, pers. comm.).

6   I include modifications of gait in this category. The bent-kneed, shuffling gait re-
        duces an individual's apparent size. However, it is not clear that the stiff-legged
        gait *increases* apparent size. Instead, the stiff-legged gait may be a consequence of
        Darwin's principle of antithesis, i.e., it may simply be a way of making it clear that
        one is *not* bending one's knees (J. Moore, pers. comm.).

7   Some forms of submissiveness involve active attention-getting, as in posterior
        presenting among many primates and "reassurance-seeking" among chimpan-
        zees. However, this does not detract from the observation that avoiding attracting
        attention is often a way of being submissive.

8   Economic analysis can also be applied to blushing, the only part of the Protoshame
        display for which there is no opposite in Protopride: Consider individual A who,
        through his behavior, claims superiority over individual B. For A, following up on
        the claim to superiority through actual aggression entails the costs of the energy
        and risk involved in the conflict but promises the benefit of definitively achieving
        the superior position. In contrast, for B, who acknowledges his own inferiority,
        conflict entails the costs of expended energy and exposure to risk (where the latter
        is likely to be greater than for A), yet there are no probable benefits. Accordingly,
        A should be willing to engage in conflict, while it is in B's best interests to ensure
        that conflict does not take place. A should be happy to forgo the costs of conflict if
        he can be certain that B acknowledges his superiority. However, B's assessment of
        their respective positions can only be communicated via behavior, and behavior is
        susceptible to manipulation. The potential for manipulation is high in Protoshame,
        as gaze, posture, and visibility are factors that are easy for mammals to control. For
        A, this means that B's signals are not as reliable as physical victory. Hence, even
        when B behaves in a subordinate manner, A may suspect a ruse and attack anyway.
        From B's perspective this makes the Protoshame display a risky enterprise, for, as
        is true of many submissive behaviors, the display makes it difficult for B to defend
        himself. What B needs in order to preserve the utility of the display is an additional
        signal which is unequivocal (or "honest"), one which A can accept as indicating
        his definitive superiority, and which therefore obviates the need for conflict. To be
        unequivocal, the additional signal must be involuntary. To be useful, the signal
        must be conspicuous so as to ensure that A notices it. Blushing fulfills both criteria
        admirably (for more on blushing as appeasement, see Stein and Bouwer [1997]
        and citations therein). Critics might object that blushing is difficult to see in people
        with very dark skin, and early hominids, living in an equatorial climate, undoubt-
        edly had dark skin. However, many present-day equatorial peoples have skin that
        is not so dark as to prevent visible blushing, and it is quite possible that the same
        was true of early hominids. Lastly, the above argument suggests that, across spe-
        cies, honest signals should be more common in appeasement displays than in
        threat displays. The specific phylogenetic roots of blushing, however, have yet to
        be investigated.

9   In addition to labeling the eliciting social condition, *humiliation* also refers to feeling-anger-because-Other-made-Ego-feel-shame. However, rather than being a discrete emotion produced by selection, this experience is an inevitable consequence of (a) the nature of Shame as a self-informing index of social standing, and (b) the relationship between rank and access to subjectively valued resources.

10   More broadly, behavioral and developmental plasticity are contingent on the ability to identify the particular circumstances characteristic of one's own surroundings, in contrast to the generic circumstances characteristic of species-typical surroundings.

11   Note that this formulation does not entail the formidable task that Ego store discrete records of all of her life experiences. Rather, self-esteem can be thought of as a running tally, with new experiences simply modifying the existing measure without necessarily being stored as independent records. Relatedly, because successes or failures are subjectively experienced via shame or pride, we can think of self-esteem as the net impact or residue of all Pride-eliciting events minus the net impact or residue of all Shame-eliciting events.

12   In a number of publications, Leary and his associates argue that self-esteem is both a trait (i.e., relatively stable over time) and a state (i.e., elicited by ongoing events). I suggest that the state of self-esteem is the cognized or articulated facet of an individual's current emotional state, particularly with regard to those emotions, such as Shame and Pride, that revolve around self-assessment.

13   Hill et al. (1997) argue that this preference is the product of a set of beliefs about how predictable, and how favorable, the future will be. This approach is congruent with some ethnographic findings. For example, in describing the violent conflict associated with the "street" culture of a poverty-stricken U.S. inner city, Anderson (1994) notes that "the most fearsome youths . . . are uncertain about how long they are going to live and believe they could die violently at any time . . . nothing intimidates them" (p. 94). However, the ethnographic literature also supplies many examples which are contrary to Hill et al.'s emphasis on cognitive schemas: Lightfoot's (1997) affluent young suburban informants risk their lives behind the wheel despite being quite optimistic about their futures. Moreover, Anderson (1994) himself explains the "street" proclivity for violence not with regard to conscious calculations about the future, but rather in terms of attempts to protect and increase self-esteem. It appears that conscious beliefs about the future influence, but do not wholly determine, the relative salience of risk or benefit. Hence, although Hill et al. (1997) take account of a number of personality factors, the authors overemphasize the contribution of abstract beliefs in decision making. This may be due to their methodology, as they rely entirely on questionnaires, yet, because decision making is importantly influenced by emotion, measures that are removed from real-world social interaction may not fully reflect actors' actual proclivities. Analogously, in assessing self-esteem, investigators must be careful to distinguish between actual self-assessment and patterned self-presentation, particularly as individuals who occupy unstable worlds may adopt an aggressively positive self-presentation as a tactic to avoid exploitation (cf. Anderson 1994).

14   In contrast to the prevailing opinion in psychology, which holds that low self-esteem is linked with violence, Baumeister et al. (1996) have argued that this is true of high self-esteem. As is often the case in such debates, both perspectives are cor-

rect. The authors point out that when an individual with high self-esteem experiences an event that is dramatically incongruent with his positive image of self, he
is likely to resort to drastic action to try to compensate. We can understand this pattern as follows: A significant difference between persons with high and low
self-esteem is the interpretation of events — whereas persons with high self-esteem are likely to interpret events in a manner which portrays them as successful or
blameless, those with low self-esteem are likely to interpret events as reflecting
poorly on them. These tendencies influence the probable frequency and character
of Shame experiences. A person with high self-esteem will only experience
Shame when his failure is a dramatic and incontestable one — any smaller or more
ambiguous failures are likely to be reinterpreted in such a fashion as to preclude
Shame. High self-esteem individuals will therefore experience Shame relatively
rarely, yet, in those instances when they do experience it, the Shame will be extremely intense. Because the degree to which benefit is focused on and risk is ignored is a function of the intensity of Shame, this means that when high
self-esteem individuals feel Shame, they will dramatically pursue high-stakes
gambles. In contrast, individuals with low self-esteem will frequently experience
Shame, sometimes at a low intensity, sometimes at a high intensity. Accordingly,
they will more frequently adopt a benefit-maximizing strategy in critical situations. Charted across the lifetime, we can therefore expect pervasive but fluctuating impulsive risk taking from those with low self-esteem, and much more
sporadic, "out of character" bursts of impulsive risk taking from those with high
self-esteem. Because much violence is a form of impulsive risk taking, we can
thus expect a greater lifetime total of violent acts from individuals with low
self-esteem, while individuals with high self-esteem may occasionally erupt in an
explosive fashion.

15   Presumably, this "design flaw" in Shame-induced risk indifference has persisted
because there is little pressure to correct it: Imagine a mutation that modified
Shame by adding the qualifier "take desperate measures, but stop short of killing
yourself." Because this mutation would only come into play in those extreme circumstances in which Ego had failed profoundly, the individuals whom it would
save would be those with the least likelihood of passing on their genes. Furthermore, to the extent that such a ceiling on risk indifference precluded engaging in
life-threatening but potentially fitness-enhancing behavior, such individuals
would be less likely to be able to improve their fitness prospects. Accordingly, the
mutation could occur and die out repeatedly, with the result that most individuals
at any one time would lack this safety feature.

16   A prominent psychologist told me that, in his own experience, taking Prozac, a se-
rotonin-specific antidepressant "diminished the gap between who I am and who I
want to be," i.e., it increased his sense of self-worth.

17   The picture here is somewhat complex, as it is unclear to what degree the
aggressivity associated with dominance and high levels of serotonin in non-mam-
mals can be equated with the *impulsive* aggression characteristic of mammals having low levels of serotonin.

18   Given the often conflicting goals of different emotions (love and anger, for example), the surprise is not that we sometimes seem to deviate from a consistent set of
values or objectives, but rather that we are ever able to experience ourselves as
consistent at all!

REFERENCES

Anderson, E. 1994. The code of the streets. *Atl. Monthly* **273**:80–94.

Barkow, J.H. 1989. Darwin, Sex, and Status: Biological Approaches to Mind and Culture. Toronto: Univ. of Toronto Press.

Baumeister, R., J. Boden, and L. Smart. 1996. Relation of threatened egotism to violence and aggression: The dark side of high self-esteem. *Psych. Rev.* **103**:5–33.

Baumeister, R., T. Heatherton, and D. Tice. 1993. When ego threats lead to self-regulation failure: Negative consequences of high self-esteem. *J. Pers. Soc. Psych.* **64**:141–156.

Belsky, J., L. Steinberg, and P. Draper. 1991. Childhood experience, interpersonal development, and reproductive strategy: An evolutionary theory of socialization. *Child Dev.* **62**:647–670.

Coccaro, E. 1989. Central serotonin and impulsive aggression. *Brit. J. Psych.* **155**:52–62.

Daly, M., and M. Wilson. 1988. Homicide. New York: de Gruyter.

Damasio, A., and G. van Hoesen. 1983. Emotional disturbances associated with focal lesions of the limbic frontal lobe. In: Neuropsychology of Human Emotion, ed. K. Heilman and P. Satz, pp. 85–110. New York: Guilford.

Fachinelli, C., S. Sargo, R. Bataller, and E. Rodriguez Echandia. 1989. Effect of 5-HTP and ketanserine on the aggressive reaction induced by food competition in dominant and submissive pigeons *(Columba livia). Behav. Brain Res.* **35**:265–270.

Fava, M., J. Rosenbaum, J. Pava, M. McCarthy, R. Steingard, and E. Bouffides. 1993. Anger attacks in unipolar depression. I. Clinical correlates and response to fluoxetine treatment. *Am. J. Psych.* **150**:1158–1163.

Fessler, D. 1999. Toward an understanding of the universality of second order emotions. In: Beyond Nature or Nurture: Biocultural Approaches to the Emotions, ed. A. Hinton, pp. 75–115. New York: Cambridge Univ. Press.

Frank, R. 1989. Passions within Reason: The Strategic Role of the Emotions. New York: Norton.

Gardner, W. 1993. A life-span rational-choice theory of risk taking. In: Adolescent Risk Taking, ed. N. Bell and R. Bell, pp. 66–83. Newbury Park, CA: Sage.

Higley, J.D., P. Mehlman, S. Higley, B. Fernald, J. Vickers, S. Lindell, D. Taub, S. Suomi, and M. Linnoila. 1996. Excessive mortality in young free-ranging male nonhuman primates with low cerebrospinal fluid 5-hydroxyindoleacetic acid concentrations. *Arch. Gen. Psych.* **53**:537–543.

Hill, E., L. Thomson Ross, and B. Low. 1997. The role of future unpredictability in human risk-taking. *Hum. Nat.* **8**:287–325.

Hollander, E., and C. Wong. 1995. Body dysmorphic disorder, pathological gambling, and sexual compulsions. *J. Clin. Psych.* **56(4)**:7–12.

Keys, A., J. Brozek, A. Henschel, O. Mickelson, and H. Taylor. 1950. The Biology of Human Starvation, vol. 2. Minneapolis: Univ. of Minnesota Press.

Leary, M., and D. Downs. 1995. Interpersonal functions of the self-esteem motive: The self- esteem system as a sociometer. In: Efficacy, Agency, and Self-esteem, ed. M. Kernis, pp. 123–144. New York: Plenum.

LeDoux, J. 1996. The Emotional Brain: The Mysterious Underpinnings of Emotional Life. New York: Simon and Schuster.

Leith, K. Pezza, and R. Baumeister. 1996. Why do bad moods increase self-defeating behavior? Emotion, risk taking, and self-regulation. *J. Pers. Soc. Psych.* **71**: 1250–1267.

Lerner, J., and D. Keltner. 1999. Beyond valence: Toward a model of emotion-specific influences on judgment and choice. *Cogn. Emot.*, in press.

Lewis, H.B. 1987. The role of shame in depression over the life-span. In: The Role of Shame in Symptom Formation, ed. H. Block Lewis, pp. 29–49. Hillsdale, NJ: Erlbaum.

Lightfoot, C. 1997. The Culture of Adolescent Risk Taking. New York: Guilford.

Malmquist, C. 1995. Depression and homicidal violence. *Intl. J. Law Psych.* **16**: 145–162.

Miller, S. 1985. The Shame Experience. Hillsdale, NJ: Analytic Press/Lawrence Erlbaum Assn.

Mineka, S., and S.K. Sutton. 1992. Cognitive biases and the emotional disorders. *Psych. Sci.* **3**:65–69.

Pine, D., G. Wasserman, J. Coplan, J. Fried, Y. Huang, S. Kassier, L. Greenhill, D. Shaffer, and B. Parsons. 1996. Platelet serotonin 2A (5-HT$_{2A}$) receptor characteristics and parenting factors for boys at risk for delinquency: A preliminary report. *Am. J. Psych.* **153**:538–544.

Raleigh, M., M. McGuire, G. Brammer, and A. Yuwiler. 1984. Social and environmental influences on blood serotonin concentrations in monkeys. *Arch. Gen. Psych.* **41**:405–410.

Reimer, M. 1996. "Sinking into the ground": The development and consequences of shame in adolescence. *Dev. Rev.* **16**:321–363.

Retzinger, S. 1991. Violent Emotions: Shame and Rage in Marital Quarrels. Newbury Park, CA: Sage.

Rosenblum, L., J. Coplan, S. Friedman, T. Bassoff, J. Gorman, and M. Andrews. 1994. Adverse early experience affect noradrenergic and serotonergic functioning in adult primates. *Biol. Psych.* **35**:221–227.

Stein, D., and C. Bouwer. 1997. Blushing and social phobia: A neuroethological speculation. *Med. Hypoth.* **49**:101–108.

Tooby, J., and L. Cosmides. 1990. The past explains the present: Emotional adaptation and the structure of ancestral environments. *Ethol. Sociobiol.* **11**:375–424.

12

Simple Reinforcement Learning Models and Reciprocation in the Prisoner's Dilemma Game

Ido Erev[1] and Alvin E. Roth[2]

[1]Faculty of Industrial Engineering and Management, Technion, Haifa 3200, Israel
[2]Dept. of Economics, and Harvard Business School, Harvard University, Cambridge, MA 02138, U.S.A.

ABSTRACT

The observation that subjects can learn to cooperate in repeated prisoner's dilemma games suggests that human players are more sophisticated and/or less self-interested than the predictions of simple adaptive learning models proposed in recent research. The present chapter demonstrates that this phenomenon is consistent with simple reinforcement learning, when learning is over a strategy set that includes a repeated game strategy that allows reciprocation to be learned. A three-parameter model that quantifies this assumption was found to outperform alternative models in predicting the results of the three experiments conducted by Amnon Rapoport and Mowshowitz (1966).

INTRODUCTION

Experimental study of the effect of experience on choice behavior typically reveals a slow adaptive adjustment process. If one of the possible alternatives yields higher return, decision makers slowly learn to prefer it. Recent research (e.g., Roth and Erev 1995; Erev and Roth 1998b; Rapoport et al. 1998; Cheung and Friedman 1999; Tang 1996; Camerer and Ho 1999; Mookerjee and Sopher 1997; Sarin and Vahid 1998; Daniel et al. 1998) demonstrates that this common adjustment process can be approximated by surprisingly simple and general adaptive learning models. For example, Roth et al. (1999) and Erev et al. (1999) show that a two-parameter reinforcement learning model that looks only at immediate reinforcement of simple, one-period actions, and assumes a very low level of rationality, can be used to predict behavior in more than 60 binary choice tasks.

An important exception to this regularity occurs in strategic settings that facilitate reciprocation (situations in which players can coordinate and benefit from mutual cooperation). For example, Anatol Rapoport and Chammah (1965) and subsequently Amnon Rapoport and Mowshowitz (1966) found that in certain two-person iterated prisoner's dilemma (PD) games (e.g., the game presented in Figure 12.2) experience reduces the frequency of selecting the alternative that yields higher payoffs (alternative D). Instead, some players learn to cooperate (the proportion of C choices increases with time).

In a recent paper (Erev and Roth 1998a) we speculated that the latter finding may not reflect a limitation of the reinforcement learning approach (and of the assumption of bounded rationality), rather that the players learn not just from immediate actions (stage-game strategies) but also from repeated game strategies. To capture learning in games, reciprocation strategies must be explicitly modeled. In this chapter, we take a preliminary step toward this goal by proposing and evaluating a reinforcement learning model in which, in addition to stage-game strategies, players can learn a reciprocation strategy. (A fuller treatment would consider more carefully how particular repeated game strategies arise. Here we simply investigate the extent to which reinforcement learning can capture the emergence of cooperation when learning is among repeated game strategies.)

We first summarize recent findings which demonstrate that behavior in simple games can be captured by models of reinforcement learning over actions. A two-parameter model that can account for behavior in matrix games in which players cannot reciprocate is presented. Next, we review the robust regularities observed in previous studies of repeated PD games, focusing on the four experiments conducted by Rapoport and Mowshowitz (1966) to test simple Markovian learning models.

In the third section, we show that a minimal generalization of the two-parameter basic reinforcement learning model, the addition of a "forgiving" reciprocation strategy, can be used to capture Rapoport and Mowshowitz's findings. We estimated the model's three parameters on the basis of the data of Experiment 1 in Rapoport and Mowshowitz (1966) and evaluated it using the results of Experiments 2, 3, and 4. We conclude with a discussion of potential extensions of the model and the main implications of the current results to the study of bounded rationality.

REINFORCEMENT LEARNING

In an earlier paper, we demonstrated the potential of reinforcement learning models (Erev and Roth 1998b). Utilizing a wide set of experiments that study the effect of long experience (more than 100 trials) in bi-matrix games in which players could not reciprocate (Suppes and Atkinson 1960; Malcolm and Lieberman 1965; O'Neill 1987; Rapoport and Boebel 1992; Ochs 1995), we showed that observed behavior is reasonably approximated by simple adaptive learning models. The results obtained from five of these games are summarized in Figure 12.1. Experimental results and equilibrium predictions are presented in the left-hand column. The three right-hand columns present the predictions of three adaptive learning models (one- and three-parameter reinforcement learn- ing models, and a four-parameter generalized fictitious play model). All models appear to capture the major trends in behavior both when it is consistent and in- consistent with equilibrium predictions.

To evaluate the predictive power of the adaptive learning models, we (in Erev and Roth 1998b) calculated the mean squared deviation (MSD) between the mean results and the different predictions. The MSD score of equilibrium was 0.035; however, all learning models considered had MSDs below 0.01. The best model, the three-parameter reinforcement learning, had an MSD of 0.006 when the three parameters were estimated to fit the data, and an MSD of 0.007 when the data of each experiment was predicted by the parameters that best fitted all other games.

More recently (Roth et al. 1999; Erev et al. 1999), we have shown that a two-parameter reinforcement learning model outperforms the three models that we studied earlier. With a single set of (two) parameters, this model captures the 11 games studied by Erev and Roth (1998b), 9 probability learning tasks (Erev et al. 1999), and 40 randomly selected constant sum games (Roth et al. 1999; a "representative sample" in Gigerenzer et al.'s [1991] terminology). This model can be summarized by the following three learning assumptions.

L1 Initial Propensities

Players have an initial propensity to play their stage-game strategies (i.e., their simple one-period actions), and only these strategies. At time $t = 1$ (before any experience has been acquired), the players are indifferent between their strate- gies. Specifically, let $A_n(1)$ be the expected payoff to n if all players choose their strategies randomly, with equal likelihood. Player n's initial propensity to select strategy j equals this expected payoff from random choices, i.e., for each player n,

$$q_{nj}(1) = A_n(1) \tag{12.1}$$

for all pure strategies j.

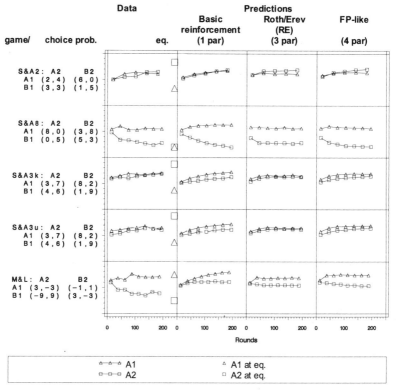

Figure 12.1   Repeated 2 × 2 games (S&A: Suppes and Atkinson 1960; M&L: Malcolm and Lieberman 1965). In the top four games, each payoff unit increases the probability of winning by 1/6 in S&A2, by 1/8 in S&A8, and by 1/10 in S&A3k and S&A3u. In the fifth game, payoffs were directly converted to money. Each cell in the left-hand column presents the experimental results: the proportion of A choices over subjects in each role (grouped in 5 to 8 blocks) as a function of time (200–210) trials in all cases. The three right-hand columns present the models' predictions in the same format. The equilibrium predictions are presented at the right-hand side of the data cells. Adapted from Erev and Roth (1998b).

L2   Average Updating

The propensity of Player n to play strategy j at trial $t + 1$ is a weighted average of the initial propensity $(q_{nj}(1))$ and the average payoff obtained by Player n from playing j in the first t trials $(AVE_{nj}(t))$. The weight of the initial propensity is a function of an initial strength parameter $N(1)$ and the number of time Player n chose strategy j $(C_{nj}(t))$. Specifically,

$$q_{nj}(t+1) = q_{nj}(1)\frac{N(1)/m_n}{C_{nj}(t) + N(1)/m_n} + AVE_{nj}(t)\frac{C_{nj}(t)}{C_{nj}(t) + N(1)/m_n}, \quad (12.2)$$

where m_n is the number of Player n's pure strategies. Thus, $N(1)$ can be naturally interpreted as the weight of the initial propensities, in units of number of experiences with the game (and $N(1)/m_n$ is the number of "initial subjective experiences" with each strategy).

This averaging assumption implies that the updating from trial to trial can be described as follows: If Player n plays his j^{th} pure strategy at time t and receives a payoff x, then the propensity to play strategy j is updated to be:

$$q_{nj}(t+1)= q_{nj}(1)W(t)+x(1-W(t)), \qquad (12.2a)$$

where

$$W(t)= \frac{C_{nj}(t)+N(1)/m_n}{C_{nj}(t)+N(1)/m_n+1}. \qquad (12.2b)$$

This trial-to-trial formulation reveals that the propensity to play strategy j increases with relatively high payoffs ($x > q_{nj}(t)$) and decreases with low payoffs ($x < q_{nj}(t)$). In addition, the updating speed decreases with experience, i.e., $W(t)$ increases with $C_{nj}(t)$.

L3 Exponential Response Rule

Probability, $p_{nj}(t)$, that Player n plays his j^{th} pure strategy at time t is given by:

$$p_{nj}(t)= \frac{EXP\left[q_{nj}(t)\lambda/S_n(t)\right]}{\sum EXP\left[q_{nk}(t)\lambda/S_n(t)\right]}, \qquad (12.3)$$

where the sum is over all of Player n's pure strategies k, λ is a free parameter that determines reinforcement sensitivity, and $S_n(t)$ is a measure of the standard deviation of the payoffs Player n has experienced up to time t. Thus the probability of selecting a strategy increases with the propensity to select it (which increases with the average payoff from past selections). The division by the standard deviation measure implies that noisy reinforcements reduce reinforcement sensitivity (leading toward more uniform choice probabilities).

The standard deviation is estimated as the average absolute difference between the recent payoff (x at trial t) and the accumulated average payoff in the first t trials ($A_n(t)$). Following the logic of Equation 12.2a:

$$S_n(t+1)= S_n(t)W'(t)+|A_n(t)-x|(1-W'(t)), \qquad (12.4)$$

where

$$W'(t)= \frac{t+N(1)}{t+N(1)+1}. \qquad (12.4a)$$

The initial value $S_n(1)$ is the expected distance of the payoff from random choices from the expected payoff given random choice. (Note that the model is defined only for positive $S_n(1)$.)

Average payoff, $A_n(t)$, is calculated in a similar manner:

$$A_n(t+1) = A_n(t)W'(t) + A_n(t)(1 - W'(t)). \qquad (12.5)$$

As noted above, $A_n(1)$ is the expected payoff from random choice.

RECIPROCATION

In contrast to the success of simple reinforcement learning of stage-game strategies in games in which players cannot reciprocate, these models are clearly violated in games that allow for reciprocation. For example, stage-game strategy learning models predict a decrease in cooperation in PD games (cf. Figure 12.2). In contrast to these predictions, previous research on the effect of experience in iterated two-person PD games reveals that players can learn to reciprocate in some games.

An extensive examination of learning under conditions that facilitate reciprocation is provided by Rapoport and Chammah (1965) and by Rapoport and Mowshowitz (1966). Both studies explored behavior in 300 repetitions of PD games. Rapoport and Chammah explored seven games under distinct conditions, while Rapoport and Mowshowitz focused on one of these games and studied the interaction between human and preprogrammed strategies. Since Rapoport and Mowshowitz replicated Rapoport and Chammah's main results and added experiments that facilitate model development and comparison, we focus here on the four experiments conducted by Rapoport and Mowshowitz. Their main results can be summarized by the following five sets of robust behavioral regularities.

Increase in Mutual Cooperation with Time

In Figure 12.2, the left-hand column presents the precentage of trials in which both players cooperated (CC choices) in 6 blocks of 50 trials over the 19 pairs participated in Experiment 1 of the Rapoport and Mowshowitz study. The payoff matrix used in that study is presented on the top of the figure. The results reveal an increase in mutual cooperation over time. The second column shows the predictions of the basic RE model with only two strategies (C = cooperative; D = defect) and with the original parameters, and reveals that the model fails to capture the data. Moreover, the incorrect prediction of a decrease in joint cooperation is robust to the choice of parameters and the specific variant of the model: all the reinforcement learning models we considered (in Erev and Roth 1998b) predicted a drop in cooperation when the only strategies are "C" and "D." The third and fourth columns are simulations of the models developed and discussed below (see section on MODELING RECIPROCATION), which enlarge the set of strategies players may learn.

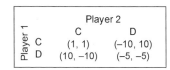

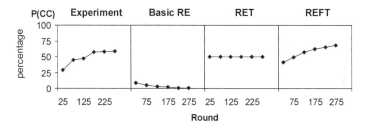

Figure 12.2 The prisoner's dilemma game studied by Rapoport and Mowshowitz (1966). The bottom panel displays the proportion of mutual cooperation (the CC [mutual] outcomes in 6 blocks of 50 trials) in Experiment 1 of Rapoport and Mowshowitz (1966) (left), and the relevant predictions of three models: the basic two-parameter model, the extension that assumes a Tit-for-Tat (TFT) strategy (RET), and the extension that assumes a forgiving TFT strategy (REFT).

Large Between-pair Variance

The first panel of Figure 12.3 presents the distribution of the proportion of cooperation (C) over the 300 trials summed across the 38 participants (Rapoport and Mowshowitz, Experiment 1). The results reveal extremely large variance. In fact, with the exception of a mode on 90–100%, the distribution is almost uniform.

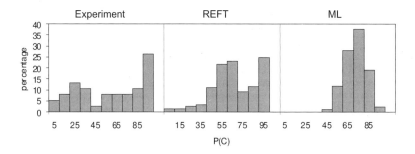

Figure 12.3 Distribution of C choices for all the subjects in Experiment 1 of Rapoport and Mowshowitz (1966) (left), and the predicted distribution by the REFT and the Markov/Learning (ML) models.

Sequential Effects

Rapoport and Mowshowitz (1966) modeled the probability of cooperation in trial *r*+1 as a function of the decisions made in trial *r* by both players. Following Rapoport and Mowshowitz, we denote the conditional probability of coopera-tion by Player *n* following a decision *X* by *n* and *Y* by Player *o* as P(C|*XY*). Summed across trials and players the observed probabilities are: P(C|CC) = 0.81, P(C|CD) = 0.43 , P(C|DC) = 0.37, and P(C|DD) = 0.22. These probabilities are displayed graphically in Figure 12.4. Note that whereas they show some responsiveness to the other player's recent choice, the responsive-ness is much weaker than the responsiveness predicted under the TFT (tit-for-tat) strategy (for further explanation, see section below, An RET Model). Under this strategy (to be discussed below) the expected probabilities are P(C|CC) = 1, P(C|CD) = 0, P(C|DC) = 1, and P(C|DD) = 0.

Sensitivity to the Opponent's Choice Probabilities

To facilitate a clean test of Markov chain models, Rapoport and Mowshowitz (1966) conducted three experiments in which human subjects played against preprogrammed opponents (using the payoff matrix of Experiment 1). In Exper-iment 2, the opponents were humans whose choices were determined by the fol-lowing conditional probabilities: P(C|CC) = 0.76, P(C|CD) = 0.25, P(C|DC) = 0.46, and P(C|DD) = 0.22. In Experiment 3 the participants played against a computer whose choice probabilities were P(C|CC) = 0.72, P(C|CD) = 0.26, P(C|DC) = 0.42, and P(C|DD) = 0.22. Finally, in Experiment 4 the game was played against a "learning" computer program. This program used three fixed choice probabilities, P(C|CD) = 0.41, P(C|DC) = 0.36, and P(C|DD) = 0.17, but increased the probability of repeated cooperation in trial

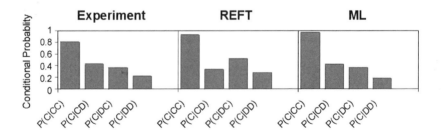

Figure 12.4 Conditional probabilities in Experiment 1 of Rapoport and Mowshowitz (1966) (left), and the predicted probabilities by the REFT model and the Markov/Learn-ing (ML) model.

$r + 1$ ($P_{r+1}(C|CC)$), following mutual cooperation. Specifically, the following linear operator model was assumed:

$$P_{r+1}(C|CC)= \begin{cases} \alpha P_r(C|CC)+(1-\alpha)\beta, \text{ if mutual cooperation was achieved at } r-1, \\ P_0(C|CC), \text{ otherwise;} \end{cases}$$

(12.6)

where $P_0(C|CC) = 0.916$, $\alpha = 0.7$, and $\beta = 0.985$. (These values were set to fit the results of Experiment 1. We return to this point below.)

The first panel of Figure 12.5 shows the proportion of C choices by the human subjects in the four experiments. It shows that whereas the identity of the opponents (human or computer) had a small effect (cf. Experiment 1 to 4 and Experiment 2 to 3), the opponent's choice probabilities had a large effect.

Failure of Simple Markov Chain Models

Rapoport and Mowshowitz (1966) tried to account for their data using a simple Markov chain model that assumes fixed and independent switching probabilities from state to state. In Experiments 2 and 3, this model has four free parameters, the conditional probabilities (P(C|CC), P(C|CD), P(C|DC), and P(C|DD)) that determine the switching probabilities. Rapoport and Mowshowitz found that when the parameters are estimated by the observed switching probabilities (in the relevant experiment), the model under-predicts the frequency of mutual cooperation. In particular, it predicts 16% of the CC outcomes in Experiment 2

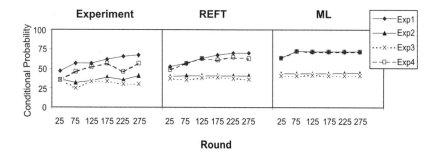

Figure 12.5 Cooperation rate (C choices by the human subjects) in the four experiments run by Rapoport and Mowshowitz (1966) (left), and the predictions of the REFT and the Markov/Learning (ML) models. Note that parameters were estimated based on Experiment 1.

and 11% of the CC outcomes in Experiment 3. The observed CC percentages were 21% and 15%, respectively.

MODELING RECIPROCATION

To distinguish among the possible explanations for the failure of the simple reinforcement learning models in games in which players can reciprocate, it is convenient to perform a "cognitive game theoretic" decomposition of these models. The model presented above and other reinforcement learning models can be decomposed into three basic submodels:

1. An abstraction of the incentive structure: all of the models we considered implicitly assume that subjects are sensitive to the objective payoff function.
2. An abstraction of the cognitive strategies considered by the subjects: in Erev and Roth (1998b), we modeled subjects as learning among simple actions (stage-game strategies).
3. An abstraction of the decision/learning rule among the relevant strategies: here we have focused on one particular reinforcement learning rule, whereas in Erev and Roth (1998b) we also studied expectation-based adaptive learning rules.

Previous explanations of reciprocation considered potential violations of all three submodels. Incentive-based explanations were provided by Kelly and Tibaut (1978) and from recent work by Bolton and Ockenfels (1998) and Fehr and Schmidt (1999). According to these accounts, reciprocation is a result of subjective incentives that differ from the objective monetary incentives. Explanations based on cognitive strategies were provided by Axelrod (1980, 1984), Komorita and Parks (1995, 1998), and Messick and Liebrand (1995). In addition, Amnon Rapoport and Mowshowitz (1966) and Macy (1991) account for reciprocation by invoking particular learning rules.

While all three classes of explanations provide insightful accounts of reciprocation in many settings, it seems that a modification of the cognitive strategies' submodel is necessary to account for reciprocation in repeated games. One of the most robust findings reported by Anatol Rapoport et al. (1976; see also Bornstein et al. 1997) is that players were able to reciprocate by alternation in chicken-type games. Since alternation is a strategy that involves memory of the previous period, it could not be observed that subjects confined their learning to stage-game strategies. A mere modification of the other two submodels (the assumed learning rule and incentive structure) cannot explain this observation.

Our main goal in this chapter is to show how this apparently necessary modification can be accomplished in a reinforcement learning model. We hope to show that this necessary modification will turn out to be sufficient to account for the five regularities described above.

An RET Model

Previous study of behavior in PD games reveals that the Tit-for-Tat (TFT) strategy can lead to efficient cooperation (e.g., Roth and Murnighan 1978; Axelrod 1980) in these settings. The TFT strategy can be thought of as the simplest quantification of the concept "reciprocation." Formally it states that:

R1   If Player n chooses to start reciprocating at trial t, he or she cooperates at that trial and cooperates at trial $t + 1$ if and only if the other player (Player o) has cooperated at t.

To apply the TFT strategy in the current adaptive learning framework, its length has to be defined. To allow learning, players should have multiple experiences with this and the alternative strategies. Moreover, it is natural to assume that the utilization length increases with experience and the potential benefit from reciprocation. These behavioral assumptions are quantified here as follows:

R2   If Player n chooses a reciprocation strategy (TFT, denoted here as strategy k) at trial t, the probability that he or she will continue to utilize it at trial $t + 1$ is:

$$\text{CONT}(t) = \begin{cases} \dfrac{C_{nk}(t)}{C_{nk}(t) + N(0)PR^{\rho}} & \text{if } PR > 0 \\ 0 & \text{otherwise} \end{cases} \tag{12.7}$$

where $C_{nk}(t)$ is the number of times that the reciprocation strategy was played, $N(0) > 0$ is "convergence speed" parameter, ρ is a "playing length" parameter, and PR is the relative potential gain from reciprocation. The potential is estimated as:

$$PR = \frac{V_n(rec) - A_n(1)}{V_n(\max) - V_n(\min)} \tag{12.8}$$

where $V_n(rec)$ is the expected payoff for Player n given successful reciprocation, $A_n(1)$ is the expected payoff from random play, and $V_n(\max) > V_n(\min)$ are the best and worst possible payoffs for Player n. In the current game $V_n(rec) = 1$, $A_n(1) = -1$, $V_n(\max) = 10$, and $V_n(\min) = -10$. Thus, the potential from reciprocation, PR, equals 0.1.

Note that the current quantification implies that when reciprocation is not expected to lead to a higher payoff than the payoff from random play ($PR \leq 0$) it will not be played more than once per strategy choice. When reciprocation is expected to lead to higher *payoff (PR > 0)*, the probability of repeated selection converges with experience to PR^{ρ}, the parameter $N(0)$ determines the speed of this convergence process. Thus, like $N(1)$, $N(0)$ can be thought of as a "conservatism" parameter. To reduce the number of free parameters we impose the constraint $N(0) = N(1)$.

The first model considered here, referred to as the RET model, is a minimal extension of the reinforcement model described above (see section on REIN- FORCEMENT LEARNING). The extension implies that players consider three strategies: the two stage-game strategies and the "probabilistic length" TFT strategy as defined by assumptions R1 and R2.

Consequently, this model has three parameters: The two learning parameters ($N(1)$ and λ) and one reciprocation length parameter (ρ). To evaluate the model we first derived its predictions of the evolution of the mutual cooperation rate in Experiment 1 of Rapoport and Mowshowitz (1966) and found the parameters that best fit the data (minimize the MSD between the observed and predicted ag- gregated 6-block learning curve).

To derive the predictions of this model for the current game, we conducted computer simulations in which 1000 virtual pairs of players played the game for 300 rounds (a replication of Experiment 1 in Rapoport and Mowshowitz). To de- scribe the simulation (and explain the model) it is useful to distinguish between the computation conducted before the first trial and during each trial. Before the first trial the (uniform) initial propensities, $A_n(1)$ and $S_n(1)$ were calculated for each player. In the current game,

$$A_n(1) = \frac{1 - 10 + 10 - 5}{4} = -1,$$

$$S_n(1) = \frac{|1 - (-1)| + |(-10) - (-1)| + |10 - (-1)| + |-5 - (-1)|}{4} = 7, \qquad (12.9)$$

$$\text{and } q_{nj}(t) = A_n(1) = -1$$

for all n and j. In addition, the players' state was set to equal "decide."

The following steps were then taken during the simulation (in trial t of the simulation of each dyad):

1. *Strategy selection.* Each player whose state was "decide" selected one of the three possible strategies (C, D, or TFT) with the probabilities given by assumption L3. The counter of the selected strategy ($C_{nj}(t)$) was up- dated (by adding 1). If the selected strategy was TFT, the player's state was set to "TFT-continue."

2. *Alternative selection.* If the state was not "TFT-continue," the selected alternative was identical to the strategy (C or D). When the state was "TFT-continue," which implies that the strategy was TFT, Player n's se- lected alternative was C if and only if at least one of the following condi- tions (from R1) were met:
   a. Player n's opponent (Player o) chose C at trial $t - 1$.
   b. Player n selected the TFT at trial t (the State was "decide" at the be- ginning of the trial).

3. *Payoff calculation.* The payoffs were determined by the chosen alterna- tives (using Figure 12.2's payoff matrix).

4. *Propensities updating.* The propensities of the selected alternatives were updated using assumption L2.
5. *Deviation and average measures.* $S(t + 1)$ and $A(t + 1)$ were calculated using the rules specified in assumption L3 (note that $S(t + 1)$ is updated based on $A(t)$).
6. *Updating the state.* If the state was TFT-continue, a virtual coin was flipped and with probability 1-CONT(t) the state was change to "decide." (CONT(t) was calculated using assumption R2).

The predictions of the RET model with the parameters that best fit the data in a grid search ($N(1) = 10$, $\lambda = 100$, $\rho = 0.03$) are presented on the third column of Figure 12.2. The results reveal that the model predicts that almost all learning will occur in the first 50 trials. Thus, it does not capture the slow increase in mutual cooperation observed by Rapoport and Mowshowitz (1966).

A More Forgiving Model (REFT)

Previous research (e.g., Axelrod 1984) suggests that the failure of the TFT strategy, as quantified above, is likely to be a result of not being "forgiving" enough to capture cooperation in a noisy environment. For example, a single mistake (deviation from TFT) by one of the players on trial t implies no mutual cooperation until the two players deviate from TFT together at the same trial. Since players are assumed to make independent choices, a single deviation is more likely to occur than a joint deviation.

To evaluate if making the reciprocation more forgiving can improve the fit of the model to the Rapoport and Mowshowitz (1966) results, the current model replaces assumption R1 with a more forgiving assumption, which implies that if both players choose to reciprocate, cooperation will be achieved within two periods. Specifically, it is assumed that:

R1f   If Player n chooses to start reciprocating at trial t, he cooperates at that trial and cooperates at trial $t + 1$ if and only if at least one of following conditions is met:
a. Player o has cooperated at trial t,
b. Player o has cooperated at trial $t - 1$, and n has not cooperated at trial t.

The predictions of the REFT model were derived using the simulation presented above after replacing the R1 conditions with the R1f condition (in step 2). The model's predictions with the parameters that best fit the data ($N(1) = 1$, $\lambda = 3.3$, $\rho = 0.05$) are presented in the fourth column of Figure 12.2. The plot shows that the forgiving model captures the increase in cooperation and outperforms the RET model.

Although the REFT model was fitted to the aggregate curve, it tends to predict large between-subject variability. Figure 12.3 compares the distribution of

C choices in the Rapoport and Mowshowitz (1966) experiment and in the simulation of the REFT model, and reveals a similar (but not identical) almost uniform distribution.

Figure 12.4 compares the observed and predicted conditional probabilities (in Experiment 1). It shows that the model captures the main experimental trends: high P(C|CC) and low P(C|DD) values. However, the model incorrectly predicts that P(C|CD) exceeds P(C|DC). This bias suggests that the current "forgiving" model is not "forgiving enough" to capture exactly the sequential dependencies in the Rapoport and Mowshowitz study.

Predictive Power and Alternative Models

The second column in Figure 12.5 shows the model's predicted C rate in the four experiments run by Rapoport and Mowshowitz. Note that the parameters were estimated based on Experiment 1 results. Thus, the fit of Experiments 2, 3, and 4 allows evaluation of the model's predictive power. Figure 12.4 shows that the model captures the rank ordering and trends observed in the three experiments: increase in cooperation in Experiment 4, a flat curve in Experiment 2, and lowest level of cooperation in Experiment 3. In addition, the simulations reveal that the current "parameter-free" predictions of Experiments 2 and 3 outperform the prediction of the four-parameter Markov chain model discussed above. The average CC percentages predicted by the current model (in the last 250 trials) are 22% and 18%.

The failure of the basic Markov chain model led Rapoport and Mowshowitz to propose a variant of this model, which assumed that the likelihood of an exit from a CC state decreases with repeated CC outcomes. This Markov/Learning (ML) model was implemented as the experimental condition in Experiment 4 and described above. Note that it has six parameters (the parameters are estimated from the observed sequential dependencies). The third column in Figure 12.5 shows the predictions of the ML model with the parameters estimated by Rapoport and Mowshowitz based on the results of Experiment 1. Whereas this model captures the main experimental trends and clearly outperforms the Markov chain model, its quantitative predictions are less accurate than the predictions of the REFT model. In all four cases the REFT model is closer to the experimental curves.

A more obvious advantage of the REFT model over the ML model is displayed in Figure 12.3. Here the ML model predicts a normal shape distribution of individual subjects and fails to capture the observation that a significant proportion of pairs appear to become stuck at a very low frequency of cooperation.

Finally, Figure 12.4 shows that the ML model outperforms the REFT model in describing the conditional probabilities. The advantage of the ML model in this case is not surprising as three of its parameters were estimated from these data.

ADDITIONAL BEHAVIORAL REGULARITIES

Research in progress (Erev and Roth, in preparation) suggests that the predictive power of the current model is not limited to the payoff matrix used by Rapoport and Mowshowitz (1966). Similarly, good fits are found for all the PD games studied by Rapoport and Chammah (1965). With the parameters estimated here (on Experiment 1 of Rapoport and Mowshowitz 1966), the model captures the effect of manipulations on the payoff matrix. Most importantly, it accurately predicts that cooperation will be obtained by most players in certain PD games, but not in others.

Erev and Roth (in preparation) also suggest that with a more general definition of the reciprocation strategy, the current model can account for behavior in all the repeated 2 × 2 games studied by Rapoport et al. (1976). For example, it can capture the conditions under which players are able to reach efficient and fair alternation outcomes.

Future research is needed to extend the current model to address repeated supergames like the prisoner's dilemma studied by Selten and Stoecker (1986).

CONCLUSIONS

Repeated games give players the opportunity to achieve cooperation through the use of repeated game strategies that make current actions contingent on the previous history of play. Learning models that do not allow players to make such contingent decisions cannot reproduce the observed behavior. In this chapter, we discussed how only a little sophistication must be added to the reinforcement learning model previously explored (a two-parameter model that captures behavior in binary decision tasks and games in which players cannot reciprocate) in order to model behavior in the repeated prisoner's dilemma. Results reveal that the addition of a single reciprocation strategy, together with the two stage-game strategies, is sufficient to permit simple reinforcement learning to capture many aspects of the observed data. A three-parameter model that quantifies this assumption was found to outperform alternative models in predicting the results of the three experiments conducted by Rapoport and Mowshowitz (1966) to compare alternative descriptive models of behavior in the PD game.

Although the current model is only an example of a strategy set sufficient to capture the effect of experience on cooperation, it has two important advantages over some previous explanations. First, most recent research focuses on the qualitative demonstrations that particular assumptions can lead to reciprocation. Current research (like the pioneering research by Anatol Rapoport and Chammah [1965] and Amnon Rapoport and Mowshowitz [1966]) shows that useful quantitative predictions can be made.

Second, the reinforcement learning "engine" is potentially general. The present reinforcement learning model is a generalization of a model that captures behavior in more than 60 games in which players cannot reciprocate and, as we hope to show in the future (Erev and Roth, in prep.), can be extended to any 2 × 2 game.

In general, the approach that we have outlined here involves separating players' learning rules from their cognitive model of the available strategies. The present example is intended to make plausible the speculation that, with an appropriate model of strategies, even very simple models of reinforcement learning may be sufficient to predict how behavior will evolve over time in repeated play of simple games.

ACKNOWLEDGMENT

This research was supported by the Henry Gutwirth Promotion of Research Fund, Israel–U.S.A. Binational Science Foundation, and the National Science Foundation (U.S.A.).

REFERENCES

Axelrod, R. 1980. Effective choice in the prisoner's dilemma. *J. Confl. Res.* **24**:3–26.
Axelrod, R. 1984. The Evolution of Cooperation. New York: Basic.
Bolton, G., and A. Ockenfels. 1998. Strategy and equity: An ERC-analysis of the Guth-van Damme game. *J. Math. Psych.* **42**:215–226.
Bornstein, G., D.V. Budescu, and S. Zamir. 1997. Cooperation in intergroup, N-person and two-person games of chicken. *J. Confl. Res.* **41**:384–406.
Camerer, C.F., and T. Ho. 1999. Experience-weighted attraction in games. *Econometrica* **67**:827–874.
Cheung, Y.W., and D. Friedman. 1999. A comparison of learning and replicator dynamics using experimental data. *J. Econ. Behav. Org.*, in press.
Daniel, T.E., D.A. Seale, and A. Rapoport. 1998. Strategic play and adaptive learning in sealed bid bargaining mechanism. *J. Math. Psych.* **42**:133–166.
Erev, I., Y. Bereby-Meyer, and A. Roth. 1999. The effect of adding constant to all payoffs: Experimental investigation, and implications for reinforcement learning models. *J. Econ. Behav. Org.*, in press.
Erev, I., and A.E. Roth. 1998a. On the role of reinforcement learning in experimental games: The cognitive game theoretic approach. In: Games and Human Behavior: Essays in Honor of Amnon Rapoport, ed. D. Budescu, I. Erev, and R. Zwick, pp. 53–78. Mahwah, NJ: Erlbaum.
Erev, I., and A.E. Roth. 1998b. Predicting how people play games: Reinforcement learning in experimental games with unique, mixed strategy equilibria. *Am. Econ. Rev.* **88(4)**:848–881.
Fehr, E., and K. Schmidt. 1999. How to account for fair and unfair outcomes — A model of biased inequality aversion. *Qtly. J. Econ.*, in press.
Gigerenzer, G., U. Hoffrage, and H. Kleinbolting. 1991. Probabilistic mental models: A Brunswikian theory of confidence. *Psych. Rev.* **98**:506–528.
Kelly, H.H., and J. Tibaut. 1978. Interpersonal Relations: A Theory of Independence. New York: Wiley.

Komorita, S.S., and C.D. Parks. 1995. Interpersonal elations: Mixed-motive interaction. *Ann. Rev. Psych.* **46**:183–207.

Komorita, S.S., and C.D. Parks. 1998. Reciprocity and cooperation in social dilemmas: Review and future directions. In: Games and Human Behavior: Essays in Honor of Amnon Rapoport, ed. D. Budescu, I Erev, and R. Zwick, pp. 315–330. Mahwah, NJ: Erlbaum.

Macy, M.W. 1991. Learning to cooperate: Stochastic and tacit collusion in social exchange. *Am. J. Soc.* **97**:808–843.

Malcolm, D., and B. Lieberman. 1965. The behavior of responsive individuals playing a two- person, zero-sum game requiring the use of mixed strategies. *Psychonomic Sci.* **12**:373–374.

Messick, D.M., and W.B.G. Liebrand. 1995. Individual heuristics and the dynamics of cooperation in large groups. *Psych. Rev.* **102**:131–145.

Mookherjee, D., and B. Sopher. 1997. Learning and decision costs in experimental constant sum games. *Games Econ. Behav.* **19**:62–91.

Ochs, J. 1995. Simple games with unique mixed strategy equilibrium: An experimental study. *Games Econ. Behav.* **10(1)**:202–217.

O'Neill, B. 1987. Nonmetric test of the minimax theory of two-person zerosum games. *Proc. Natl. Acad. Sci. USA* **84**:2106–2109.

Rapoport, Amnon, and R.B. Boebel. 1992. Mixed strategies in strictly competitive games: A further test of the minmax hypothesis. *Games Econ. Behav.* **4**:261–283.

Rapoport, Amnon, and A. Mowshowitz. 1966. Experimental studies of stochastic models for the prisoner dilemma. *Behav. Sci.* **11**:444–458.

Rapoport, Amnon, D.A. Seale, I. Erev, and J.A. Sundali. 1998. Coordination success in market entry games: Tests of equilibrium and adaptive learning models. *Manag. Sci.* **44**:129–141.

Rapoport, Anatol, and A.M. Chammah. 1965. Prisoner's Dilemma: A Study in Conflict and Cooperation. Ann Arbor: Univ. of Michigan Press.

Rapoport, Anatol, M.J. Guyer, and D.G. Gordon. 1976. The 2 × 2 Game. Ann Arbor: Univ. of Michigan Press.

Roth, A.E., and I. Erev. 1995. Learning in extensive-form games: Experimental data and simple dynamic models in the intermediate term. *Games Econ. Behav. (Spec. Iss.: Nobel Symp.)* **8**:164–212.

Roth, A.E., I. Erev, R.L. Slonim, and G. Barron. 1999. Learning and equilibrium as useful approximations: Accuracy of predictions in randomly selected constant sum games. Haifa: Technion. Mimeo.

Roth, A.E., and J.K. Murnighan. 1978. Equilibrium behavior and repeated play of the prisoners' dilemma. *J. Math. Psych.* **17**:189–198.

Sarin, R., and F. Vahid. 1998. Predicting how people play games: A procedurally rational model of choice. Texas A&M Univ. Mimeo.

Selten, R., and R. Stoecker. 1986. End behavior in sequences of finite prisoner's dilemma supergames: A learning theory approach. *J. Econ. Behav. Org.* **7**:47–70.

Suppes, P., and R.C. Atkinson. 1960. Markov Learning Models for Multiperson Interactions. Palo Alto: Stanford Univ. Press.

Tang, F. 1996. Anticipatory learning in two-person games: An experimental study. II. Learning. Discussion Paper B–363. Bonn: Univ. of Bonn.

13

Imitation, Social Learning, and Preparedness as Mechanisms of Bounded Rationality

Kevin N. Laland

Sub-Dept. of Animal Behaviour, University of Cambridge, Madingley,
Cambridge CB3 8AA, U.K.

ABSTRACT

The behavioral decisions made by many animals are to a large part influenced by what other animals are doing. Social learning is not restricted to humans, or clever animals, but is a fundamental feature of vertebrate life. In an array of different contexts, numerous animals adopt a "do-what-others-do" strategy and, in the process, learn an appropriate behavior. The main focus of this chapter is social learning in animals. A summary of the field is given, describing the different ways in which animals learn from each other, the different types of information they acquire, and the rules that they employ. Theoretical findings exploring the circumstances under which natural selection should favor reliance on social cues are also described. The penultimate section considers to what extent human social learning differs from that of animals. The chapter concludes by asking what social learning can tell us about bounded rationality.

ANIMAL SOCIAL LEARNING

Social learning occurs when an animal learns a behavioral pattern or acquires a preference as a consequence of observing or interacting with a second animal. The term "social learning" is a general term that represents learning that is influenced socially, in contrast to instances of individual learning in which behavior acquisition is not influenced by interaction with others. This general term should not be confused with "imitation," which loosely describes one psychological process that can result in social learning. Imitation refers to instances where, by observation of another individual performing an act, an animal is able to reproduce the same motor pattern. Note that the term "imitation" is not a synonym for social learning, since it is quite possible to imitate without learning anything. Moreover, imitation is just one of several processes that can result in social learning, including "local enhancement," "stimulus enhancement," "social facilitation," "goal emulation," "observational conditioning," and others.

Local (or stimulus) enhancement refers to a process in which one animal directs another animal's attention to a location (or object) in the environment. If, as a consequence of this tip-off, the observer expresses an equivalent behavior to the observed, local enhancement can result in a behavior pattern spreading through a population. Social facilitation occurs when the perception of other animals performing a behavior (e.g., pecking) directly elicits the same behavior in the observer. Like imitation and local enhancement, social facilitation does not always result in learning; however, when it does (i.e., if by pecking the observer identifies a new food source), a simple form of social learning has occurred. Other terms, such as "observational conditioning" and "goal emulation," refer to the learning of emotional responses and goals from other animals. Imitation is generally regarded as requiring more complex or advanced psychological processing than local enhancement and other processes leading to social learning, although this is unproven. In reality, the terms that describe "types" of social learning have very little real explanatory power: They do not, for example, explain how social and environmental stimuli are analyzed, representations are constructed, associations are formed between events, and like motor acts produced.

I begin with these distinctions for two reasons. First, there is a great deal of confusion about the meaning of terms such as "social learning" and "imitation," and thus a clear definition at the outset may be useful. It is important to be aware of the fact that discussions of social learning phenomena in different disciplines use terms, and make distinctions, with various degrees of rigor. Accounts of human social learning frequently treat social learning and imitation as synonyms, yet in the vast majority of cases where humans are described as imitating, this is unproven. Second, it is also important to recognize that neither imitation, nor teaching, nor any other cognitively sophisticated psychological process, is necessary for a socially transmitted behavioral tradition to be established. There is no evidence that simple processes such as local enhancement are any less likely than cognitively complex processes such as imitation to result in social learning, behavioral conformity, or stable transmission. On the contrary, numerous animal traditions appear to be supported by psychologically simple mechanisms. For the purposes of this chapter, it does not matter by what mechanism one individual learns from a second; what is important is that the learning is contingent on social interaction, and the social processes involved can result in the diffusion of a pattern of behavior through a population.

Animal social learning is a manifestation of the use of simple heuristics to bias decision making. Ethologists and behavioral ecologists have been interested in social learning because it seems to allow animals to learn about their environments rapidly and efficiently, without having to engage in potentially hazardous learning trials or waste a large amount of time on exploration. One only has to consider the potential fitness costs associated with having to learn the identity of an unfamiliar predator or a poisonous food, or reflect on the energy expended in searching the local environment for a water source, to envisage how the "do-what-others-do" strategy might pay off. Such a strategy is particularly beneficial if the observer is in a position immediately to assess the consequences of the observed behavior, and can use this information to bias whether or not it adapts.

There are several well-known examples of animal social learning (for an overview of the field, see Heyes and Galef 1996). Perhaps the most celebrated of all cases is the washing of sweet potatoes by Japanese macaques. A young female macaque discovered that she could wash the sand grains off her sweet potatoes in water, and this habit spread throughout the troop. The younger individuals were thought to learn from the older animals, and this transmission was referred to as a preculture or protoculture, the implication being that is was a primitive homologue of human culture. In another famous example, Jane Goodall (1964) reported that infant chimps learned the skills necessary for foraging for termites using stalks and twigs by imitating adults. While nearly all members of the chimpanzee population in the Gombe National Park in Tanzania fish for termites, chimpanzees in other populations do not exhibit this behavior, and this has led to the suggestion that primitive cultural traditions account for the between-population variation in this behavior.

These high-profile, textbook cases present a slightly misleading picture of social learning. Most animal social learning is not from parents to offspring, does not involve cognitively demanding transmission mechanisms, and will not maintain alternative traditions between populations; indeed, there is some doubt whether even the potato washing and termiting traditions have these qualities. A more prototypical example is the acquisition of dietary preferences by rats that attend to cues on the breath of conspecifics (Galef 1996). In general, rats prefer to eat foods that other rats have eaten than alternative novel diets, and this simple mechanism probably maintains short-term dietary traditions in rat populations. Another representative example is the spread of milk bottle top opening in British tits (Hinde and Fisher 1951). These birds learned to peck open the foil cap on milk bottles and to drink the cream. Hinde and Fisher found that this behavior probably spreads by local enhancement, where the tits' attention is drawn to the milk bottles by a feeding conspecific, and after this initial tip-off, they subsequently learn on their own how to open the tops.

Much, perhaps most, animal social learning involves the short-term transmission of feeding and foraging information among populations of social foragers, by very simple mechanisms such as local enhancement. A considerable amount of empirical evidence has accumulated for this kind of animal social transmission (Lefebvre and Palameta 1988). It occurs among populations of rats, pigeons, starlings, bats, gulls, and literally hundreds of other species that acquire up-to-date foraging and feeding information from unrelated conspecifics. This is what characterizes animal social learning. Animals learn what to eat and where to find it by very simple mechanisms. These social foragers typically live in patchy and variable environments, and the information they acquire through social learning is usually only of transient value. Nonetheless, short-term traditions are established. It would be misleading, however, to imply that animal social learning is restricted to the transmission of foraging information. Several studies, among mammals, birds, and fish, have suggested that individuals can learn to identify predators by responding to the fright reactions, alarm calls, or alarm substances of experienced conspecifics and heterospecifics (e.g., Mineka and Cook 1988). Other studies have suggested that females of several species may copy the mate choices of other females, although this claim remains contentious (Dugatkin 1992). There is some evidence suggesting the traditional use of migratory routes and the return to specific locations for breeding in birds and fish. There is probably some transmission of information concerning territorial resources, territorial boundaries, and pathways in many species, although this has been subject to little investigation.

Not all cases of animal social learning fit a stereotype of simple psychological mechanisms and horizontal transmission. There are several examples of behavior patterns that are transmitted vertically (i.e., from parents to offspring) or obliquely (i.e., from the parental to the offspring generation, but not via parents). The development of a fear of snakes by rhesus monkeys that perceive conspecifics acting fearfully in the presence of a snake is one example (Mineka and Cook 1988). The transmission from mother to offspring of a method for extracting the seeds from pine cones in black rats is a second (Terkel 1996). Moreover, the social transmission of bird song could be considered a general category of vertical or oblique cultural transmission. What is more, animals do sometimes exhibit sophisticated forms of social learning. There is clear evidence for imitation in chimpanzees (Whiten and Custance 1996) and some birds (Atkins and Zentall 1996), and slightly less rigorous evidence in orangutans and gorillas. Nonetheless, the current view of animal social learning implies that such cases are exceptions and that most animal social learning can be thought of as an adjunct to individual learning that allows animals to enhance their foraging efficiency and acquire other valuable information in changing, unpredictable environments. This is known as "highly horizontal" transmission.

WHEN SHOULD NATURAL SELECTION FAVOR SOCIAL LEARNING?

Highly horizontal forms of transmission are phylogenetically much more widespread than vertical forms. Most of the cases of vertical transmission involve traits such as bird song, sexual imprinting, or habitat selection, which are highly constrained and have a very specific function. Such traits cannot be regarded as homologues of the flexible and information-rich vertical transmission system that characterizes human culture. In contrast to animal proto-cultures, it would seem that the "traditional" transmission that characterizes human culture addresses a different kind of adaptive problem germane to features of the environment, which are stable for long periods of time relative to the lifetime of an individual organism. A comparative perspective suggests that it was horizontal social learning that evolved first, and that in hominid, and in a relatively restricted number of other species, a general capacity for vertical transmission subsequently evolved. Thus the problem of how human culture evolved has been transformed into two quite separate questions: (a) how did social learning evolve (where the appropriate focus is on the adaptive advantages of a highly horizontal transmission system), and (b) how did a highly horizontal system of social learning evolve into a traditional system with the characteristics of human culture? Both of these questions have been addressed using mathematical models.

Figure 13.1, taken from Laland et al. (1996), is an illustration of the results of a mathematical analysis that used population genetics models to explore when natural selection should favor horizontal social transmission in a population already capable of learning. Two key variables turned out to be (a) the probability that a naive forager will successfully locate a highly nutritional but patchily distributed food source (ε), and (b) the rate at which the environment varies (e), for

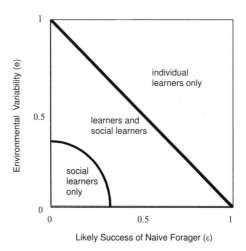

Figure 13.1 Horizontal social learning is favored by natural selection in changing environments when the probability of individual foraging success is low, either because individuals can only search a small section of their environment, or because food sources are sparsely dispersed. Figure reprinted with permission from Academic Press, Inc.; taken from Laland et al. (1996).

example, reflecting a change in the location of that food source. Note that this measure of environmental variability is relative to daily, or more frequent, foraging bouts, and hence even when e is small it can represent rapid environmental change relative to the lifetime of an organism. When the probability is high that (individual) foraging will allow a naive animal to locate the nutritional diet, or when the environment changes very rapidly, social learning is of no adaptive advantage and cannot evolve. Where the likely success of a naive forager is low, and when the rate of change in the environment is fast but not too fast, all individuals in the population should be social learners. There are also circumstances where populations should be polymorphic for individual and social learners. This means that social learning can evolve in a rapidly changing environment when the probability of individual foraging success is low, either because individuals can only search a small section of the population range, or because food sources are sparsely dispersed. These are precisely the kind of environments in which most animal social learning is found. A similar conclusion was reached by Giraldeau et al. (1994) in a related analysis that explored the advantages of social learning in a population competing for limited food resources. Giraldeau et al. hypothesized that a further adaptive function of social learning may be that it allows individuals to circumvent some of the inhibitory effects that scrounging (i.e., exploitation of food discovered by others) has on the individual learning of a foraging skill. Their model suggests that there are circumstances in which foraging tasks will be difficult to learn exclusively through individual experience, because scrounging reduces payoffs, but can be learned through observation. They state that scrounging may drive the evolution of social learning.

The second question raised by the comparative perspective is how a highly horizontal system of social learning evolved into a traditional system with the characteristics of human culture. To address this question, it is imperative to conduct a similar mathematical analysis of the adaptive advantages of a system of vertical cultural transmission. Boyd and Richerson (1985) explored under what circumstances natural selection should favor such a transmission in a population of individuals that can learn about their environment on their own but not from each other. They concluded that when environments change very slowly, all information should be transmitted genetically, since the modest demands for updating are easily met by the genetic system responding to selection. At intermediate rates of change vertical social learning is an advantage, i.e., when changes are not so fast that parents and offspring experience different environments, but not so slow that appropriate genetically transmitted behavior could evolve. Finally, when environmental change is very rapid, tracking by individual learning is favored, (although the analysis presented above suggests that under certain conditions horizontal social transmission will be beneficial). The models of other authors reach similar conclusions (for a review of this literature, see Laland et al. 1996).

Unfortunately, the assumptions and conclusions of these theoretical analyses have not been subject to a great deal of empirical investigation. However, Laland and Williams (1998) have carried out an experiment designed to test the theoretical prediction that social learning should be maladaptive in an environ-ment with rapid or sudden changes. Populations of fish were established with socially transmitted traditions for taking different routes to a food source by training founders to take particular routes and then gradually replacing the trained animals with naïve fish. In the experimental tanks there were two routes, with one route substantially longer than the other. The long route was designed to represent an environment in which the optimal route to feed had suddenly changed, thus fish in shoals whose founders were trained to take the long route have to learn to "track this change" by switching preference to the short route. The experiment found that swimming with founders that had a prior preference for the long route slowed down the rate at which subjects adjusted to the new pat-terns of reinforcement in their environment, relative to fish that swam alone (see Figure 13.2). Consistent with the theoretical predictions, shoaling fish utilizing public information tracked the environment less effectively than lone fish. If this finding applies to natural populations of animals, where behavioral traditions lag behind the environmental state, the lag may be greater for animals that aggre-gate and rely on social information than it would be for isolates relying exclu-sively on their own experience. If this is the case, suboptimal traditions may be fairly common in animal populations.

The findings of this experiment should be interpreted with some caution. While the experiment can legitimately be described as providing evidence for

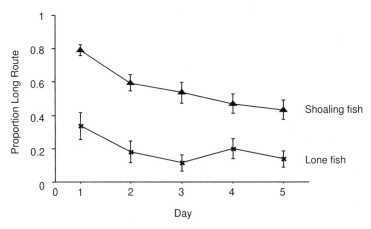

Figure 13.2   Fish that swam with conspecifics that had a preestablished preference for a circuitous route to a food source learned to take a short route more slowly than fish that swam alone. This suggests that animals utilizing public information may sometimes track the environment less effectively than loners. Figure reprinted with permission from Oxford University Press; taken from Laland and Williams (1998).

the social transmission of maladaptive information, neither the behavior of the fish, nor the general capacity for social learning should be described as maladaptive. Taking an energetically costly route (indicating similar behaviors, such as foraging at a relatively low profitability patch) may well be an adaptive strategy for animals that gain protection through aggregation, provided that conspecifics are doing the same. Furthermore, although in this instance the information that was transmitted between fish in the long-route conditions was suboptimal, in general there is no doubt that animal social learning is typically adaptive and results in the transmission of "good" information (Galef 1995). This is, in part, because the germane features of the environment are frequently sufficiently stable to afford equivalent levels of reinforcement to the transmitter and receiver of information. It also probably reflects the fact that social animals have evolved mechanisms that prevent bad information from spreading. For example, several species of animals can identify cues associated with illness caused by toxic substances in conspecifics, and consequently will not adopt toxic diets, while for others the transmission of dietary preferences only works effectively for adaptive traits (Laland et al. 1996). Nonetheless, the behavioral tradition for guppies taking the long route may legitimately be described as maladaptive, since if all of the members of the population were to switch to the short route, they would all have to expend less energy in locating food, and their search time would be reduced. The behavioral tradition favoring the long route is associated with a potential reduction in the long-term rate of net energy gain relative to a tradition favoring the short route.

The finding that historical as well as economic factors are important in the foraging decisions of animals is supported by experimental studies of the diet choices of rats influenced by social cues. Laland and Plotkin (1991) found that the equilibrium mean proportion of the diet represented by food items for which there is socially transmitted information cannot always be predicted from animals' consumption of such food items in the absence of social information. Here diet composition depends on past traditions for exploiting particular resources, and cannot always be predicted from palatability, profitability, or patterns of reinforcement. These laboratory findings are mirrored by observations from the field, which provide compelling, yet generally unproven, evidence for the importance of historical factors. For instance, the characteristic tool-using repertoires of particular chimpanzee populations probably reflect cultural traditions, although differences in the ecological environments may be important. The take home message is that, while there is no evidence that animal cultures support maladaptive behavior, we cannot always predict a priori what the adaptive behavior of social learners will be, since historical and frequency-dependent processes allow traditions to stray from the optimal.

WHAT RULES DO ANIMALS EMPLOY?

I have described animal social learning as if animals copy the behavior of others indiscriminately. However it is difficult to see how such an unconditional "do-what-others-do" strategy could be successful, since at least some members of the population must gauge whether the transmitted information is appropriate to the immediate environment for it to maintain its utility. Unfortunately, most studies of social learning in animals have not attempted to investigate the nature of the strategy adopted by animals when they copy others. However, a number of incidental findings suggest that, at least some of the time, animals are employing more complex strategies than an unconditional "do-what-others-do."

The simplest alternative strategy is perhaps to adopt the behavior of others only when the current, or tried-and-tested, behavior is unproductive. For example, Lefebvre and colleagues investigated the spread of a food-finding behavior in populations of pigeons, in which the birds were required to peck open a carton containing seed. They found that pigeons would scrounge (steal) food from other birds if possible, and only when there were not enough birds producing food did some scroungers switch to adopting the food-finding behavior. (Lefebvre and Palameta 1988). The suggestion that this reflects a strategy of "do-what-others do" only when there is no easier option is supported by the fact that scroungers and producers switch strategy to maintain a frequency-dependent balance and that the proportion of scroungers diminishes as the share of producers increases (Giraldeau and Beauchamp 1999).

Boyd and Richerson (1988) presented a theoretical model which assumed that animals would copy the behavior of conspecifics when uncertain as to what to do themselves. This assumption has never been explicitly tested on animal populations, although some empirical evidence does bear on it. For example, in a series of studies, Galef and colleagues have established that rats, when confronted with two alternative novel foods, will preferentially adopt the diet consumed by conspecifics by utilizing odor cues on their breath (Galef 1996). In the absence of these social cues rats consume less food in total. Interestingly, when the foods were familiar, the demonstrators influence was much weaker, suggesting that public information is of greatest utility when the rat is uncertain. Other studies reach a similar conclusion (Laland and Plotkin 1991).

Studies of social learning in species as diverse as rats, pigeons, and guppies suggest that these animals sometimes adopt a "do-what-the-majority-do" strategy (Laland et al. 1996). In such cases, the probability that individuals learn a behavior from others depends on the number of individuals expressing the behavior. If some strategies are widespread they are likely to generate a conformist transmission, which may act to prevent novel behavior patterns from invading.

Obviously learning from others is more effective if one adopts the behavior of the most successful individuals. There is also some evidence that individuals in some species adopt a "do-what-the-successful-individuals-do" strategy. For example, bats that are unsuccessful in locating food alone follow previously successful bats to feeding sites (Wilkinson 1992). Starlings can use the foraging success of other birds to assess patch quality, and exploit this information in their judgements as to whether to stay or switch patches (Templeton and Giraldeau 1996). For redwing blackbirds, the social learning of a food preference is affected by whether the demonstrator bird becomes sick or remains well (Mason 1988). At this stage it is not clear which, if any, of these heuristics provides the best description of the rules that animals employ when they learn from others.

INNOVATION AND DIFFUSION

When a novel behavior pattern spreads through an animal population, typically one individual will be its inventor or discoverer. There have been precious few empirical investigations of who these innovators are. However, evidence is beginning to emerge that innovators are sometimes individuals for whom the current prevailing risk-averse foraging strategies are unproductive, and who are driven to search for alternatives, perhaps incurring some risk. Such animals are often small, young, low-ranking, or poor competitors. Primate studies appear to indicate that innovators are frequently low in rank or poor competitors on the outskirts of the social group (Kummer and Goodall 1985). For instance, Sigg (1980) found that peripheral female hamadryas baboons were significantly better at learning novel tasks than central females. A recent review found that of 38 independent cases of innovation reported in the primate literature, 25 were by low-ranking individuals (S.M. Reader, pers. comm.).

Kummer and Goodall (1985) found no shortage of innovation in primate populations, but these innovative behaviors rarely spread, in spite of their apparent utility. It seems that often individuals do not adopt a better alternative, even when other members of the population exhibit such behavior. This is perhaps because on many occasions when ecological and technical innovations occur, the innovator is alone, or at least freed from social distractions (Kummer and Goodall 1985). If the twin observations, that it is poorer competitors that innovate, and that poorer competitors find themselves on the outskirts of aggregations, are common to many species, much innovation will tend to occur unobserved by others, decreasing the chance that the novel behavior pattern will spread. This may be one explanation for both the slow diffusion of new behaviors in the wild (Kummer and Goodall 1985), and the rarity of stable animal traditions (Boyd and Richerson 1988).

Empirical research has established a number of factors that influence the stability of animal traditions, including the number of individuals in a social group, the rate of change of group composition, and the amount of time available to forage (Galef and Allen 1995). Social transmission may be more stable when it reinforces a prior preference (i.e., for a more palatable diet) than when it conflicts with one (Laland and Plotkin 1991). Whether such pre-established biases reflect earlier learning, familiarity, or preparedness has not been established. Thus it is not clear to what extent animal traditions can be considered highly constrained by past natural selection or quasi-independent processes propagating arbitrary behavioral alternatives.

ARE HUMANS DIFFERENT?

There are obvious differences between human culture and animal behavioral traditions, although the distinction is not as clear cut as it might appear at first sight. In contrast to animal traditions, human culture is principally vertically (or obliquely) transmitted, i.e., information flows from the parental to the offspring generation. This can be seen by focusing on the correlations between parent and offspring for personality traits, and behavior patterns (Cavalli-Sforza et al. 1982; Boyd and Richerson 1985). Nonetheless, in post-industrial societies information may increasingly be transmitted horizontally. Human culture utilizes complex social learning mechanisms such as imitation and teaching. However, the role of local enhancement and other simple processes is undoubtedly underestimated, and that of imitation overestimated. Boyd and Richerson (1985) stress a powerful conformist transmission in human societies, in the same way that many animals adopt the behavior of the majority. As in animals, human cultural transmission is based on the transmission of acquired information, but this is facilitated by a complex form of communication, namely language, which may in part account for its greater stability, and for the existence of traditions in which information accumulates from generation to generation. However, the principal consequence of the differences between human and animal "cultures" is that socially transmitted information has a stronger influence on human decision making than it does in animals.

This is not to say that human culture is so powerful that it no longer interacts with genetic inheritance at all, but rather overrules it. Such a position fails to explain many relevant data that indicate that, to varying degrees, human cultural processes are constrained by human genes, and could not work unless they were, since they need "a priori" knowledge in the form of evolved, genetically encoded information, to get started (Durham 1991; Barkow et al. 1992). For example, there is now considerable evidence that evolved linguistic predispositions, as well as other generative capacities, exist in human brains, and presumably they are subject to developmental processes that are constrained by genes (Barkow et al. 1992; Pinker 1994). Culture cannot always be meaningfully decoupled from genetics. However, neither can culture (in humans or animals) merely be treated as the expression of naturally selected genes, i.e., like any other feature of the phenotype, as early human sociobiologists advocated. This is because such a position neglects the power of cultural inheritance to bias behavior away from fitness peaks, maintain suboptimal traditions, and shape natural selection pressures.

A focus on social learning suggests a conception of human behavior that is significantly frequency-dependent, and largely shaped by shared learned information, in the form of ideas, beliefs, and values. The transmission and reception of this information is constrained by naturally selected predispositions and past learning. Similar views have been advocated by proponents of gene-culture coevolutionary theory (Boyd and Richerson 1985; Durham 1991; Feldman and Laland 1996) and by economists who stress informational cascades (Bikhchandani et al. 1998).

WHAT DOES SOCIAL LEARNING TELL US ABOUT BOUNDED RATIONALITY?

Making "perfect" decisions about how to maximize reproductive success would take considerable time, and have significant costs in terms of delay and computational brain structures. Of course, animals do not have that luxury. They are required to make rapid decisions that may have significant effects on fitness, and that may sometimes even have life or death consequences, on the basis of inadequate information. This in itself puts an upper ceiling on the level of rational behavior we can expect from animals. In spite of this, animals consistently avoid predators, find food, select mates, and reproduce effectively, often with extraordinary efficiency. This is in part a tribute to the power of natural selection to shape the behavior and decision-making processes of animals. However, for many animals, adaptive behavior results in part from copying the behavior of others. Social learning is usually a shortcut to adaptive behavior, by which animals acquire valuable information about the environment by exploiting the knowledge base of other members of the population, without having to explore, invent, or investigate for themselves. Social learning provides animals with cheap and dirty solutions to problems such as what to eat, how to process it, where to find food, how to identify predators, how to choose mates, and much more. "Do-what-others-do" is an effective heuristic in many situations, particularly those in which both the observer and demonstrator of the target behavior are exposed to equivalent environments, and those in which the observer is in a position to assess the consequences to the target behavior. Animals probably do not copy other animals indiscriminately, although this has yet to be established empirically. Nonetheless, there is evidence that animals employ strategies such as "Do-what-others-do" when they are uncertain, or, when there is no easier solution, they use "Do-what-the-majority-do," or "Do-what-the-successful-individuals-do."

Distinctions can be drawn between the capacity for social learning, behavior that results from or is influenced by socially transmitted information, the transmitted information, and socially maintained traditions. The capacity for social learning is an adaptation that we can assume would not have been favored by natural selection if it did not generate adaptive behavior most of the time.

Socially learned behavior is typically adaptive, although it may be suboptimal, since the adaptive solution depends on the behavior of others. Socially transmit ted information is typically adaptive, and several species of animals have evolved mechanisms to reduce the likelihood that maladaptive information can spread. Nonetheless, in rapidly or suddenly changing environments, socially transmitted information may be outdated, and individuals that rely on public in formation may track the environment less effectively than those that do not. Em pirical evidence suggests that animal traditions may sometimes be arbitrary or suboptimal.

Most socially learned behaviors are invented or discovered by an "innova tor." Much of the time innovators appear to be poor competitors who are low in the dominance hierarchy. Perhaps in many cases innovators can be regarded as individuals who have not achieved a satisfactory level of food consumption or mating success, i.e., who have not reached aspirational levels, and who search for new solutions, sometimes incurring some risk in the process. In contrast, per haps the majority of the population are content to express established behavior patterns because they have reached their aspiration levels, and perhaps they do not adopt the novel adaptive behavior patterns of innovators because they can afford to be risk averse. Similarly, for those quick or powerful enough, scroung ing food from others is undoubtedly an easy an effective foraging strategy. How ever, as soon as this strategy becomes unproductive, because there are insufficient producers of food, scroungers are prepared to search for a new strat egy and sometimes copy the food-producing behavior of others.

Humans cannot be regarded as maximizing reproductive success, in part be cause social learning processes are quasi-independent of biological processes, and sufficiently powerful to bias human behavior towards conformist norms. Past learning and evolved predispositions bias the probability that information will be transmitted and received, and affect the stability of traditions.

REFERENCES

Atkins, C.K., and T.R. Zentall. 1996. Imitative learning in male Japanese quail (*Coturnix japonica*) using the two-action method. *J. Comp. Psych.* **110**:316–320.

Barkow, J., L. Cosmides, and J. Tooby. 1992. The Adapted Mind: Evolutionary Psychology and the Generation of Culture. Oxford: Oxford Univ. Press.

Bikhchandani, S., D. Hirshleifer, and I. Welch. 1998. Learning from the behaviour of others: Conformity, fads and informational cascades. *J. Econ. Persp.* **12(3)**:151–170.

Boyd, R., and P.J. Richerson. 1985. Culture and the Evolutionary Process. Chicago: Univ. of Chicago Press.

Boyd, R., and P.J. Richerson. 1988. The evolution of reciprocity in sizable groups. *J. Theor. Biol.* **132**:337–356.

Cavalli-Sforza, L.L., M.W. Feldman, K.H. Chen, and S.M. Dornbusch. 1982. Theory and observation in cultural transmission. *Science* **218**:19–27.

Dugatkin, L.A. 1992. Sexual selection and imitation: Females copy the mate choice of others. *Am. Nat.* **139**:1384–1389.

Durham, W.H. 1991. Coevolution: Genes, Culture and Human Diversity. Palo Alto: Stanford Univ. Press.

Feldman, M.W., and K.N. Laland. 1996. Gene-culture coevolutionary theory. *Trends Ecol. Evol.* **11**:453–457.

Galef, B.G., Jr. 1995. Why behaviour patterns that animals learn socially are locally adaptive. *Anim. Behav.* **49**:1325–1334.

Galef, B.G., Jr. 1996. Social enhancement of food preferences in Norway rats: A brief review. In: Social Learning in Animals: The Roots of Culture, ed. C.M. Heyes and B.G. Galef, Jr., pp. 49–64. New York: Academic.

Galef, B.G., Jr., and C. Allen. 1995. A new model system for studying behavioural traditions in animals. *Anim. Behav.* **50(3)**:705–717.

Giraldeau, L.A., and G. Beauchamp. 1999. Food exploitation: Searching for the optimal joining policy. *Trends Ecol. Evol.* **14**:102–106.

Giraldeau, L.A., T. Caraco, and T.J. Valone. 1994. Social foraging: Individual learning and cultural transmission of innovations. *Behav. Ecol.* **5(1)**:35–43.

Goodall, J. 1964. Tool-using and aimed throwing in a community of free-living chimpanzees. *Nature* **201**:1264–1266.

Heyes, C.M., and B.G. Galef, Jr. 1996. Social Learning in Animals: The Roots of Culture. New York: Academic.

Hinde, R.A., and J. Fisher. 1951. Further observations on the opening of milk bottles by birds. *Brit. Birds* **44**:393–396.

Kummer, H., and J. Goodall. 1985. Conditions of innovative behaviour in primates. *Phil. Trans. Roy. Soc. Lond. B* **308**:203–214.

Laland, K.N., and H.C. Plotkin. 1991. Excretory deposits surrounding food sites facilitate social learning of food preferences in Norway rats. *Anim. Behav.* **41**:997–1005.

Laland, K.N., P.J. Richerson, and R. Boyd. 1996. Developing a theory of animal social learning. In: Social Learning in Animals: The Roots of Culture, ed. C.M. Heyes and B.G. Galef, Jr., pp. 129–154. New York: Academic.

Laland, K.N., and K. Williams. 1998. Social transmission of maladaptive information in the guppy. *Behav. Ecol.* **9**:493–499.

Lefebvre, L., and B. Palameta. 1988. Mechanisms, ecology and population diffusion of socially learned food finding behavior in feral pigeons. In: Social Learning: Psychological and Biological Perspectives, ed. T. Zentall and B.G. Galef, Jr., pp. 141–164. Hillsdale, NJ: Erlbaum.

Mason, J.R. 1988. Direct and observational learning by redwing blackbirds (*Agelaius phoeniceus*): The importance of complex visual stimuli. In: Social Learning: Psychological and Biological Perspectives, ed. T. Zentall and B.G. Galef, Jr., pp. 99–115. Hillsdale, NJ: Erlbaum.

Mineka, S., and M. Cook. 1988. Social learning and the acquisition of snake fear in monkeys. In: Social Learning: Psychological and Biological Perspectives, ed. T. Zentall and B.G. Galef, Jr., pp. 51–73. Hillsdale, NJ: Erlbaum.

Pinker, S. 1994. The Language Instinct: The New Science of Language and Mind. Harmondsworth: Penguin.

Sigg, H. 1980. Differentiation of female positions in Hamadryas one-male-units. *Z. Tierpsych.* **53**:265–302.

Templeton, J.J., and L.A. Giraldeau. 1996. Vicarious sampling: The use of personal and public information by starlings foraging in a simple patchy environment. *Behav. Ecol. Sociobiol.* **38**:105–112.

Terkel, J. 1996. Cultural transmission of feeding behaviour in the black rat (*Rattus rattus*). In: Social Learning in Animals: The Roots of Culture, ed. C.M. Heyes and B.G. Galef, Jr., pp. 17–47. New York: Academic.

Whiten, A., and D. Custance. 1996. Studies of imitation in chimpanzees and children. In: Social Learning in Animals: The Roots of Culture, ed. C.M. Heyes and B.G. Galef, Jr., pp. 291–318. New York: Academic.

Wilkinson, G. 1992. Information transfer at evening bat colonies. *Anim. Behav.* **44**:501–518.

14

Decision Making in Superorganisms

How Collective Wisdom Arises from the Poorly Informed Masses

Thomas D. Seeley

Section of Neurobiology and Behavior, Cornell University,
Ithaca, NY 14853, U.S.A.

ABSTRACT

This chapter considers the mechanisms of decision making in groups that possess a high level of functional integration (superorganisms). Such groups, which include colonies of social insects, often possess impressive powers of decision making, especially with respect to simultaneous-option decisions. Since no one member of a social insect colony can possess a synoptic knowledge of its colony's options, or can perform the complex information processing needed to estimate the utility of each option and then choose among them, the concepts of bounded rationality and heuristics are highly relevant to solving the mystery of how colonies of social insects make decisions. To give substance to these ideas, one specific example of group decision making is examined: how honeybee swarms choose a home site. Experimental studies of this subject indicate that even though the swarm as a whole is a sophisticated and skilled decision-making agent, the cognitive skills required of the individual bees involved appear to be surprisingly simple.

INTRODUCTION

The term "superorganism" refers to a group of organisms that is functionally organized to work as an integrated whole (Maynard Smith and Szathmary 1997). Examples of groups that can be properly regarded as superorganisms are colonies of ants, bees, wasps, and termites in which most of the members (the workers) have lost the capacity to reproduce. Worker individuals can propagate their genes only by ensuring the success of the colony, just as somatic cells can propagate their genes only by ensuring the success of the organism. Hence, the colony can be expected to be functionally organized, i.e., to be organized in ways that favor the colony's success relative to other colonies. It is, therefore, reasonable to apply the concepts of optimization and adaptation to entire colonies, as was done, for example, by Oster and Wilson (1978) in their book on the caste systems of social insects.

The goal of this workshop was to examine bounded rationality as the key to understanding how animals (including people) actually make decisions. In this chapter I will maintain the focus on how decisions are made, but will do so by examining the mechanisms of decision making in superorganisms rather than organisms. We shall see that the superorganismal colonies of social insects provide us with excellent opportunities to investigate the surprisingly simple strategies of individual behavior that underlie the functioning of a group as a decision-making agent. In addition, we shall see that the concept of bounded rationality of individuals applies as much, if not more so, in the context of group decision making as in individual decision making.

GROUPS MAKE SIMULTANEOUS-OPTION DECISIONS

In essence, decision making has two components: (a) gathering information about the options from which a choice will be made, and (b) processing the information to choose an option and so arrive at a decision. If a decision is made by gathering and processing information about options one at a time in a temporal sequence, we call this a *sequential-option decision*; however, if a decision is made by gathering information about multiple options simultaneously and then processing a pool of information, we call this a *simultaneous-option decision* (Todd and Miller 1999). One of the principal features of decision making in groups is that it nearly always produces simultaneous-option decisions. This is because a group, unlike an individual, can conduct its search for alternatives as a parallel process, with different individuals exploring different places or different ideas at the same time. Given this reality, we can see that a central puzzle regarding group decision making is what heuristics — short-cut methods of problem-solving (Gigerenzer and Todd 1999) — a group's members use to sort through numerous options simultaneously and eventually produce a decision.

MAIN FEATURES OF DECISION MAKING
BY SOCIAL INSECT COLONIES

The natural history of social insects is filled with examples of real-world choice problems faced by colonies. These include choosing where to build the nest

(Lindauer 1955), deciding when to enlarge the nest (Pratt 1998), selecting the best route for a trail linking the nest site and a food source (Deneubourg and Goss 1989), deciding how to allocate the investment in reproductives between males and females (Crozier and Pamilo 1996), and choosing which males from outside the colony will be allowed to mate with a new queen inside the colony (Franks and Hölldobler 1987). Thus, social insects present us with a multitude of group decision-making processes that have been honed by natural selection to work well in nature.

Equally importantly, the colonies of social insects are groups that are unusually open to analysis through observation and experimentation. With proper care, colonies of ants and bees will thrive in brightly illuminated, glass-walled enclosures (e.g., observation hives) where one can watch everything that happens inside the colony's nest. This, coupled with the fact that insects generally do not mind humans peering at them, means that each step of any particular decision-making process of a colony is open to scrutiny. While it is true that individual insects are small, at least compared to ourselves, they are macroscopic entities that can be watched with the naked eye and labeled for individual identification. The small size of the members of a social insect colony is actually an advantage, for often it means that a whole colony is a compact unit. It is not unusual for an entire decision-making process to transpire within a nest or an arena situated in a laboratory where it is easily watched, videorecorded, and experimentally analyzed.

A third feature of decision-making processes in social insect colonies is that they are highly distributed processes. This is especially true for those species, such as army ants and honeybees, whose colonies show the highest degree of functional integration. In these species a colony typically consists of one mated queen which serves as an egg-laying machine, thousands upon thousands of sterile workers that perform all tasks other than egg production, and in certain seasons a number of future reproductives (unmated queens and males) that will eventually leave the nest to establish new colonies. In honeybees, the best-studied species, for example, there is no evidence of a control hierarchy within colonies, with a central authority functioning as a central decision-making unit. In particular, it is clear that the queen of a honeybee colony does not supervise the actions of her colony. As the biblical King Solomon observed for colonies of ants, there is "neither guide, overseer, nor ruler." The queen of a honeybee colony does emit a chemical signal, the blend of "queen substance" pheromones, which provides negative feedback regulating the colony's production of replacement queens (Winston and Slessor 1992), but neither this nor any other signal from the queen provides comprehensive instructions to the thousands of workers within a hive (Seeley 1995).

Why is the decision making of the superorganismal insect societies so decentralized? Centralized control of any cooperative group requires that a tremendous amount of information — usually dispersed among all the members of the group — be communicated to a central decision-making individual, that this individual then integrates all this information, and finally that it issues instructions to the other group members (Simon 1981). However, no species of social insect has evolved anything like a colony-wide nervous system which would allow information to flow rapidly and efficiently to a central decision maker. Moreover, there is no individual within a colony capable of processing a huge mass of information. It is not surprising, therefore, that social insect colonies have evolved highly distributed mechanisms of group decision making. Given that no one member of a social insect colony can possess a synoptic knowledge of her colony's options, or can perform the complex information processing needed to estimate the utility of each option, it is not surprising that the concepts of bounded rationality and heuristics are highly relevant to understanding how superorganisms make their decisions.

HOW HONEYBEE SWARMS CHOOSE A HOME SITE

Natural History

One of the most spectacular and best-studied examples of an animal group functioning as a collective decision-making agent is a swarm of honeybees choosing its future home. This phenomenon occurs in the late spring and early summer when a colony outgrows its hive and proceeds to divide itself by swarming. The mother queen and approximately half of the worker bees (approximately 10,000 bees) leave the parental hive to establish a new colony, while a daughter queen and the remaining workers stay behind to perpetuate the old colony. The swarm bees leave en masse, quickly forming a cloud of bees just outside the parental hive; they then coalesce into a beard-like cluster at an interim site (usually a nearby tree branch) where they choose their future dwelling place. The nest-site selection process starts with several hundred scout bees flying from the swarm cluster to search for tree cavities and other potential nest sites that meet the bees' real-estate preferences: cavity volume greater than 20 liters; cavity walls thick and strong; and a cavity opening smaller than 30 cm^2, at least 3 meters above the ground, facing south for sunlight, and located at the floor of the cavity. The scouts then return to the cluster, report their findings by means of waggle dances, and work together to decide which one of the dozen or more possible nest sites that they have discovered should be the swarm's new home. Once the scouts have completed their deliberations, they stimulate the other members of the swarm to launch into flight and then steer them to the chosen site (the biology of swarming is reviewed in Winston 1987).

How exactly do the several hundred scout bees jointly decide which of the several sites found should be their future home? The first step toward solving this mystery came in the early 1950s when Martin Lindauer (1955, 1961) discovered that a scout bee can report the location of a potential nest site to other scouts on the swarm cluster by means of the waggle dance (von Frisch 1967; see Figure 14.1). He also observed that initially the scouts' dances denote various sites, but that eventually all of their dances are for just one site. Shortly thereafter, the swarm lifts off and flies to this site. Lindauer suggested that the dancers achieve a consensus by influencing one another, for he observed bees that

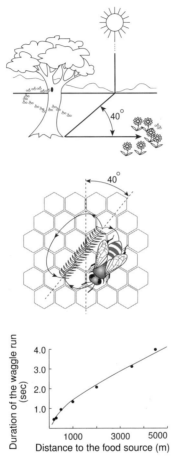

Figure 14.1   The waggle dance of the honeybee. As shown here, the dance is used to indicate the location of a flower patch, but it can also be used to indicate the location of a nest site. Top: The patch of flowers lies along a line 40° to the right of the sun as a bee leaves her colony's nest inside a hollow tree. Middle: To report the location of this food source when inside the nest, the bee runs through a figure-eight pattern, vibrating her body laterally as she passes through the central portion of the dance, the waggle run. A single dance can consist of 100 or more dance circuits, each with a waggle run. Bottom: the relationship between the distance to the flowers and the duration of the waggle run. (From *The Wisdom of the Hive* by Thomas D. Seeley, copyright © 1995 by the President and Fellows of Harvard College, reprinted by permission of Harvard University Press.)

ceased to dance for one site and later danced for another site after being recruited to it. However, the precise mechanisms of the decision-making process in honeybee swarms remained a mystery until recently, even though they were the subject of much discussion (see Wilson 1971; Dawkins 1982; Markl 1985; Griffin 1992).

One thing that has favored the analysis of group decision making in honeybee swarms is that this process is an external one: it occurs on the surface of the swarm cluster where it is easily observed. The swarm's surface is where the scout bees produce the waggle dances that advertise the sites they favor. Thus one can monitor the building of a consensus among a swarm's scouts by video-recording their dances. Recently, complete records of the scout bees' dances in three swarms were made using swarms that consisted entirely of bees labeled for individual identification (Seeley and Buhrman 1999). With each bee so labeled, it was possible to follow each bee's history of dancing throughout the decision-making process of each swarm. In each case, the videorecords yielded not only a synoptic view of this process at the level of the whole swarm, but also key insights into the rules of behavior used by individual bees in collectively producing a decision.

Group-level View

The record of dances performed on one of the swarms is shown in Figure 14.2. Each panel in this figure shows, for an approximately two-hour period, the number of bees that danced for each potential nest site and the total number of waggle runs that the dancing bees performed for each site. We can see that the time when dances were performed was spread over three days and totaled some 16 hours of active deliberations. During the first half of the decision-making process (i.e., what is shown in the first four panels), the scout bees reported all 11 of the potential nest sites that they would consider. We can also see that during the first half of the process the scouts did not advertise any one of the alternative sites more strongly than the others; during the second half, however, one of the sites gradually began to be advertised more strongly than all the others. Indeed, during the last few hours of the decision making, the site that had emerged as the front-runner (site G) became the object of all the dances performed on the swarm: by the end there was unanimity among the dancing bees.

Besides the conspicuous transition from diversity to uniformity in the sites advertised by the dances, we also see a crescendo in dancing at the end of the decision making. If one compares the last panel with the seven prior panels in terms of number of dancing bees, dances, and number of waggle runs, one sees that the last panel has by far the highest number of each. Note too that the site that was ultimately chosen (site G) was not the first site advertised on the swarm; it was seventh out of 11 sites. Also, we see that many potential nest sites are advertised only weakly and briefly on the swarm, i.e., by just one to three bees and often in just one or two panels (sites C, E, F, H, I, J, and K).

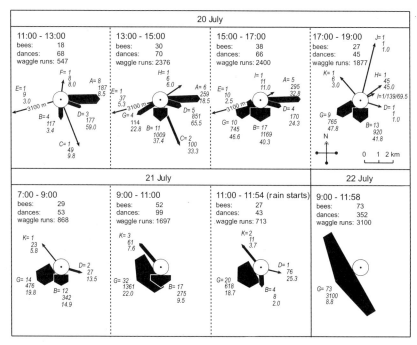

Figure 14.2 History of a swarm's decision-making process from the time that the first potential nest site was advertised on the swarm (shortly after 11:00 hours on July 20, 1997) to until it lifted off to fly to its new home (at 11:58 hours on July 22, 1997). The circle within each of the panels represents the location of the swarm; each arrow pointing out from the circle indicates the distance and direction of a potential nest site; the width of each arrow denotes the number of different bees that danced for the site in the time period shown. The set of numbers at the tip of each arrow denotes three things: *top* the number of bees that danced for the site, *middle* the number of waggle runs performed for the site, *bottom* the mean number of waggle runs per dance for the site. The numbers after "bees," "dances," and "waggle runs" within each panel denote the total number of each (summed over all the potential nest sites) for the time period shown. (From Seeley and Buhrman (1999); reprinted by permission of Springer-Verlag.)

There was, however, a real "debate" among the dancing bees. The scout bees found three sites — sites A, B, and G — which elicited dancing by several bees over periods lasting several hours, and so were represented by hundreds or thousands of waggle runs. While watching this swarm, we thought at first that site A would be the chosen site, for during the first two hours of dancing it gained a strong lead among the dancers. However, the advertising of site A faded after several hours. Meanwhile the dancing for sites B and G became stronger and stronger. By the end of the first day (July 20), it was clear that these two sites were the leading candidates, though it was not clear which site would ultimately be chosen. Between 17:00 and 19:00 hours, site B led site G in terms of both dancers (13 vs. 9) and waggle runs (920 vs. 765), but there was no doubt that the scout bees were still far from an agreement. The second day (July 21) began with both sites continuing to receive strong, nearly equal advertising by the dancers; however, over the course of the morning, the dancing for site G strengthened while that for site B weakened. If rain had not shut off the debate at the end of the morning, it seems likely that all the dances would have been for site G by some-time in the afternoon of July 21. As it was, the bees that danced on the morning of July 22 were unanimous in advertising site G, and at 11:58 hours the swarm lifted off and flew in the direction of site G.

Is the site chosen by a swarm the best of the sites discovered by the swarm's scout bees? Although we cannot answer this question for the case just shown, because the 11 sites located by the bees were never located by us in the surround-ing woodlands, the results of another study indicate that swarms are actually quite accurate in choosing the best site (Seeley and Buhrman, unpublished work). In this study, three swarms of bees were transported one at a time to a windswept, treeless island along the coast of Maine. There we presented each swarm with an array of five nestboxes in a fan-shaped array, with each nestbox 200 m from the swarm. Of the five nestboxes, four offered a mediocre home site — a 15-liter cavity — and one offered an excellent home site — a 40-liter cavity. (A 15-liter cavity provides barely enough space for the honey-filled combs that will fuel a colony's heat production during the cold, flowerless months of winter, whereas a 40-liter cavity provides ample storage space.) The record of each swarm's search for and choice among these five alternative nest sites is shown in Figure 14.3. We see that in each case the scout bees discovered one or more of the mediocre sites well before they located the excellent site, sometimes several hours in advance, and that they recruited other bees to the me-diocre site. However, we also see in each case that once the excellent site was discovered, the bees recruited very strongly to this site so that within a few hours the number of scout bees at the excellent site greatly exceeded the number of scouts at any of the mediocre sites. Ultimately, each swarm lifted off and flew to-ward the excellent site. It is clear, therefore, that these three swarms demon-strated high accuracy in making the decision of where to live.

Individual-level View

It is tempting to think of the individual scout bees operating like the members of a human jury to produce a consensus: different options are presented, each indi-vidual evaluates the various options and forms an opinion, and if there is not a consensus then the members discuss the relative strengths of the leading options until the discordant individuals change their minds and everyone is in agree-ment. For bees, this would require rather complex cognitive skills. In particular, it would require that each bee acquire knowledge of the alternative nest sites, compare these alternatives and decide which seems best, and yet remain open to switching its opinion under the influence of additional information from other

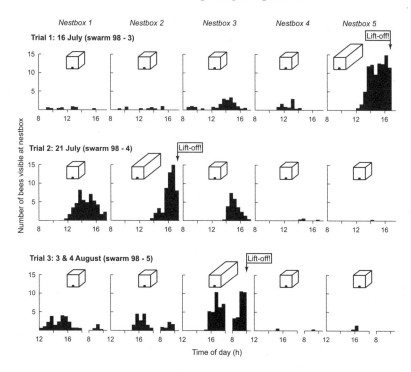

Figure 14.3   Results of three trials of a test of the ability of swarms to select the best nest site in an array of five sites. The test was conducted on Appledore Island, Maine, which is devoid of natural nest sites. Five nestboxes were arranged in a fan-shaped array on the island so that each box was equidistant (230 m) from the swarm. One nestbox was an excellent nest site (40-liter cavity) while the other four were only mediocre sites (15-liter cavities). A count of the number of scout bees visible at each nestbox was made every 30 min. In each trial, one or more of the mediocre sites was discovered long before (1–14 hours) the excellent site. Nevertheless, in each trial the excellent site was ultimately chosen by the swarm. Thus we see that these three swarms were all accurate decision makers.

bees. In reality, however, each scout bee in a swarm uses much simpler cognitive tools than does a human in a jury. Nevertheless, as we have just seen, collectively the scouts form accurate decisions.

The first indication that simple heuristics might underlie the scouts' consensus-building process came from examining the dance records of individual bees. We found that of the 149 bees that performed dances in the swarm whose decision-making history is depicted in Figure 14.2, 72 danced initially for a nonchosen site while 77 danced initially for the chosen site. Since eventually the dancers were unanimous in advertising the chosen site (see Figure 14.2), one might think that the scouts possess a means whereby all the bees that danced initially for a nonchosen site switched their dancing for the chosen site. To our surprise, however, we found that most (48, or 67%) of these 72 bees instead simply *ceased* their dancing; only a minority (24, or 33%) *switched* their dancing. Thus we had a very curious result: the process of building a consensus among the dancing bees relies much more upon bees ceasing to dance than upon bees switching their dances to the chosen site. In other words, in a honeybee swarm, consensus building is more a matter of those favoring the losing option dropping out of the debate than it is a matter of them changing their minds. The former seems a good deal simpler than the latter.

When we next examined the behavior records of those relatively few (24) individuals that did switch their dancing from the nonchosen to the chosen site, we found a hint that even these bees were doing something simpler than one might think at first: all had a long period (2–10 hours) between stopping dancing for the nonchosen site and starting dancing for the chosen site. It looked, therefore, like these bees did not quit dancing for the nonchosen site by encountering a "persuasive" dancer for the chosen site and then comparing the two sites. Instead, it looked like these bees switched their dancing by first losing the desire to produce dances for one site and then, several hours later, gaining the desire to produce dances for anothert site, one that they probably visited after following a dancer advertising this second site. (By this time, all the dances on the swarm were advertising the chosen site, hence when these 24 switching bees resumed their dancing, they all did so with dances for the chosen site.) This finding suggested that the phenomenon of a bee switching her dancing between sites may not be based on her having knowledge of multiple sites simultaneously and comparing the sites ("comparison tactic"), but may instead be based on her having knowledge of just one site at a time ("noncomparison tactic"). A conclusive test of these two hypotheses remains to be done; however, for now it is useful to recognize that the cognitive tools underlying the phenomenon of dance switching may be simpler than they appear at first glance.

If all of the bees that initially dance on a swarm eventually cease dancing, and if most bees that subsequently dance on a swarm start dancing after following a dancer chosen at random, then it is not hard to see how a consensus will emerge among the dancing bees. All sites will eventually lose their old supporters, and only those sites that elicit strong dancing will gain new ones. In addition, because strong dancing for a site recruits many bees to this site, and because these recruited bees will also dance strongly for the site, there is positive feedback on the number of bees at a site. Eventually, the site that most strongly stimulates bees to dance will become the target of all the dances. But what ensures that the consensus will settle on the best site, or at least one of the better sites, in the array of alternatives discovered by the scout bees? One mechanism for achieving this would be for the bees to adjust dance strength in relation to site quality, so that the higher the nest-site quality the greater the waggle-dance strength.

There is evidence now that scout bees that have visited an excellent site will indeed produce dances that contain more waggle runs than do bees from a mediocre site (Seeley and Buhrman, unpublished results). They accomplish this by varying as a function of site quality both the *duration* of the dance and the *rate* at which waggle runs are produced during the dance. This requires, of course, that the bees are able to evaluate a nest site and then convert a sense of overall "site goodness" into a dance of appropriate duration and tempo. This is not a trivial task, especially given the fact that scout bees assess multiple variables of a site (cavity volume, entrance size and height, etc.). Yet except for cavity volume (Seeley 1977), we know nothing of how a bee gathers information about the properties of a potential home site, and we know nothing at all about how a bee integrates this information into an overall sense of site goodness. Only future studies can reveal whether the accurate evaluation of a potential home site entails surprisingly simple or impressively complex cognitive skills.

Whether simple or complex, there is strong evidence that most scout bees use their nest-site evaluation tools only once during the swarm's entire decision-making process. Seeley and Buhrman (1999) found that in each of the three swarms they studied, a large majority (76–86%) of the bees that performed dances did so for just one of the several potential nest sites that were reported on their swarm. A small minority (11–22%) of the dancers danced for two sites, and only a tiny percentage (2–3%) danced for three or more sites. These results suggest that most scouts actually visit just one potential nest site. When Visscher and Camazine (1999) set up swarms in a Californian desert, gave them two nestboxes from which to choose, and dotted each bee visiting a nestbox with one of two colors of paint, they showed directly that more than 80% of the bees visited just one site. Thus it is clear that however complex the task of evaluating a potential nest site, most scout bees perform this task at just one site.

CONCLUSIONS

We ordinarily think of decision making as a process performed by individual organisms, but sophisticated acts of decision making are also performed by groups, most notably those groups that have evolved a high level of functional organization, such as the superorganismal colonies of social insects. Since groups can perform multiple activities simultaneously, when it comes to decision making they have a natural ability to gather and process information about several options simultaneously. Thus one of the main challenges in understanding decision making by groups is identifying the heuristics that the group members use to digest collectively the mass of information that the group has assembled.

Colonies of social insects provide us with countless examples in which a group operates smoothly to make ecologically important decisions, ones that determine the success or failure of the entire group. By peering inside these colonies and analyzing the inner workings of their decision-making processes, we can learn about distributed systems of decision making that function well in nature. There is no central authority in these colonies. Rather, each individual

operates with extremely limited information and yet, somehow, correct decisions are made.

To gain some feeling for the specific tricks that enable a group of poorly informed individuals to work together to produce wise decisions, we have examined the means by which a honeybee swarm selects a dwelling place. Viewing
the process at the group level, we see an impressive decision-making process:
the scout bees in a swarm locate a dozen or so potential dwelling places, each of
these alternatives is evaluated with respect to numerous attributes, and the best
of these alternatives is ultimately chosen for the swarm's new home. Looking at
the process at the individual level, we see that the search for and evaluation of
the alternatives is somewhat simplified for individual bees by the fact that most
bees visit just one site during the entire decision-making process. It remains unclear, however, whether it is appropriate to consider the evaluation of one site a
simple process, since we know almost nothing about how bees evaluate a site.
Perhaps bees possess an ingenious heuristic that enables them to judge easily the
overall goodness of a site, or perhaps they perform an amazing feat of information acquisition and integration.

We understand in greater detail the mechanisms by which individuals work
together to identify the best site, once the information about the different sites
has been reported on the swarm by means of waggle dances. The bees decide
which site is best by building a consensus among the dancers advertising the various sites. The bees' consensus-building technique illustrates the way that simplifying tricks can evolve that reduce the information processing required of
individual bees. Instead of having each dancing bee compare the quality of her
site with that of other sites and switch her dance if she detects a superior site, it
appears that the dancing bees build a consensus by having each bee eventually
cease her dancing, by having each bee adjust the strength of her dancing in accordance with site quality, and by having new dancers become recruited to each
site in accordance with the strength of the dancing for each site (perhaps simply
by having bees choose at random a dancer to follow). In this way, mediocre sites
will soon lose all their dancers, only good sites will gain dancers, and eventually
(because strong dancing exerts positive feedback on itself) the best site will acquire all the dancers.

It now appears that even though a honeybee swarm is composed of
tiny-brained bees, it is able to perform a sophisticated decision-making process
because it distributes among many bees the task of evaluating the numerous potential sites and the task of identifying the one best site for its new home. Moreover, it now seems that the cognitive tools used by the swarm bees are
surprisingly simple, especially compared to the complex information processing performed by the swarm as a whole.

ACKNOWLEDGMENTS

The author's research discussed here was supported by National Science Foundation grant IBN96–30159. I am deeply grateful to the NSF for this financial support, and to Dr. James G. Morin, Director of the Shoals Marine Laboratory, for facilities and support during the experimental work on the accuracy of swarm decision making.

REFERENCES

Crozier, R.H., and P. Pamilo. 1996. Evolution of Social Insect Colonies: Sex Allocation and Kin Selection. Oxford: Oxford Univ. Press.

Dawkins, R. 1982. The Extended Phenotype. Oxford: Oxford Univ. Press.

Deneubourg, J.L., and S. Goss. 1989. Collective patterns and decision-making. *Ethol. Ecol. Evol.* **1**:295–311.

Franks, N.R., and B. Hölldobler. 1987. Sexual competition during colony reproduction in army ants. *Biol. J. Linnean Soc.* **30**:229–243.

Gigerenzer, G., and P.M. Todd. 1999. Fast and frugal heuristics: The adaptive toolbox. In: Simple Heuristics That Make Us Smart, G. Gigerenzer, P.M. Todd, and the ABC Research Group, pp. 3–34. New York: Oxford Univ. Press.

Griffin, D.R. 1992. Animal Minds. Chicago: Chicago Univ. Press.

Lindauer, M. 1955. Schwarmbienen auf Wohnungssuche. *Z. vergl. Physiol.* **37**:263–324.

Lindauer, M. 1961. Communication among Social Bees. Cambridge: Harvard Univ. Press.

Markl, H. 1985. Manipulation, modulation, information, cognition: Some of the riddles of communication. In: Experimental Behavioral Ecology and Sociobiology, ed. B. Hölldobler and M. Lindauer, pp. 163–194. Stuttgart: Fischer.

Maynard Smith, J., and E. Szathmary. 1997. The Major Transitions in Evolution. Oxford: Oxford Univ. Press.

Oster, G.F., and E.O. Wilson. 1978. Caste and Ecology in the Social Insects. Princeton: Princeton Univ. Press.

Pratt, S. 1998. Condition-dependent timing of comb construction by honeybee colonies: How do workers know when to start building? *Anim. Behav.* **56**:603–610.

Seeley, T.D. 1977. Measurement of nest-cavity volume by the honeybee (*Apis mellifera*). *Behav. Ecol. Sociobiol.* **2**:201–227.

Seeley, T.D. 1995. The Wisdom of the Hive. Cambridge: Harvard Univ. Press.

Seeley, T.D., and S.C. Buhrman. 1999. Group decision making in swarms of honeybees. *Behav. Ecol. Sociobiol.* **45**:19–31.

Simon, H.A. 1981. The Sciences of the Artificial. 2d ed. Cambridge: MIT Press.

Todd, P.M., and G.F. Miller. 1999. From pride and prejudice to persuasion: Satificing in mate search. In: Simple Heuristics That Make Us Smart, G. Gigerenzer, P.M. Todd, and the ABC Research Group, pp. 287–308. New York: Oxford Univ. Press.

Visscher, P.K., and S. Camazine. 1999. Collective decisions and cognition in bees. *Nature* **397**:400.

von Frisch, K. 1967. The Dance Language and Orientation of Bees. Cambridge: Harvard Univ. Press.

Wilson, E.O. 1971. The Insect Societies. Cambridge: Harvard Univ. Press.

Winston, M.L. 1987. The Biology of the Honeybee. Cambridge: Harvard Univ. Press.

Winston, M.L., and K.N. Slessor. 1992. The essence of royalty: Honeybee queen pheromone. *Am. Sci.* **80**:374–385.

Seated, left to right: Ido Erev, Barbara Mellers, Charlotte Hemelrijk, Reinhard Selten
Standing, left to right: Dan Fessler, Tom Seeley, Ralph Hertwig, Klaus Scherer, Kevin Laland

15

Group Report: Effects of Emotions and Social Processes on Bounded Rationality

Barbara A. Mellers, Rapporteur
Ido Erev, Daniel M.T. Fessler, Charlotte K. Hemelrijk,
Ralph Hertwig, Kevin N. Laland, Klaus R. Scherer,
Thomas D. Seeley, Reinhard Selten, and Philip E. Tetlock

INTRODUCTION

People facing decisions are constrained by computational capacities of the human mind, i.e., they are limited in their perceptions, their attention, their memories, as well as their information-processing abilities. Rather than optimizing, they resort to simplifying rules and heuristics. Gigerenzer et al. (1999) explore fast and frugal heuristics and argue that these tools work remarkably well because they exploit structural regularities in the environment. The heuristics they discuss are largely based on cognitive processes. In this chapter, we discuss heuristics that exploit structure in the social and emotional world.

EMOTIONAL PROCESSES IN THE ADAPTIVE TOOLBOX

Emotions have traditionally been regarded as impediments to rationality. They wreak havoc on orderly thought, interfere with logical reasoning, and subvert the most carefully laid plans. In the past, emotions have been linked to madness; the Romans, for example, treated anger as a temporary bout of insanity (de Sousa 1987). Although emotions can be detrimental, we focus here on their adaptive properties.

Darwin (1872) was one of the first to make the case that emotional expressions are beneficial. Threatened animals often show their teeth and, in the process, signal their ability, and perhaps their intention, to attack an aggressor. People who are surprised open their eyes widely and, in that way, obtain as much new information as possible. These expressions have evolved to provide advantages to survival and reproduction.

More recently, Damasio (1994) demonstrated the importance of emotions by examining what happens to those who cannot experience them. He describes a patient named Elliot who suffered from a particular form of frontal lobe damage. Although Elliot's reasoning processes were excellent, he was unable to experience feelings. The absence of emotions was disruptive enough to render him incapable of functioning as a social being.

Damasio argues that Elliot is a modern-day version of Phineas Gage. Gage worked for the railroad and often set off explosives to clear away rocks and debris. On a fateful day in 1848, an accident occurred. An iron rod pierced his cheek, came out through the top of his skull, and damaged his frontal lobe in the same region as that of Elliot. Gage survived the accident and, miraculously, retained his capacity for rational thought. However, his personality was different: he was unable to experience emotions. Damasio argues that Gage's tragic decline and eventual death were caused by his inability to experience emotions and behave appropriately as a social being.

Emotions have beneficial effects from the first day of life. Infants typically smile in their first or second day and laugh in their fourth or fifth month. Smiling, laughing, and crying increase the infant's chances of obtaining parental attention (Freedman et al. 1967). By the eighth month, infants smile selectively in response to familiar faces and cry in response to unfamiliar ones. Such smiles further reinforce attachments between parent and child.

Later in life, emotions serve a wider array of functions. Damasio (1994) suggests that, when considering the consequences of our actions, we associate anticipated outcomes with bodily feelings. For example, bad outcomes are linked to unpleasant gut reactions. Those visceral feelings can direct our attention away from decisions with unpleasant feelings and toward decisions with more pleasurable ones. Damasio refers to the process as the somatic marker hypothesis. This process, he claims, implicitly reduces the number of options we consider and makes our decisions more manageable.

Frank (1988) stresses the economic advantages of emotions. Emotions promote self-interest, not because of any hidden gains in their expression, but rather because they solve commitment problems. Some decisions require difficult-to-reverse commitments from individuals, even though the commitments may be contrary to their short-term interests. Consider a couple who wants to marry and have children. They may be reluctant to do so for fear of their partner leaving if and when a more attractive mate becomes available. The couple could solve the problem by writing a contract with large penalties on divorce, or they could rely on the bonds of romantic love. Strong emotional commitments may be the best way for the couple to achieve their long-term goals.

Emotions also solve problems of social control. Feelings of guilt and shame keep most people from cheating, even when cheating serves their short-term in-terests. Furthermore, people recognize that if others perceive them as cheaters, they may be denied future opportunities. In this way, guilt and shame constrain behavior and provide strong social constraints on respectable members of a community.

In a similar vein, feelings of fairness can deter selfish behavior. The ultima-tum game provides an example. In this game, two individuals are typically paired up, and one is given a fixed sum of money to divide between them. That individual makes an offer, and if the other accepts, the money is divided between them according to that offer. If the offer is rejected, both individuals receive nothing. Suppose a player has $10 to divide. The rational offer is to keep $9.99 for oneself and offer 1 cent to the other player. The rational response is to accept. In fact, many people often reject such offers and act angered by the unfairness of the offer. This "irrational" response conflicts with notions of self-interest, (i.e., a penny is better than nothing, isn't it?) when in fact, the response may protect that player from future injustices in games with repeated play. Would-be players tempted to offer sharply unequal allotments recognize the likelihood of the other player's anger and may be deterred from acting unfairly.

What Are Emotions?

Emotions are relatively brief episodes of synchronized responses that produce noticeable changes in the functioning of an organism. Such changes are brought about by triggering events of major significance (Scherer 1999). The term, "emotion," refers to a combination of components, including physiological arousal, motor expression, and subjective feelings with emotional and motivational consequences. Emotions usually last for a relatively short period of time and disappear fairly rapidly, generally ranging from several minutes to a few hours, with the exception of sadness. Other affective phenomena longer in duration include moods (e.g., cheerful, gloomy, irritable, listless, depressed, buoyant), interpersonal affective stances (e.g., distant, cold, warm, supportive, contemptuous), attitudes (e.g., liking, loving, hating, valuing, desiring), and affectively pertinent personality traits (nervous, anxious, reckless, morose, hos-tile, envious, jealous).

Most researchers agree on at least eight emotions, including anger, sadness, joy, fear, shame, pride, disgust, and guilt (Ekman 1992; Frijda 1986; Izard 1991). Others include surprise. There is still considerable debate about whether some emotions are "basic" in an evolutionary sense (Ortony and Turner 1990; Izard 1992). The specific effects of an emotion are not always obvious, so many researchers consider their adaptive functions within an evolutionary context

(Mesquita et al. 1997). Some emotions, such as disgust, have undoubtedly evolved to protect animals from toxins. After becoming sick from a particular food, animals are usually repulsed by the same food on another encounter. Taste aversion can occur after a single trial. Furthermore, the conditioned stimulus and the unconditioned stimulus need not occur together; animals still avoid the food, even with gaps of up to 75 minutes between food and sickness (Garcia and Koelling 1966). Taste aversion can also be culturally defined. A particular food may be a delicacy in one culture, but repulsive in another.

Fear is another emotion with evolutionary implications. Animals that are fearful are more likely to take flight and escape their predators. However, when they become too fearful, they miss opportunities for survival and reproduction. It has long been thought that fear was innate; for example, many primates who see a snake for the first time exhibit fearful reactions, including flight, facial expressions indicative of fear, visual monitoring of the snake, and alarm or distress calls. However, recent evidence suggests that fear also can be learned (Mineka and Cook 1988).

Three classes of theories have been offered to describe emotions: discrete, dimensional, and appraisal-based. Discrete theories, stemming from Darwin, postulate a number of basic emotions characterized by early ontogenetic onset and universal facial expressions. Dimensional theories, following Wundt's example, characterize emotions as values along one or more continua, such as pleasantness vs. unpleasantness, restfulness vs. activation, and relaxation vs. attention. The simplest version postulates a single dimension of negative and positive affect, fundamental to approach and avoidance tendencies. More complex versions have three or more dimensions. The third class of theories are appraisal-based approaches as pioneered by Arnold (1962) and Lazarus (1968). They assert that emotions are elicited by a cognitive, but not necessarily conscious or controlled, evaluation of antecedent conditions. For example, the component-process theory (Scherer 1984) predicts that the organism uses a limited number of evaluation checks on the stimulus (novelty, intrinsic pleasantness, goal conduciveness, coping potential, and comparability of standards) to monitor events in the environment. Emotions are part of this appraisal process. Anger is produced by an event appraised as interfering with goal attainment, fear is produced by expectations of future events that exceed one's potential for coping, and joy is produced by achievement of a goal.

Emotions and Bounded Rationality

Emotions facilitate rapid, automatic, and survival-oriented actions. Frijda (1986) argues that emotions serve as "relevance detectors," where relevance is determined by an individual's perceptions of a situation. Scherer (1984) emphasizes the role of emotions as replacements for reflexes, instincts, and simple stimulus-response chains that involve the automatic execution of a response. By decoupling the stimulus and response, the organism has time to reevaluate the eliciting event and consider more than one behavioral response.

It is helpful to distinguish among three routes by which emotions can influence choice. We refer to these as background emotions, task-related emotions, and anticipated emotions. Background emotions are those that the decision maker experiences at the time of the choice, but are not elicited from the decision itself. Task-related emotions, such as frustration and anxiety, arise in the course of making a decision. Finally, anticipated emotions are those that the decision maker imagines about future courses of action. We now discuss each in turn.

Background Emotions

Everyone who has ever made a decision remembers occasions in which unrelated moods and emotions took charge. These background emotions also affect perceptions and memories. When happy, we are better at retrieving happier memories, and when sad, we are better at recalling unhappy events (Bower 1981). If memories are marked with somatic tags, background moods may facilitate retrieval of similarly tagged memories. Damasio (1994) notes that emotions direct perceptions to our bodies, and those visceral sensations send instructive signals for action.

Background emotions can also influence attention by focusing it on particular stimuli and influencing the search for information and alternatives. Positive emotions, such as satisfaction, joy, and pride, can shorten the search for alternative options, especially when the decision maker is satisfied with current achievements relative to an aspiration level. Conversely, mild forms of anxiety may foster a more intensive search for alternatives. Anger may focus the individual on actions that lead to revenge and bring the search for new alternatives to a standstill.

Last but not least, background emotions can influence the strategies or heuristics we use to process information. Some positive emotions can promote more flexible and creative problem solving (Isen 1993), and some negative emotions, such as sadness, can lead to more analytical thinking, greater processing of cues, and longer response times (Luce et al. 1997; Luce 1998). Both positive and negative emotions vary in strength or arousal, and psychologists have shown that task performance and arousal are often nonlinearly related, i.e., task performance is best when arousal is moderate.

Task-related Emotions

Some decisions create conflict. We are uncertain about what to do because no single option clearly dominates all others. Bettman et al. (1993) and Einhorn and Hogarth (1981) have operationalized decision conflict as the degree to which valued attributes are negatively correlated. For example, professors making selection decisions for graduate school often find that applicants have either high test scores or high grades, but not both. Families purchasing houses often find that they must face difficult trade- offs, such as whether to have more space in their home or a shorter commute time.

When there is no single best option, people look for reasons to justify their choices (Tversky and Shafir 1992a). People may also prolong the search and/or delay the decision (Tversky and Shafir 1992b; Dhar 1997). Luce (1998) has found that, when consumers experience decision conflict about which product to purchase, they often process more information, but then use simpler decision heuristics that permit them to avoid emotionally difficult trade-offs.

One strategy that people appear to use when making difficult trade-offs is to weight the most important attribute more heavily (Tversky et al.1988). Another strategy is to use simple rules of thumb based on emotions. Hsee (1995, 1996) has shown that, as the difficulty of a choice increases, people tend to select their affectively preferred options more frequently.

Many important decisions are made under severe time pressure. Janis and Mann (1977) discuss the feelings of extreme ambivalence and stress that individuals feel in military, political, and economic domains. They also identify some common maladaptive coping patterns that people adopt, such as defensive avoidance, panic, and hypervigilance. When groups make decisions, additional problems can occur. Conformity pressures can increase and produce "group think," in which group members suppress their doubts about a plan of action and fail to explore the subtleties and complexities that should be discussed.

Tetlock et al. (1996) have examined how people make decisions requiring difficult trade-offs between core values, such as money and love. In these cases, decision makers lack a common metric for comparing values. This problem, sometimes called "value incommensurability" contributes to emotional conflict, cognitive dissonance, and social awkwardness. In other cases, decisions involve transgressions of personal and cultural taboos that are even more severely charged with affect and symbolism. Such trade-offs are sometimes called "constitutively incommensurable." They are not just cognitively dissonant, they are also morally corrosive in the sense that the longer we spend thinking about proposals that breach cultural limits on markets — proposals to auction off body organs to medically needy recipients or to permit the buying and selling of adoption rights for children — the more we undercut our identities as members in good standing in a moral community. The anger and indignation that people feel upon being asked such questions, and the anger they know observers feel at those willing to entertain such proposals, serve as a warning signal to pursue this line of thought no further.

Anticipated Emotions

Decisions are often made with the help of a process of imagination in which we try to experience outcomes "before the fact." Anticipated feelings, such as guilt, shame, fear, and joy, are ways of testing ourselves to see how we feel about possible outcomes. A variety of anticipated emotions have been studied, especially anticipated regret (Landman 1993). Anticipated regret of a new product that malfunctions can increase the chances that people will buy a familiar product (Simonson 1992). Anticipated regret of a child becoming ill or dying from a vaccination increase the chances that people will not vaccinate their children (Ritov and Baron 1990). Anticipated regret of losing a lottery increases the chances that students will refuse to trade their original lottery tickets for new lottery tickets with objectively better odds (Bar-Hillel and Neter 1996). Finally, anticipated regret of a new medical procedure failing increases the chance that physicians will take the safer, more familiar route when treating a patient.

The anticipation of emotions may involve cognitive processing, consistent with appraisal-based theories, or more visceral processing, as suggested by Damasio's somatic marker hypothesis. Results from studies that ask participants to imagine fearful stimuli suggest that the mere thought of extreme negative experiences can activate fearful facial expressions, heart rate, and respiration (Schwartz et al. 1976; Lang et al. 1980). Most likely, both cognitive and emotional processes are involved. Cognitive processing seems plausible with milder emotions, and more visceral processes may dominate with extreme emotions (Le Doux 1996).

Some efforts have been made to formalize the process by which anticipated emotions influence choice. Loomes and Sugden (1982) and Bell (1982) proposed an account of risky choice based on anticipated regret. Regret is the feeling that occurs when one's outcome is worse than the other outcome that would have occurred under another choice. According to regret theory, people anticipate regret and modify their utilities to reflect it. Then they select the option with the greater expected utility, modified by anticipated regret. Later, Loomes and Sugden (1986) and Bell (1985) developed another account of risky choice called disappointment theory. Disappointment is the feeling that occurs when one's outcome is worse than the outcome one would have received under another state of the world.

Both regret theory and disappointment theory have been successful at describing some aspects of risky choice, but the assumptions about emotions were never tested directly. Mellers et al. (1997, 1999) measured anticipated emotions and then obtained risky choices. They developed a theory of anticipated affect and used it to describe risky choice. Their account, called subjective expected pleasure, expands upon disappointment and regret theories by assuming that people anticipate how they will feel about all outcomes of a decision, weight each anticipated emotion by the chances it will occur, and select the option that provides the greater average pleasure. This account gives a good description of risky choices between gambles with monetary outcomes.

With some decisions, such as whether to move, take a new job, have a child, or get married, it is impossible to anticipate all possible outcomes. With other decisions, one may not be interested in more than a few possible outcomes. Feel-ings about those outcomes can be strong enough that we simply avoid an alterna-tive with a potentially severe consequence. Some people avoid California for fear of earthquakes, some avoid alcohol for fear of getting addicted, and some avoid the stock market for fear of financial disaster.

Avoiding pain is not the only emotional basis for decisions. In other in-stances, people pursue pleasure. Teenagers who race cars at high speeds, take dangerous drugs, and engage in unsafe sex may be so immersed in momentary pleasure that they disregard the possibility of future pain and suffering. Loewenstein (1996) discusses a variety of cases in which people make deci-sions, but are essentially "out of control," including those with addictions and cravings. Simple emotion-based heuristics can be both adaptive and maladaptive, depending on the context and the consequences.

SOCIAL PROCESSES IN THE ADAPTIVE TOOLBOX

We live in social networks, adopt social norms, feel social pressures, and make social comparisons. In this section, we discuss three ways in which social pro-cesses influence decision making. First, we discuss the social context that shapes our decisions. Then we discuss fast and frugal heuristics based on social processes.

The Social Context

The mere presence of others influences our behavior. Zajonc (1965) argued that the social context is arousing, and arousal facilitates dominant responses. That is, it boosts performance on easy tasks and hinders performance on harder tasks. For example, ants excavate more sand in the presence of other ants, and chickens eat more grain in the presence of other chickens (Bayer 1929; Chen 1937). A large body of research shows that people tended to perform better on relatively simple tasks, such as easy multiplication problems. However, their performance is hindered by the presence of other people with more difficult tasks. They are slower at learning mazes, nonsense syllables, and complex multiplication prob-lems in the presence of other people. Cockroaches, parakeets, and green finches also learn mazes more slowly in the presence of others (Allee and Masure 1936; Gates and Allee 1933; Klopfer 1958).

The presence of others can do more than facilitate dominant responses. It can also increase social loafing; individuals working in groups do not work as hard as individuals working alone (Latane et al. 1979). It can interfere with automatic responses, such as speaking. Stutterers stutter more in front of others (Mullen 1986). It can intensify emotions (Storms and Thomas 1977). People who sit close to each other in a room behave different from people who sit far apart. When sitting together, people are more likely to laugh and clap at amusing stimuli (Freedman et al. 1980). They are also more likely to express anger and outrage at stimuli perceived as unfair and unjust. Finally, the presence of others can increase conformity. Asch (1956) was one of the first to demonstrate the powerful effects people can have on each other. He asked students in a room to judge the length of a line relative to a standard. Students seated around a table gave their answers, one after the next. Asch manipulated the number of students who gave the incorrect answer before a naive subject was asked the question. Naive subjects were more likely to give incorrect responses, even when they knew their answers were wrong, as the number of wrong answers given before them increased.

Social networks have powerful effects on decisions, especially those regarding interpersonal relationships. One of the best predictors of friendship is proximity in living quarters. Festinger et al. (1950) observed the friendships in MIT married student apartments. Couples were assigned to apartments at random, but the friendships that developed were anything but random. When asked to name their three closest friends, students in the apartments tended to name others living in the same building or on the same floor. The individual chosen most often was the person living next door.

Finally, social norms and social expectations influence choice. Individuals who accept a role, such as a parent, a dentist, an accountant, or a secretary, also tend to accept a set of rules that prescribes their behavior. Doctors in hospitals, professors in classrooms, and workers on assembly lines adopt heuristics for decisions as part of their identities. These social norms often free people from evaluating the appropriateness of their behavior and permit them to direct their attention to other matters (March 1994).

Many social norms are so subtle that they often go unnoticed. Consider the norm of cleanliness in a particular environment. Such norms are quickly altered by the behavior of others in that environment. Cialdini et al. (1990) showed that people tended to litter more when a given environment was already littered than when it was clean. Rule violators are often punished, and punishments can range from embarrassment to execution. Tolerance of rule violators also differs across cultures and is a type of social norm.

Social Learning

Bismarck is reputed to have once said, "Fools learn from experience; wise men learn from the experience of others." Animals facing problems such as finding food, avoiding predators, and selecting mates often turn to each other for solutions. Laland (this volume) notes that social learning has many forms, each reflecting the nature of what is learned (motor patterns, locations, objects to interact with, goals, etc.). When animals imitate, they learn by copying the motor patterns of another animal in a particular context. With local enhancement, animals learn by directing their attention to the same object as another animal.

Imitation and local enhancement are useful heuristics, but they both require further decisions. To imitate, one must decide who to imitate as well as what and when to imitate. Strategies such as "do-what-the-majority-do" or "do-what-the-successful-do" are plausible rules. Animals would presumably use such heuristics when there were high costs associated with asocial learning, frequent variation in the environment, and few opportunities for scrounging (or stealing) (Boyd and Richerson 1985; Giraldeau et al. 1994). Social learning may also be advantageous when competition for resources is relatively light or when animals band together in unfamiliar or threatening environments. Asocial strategies may be desirable for less successful animals. Laland believes that less successful animals may be those most likely to try innovative strategies. These animals may try imitation, but if that fails, they resort to innovative heuristics.

Imitation is also a successful heuristic with humans, especially with social dilemmas. Social dilemmas are situations in which people who pursue their self-interests eventually make the group worse off. The prisoner's dilemma game is a well-known example of such a problem. In prisoner's dilemma games with repeated play, one strategy seems to outperform all others. This strategy, called Tit-for-Tat, is one in which a player cooperates on the first trial and then imitates the other player on all remaining trials. Axelrod (1984) has shown that Tit-for-Tat outperforms all other strategies in computer tournaments. He attributes its success to four key functional properties: one who adopts the Tit-for-Tat strategy is nice (never defects first), cooperative (always reciprocates cooperation), forgiving (returns to cooperation as soon as the other player does), and retaliatory (strikes back as soon as the other player defects).

Group Decision Making

Individuals often meet to solve problems through give-and-take interactions. Which heuristics facilitate group decisions? One rule is called the Delphi method. This rule dates back to sometime around 250 B.C., when King Ptolemy decided to translate some biblical writings into Greek. The king asked the high priest of Judea to help. The priest selected seventy scholars, sent them to Alexandria, put each in a separate room, and asked each to do his translation independently. When the job was done, a committee that examined the seventy translations found that they were identical. Word spread, and everyone was astonished. But when an old Rabbi heard what had happened, he said, "Seventy scholars in separate rooms, and this you call a miracle? Put them in one room and get the same translation — this is a miracle."

The translation story illustrates the idea behind the Delphi method, a procedure for group decision making in which individuals give separate opinions, receive information about the views of others, give their separate opinions again, and eventually converge on a decision without face-to-face confrontations. This simple heuristic has proven to be an effective strategy for reaching agreement using impersonal debate (Dalkey 1975; Dalkey and Helmer 1963).

The natural competitor to the Delphi method is free-form discussion. Other more mathematical rules have also been proposed for aggregating individual judgments. The Delphi method exploits the idea that individuals come with different forms of expertise, different knowledge bases, and different biases, all of which should enter into a consensus decision. More recently, Delbecq et al. (1975) proposed an alternative in which individuals make silent judgments, learn the judgments of the group, discuss the problem, and then reconsider their judgments individually. Final judgments are aggregated mathematically. This procedure has also shown promise and some have argued that it can improve on the Delphi method (Gustafson et al. 1973).

EXPLORING HEURISTICS BASED ON EMOTIONS AND SOCIAL PROCESSES

Mate choice is an important decision based on social and emotional processes. Buss (1989) describes rules used in mate choice among humans. He argues that selection pressures have influenced human mate preferences in systematic ways. Male reproductive success depends on mating with females who are fertile, and fertility is correlated with youth and beauty. Female reproductive success depends on finding males who show the ability and willingness to invest resources in their offspring. Buss (1989; Buss et al. 1990) investigates mate preferences cross-culturally and finds that males placed greater value than females on relative youth and physical attractiveness in potential mates. Females placed greater value than males on earning capacity and variables related to resource acquisition in potential mates. He attributes these preferences, which presumably guide mate selection, to adaptive pressures over time.

In any real world setting, there are multiple explanations for mate choice. For example, ethologists have described two types of primate species belonging to the genus *Macaca*: "despotic" (e.g., rhesus macaques, *Macaca mulatta*) and "egalitarian" (e.g., Sulawesi macaques, *Macaca tonkeana*) species. Despotic macaques have a steep dominance hierarchy, loose grouping, and fierce displays of aggression that are relatively rare. Egalitarian macaques have a weak dominance hierarchy, cohesive grouping, and mild aggressive tendencies that occur quite frequently. Females in the two types of species display different types of mating behavior. Females in the despotic species select only high-ranking males, whereas those in the egalitarian species are highly promiscuous. What accounts for this difference in mate choice?

Some have argued that females in each type of species have different rules for mate choice (Caldecott 1986). By means of an individual-oriented computer model, Hemelrijk (1999) proposed, as an alternative explanation, that females differ in their opportunities for mating rather than their heuristics for choosing. Opportunities for mating are implicit constraints. Hemelrijk's model asserts that individuals within each sex have identical dominance ranks, although males are more dominant than females. Individuals in both types of species aggregate and perform interactions that eventually produce a dominance hierarchy.

The two virtual species are identical with one exception — the intensity of their aggression. Despotic species are more aggressive, an assumption consistent with observations of real macaques. According to the model, in the despotic species, competitive interactions result in a steep dominance hierarchy, and a clear spatial structure emerges, with high-ranking individuals in the central area and subordinates in the periphery. In the egalitarian species, both the dominance hierarchy and the spatial structure are much weaker. Now something peculiar starts to happen.

Hemelrijk predicts that, in the egalitarian species, males will maintain higher ranks and females will keep their lower ranks. In the despotic species, there is stronger differentiation. Consequently, some females become more dominant than males. This intersexual overlap in ranks is likely to influence sexual behavior. For instance, Rosenblum and Nader (1971) showed that, with Bonnet macaques, males with lower rankings are often inhibited with higher-ranking females. Hemelrijk (1999) argues that if a similar inhibition took place with despotic males, despotic females, because of their higher ranks, would have fewer mating partners than egalitarian females, holding all else constant. In Hemelrijk's model, if intersexual rank overlap is larger in despotic macaques, despotic females show selective mate choice because the number of mates available to them is limited. Females in the egalitarian species not only have more partners, they are also less capable of refusing their partners because of their subordinate ranks relative to males. Whether or not there are real differences in female mate choice remains to be seen.

Hertwig proposed an exercise in computer simulation to examine the effects of romantic love in mate search (see also Miller and Todd 1998). Consider a population that is comprised of female and male agents, each characterized by several cues. Female agents are described in terms of their reproductive potential, and male agents are described in terms of their ability to acquire resources and invest them in offspring (Buss 1992). Each agent has an aspiration level that must be met before an agent accepts a partner. This aspiration level could be acquired via individual learning (e.g., feedback concerning one's own mate quality) or social learning (e.g., imitating peers, that is, adopting the aspiration level of proximal agents). Furthermore, aspiration levels of females are higher than those of males. An agent combines cues to assess another agent's mate value, for example, using a weighted additive rule (see Payne and Bettman, this volume). Then the agent compares the overall mate value to his or her aspiration level, and if the overall assessment exceeds the aspiration level, the potential mate would be accepted. Furthermore, if a "good" match occurs, romantic love might be evoked in one or both of the individuals.

Hertwig identifies three potential functions of romantic love. First, an expression of romantic love will increase an agent's mate value in the eyes of the recipient. Second, romantic love will change the agent's perceptions of the loved one (i.e., increase cues values or importance weights on favorable attributes), thereby strengthening the bond. Third, an agent who expresses romantic love will stop his or her search for a mate, at least for some time. In this sense, romantic love becomes a commitment device, as described by Frank (1988).

By examining these functions, one can gain insight into the effects of romantic love on population size, number of matings, number of offspring, and other variables. One can also investigate the conditions under which romantic love would be advantageous to selected groups within the population, such as males, females, or agents with lower mate values. These exercises help us understand plausible functions of romantic love in different environments and their effects on population survival.

CONCLUSION

Models of bounded rationality are based on assumptions about limited time, resources, and mental capacities. Because of these limitations, people often rely on simple rules that exploit the structure in the environment. Fast and frugal heuristics proposed thus far have focused on cognitive strategies. We have examined heuristics based on emotions and social processes.

Emotions can influence all aspects of decision making. We discussed background emotions, task-related emotions, and anticipated emotions. Background emotions are those that the decision maker experiences at the time of the choice, but are not elicited from the task itself. Task-related emotions, such as frustration and anxiety, arise in the course of making a decision. Finally, anticipated emotions are those that the decision maker imagines about future courses of action. In some cases, choices can be predicted by a Which-Feels-The-Best? heuristic. In other cases, people may use more complex heuristics, such as a Which-Feels-Best-On-Average? heuristic.

Many decisions can be solved by more than one fast and frugal rule and, over time, decision makers learn which heuristics work. Emotions are an important part of the learning process. When the consequence is rewarding, feelings are pleasurable, and when the consequence is punishing, feelings are painful. In this way, emotions serve as secondary reinforcers to learning.

Social processes also influence fast and frugal heuristics. We live in social networks, adopt social norms, feel social pressures, and make social comparisons. We discuss the social context or background factors that shape our decisions. Then we discuss social heuristics for individual and group decision making.

Finally, we examine the use of fast and frugal heuristics in mate choice and show how both empirical work and computer simulations can shed light on underlying processes and functions of emotions. We eagerly await future research on fast and frugal heuristics that exploits additional structure in our social and emotional worlds.

REFERENCES

Allee, W.C., and R.M. Masure. 1936. A comparison of maze behavior in paired and isolated shell-parakeets (*Melopsittacus undulatus Shaw*) in a two-alley problem box. *J. Comp. Psych.* **22**:131–155.

Arnold, M.B. 1962. Emotion and Personality, vol. 1: Psychological Aspects. New York: Columbia Univ. Press.

Asch, S.E. 1956. Studies of independence and conformity: A minority of one against a unanimous majority. *Psych. Mono.* **70 (9, No. 416)**.

Axelrod, R. 1984. The Evolution of Cooperation. New York: Basic.

Bar-Hillel, M., and E. Neter. 1996. Why are people reluctant to exchange lottery tickets? *J. Pers. Soc. Psych.* **70**:17–27.

Bayer, E. 1929. Beiträge zur Zweikomponenten Theorie des Hungers. *Z. Psych.* **112**:1–54.

Bell, D.E. 1982. Regret in decision making under uncertainty. *Operations Res.* **30**:961–981.

Bell, D.E. 1985. Disappointment in decision making under uncertainty. *Operations Res.* **33**:1–27.

Bettman, J., E.J. Johnson, M.F. Luce, and J.W. Payne. 1993. Correlation, conflict, and choice. *J. Exp. Psych.: Learn. Mem. Cogn.* **19**:931–951.

Bower, G.H. 1981. Mood and memory. *Am. Psych.* **36**:129–148.

Boyd, R., and P.J. Richerson. 1985. Culture and the Evolutionary Process. Chicago: Univ. of Chicago Press.

Buss, D.M. 1989. Sex differences in human mate preferences: Evolutionary hypotheses tested in 37 cultures. *Behav. Brain Sci.* **12**:1–49.

Buss, D.M. 1992. Mate preference mechanisms: Consequences for partner choice and intrasexual competition. In: The Adapted Mind, ed. J.H. Bakow, L. Cosmides, and J. Tooby. New York: Oxford Univ. Press.

Buss, D.M., et al. 1990. International preferences in selecting mates. *J. Cross Cult. Psych.* **21**:5–47.

Caldecott, J.O. 1986. Mating patterns, socieities, and ecogeography of macaques. *Anim. Behav.* **34**:208–220.

Chen, S.C. 1937. Social modification of the activity of ants in nest-building. *Physio. Zool.* **10**:420–436.

Cialdini, R.B., R.R. Reno, and C.A. Kallgren. 1990. A focus theory of normative conduct. *J. Pers. Soc. Psych.* **6**:1015–1026.

Dalkey, N.C. 1975. Toward a theory of group estimation. In: The Delphi Method: Techniques and Applications, ed. H.A. Linstone and M. Turoff, pp. 236–261. Reading, MA: Addison-Wesley.

Dalkey, N.C., and O. Helmer. 1963. An experimental application of the Delphi method to the use of experts. *Manag. Sci.* **3**:458.

Damasio, A. 1994. Descartes' Error. New York: Grosset/Putnam.

Darwin, C. 1872. The Expression of the Emotions in Man and Animals. New York: New York Philosophical Library.

Delbecq, A., A. Van de Ven, and D. Gustafson. 1975. Group Techniques for Program Planning. Glenview, IL: Scott Foresman.

de Sousa, R. 1987. The Rationality of Emotions. Cambridge, MA: MIT Univ. Press.

Dhar, R. 1997. Consumer preference for a no-choice option. *J. Consumer Res.* **24**:215–231.

Einhorn, H.J., and R.M. Hogarth. 1981. Behavior decision theory: Processes of judgment and choice. *Ann. Rev. Psych.* **32**:53–88.

Ekman, P. 1992. An argument for basic emotions. *Cogn. Emot.* **6**:169–200.

Festinger, L., S. Schachter, and K. Back. 1950. Social Pressures in Informal Groups: A Study of Human Factors in Housing. New York: Harper.

Frank, R. 1988. Passions within Reason. New York: Norton.

Freedman, J.L., J. Birsky, and A. Cavoukian. 1980. Environmental determinants of behavioral contagion. *Basic Appl. Soc. Psych.* **1**:155–161.

Freedman, D.G., C.B. Loring, and R.M. Martin. 1967. Emotional behavior and personality development. In: Infancy and Early Childhood, ed. Y. Brackbill. New York: Free Press.

Frijda, N.H. 1986. The Emotions. Cambridge: Cambridge Univ. Press.

Garcia, J., and R. Koelling. 1966. Relation of cue to consequence in aviodance learning. *Psych. Sci.* **4**:123–124.

Gates, M.F., and W.C. Allee. 1933. Conditioned behavior of isolated and grouped cockroaches on a simple maze. *J. Comp. Psych.* **15**:331–358.

Gigerenzer, G., P.M. Todd, and the ABC Group. 1999. Simple Heuristics That Make Us Smart. New York: Oxford Univ. Press.

Giraldeau, L.A., T. Caraco, and T.J. Valone. 1994. Social foraging: Individual learning and cultural transmission of innovations. *Behav. Ecol.* **5(1)**:35–43.

Gustafson, R.U., D.H. Shukla, A. Delbecq, and G.W. Walster. 1973. A comparative study of differences in subjective likelihood estimates made by individuals, interacting groups, Delphi groups, and nominal groups. *Org. Behav. Human Decis. Proc.* **9**:280–291.

Hemelrijk, C.K. 1999. An individual-oriented model of the emergence of egalitarian and despotic societies. *Proc. Roy. Soc. Lond. B* **266**:361–369.

Hsee, C.K. 1995. Elastic justification: How tempting but task-irrelevant factors influence decisions. *Org. Behav. Human Decis. Proc.* **62**:330–337.

Hsee, C.K. 1996. Elastic justification: How unjustifiable factors influence judgments. *Org. Behav. Human Decis. Proc.* **66**:122–129.

Isen, A.M. 1993. Positive affect in decision making. In: Handbook of Emotions, ed. M. Lewis and J.M. Haviland. New York: Guilford.

Izard, C.E. 1991. The Psychology of Emotions. New York: Plenum.

Izard, C.E. 1992. Basic emotions, relations among emotions, and emotion–cognition relations. *Psych. Rev.* **99**:561–565.

Janis, I.L., and L. Mann. 1977. Decision making: A psychological analysis of conflict, choice, and commitment. New York: Free Press.

Klopfer, P.M. 1958. Influence of social interaction on learning rates. *Science* **128**:903–904.

Landman, J. 1993. Regret. New York: Oxford Univ. Press.

Lang, P.J., M.J. Kozak, G.A. Miller, D.N. Levin, and A. McLean. 1980. Emotional imagery: Conceptual structure and pattern of somato-visceral response. *Psychophysiology* **17**:179–192.

Latane, B., K. Williams, and S. Harkins 1979. Many hands make light the work: The causes and consequences of social loafing. *J. Pers. Soc. Psych.* **37**:822–832.

Lazarus, R.S. 1968. Emotions and adaptation: Conceptual and empirical relations. In: Nebraska Symp. on Motivation, vol. 16, ed. W.J. Arnold, pp. 175–270. Lincoln, NE: Univ. of Nebraska Press.

Le Doux, J.E. 1996. The Emotional Brain. New York: Simon and Schuster.

278 *Barbara A. Mellers et al.*

Loewenstein, G. 1996. Out of control: Visceral influences on behavior. *Org. Behav. Human Decis. Proc.* **65**:272–292.

Loomes, G., and R. Sugden. 1982. Regret theory: An alternative of rational choice under uncertainty. *Econ. J.* **92**:805–824.

Loomes, G., and R. Sugden. 1986. Disappointment and dynamic consistency in choice under conflict. *Rev. Econ. Stud.* **53**:271–282.

Luce, M.F. 1998. Choosing to avoid: Coping with negatively emotion-laden consumer decisions. *J. Consumer Res.* **24**:409–433.

Luce, M.F., J. Bettman, and J. Payne. 1997. Choice processing in emotionally difficult decisions. *J. Exp. Psych.: Learn. Mem. Cogn.* **23**:384–405.

March, J.G. 1994. A Primer of Decision Making. New York: Free Press.

Mellers, B.A., A. Schwartz, K. Ho, and I. Ritov. 1997. Decision affect theory: Emotional reactions to the outcomes of risky options. *Psych. Sci.* **8**:423–429.

Mellers, B.A., A. Schwartz, and I. Ritov. 1999. Emotion-based choice. *J. Exp. Psych.: Gen.* **128**:332–345.

Mesquita, B., N.H. Frijda, and K.R. Scherer. 1997. Culture and emotion. In: Handbook of Cross Cultural Psychology, vol. 2: Basic Processes and Human Development, 2d ed., ed. J.W. Berry, pp. 255–298. Boston: Allyn and Bacon.

Miller, G.F., and P.M. Todd. 1998. Mate choice turns cognitive. *Trends Cogn. Sci.* **2**:190–198.

Mineka, S., and M. Cook. 1988. Social learning and the acquisition of snake fear in monkeys. In: Social Learning. Psychological and Biological Perspectives, ed. T.R. Zentall and B.G. Galef, Jr. Hillsdale, NJ: Erlbaum.

Mullen, B. 1986. Stuttering, audience size, and the other-total ratio: A self-attention perspective. *J. Appl. Soc. Psych.* **27**:297–323.

Ortony, A., and T.J. Turner. 1990. What's basic about basic emotions? *Psych. Rev.* **97**:315–331.

Ritov, I., and J. Baron. 1990. Reluctance to vaccinate: Omission bias and ambiguity. *J. Behav. Decis. Mak.* **3**:263–277.

Rosenblum, L.A., and R.D. Nader. 1971. The ontogency of sexual behavior in male bonnet macaques. In: Influence of Hormones on the Nervous System, ed. D.H. Ford, pp. 388–400. Basel: Karger.

Scherer, K.R. 1984. On the nature and function of emotion: A component process approach. In: Approaches to Emotion, ed. K.R. Scherer and P. Ekman, pp. 293–318. Hillsdale, NJ: Erlbaum.

Scherer, K.R. 1999. Psychological models of emotion. In: The Neuropsychology of Emotion, ed. J. Borod. New York: Oxford Univ. Press

Schwartz, G.E., P.L. Fair, P. Salt, M.R. Mandel, and G.L. Klerman. 1976. Facial muscle patterning to affective imagery in depressed and nondepressed subjects. *Science* **192**:489–491.

Simonson, I. 1992. The influence of anticipated regret and responsibility on purchase decisions. *J. Consumer Res.* **19**:1–14.

Storms, M.D., and G.C. Thomas. 1977. Reactions to physical closeness. *J. Pers. Soc. Psych.* **35**:412–418.

Tetlock, P.E., R.S. Peterson, and J.S. Lerner. 1996. Revision the value pluralism model: Incorporating social content and context postulates. In: The Psychology of Values: The Ontario Symp. on Personality and Social Psychology, vol. 8, ed. C. Seligman et al., pp. 25–51. Hillsdale, NJ: Erlbaum

Tversky, A., S. Sattah, and P. Slovic. 1988. Contingent weighting in judgment and choice. *Psych. Rev.* **95**:371–384.

Tversky, A., and E. Shafir. 1992a. Choice under conflict: The dynamics of deferred decision. *Psych. Sci.* **3**:358–361.

Tversky, A., and E. Shafir. 1992b. The disjunction effect in choice under uncertainty. *Psych. Sci.* **3**:305–309.

Zajonc, R.B. 1965. Social facilitation. *Science* **149**:269–274.

16

Norms and Bounded Rationality

Robert Boyd[1] and Peter J. Richerson[2]

[1]Dept. of Anthropology, University of California, Los Angeles, CA 90095, U.S.A.
[2]Division of Environmental Studies, University of California, Davis, CA 95616, U.S.A.

ABSTRACT

Anthropologists believe that human behavior is governed by culturally transmitted norms and that such norms contain accumulated wisdom that allows people to behave sensibly even though they do not understand why they do what they do. Economists and other rational choice theorists are skeptical about functionalist claims because anthropologists furnish no plausible mechanisms to explain why norms have this property. In this chapter, we outline two such mechanisms. We show that occasional learning, when coupled with cultural transmission and a tendency to conform, can lead to the spread of sensible norms even though very few people understand why they are sensible. We also show that norms that help solve problems of self-control, which arise from time-inconsistent preferences, can spread if individuals tend to imitate successful people and are occasionally influenced by members of other groups with different norms. On the other hand, nonadaptive norms can also spread, and maladaptive norms can persist.

DO NORMS HELP PEOPLE MAKE GOOD DECISIONS
WITHOUT MUCH THOUGHT?

Many anthropologists believe that people follow the social norms of their society without much thought. According to this view, human behavior is mainly the result of social norms and rarely the result of considered decisions. In recent years, there has been increased interest within anthropology in how individuals and groups struggle to modify and reinterpret norms to further their own interests. However, we think it is fair to say that most anthropologists still believe that culture plays a powerful role in shaping how people think and what they do.

Many anthropologists also believe that social norms lead to adaptive behavior, i.e., by following norms, people can behave sensibly without having to understand why they do what they do. For example, throughout the New World, people who rely on corn as a staple food process the grain by soaking it in a strong base (such as calcium hydroxide) to produce foods like hominy and masa (Katz et al. 1974). This alkali process is complicated, requires hard work, and substantially reduces the caloric content of corn. However, it also increases the amount of available lysine, the amino acid in which corn is most deficient. Katz et al. (1974) argue that alkali processing plays a crucial role in preventing protein deficiency disease in regions where the majority of calories are derived from corn. Traditional peoples had no understanding of the nutritional value of alkali processing, rather it was a norm: we Maya eat masa because that is what we do. Nonetheless, by following the norm, traditional people were able to solve an important and difficult nutritional problem. The work of cultural ecologists, such as Marvin Harris (1979), provides many other examples of this kind, although few are as well worked out. Other varieties of functionalism (for a discussion, see Turner and Maryanski 1979) also hold that social norms evolve to adapt to the local environment. While nowadays anthropologists are explicitly critical of functionalism, cryptic functionalism still pervades much thinking in anthropology (Edgerton 1992).

Norms may also lead to sensible behavior by proscribing choices that people find tempting in the short run, but which are damaging in the long run. Moral systems around the world have proscriptions against drunkenness, laziness, gluttony, and other failures of self-control. There is evidence that such proscriptions can increase individual well-being. For example, Jensen and Ericson (1979) show that Mormon youths in Tucson are less likely to be involved in "victimless crimes," such as drinking and marijuana use, than members of a nonreligious control group. Moreover these differences seem to have consequences. McEvoy and Land (1981) report that age-adjusted mortalities for Mormons in Missouri are approximately 20% lower than control populations, and the differences were biggest for lung cancer, pneumonia/influenza, and violent death, sources of mortality that should be reduced if the abstentious Mormon norms are being observed. Apparently, living in a group in which there are norms against alcohol use makes it easier for young Mormons to do what is in their own long-term interest.

WHAT ARE NORMS, AND WHY DO PEOPLE FOLLOW THEM?

Examples like these present a series of interesting questions to economists, psychologists, and others who start with individuals as the basic building blocks of social theory. First, what are norms? How can we incorporate the notion that there are shared social rules into models that assume that people are goal-oriented decision makers? Second, why should people follow norms? Norms will change behavior only if they prescribe behavior that differs from what people would do in the absence of norms. Finally, why should norms be sensible? If individuals cannot (or do not) determine what is sensible, why should norms prescribe sensible behavior? It seems more plausible that they will simply represent random noise or even superstitious nonsense.

A recent efflorescence of interest in norms among rational choice theorists provides one cogent answer to the first two questions. Norms are the result of shared notions of appropriate behavior and the willingness of individuals to reward appropriate behavior and punish inappropriate behavior (for a review, see McAdams 1997). Thus, it is a norm for men to remove their hats when they enter a Christian church because they will suffer the disapproval of others if they do not. In contrast, it is not a norm for men to remove their hats in an overheated country and western bar, even if everyone does so. By this notion, people obey norms because they are rewarded by others if they do and punished if they do not. As long as the rewards and punishments are sufficiently large, norms can stabilize a vast range of different behaviors. Norms can require property to be passed to the oldest son or to the youngest; they can specify that horsemeat is a delicacy or deem it unfit for human consumption.

There is no consensus in this literature about why people choose to punish norm violators and reward norm followers. There have been a number of proposals: Binmore (1998) argues that social life is an infinite game and that norms are game theoretic equilibria of the kind envisioned in the folk theorem. Norm violators are punished, and so are people who fail to punish norm violators, people who fail to punish them, and so on ad infinitum. McAdams (1997) suggests that all people desire the esteem of others, and because esteem can be "produced" at very low cost, it is easy to punish norm violators by withholding esteem. Bowles and Gintis (1999) and Richerson and Boyd (1998) argue that group selection acting over the long history of human evolution created a social environment in which natural selection favored genes leading to a reciprocal psychology. Here we will simply assume that the problem of why people choose to enforce norms has somehow been solved.

HOW DO NORMS SOLVE PROBLEMS THAT PEOPLE CANNOT SOLVE ON THEIR OWN?

Virtually all of the recent literature on norms focuses on how norms help people solve public goods and coordination problems (e.g., Ostrom et. al. 1991; Ellickson 1994). It does not explain why norms should be adaptive. If people do not understand why alkali treatment of corn is a good thing, why should they require their neighbors to eat masa and hominy, and be offended if they do not? Nor does the recent literature on norms explain why norms should commonly help people with problems of self-control. If people cannot resist the temptations of alcohol, why should they insist that their neighbors do so? Below we sketch possible answers to these questions.

Occasional Learning Plus Conformism Leads to Adaptive Norms

In this section we show how a small amount of individual learning, when coupled with cultural transmission and a tendency to conform to the behavior of others can lead to adaptive norms, even though most people simply do what everyone else is doing.

Why It May Be Sensible for Most People to Imitate

It is easy to see why people may choose to imitate others when it is costly or difficult to determine the best behavior — copying is easier than invention, and plagiarism is easier than creation. However, as these examples illustrate, it is not clear that by saving such costs, imitation makes everybody better off; this is why we have patents and rules against plagiarism. We have analyzed a series of mathematical models which indicate that when decisions are difficult, everyone can be better off if most people imitate the decisions of others under the right circumstances (Boyd and Richerson 1985, 1988, 1989, 1995, 1996). The following simple model illustrates our reasoning.

Consider a population that lives in an environment that switches between two states with a constant probability. Further assume that there are two behaviors, one best in each environmental state. All individuals attempt to discover the best behavior in the current environment. First, each individual experiments with both behaviors and then compares the results. The results of such experiments vary for many reasons, and so the behavior that is best during any particular trial may be inferior over the long run. To represent this idea mathematically, assume that the observed difference in payoffs is a normally distributed random variable, X (Figure 16.1). Second, each individual can observe the behavior of an individual from the previous generation who has already made the decision.

We assume that individuals combine sources of information by adopting a particular behavior if its payoff appears *sufficiently* better than its alternative; otherwise they imitate. The larger the observed difference in the payoffs between the two behaviors, the more likely it is that the behavior with the higher payoff actually is best. By insisting on a large difference in observed payoff, individuals can reduce the chance that they will mistakenly adopt the inferior behavior. Of course, being discriminating will also cause more trials to be indecisive, and then, they must imitate. Thus, there is a tradeoff. Individuals can increase the accuracy of learning but only by also increasing the probability that learning will be indecisive and having to rely on imitation.

The optimal decision rule depends on what the rest of the population is doing. Assume that most individuals use a learning rule that causes them to imitate x%

Learning Rule

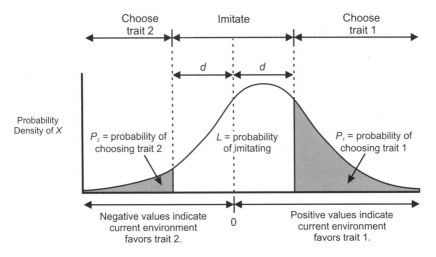

Figure 16.1   A graphical representation of the model of individual and social learning. Each individual observes an independent, normally distributed environmental cue, X. A positive value of X indicates that the environment is in state 1; a negative value indicates that the environment is in state 2. If the value of X is larger than the threshold value, d, an individual adopts trait 1. This occurs with probability, p_1. If the value of the environmental cue is smaller than $-d$, the individual adopts trait 2 which occurs with probability, p_2. Otherwise the individual imitates. Thus, the larger the standard deviation of the cue compared to its mean value, the greater is the predictive value of the cue.

of the time — call these "common-type individuals." There are also a few rare invaders who imitate slightly more often. Compared to the common type, invaders are less likely to make learning errors. Thus, when invaders learn, they have a higher payoff than the common-type individuals when they learn. When invaders imitate, they have the same payoff as the common-type individuals. However, invaders must imitate more often and those who must imitate always have lower fitness than those whose personal information is above the learning threshold. To see why, think of each imitator as being connected to a learner by a chain of imitation. If the learner at the end of chain learned in the current environment, then the imitator has the same chance of acquiring the favored behavior as does a learner. If the learner at the end of the chain learned in a different environment, the imitator will acquire the wrong trait. Thus, the invading type will achieve a higher payoff if the advantage of making fewer learning errors is sufficient to offset the disadvantage of imitating more.

This tradeoff depends on how much the common type imitates. When the common type rarely imitates, the payoff of individuals who imitate and

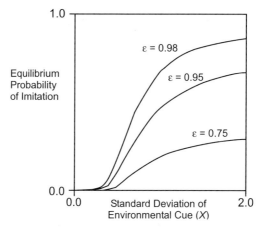

Figure 16.2   Probability that individuals imitate (L) at evolutionary equilibrium as a function of the quality of the environmental cue for three different rates of environmental change. The mean of the environmental cue (X) is 1.0, so as the standard deviation of X increases, the extent to which the cue predicts the environmental state decreases. Thus, the results plotted here indicate that as the predictive quality of the cue decreases, the probability of imitation at evolutionary equilibrium increases. The parameter ε is the probability that the environment remains unchanged from one time period to the next. Thus as the rate of environmental change decreases, the probability of imitation at evolutionary equilibrium increases. See Boyd and Richerson (1988) for details.

individuals who learn will be similar because most imitators will imitate somebody who learned, and the fact that mutants make fewer learning errors will allow them to invade. However, as the amount of imitation increases, the payoff of imitating individuals relative to those who learn declines because increased imitation lengthens the chain connecting each imitator to a learner. Eventually the population reaches an equilibrium at which the common type can resist invasion by mutants that change the rate of imitation. Figure 16.2 plots the probability that individuals imitate (denoted as L in Figure 16.1) at evolutionary equilibrium as a function of the quality of the information available to individuals for three different rates of environmental change (for details of the calculation, see Boyd and Richerson 1988). Notice that when it is difficult for individuals to determine the best behavior and when environments change infrequently, more than 90% of a population at equilibrium simply copies the behavior of others.

As long as environments are not completely unpredictable, the average payoff at the evolutionary equilibrium is greater than the average payoff of individuals who do not imitate (Boyd and Richerson 1995). The reason is simple: imitation allows the population to learn when the information is good and imitate when it is bad. Figure 16.3 plots the average payoff of imitating and learning individuals as a function of the fraction of individuals who imitate. The payoff of learning individuals increases as the amount of imitation increases because individuals are demanding better evidence before relying on their individual

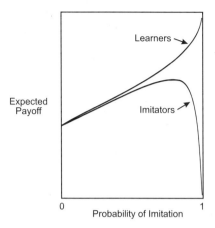

Figure 16.3   Individuals either learn or imitate according to the outcome of their learning trial. As individuals become more selective, the frequency of imitating individuals increases. This figure plots the expected fitness of individuals who imitate and those who learn as a function of the probability that an individual randomly chosen from the population imitates (assuming the outcome of learning experiments is normally distributed with mean 0.5 and variance 1).

experience and therefore are making fewer learning errors. The payoff of individuals who imitate because their evidence does not happen to meet rising standards *also* increases at first because they are directly or indirectly imitating learners who make fewer errors. If imitation is too common, the payoff to imitation declines because the too-discriminating population does too little learning to track the changing environment. The first effect is sufficient to lead to a net increase in average payoff at evolutionary equilibrium.

We believe that the lessons of this model are robust. It formalizes three basic assumptions:

1. The environment varies.
2. Cues about the environment are imperfect, so individuals make errors.
3. Imitation increases the accuracy (or reduces the cost) of learning.

We have analyzed several models that incorporate these assumptions, but differ in other features. All of these models lead to the same qualitative conclusion: when learning is difficult and environments do not change too fast, most individuals imitate at evolutionary equilibrium. At that equilibrium, an optimally imitating population is better off, on average, than a population that does not imitate.

Adding Conformism

So far we have only shown that it may be best for most people to copy others rather than try to figure out things for themselves. Recall that for something to be

a norm, there has to be a conformist element. People must agree on the appropriate behavior and disapprove of others who do not behave appropriately. We now
show that individuals who respond to such disapproval by conforming to the social norm are *more* likely to acquire the best behavior. We will also show that as
the tendency to conform increases, so does the equilibrium amount of imitation.

To allow the possibility for conformist pressure, we add the following assumption to the model described above: when an individual imitates, she may be
disproportionately likely to acquire the more common variant. Let q be the fraction of the population using trait 1. As before, individuals collect information
about the best behavior in the current environment, and then if the information is
not decisive, they imitate. However, now the probability (Prob) that an imitating
individual acquires trait 1 is:

$$\text{Prob}(1) = q + \Delta q(1-q)(2q-1) . \qquad (16.1)$$

Thus Δ represents the extent to which individuals respond to the blandishments
of others. When $\Delta = 0$, individuals ignore conformist pressures, and the model is
the same as the one described in the previous section. When $\Delta > 0$, social pressure (or merely a desire to be like others) induces individuals to adopt the more
common of the two behaviors. When $\Delta \approx 1$, individuals almost always adopt the
same behavior as the majority.

We now determine the equilibrium values of Δ and L (the probability of relying on imitation) in the same way that we determined the equilibrium amount of
imitation above. Assume that most of the population is characterized by one pair
of values of Δ and L. Then, consider whether that population can be invaded by
individuals using slightly different values of Δ and L. The evolutionary equilibrium is the combination of values of Δ and L that cannot be invaded in this way.

This analysis leads to two robust results. First, all conditions that lead a substantial fraction of the population to rely on imitation also lead to very strong
conformity. Consider, for example, Figure 16.4, which plots the equilibrium values of Δ and L as a function of the rate of environmental change. Notice that as
long as the environment is not completely unpredictable, the equilibrium value
of Δ is near its maximum value — when people imitate, they virtually always do
what the majority of the population is doing. As detailed in Henrich and Boyd
(1998), the equilibrium values of Δ and L are equally insensitive to other parameters in the model. Second, as conformism increases, so does the fraction of the
population that relies on imitation. Figure 16.4 shows that the equilibrium value
of L, when both L and Δ are allowed to evolve, is larger than the equilibrium
value of L in a model in which Δ is constrained to be zero. Thus, a tendency to
conform increases the number of people who follow social norms and decreases
the numbers who think for themselves.

These results are easy to understand. Just after the environment switches,
most people acquire the wrong behavior. Then, the combination of occasional

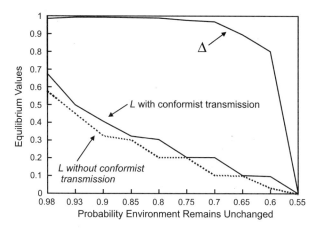

Figure 16.4 Equilibrium values of L and Δ for different rates of environmental variation. At evolutionary equilibrium, the strength of conformist transmission is high for a
wide range of rates of environmental change. However, reliance on social learning (L as
proportion ranging from 0 to 1.0) decreases rapidly over the same range of environmental
stability. When there is no conformist effect (Δ is constrained to be zero), the evolutionary equilibrium value of L is lower than when Δ is free to evolve to its equilibrium value.
Since the conformist effect causes the population to track the environment more effectively, it makes social learning more useful. For more details on this calculation, see
Henrich and Boyd (1998).

learning and imitation causes the best behavior to become gradually more common in the population until an equilibrium is reached at which most of the people are characterized by the better behavior. For rates of environmental change
that favor substantial reliance on imitation, the best behavior is more common
than the alternative averaged over this entire cycle. Thus, individuals with a conformist tendency to adopt the most common behavior when in doubt are more
likely to acquire the best behavior. Conformism continues to increase until it becomes so strong that it prevents the population from responding adaptively after
an environmental shift. Optimal conformism leads to increased imitation because on average conformism causes imitators to be more likely to acquire the
best behavior in the current environment.

Imitation of Successful Neighbors Leads to the Spread of Beneficial Norms

There is a large literature that indicates that people often have time-inconsistent
preferences and, as a result, they often make choices in the short run that they
know are not in their long-term interest. It is plausible that social norms help
people solve these problems by creating short-term incentives to do the right
thing. I may not be able to resist a drink when the costs are all in the distant future, but will make a different decision if I suffer immediate social disapproval.
It is also easy to see why such norms persist once they are established. If

everyone agrees that self-control is proper behavior and punish people who disagree, then the norm will persist. The problem is that the same mechanism can stabilize any norm. People could just as easily agree that excessive drinking is proper behavior and punish teetolars. If it is true that norms often promote self-control, then we need an explanation of why such norms are likely to arise and spread. In this section, we sketch one such mechanism.

Suppose people modify their beliefs by imitating the successful. If they sometimes imitate people from neighboring groups with different norms, then under the right circumstances norms that solve self-control problems will spread from one group to another because their enforcement makes people more successful and therefore more likely to be imitated.

Consider a model in which a population is subdivided into n social groups (number $d = 1,...,n$). There are two alternative behaviors: Individuals can be self-indulgent or abstentious. Self-indulgent individuals succumb to the temptations of strong drink, while abstentious individuals restrain themselves. Abstentious individuals are better off in the long run. They make more money, live longer, are healthier, and so on, and everyone agrees that the short-term pleasures of the bottle are not sufficient to compensate for the long-term costs that result. Nonetheless, because individuals do not have time-consistent preferences, everyone succumbs to the temptations of the table and drinks to excess.

Next, assume that there are two social norms governing consumption behavior. People can be *puritanical* or *tolerant*. Puritans believe that alcohol consumption is wrong and disapprove of those who drink. Tolerant people believe everyone should make their own consumption decisions. Each type disapproves of the other: puritans believe that no one should tolerate excess, and the tolerant think that others should be tolerant as well. These norms affect the costs and benefits of the two behaviors. When puritans are present, the people who drink suffer social disapproval, and because this cost is incurred *immediately*, it can cause people to choose not to drink when they otherwise might. Thus as the proportion of the population who hold puritanical beliefs increases, the proportion of people who drink decreases, and people are better off in the long run. To formalize these ideas, let p_d be the frequency of the puritanical norm in group d. Then W_1, the average payoff of puritanical individuals in group d, is given by:

$$W_1(p_d) = W_0 - s(1 - p_d) + gp_d . \qquad (16.2)$$

W_2, the average payoff of tolerant individuals in group d, is given by:

$$W_2(p_d) = W_0 - sp_d + (g + \delta)p_d . \qquad (16.3)$$

W_0 is the baseline payoff of drinkers in a completely tolerant group. Individuals of each type suffer disapproval and a reduction in welfare when the other type is present in their social group. These social effects on welfare are represented by the terms proportional to s in two expressions above. However, the welfare of all individuals is increased by the fraction of puritanical individuals because everybody is less likely to drink when puritans are present to shame them. These effects are represented by the terms proportional to g and $g + \delta$. The parameter δ captures the idea that puritans may have a different effect on each other than they do on the tolerant: perhaps bigger because they are more sensitive to the opinions of their own kind; perhaps smaller because they are already avoiding strong drink.

Next, the following process governs the evolution of these norms within a group. During each time period, each individual encounters another person, compares her welfare to the person she encounters, and then with probability proportional to the difference between their payoffs during the last time period, adopts that person's norm. In particular, suppose that an individual with norm i from group f encounters an individual with norm j from group d. After the encounter, the probability that an individual switches to j is:

$$\text{Prob}\,(j\,|i,j) = \frac{1}{2}\left\{1 + \beta\left[W_j\left(p_f\right) - W_i(p_d)\right]\right\} . \tag{16.4}$$

When the parameter β equals zero, payoffs do not affect imitation — people imitate at random. When $\beta > 0$, people are more likely to imitate high payoff individuals. Notice that since an individual's payoff depends on the composition of his group, there will be a tendency for ideas to spread from groups in which beneficial norms are common to groups in which less beneficial norms are common.

Let m_{df} be the probability that an individual from group f encounters an individual from group d. Δp_f, the change in p_f during one time period, is given by:

$$\begin{aligned}
\Delta p_f = {}& \beta p_f\left[W_1\left(p_f\right) - \overline{W}\left(p_f\right)\right] \\
&+ \sum_{def} m_{df}\beta\left\{p_d\left[W_1\left(p_d\right) - \overline{W}\left(p_d\right)\right] - p_f\left[W_1\left(p_f\right) - \overline{W}\left(p_f\right)\right]\right\} \\
&+ \sum_{def} m_{df}\left(p_d - p_f\right)\left\{1 + \beta\left[\overline{W}\left(p_d\right) - \overline{W}\left(p_f\right)\right]\right\} .
\end{aligned} \tag{16.5}$$

To make sense of this expression, first assume that people only encounter individuals from their own social group. Then

$$\Delta p_f = \beta p_f\left[W_1\left(p_f\right) - \overline{W}\left(p_f\right)\right] . \tag{16.6}$$

This is the ordinary replicator dynamic equation. This equation simplifies to have the form:

$$\Delta p_f = \alpha p_f\left(1 - p_f\right)\left(p - \tilde{p}\right) , \tag{16.7}$$

where $\alpha = \beta(2s - \delta)$ and $\tilde{p} = s/(2s - \delta)$. Thus, when each social group is isolated and the effects of social sanctions are large compared to the effects of drinking ($2s > \delta$), there are two stable evolutionary equilibria: groups consisting of all puritans or all tolerant individuals. If the presence of puritans benefits other puritans more than it benefits the tolerant ($\delta > 0$), then the all-puritan equilibrium has a larger basin of attraction. If puritans benefit the tolerant more, then the all-tolerant equilibrium has a larger basin of attraction.

When there is contact between different groups, the last two terms in Equation 16.5 affect the change in frequency of norms within social groups. The third term is of most interest here. If $\beta = 0$, this term is proportional to the difference in the frequency of puritanism between the groups and simply represents passive diffusion. If, however, $\beta > 0$, there is a greater flow of norms from groups with high average payoff to groups with lower average payoff. This differential flow arises because people imitate the successful and norms affect the average welfare of group members. Can this effect lead to the systematic spread of beneficial norms?

For the beneficial puritanical norm to spread, two things must occur. First, such a norm must increase to substantial frequency in one group. Second, it must spread to other groups. Here we address only the second question. To keep things simple, we further assume that social groups are arranged in a ring and that individuals only have contact with members of two neighboring groups. Now, suppose that a random shock causes the puritan norm to become common in a single group. Will this norm spread? To answer this question we have simulated this model for a range of parameter values. Representative results are shown in Figure 16.5 that plots the ranges of parameters over which the beneficial norm spreads. The vertical axis gives the ratio of m (the probability that individuals interact with others outside of their group) to α (rate of change due to imitation within groups), and the horizontal axis plots $\tilde{p}$ (the unstable equilibrium that separates the domains of attraction of puritanical and tolerant equilibria in isolated groups). The shaded areas give the combinations of m/α and $\tilde{p}$, which lead to the spread of the puritanical norm to all groups given that it was initially common in a single group for two values of g.

First, notice that the beneficial norm spreads most easily when the level of interaction between groups is intermediate. If there is too much mixing, the puritanical norm cannot persist in the initial population. It is swamped by the flow of norms from its two tolerant neighbors. If there is too little mixing, the puritanical norm remains common in the initial population but cannot spread because there is not enough interaction between neighbors for the beneficial effects of the norm to cause it to spread.

Second, to understand the effect of g, consider the case in which $g = 0$. Even when the norm produces no benefit to individuals as it becomes common, it can still spread if the puritanical norm has a larger basin of attraction in an isolated population ($\delta < 0$). In this case, the costly disapproval of harmless pastimes can seriously handicap the tolerant when puritans are only moderately common. To understand why, consider a focal group at the boundary between the spreading front of puritan groups and the existing population of tolerant groups. The focal group, in which both norms are present, is bounded on one side by a group in which puritan norms are common, and on the other side a group in which

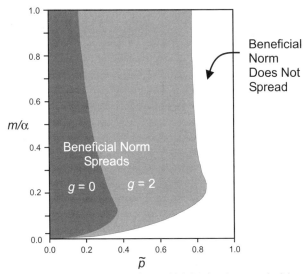

Figure 16.5   Plots parameter combinations which lead to the spread of the group beneficial norm between groups. The vertical axis gives the ratio of m, the probability that individuals interact with others outside of their group to α, the rate of change due to imitation within groups. The horizontal axis plots $\tilde{p}$, the unstable equilibrium that separates the domains of attraction of all puritanical and tolerant equilibria in isolated groups. The shaded areas give the combinations of m/α and $\tilde{p}$ which lead to the spread of the puritanical norm given that it has become common in a single group for two values of g, the extent to which individual behavior is affected by norms. Notice that the beneficial norm spreads when the level of interaction between groups is intermediate. If there is too much mixing the puritanical norm cannot persist in the initial population. If there is too little mixing, it can persist in the initial population but cannot spread.

tolerant norms are common. Since groups on both sides of the boundary have the same average payoff, the flow of norms will tend to move the focal group towards an even balance of the two norms. If the domain of attraction of the puritanical norm includes 0.5 and if there is enough mixing, then mixing with neighboring groups can be enough to tip the focal group into the basin of attraction of the puritanical norm. This is true even though the differential success owes only to puritans avoiding the costs imposed on the tolerant by puritans. To see why increasing g increases the range of values of $\tilde{p}$ which allow the beneficial norm to spread, consider again a focal group on the boundary between the regions in which the puritanical norm is common and uncommon. When $g > 0$, individuals in the focal group are more likely to imitate someone from the neighboring group, where the puritanical norm is common, than the other neighboring group, where tolerant individuals are common, because individuals from the former group are more successful. Therefore, the flow of norms will tend to move the focal group toward a frequency of puritans greater than 0.5.

It is interesting to note that the rate at which this process of equilibrium selection goes on seems to be roughly comparable to the rate at which traits spread within a single group under the influence of the same learning process. Game theorists have considered a number of mechanisms of equilibrium selection that arise because of random fluctuations in outcomes due to sampling variation and finite numbers of players (e.g., Samuelson 1997). These processes also tend to pick out the equilibrium with the highest average payoff and the largest domain of attraction. However, unless the number of individuals in the population is very small, the rate at which this occurs is very slow. In contrast, in the simulations we performed, the group beneficial trait spread from one population to the next at a rate roughly half the rate at which the same imitate-the-successful mechanism led to the spread of a trait within an isolated group. Of course, we have not accounted for the rate at which the beneficial norm becomes common in an initial group. This requires random processes. However, only the group, not the whole population, needs be small, and the group must be small only for a short period of time for random processes to give rise to an initial "group mutation," which can then spread relatively rapidly to the population as a whole.

CONCLUSION: ARE NORMS USUALLY SENSIBLE?

We have shown that it is possible for norms to guide people towards sensible behavior that they would not choose if left to their own devices. Norms could be sensible, just as functionalists in anthropology have claimed. However, the fact that they could be sensible does not mean that they *are* sensible. There are some well-studied examples, like the alkali treatment of corn, and there are many other plausible examples of culturally transmitted norms that seem to embody adaptive wisdom. However, as documented in Robert Edgerton's book, *Sick Societies* (1992), there are also many examples of norms that are not obviously adaptive and in fact some seem spectacularly maladaptive. Such cases might result from the pathological spread of norms that merely handicap the tolerant without doing anyone any good (and perhaps harm puritans as well?). Or, they might result from antiquated norms that persist in a frequency above a large basin of attraction for tolerance, having lost their original fitness-enhancing effect due to social or environmental change. More careful quantitative research on the costs and benefits of alternative norms would clearly be useful.

We believe that it is also important to focus more attention on the processes by which norms are shaped and transmitted. Anthropologists and other social scientists have paid scant attention to estimating the magnitude of evolutionary processes affecting culture change in the field or lab, although several research programs demonstrate that such estimates are perfectly practical (Aunger 1994; Insko et al. 1983; Labov 1980; Rogers 1983; Rosenthal and Zimmerman 1978; Soltis et al. 1995). What happens to a Maya who does not utilize the normative form of alkali treatment of corn in her traditional society? What are the nutritional effects? The social effects? From whom do people learn how to process corn? How does this affect which variants of the process are transmitted and which are not? Only by answering such questions will we learn why societies have the norms they have and when norms are adaptive.

REFERENCES

Aunger, R. 1994. Are food avoidances maladaptive in the Ituri Forest of Zaire? *J. Anthro. Res.* **50**:277–310.

Binmore, K.G. 1998. Just Playing: Game Theory and the Social Contract. Cambridge: MIT Press.

Bowles, S., and H. Gintis. 1999. The evolution of strong reciprocity. Santa Fe Institute Working Paper 98-08-073E. Santa Fe, NM.

Boyd, R., and P.J. Richerson. 1985. Culture and the Evolutionary Process. Chicago: Univ. of Chicago Press.

Boyd, R., and P.J. Richerson. 1988. An evolutionary model of social learning: The effects of spatial and temporal variation. In: Social Learning: Psychological and Biological Perspectives, ed. T. Zentall and B.G. Galef, pp. 29–48. Hillsdale, NJ: Erlbaum.

Boyd, R., and P.J. Richerson. 1989. Social learning as an adaptation. *Lect. Math. Life Sci.* **20**:1–26.

Boyd, R., and P.J. Richerson. 1995. Why does culture increase human adaptability? *Ethol. Sociobiol.* **16**:125–143.

Boyd, R., and P.J. Richerson. 1996. Why culture is common, but cultural evolution is rare. *Proc. Brit. Acad.* **88**:77–93.

Edgerton, R. 1992. Sick Societies: Challenging the Myth of Primitive Harmony. New York: Free Press.

Ellickson, R.C. 1994. Order without Law: How Neighbors Settle Disputes. Cambridge, MA: Harvard Univ. Press.

Harris, M. 1979. Cultural Materialism: The Struggle for a Science of Culture. New York: Random House.

Henrich, J., and R. Boyd. 1998. The evolution of conformist transmission and the emergence of between-group differences. *Evol. Human Behav.* **19**:215–242.

Insko, C.A., R. Gilmore, S. Drenan, A. Lipsitz, D. Moehle, and J. Thibaut. 1983. Trade versus expropriation in open groups: A comparison of two types of social power. *J. Pers. Soc. Psych.* **44**:977–999.

Jensen, G.F., and M.L. Erickson. 1979. The religious factor and delinquency: Another look at the hellfire hypothesis. In: The Religious Dimension: New Directions in Quantitative Research, ed. R. Wenthow, pp. 157–177. New York: Academic.

Katz, S.H., M.L. Hediger, and L.A. Valleroy. 1974. Traditional maize processing techniques in the New World. *Science* **184**:765–476.

Labov, W. 1980. Locating Language in Time and Space. Philadelphia: Univ. of Pennsylvania Press.

McAdams, R.H. 1997. The origin, development, and regulation of norms. *Mich. Law Rev.* **96**:338–443.

McEvoy, L., and G. Land. 1981. Life-style and death patterns of Missouri RLDS Church members. *Am. J. Public Health* **71**:1350–1357.

Ostrom, E. 1991. Governing the Commons: The Evolution of Institutions for Collective Action. Cambridge: Cambridge Univ. Press.

Richerson, P.J., and R. Boyd. 1998. The evolution of human ultra-sociality. In: Indoctrinability, Ideology, and Warfare: Evolutionary Perspectives, ed. I. Eibl-Eibisfeldt and F. Salter, pp. 71–96. New York: Berghahn.

Rogers, E.M. 1983. Diffusion of Innovations. 3d ed. New York: Free Press.

Rosenthal, T., and B. Zimmerman. 1978. Social Learning and Cognition. New York: Academic.

Samuelson, L. 1997. Evolutionary Games and Equilibrium Selection. Cambridge, MA: MIT Press.

Soltis, J., R. Boyd, and P.J. Richerson. 1995. Can group-functional behaviors evolve by cultural group selection? An empirical test. *Curr. Anthro.* **36**:473–494.

Turner, J.H., and A. Maryanski. 1979. Functionalism. Menlo Park, CA: Benjamin/Cummings.

17

Prominence Theory as a Tool to Model Boundedly Rational Decisions

Wulf Albers

Institute of Mathematical Economics, University of Bielefeld, Postfach 10 01 31,
33501 Bielefeld, Germany

ABSTRACT

Prominence theory models the construction of numerical responses and the perception of numerical stimuli in the decimal system. It is process based and does not conform with traditional approaches using universal utility and probability functions that are independent of the specific task.

The basic components of the model are the prominent or full-step numbers, ...,1, 2, 5, 10, 20, 50, 100,....., i.e., the powers of ten, their halves, and their doubles. Processes that construct numerical responses use these numbers as components, which are added and subtracted where every number is used at most once, with a coefficient +1, –1, or 0, such as 17 = 20 – 5 + 2. Responses are constructed in processes in which the decision maker runs through the full-step numbers in decreasing order and asks, at each step, whether to add, subtract, or not use this number to improve the current tentative response. The process stops when the decision maker reaches the boundary of her ability to judge. Knowledge of this process permits us to draw conclusions as to the exactness with which the decision is made. This exactness is determined by the size of the window of "reasonable alternatives." The exactness is selected such that there are between three and five alternatives in the window that can be percieved on this level of exactness. Awareness of this rule permits us to reconstruct decision-making processes that are behind given responses and to deduce information about motivation.

Full-step numbers determine the steps of a scale on which differences of numbers are measured (e.g., the distance between 20 and 100 is two full steps). Between full-step numbers, linear interpolation is applied. This evaluation induces logarithmic perception. In a given task, the window of logarithmic perception is limited at most to three consecutive full-step numbers. The window is selected as fine (i.e., as near to zero) as possible, but such that the greatest number that occurs in the task is inside the window. The next full step below the lowest full-step number of the window is the zero point. Full-step numbers between the window and zero are not perceived as full steps. Since the position of the window depends on the task, the measurement of numerical differences is task-dependent. This basic idea structures the perception of payoffs, probabilities, and other numerical quantities. It organizes the evaluation of the perception of prospects and structures in negotiation processes, fairness criteria of multiperson agreements, multiattributive decisions, and the implementation of aspiration levels in decision and negotiation tasks.

Boundedly rational principles of the aggregation of the components of utility and the construction of fairness criteria are presented. The approach is supported by a collection of confirming experiments and applications. In addition, the relationships of prominence theory to the Weber–Fechner law and the prospect theory of Kahneman and Tversky are discussed.

PROMINENT NUMBERS OF THE DECIMAL SYSTEM[1]

Perception and construction of numerical responses are guided by a system of numbers, called *prominent* or *full-step numbers*:

$$..., 0.1, 0.2, 0.5, 1, 2, 5, 10, 20, 50, 100, 200, 500, 1000,...$$

These are the integer powers of ten, their doubles, and their halves. They have the property that every number is either approximately or exactly the double of the preceding one.

Halving and doubling are the basic mental processes for the comparison of numerical data. Doubles and halves can be emotionally perceived, so that the abstract process of halving is related to emotional perception of difference. Therefore, the system of prominent numbers serves as a scale that permits the evaluation of differences. The idea is to evaluate the distance between any two neighboring full-step numbers as one step and to apply linear interpolation. For example: the difference between 20 and 100 is two steps (from 20 to 50, and from 50 to 100); the difference between 50 and 70 is two-fifths of the full step between 50 and 100.

Full-step numbers are also used for the identification of numbers. The idea is that every number can be presented as a sum of full-step numbers, e.g., $17 = 20 - 5 + 2$. When a person is asked for a numerical response, she

---

[1] Boundedly rational decision processing is not as simply structured as we expected when we started our investigations on prominence theory. In our research we observed partial phenomena, which at first seemed to contradict the general model. By looking more closely at these phenomena, we were able to explain them by adding additional rules, which delineated behavior under specific conditions. For purposes of clarification, I therefore include sections that provide more technical details, so that those readers who wish to apply this theory can avoid the initial pitfalls.

constructs her answer as the sum of full-step numbers in a process by which the respective tentative response is refined stepwise by adding or subtracting the next finer full-step number. In this process, every full-step number is used at most once, with a coefficient of $+1$, -1, or 0.

The principles of doubling and halving would be more adequately verified by the system of dual numbers, i.e., .., 1, 2, 4, 8, 16, 32,.... The full-step structure would then have exact doubles in every step, and the presentation of numbers could be restricted to sequences with alternating signs. In the decimal system, this works for $17 = 20 - 5 + 2$, but it does not function for the presentation of numbers between 20 and 30, e.g., $22 = 20 + 2$. Our culture selected the decimal system.

PERCEPTION OF NUMERICAL STIMULI

The Signal Identification Process

Object identification can be performed at different levels of graininess or exactness. A greater level of exactness is obtained under finer zoom. Let us assume that we have to identify an animal that is drawn by a four-year-old child. We may be able to identify it as a horse, dog, or cat, but we will probably not be able to decide what sort of horse, dog, or cat it is. By contrast, when we look at a photo, we can identify more detailed attributes and specify our responses more precisely.

My view of object identification generally follows a process of stepwise refinement of the graininess of analysis. Using the above example, our first decision happens on a crude level: we determine that the drawing (or photo) is an animal. Next, under finer graininess, we refine our decision to indicate general species, e.g., a horse. Under even finer graininess, we indicate the type of object, e.g., Arabian.

In this process, the specification of the object on a given level of graininess reduces the number of possible objects, and thereby permits further grain refinement in the next step of analysis.

The identification of a numerical response follows the same principle. We describe the process by means of an example. To identify the signal 17, we start with a sufficiently crude full-step number and go down the sequence of full-step numbers until a full-step number is found for which the signal is nearer to the full-step number than to zero. We obtain 20. This is our preliminary result on a crude level of exactness. We can now refine the level of analysis by taking the next finer full-step number, 10, and asking whether this number should be added to or subtracted from the current preliminary result, or if it should not be used at all. This level yields the alternatives $20 - 10$, 20, and $20 + 10$, among which we select 20. Next, we again refine the level of analysis by taking the next finer full-step number, 5, and asking whether $20 - 5$, 20, or $20 + 5$ is the best response. We decide for $20 - 5$. In the next step, we turn to the full-step number 2 and must decide between $20 - 5 - 2$, $20 - 5$, and $20 - 5 + 2$. We select $20 - 5 + 2$ and have identified the signal.

This process requires an ability to answer the question: which of two given alternatives, x or y, is nearer to the signal? Possible responses are: "x is nearer," "y is nearer," "x and y are equally near," or "my exactness of judgment does not allow selection of either x or y." The first two responses cause the selection of x or y. The fourth alternative implies that the response cannot be refined, and thus the decision maker must stop the process and give the current preliminary response as the final response. When "x and y are equally near," the decision maker also stops the process and takes the midpoint of x and y as the final response.[2]

The process is usually not used to identify a number that is given in advance (as in the example above), but rather to identify a response that adequately describes a diffuse signal. The signal is usually not precise, similar to the situation in which an object must be identified. The decision must specify two variables: (a) the level of graininess or the exactness of analysis and (b) the given response. The procedure solves both problems in a way that selects the finest possible response. It is interesting to note that the decision maker obtains information about the exactness of her analysis but does not provide explicit information. This is only possible to conclude from the response on the exactness via the finest full-step number that is used in the presentation.

We denote the described process as signal identification process. Albers and Güntzel (1999) perform an extended analysis of the reports of subjects concerning the numbers that came to their minds when they constructed numerical responses. The observed results strongly support the described process model.

Presentations and Exactness

In general, when we are confronted with the result of such a process, we want to draw conclusions from the response regarding the decision maker's exactness of analysis. We first characterize the possible results of such processes and denote them as presentations. Thereafter we define the exactness of a presentation:

- a *presentation* is a sum of full-step numbers in which every full-step number appears at most once and has the coefficient +1, −1, or 0;
- the finest full-step number of the presentation for which the coefficient does not equal zero is the *exactness* of the presentation.

---

2 This permits responses such as 25 or 75 on a crude level of exactness, i.e., when the decision maker perceives the signal as equally near to 0 and 50 (or 50 and 100). This observation caused us to identify incorrectly the numbers $25 \cdot 10^i$ (i integer) as prominent. However, these terms only occur as the last terms of presentations. Nevertheless, we denote the exactness on which such a response is given as $25 \cdot 10^i$.

The presentation of a given number need not be unique. For example, 17 can be presented as 10 + 5 + 2, or 20 − 5 + 2, or 20 − 2 − 1. Not all presentations of the same number must have the same exactness. Here, we are interested in the crudest level of exactness on which it is possible to construct the number. For 17, this is the exactness 2. Therefore, we define the *exactness of a number* as the crudest exactness over all presentations of the number.[3,4]

The signal identification process described above selects the presentation of the response in such a way that the exactness of the presentation equals the exactness of the response (i.e., it selects one of the crudest possible presentations of the response).

The exactness of an arbitrary number is $x = X \cdot 10^i$ with i integer and X integer with the last digit unequal to zero. Let $d(X)$ equal this last digit of X. Then the exactness of x is $e(x) = e(X) \cdot 10^i$ with $e(X)$ related to $d(X)$ as follows:[5]

last nonzero digit $d(X)$	1 2 3 4 5 6 7 8 9
exactness digit $e(X)$	1 2 2 1 5 1 2 2 1

Sometimes it makes sense to consider the exactness as a proportion of the given response. The *relative exactness* is the exactness as a proportion of the response. For example, the relative exactness of 17 is 2/17 = 11.8%. The relative exactness is a useful tool for describing the exactness of perception. Consumers usually reach an exactness of perception of 5–10%. Price setting in Germany used to reach an exactness of 5% (after rounding prices as 7.98 to 8.00). Spontaneous judgments of subjects are frequently given with a relative exactness of just cruder than 25%.

People do not select arbitrarily fine exactness of responses. In general we expect that the frequency of responses decreases as the level of exactness becomes finer. We addressed this issue by investigatig 200 subjects, each of whom gave price estimates for sixty articles. It was shown that the logarithm of the frequency of choices of a number was a linear decreasing function of the logarithm of the inverse of the relative exactness.

Level of Exactness

It is important to distinguish between the exactness with which a response can be given and the exactness of the numerical response. A decision maker who gives a response has *level of exactness, a,* if she can distinguish two numbers (x, y) if

---

[3] The exactness of zero is defined as infinity. This follows from the idea that the response zero is possible under any given lower bound of exactness.
[4] In general a crude (great, high) exactness corresponds to a crude analysis, and a fine (small, low) exactness corresponds to a fine analysis. I recommend using the terms "crude" or "fine," rather than other terms to make the direction clear.
[5] This definition of exactness was suggested by Reinhard Selten (pers. comm.).

and only if their difference is $|x - y| \geq a$. The level of relative exactness is defined correspondingly:

> A decision maker who gives a response has a *level of relative exactness,*
> r, if she can distinguish any two numbers (x, y) if and only if
> $|x - y| / \max(|x|,|y|) \geq r$.

Assume the decision maker gives the response 20. This is possible, for instance, in a situation where the decision maker can distinguish between 20 and 10, but not between 20 and 15 (exactness level 10), or in a situation in which she can distinguish between 20 and 18 but not between 20 and 19 (exactness level 2). The response does not provide information concerning the level of exactness on which it was produced.

Conclusions regarding the exactness level of the decision maker (or of a group of decision makers) can be drawn when sets of responses are available. For instance, when the responses 30, 35, 40, and 45 are given with nearly equal frequency, we may conclude that the level of exactness was 5. When 30 and 40 are about three times as frequent as 35 and 45, we may conclude that half of the subjects had an exactness level of 5 (i.e., they provided responses of 30, 35, 40, and 45 with equal frequency) and half of the subjects had an exactness level of 10 (i.e., they provided responses of 30 and 40 with equal frequency and each number was selected by each person twice as often).[6]

For certain data sets, part of the subjects responded with relatively fine exactness, while most selected a cruder level of exactness. Therefore, we define the level of exactness of a data set as the crudest level of exactness that is fulfilled by 80% of the data. (A less *ad hoc* measure is presented in Selten [1987].)

Natural Scales

A frequently used refinement of the structure of full-step numbers is represented by spontaneous numbers. They insert one additional step (i.e., a "midpoint") between any two consecutive full-step numbers. The most prominent number between the two full steps is selected as the midpoint. This criterion immediately selects 15 as the midpoint between 10 and 20, and 30 as the midpoint between 20 and 50 (as the numbers with the crudest level of exactness within the respective intervals; note that 30 = 50 – 20 is the crudest number between 20 and 50, since 40 = 50 – 10). Between 50 and 100 there are two candidates with the crudest level of exactness: 70 and 80. 70 = 100 – 50 + 20 is cruder in that it has a slightly

---

[6] The idea behind this example can be generalized using the following rules of thumb for the relations of frequencies of numbers with different exactness: numbers with exactness 5 are twice as frequent as numbers with exactness 10 (last digits are 5, 0 versus 0); numbers with exactness 2 are three times as frequent as numbers with exactness 5 (last digits 2, 3, 5, 7, 8, 0 versus 5, 0); numbers with exactness 2 are three-fifths as frequent as numbers with exactness 2 (last digits 1, 2, 3, 4, 5 vs. 2, 3, 5).

cruder relative exactness, while $80 = 100 - 20$ is easier to obtain in that it requires only one step of refinement for construction; 70 needs two steps from 100 to $100 - 50$ and from there to $100 - 50 + 20$. In my research I have found that — under the evaluation condition — subjects tend to select 80 as the more prominent of the two candidates. However, in judgment situations, they select 70 and 80 with equal frequency. Therefore, 70 and 80 are both acceptable as midpoints. Applying the same consideration to all multiples of these numbers with integer powers of ten, we obtain the spontaneous numbers:

..., 10, 15, 20, 30, 50, (70 or 80), 100, 150, 200, 300, 500, (700 or 800), ...

Like full-step numbers, these numbers also permit us to define a scale, i.e., the scale of half steps. To identify the structure, we interpret the pairs $7 \cdot 10^i$ and $8 \cdot 10^i$ (i integer) as different notations of the "midpoint" between $5 \cdot 10^i$ and $10 \cdot 10^i$, i.e., as two possible notations of the same half step. The QuickEst heuristic of Hertwig et al. (1999) relies on spontaneous numbers to estimate numerical values.

Refining the set of spontaneous numbers by inserting midpoints raises certain problems. For example, empirical data clearly show that after 80 inserted between 50 and 100, in the next step only one number, 90, is inserted on one side of 80; however, two numbers, 60 and 70, are inserted on the other side, and the same holds for the corresponding integer multiples with ten (Albers, unpublished manuscript).

Exactness Selection Rule

Empirical results show that the exactness of subjects' responses is related to the respective task. This relationship is given by the following rule:

> *Exactness selection rule*: Exactness and relative exactness are selected such that there are 3 to 5 values that fulfill the exactness constraints in the range of reasonable alternatives.[7]

This rule makes sense if one assumes that the attention of the decision maker is restricted to a window within which at most five different values can be determined. This window is described as the *range of reasonable alternatives*. My impression is that this is a term which is spontaneously understood by decision makers, who frequently substructure their analysis of the possible consequences of their decisions according to a worst case/best case scenario. They evaluate potential "worst case" and "best case" scenarios under sufficiently reasonable conditions. Alternatives outside the range of worst case and best case are not

---

[7] The prediction of absolute exactness is given in a separate rule below, so that this rule only specifies the selection of relative exactness.

considered. Thus, the use of the range of reasonable alternatives as a fundamental behavioral term requires no further explanation.[8]

The phenomenon that subjects are able to distinguish reliably, and without
use of additional tools, at most five categories of perception within the range of
reasonable alternatives has been confirmed in several psychophysical experiments under very different conditions (see, e.g., Huttenlocher et al. [1988], who
explain the forward telescoping effect in the same way). The number
Huttenlocher et al. reported varies between 5 and 9, while more recent studies
tend to report lower values. Our investigations confirmed 5 as the normal
restriction.

Results Confirming the Exactness Selection Rule

The exactness selection rule has been confirmed by several studies. The first
study (Albers et al. 1997) considered retail prices of food. The prices of 30
(mostly brand-name) articles were collected from 35 shops. The prices of the
brand-name articles fulfilled the exactness selection rule.[9] For offbrand articles,
which included different kinds of bread, apples, and tomatoes, the quality
dispersion was much higher and thus the exactness selection rule was not
fulfilled.

Another study supporting the rule involves the following experiment. On the
bottom of a screen there is a horizontal line with a small vertical mark. On the top
of the screen, there is a horizontal line with a scale on which all multiples of ten
are marked by small vertical lines, and the numbers (multiples of ten) are written
next to the marks. The subject's task was (a) to identify the position of the mark
on the bottom of the scale with a position on the scale by bearing vertically upward, and (b) to describe the obtained position by a number. By bearing upward,
the mark on the bottom of the screen creates an imprecise image on the scale,
which becomes more diffuse the longer the distance between the mark and scale
is. The variation of the distance between the bottom line with the mark and the
scale allowed us to manipulate the decision maker's level of exactness of judgment. We varied the horizontal position of the mark on the bottom horizontal
line in such a way that (for every distance between mark and scale) the last digits
of the exact responses would have selected all numbers 0, 1, 2, ..., 9 with equal

---

8   A more formal but still *ad hoc* approach is to define, in a choice situation, the range of
    reasonable alternatives as the range between the two endpoints of the 10% tails of the
    observed distribution of selected values. This gives an impression of the meaning of
    the term. However, I am aware that the length of the tails that are cut off by a worst
    case/best case analysis can itself be part of a learning process that avoids undesired
    results.
9   This involves the assumption that for every article, the range of reasonable alternatives
    was given as the range between the two endpoints of the 10% tails of the respective
    distribution of prices.

frequency. We observed that for a great distance of bottom line and scale, sub-jects only selected multiples of ten as responses (exactness level 10); for about half the distance, they selected all multiples of 5 with equal frequency (exact-ness level 5); for about a quarter of the first distance, 2 and 8 were selected as ad-ditional responses; and for short distances, multiples of 1 were selected with about equal frequency when the line with the mark was near the line with the scale. Results clearly indicate that the exactness of the responses was influenced by the exactness of perception. An estimate of the extension of the respective ranges of reasonable alternatives can be obtained from the distribution of the er-rors of the selected data. The exactness selection rule could be verified (for fur-ther details, see Albers et al. [1997], section 4.)

A frequency diagram is a useful tool to describe the selected exactness. For every exactness, it gives the frequency with which it occured as an exactness of a response. In the bearing experiment, we obtained different frequency diagrams for different distances. The same kind of diagrams can be computed, for exam-ple, for the prices of contracts on the stock market. Stocks with a higher fre-quency of trading show finer exactness of prices. Using the diagrams, comparison of stock market data and the bearing experiment permits informa-tion about the exactness of analysis of the persons that made the prices (see Uphaus et al. 1998).[10] A more detailed analysis considers the sequence of offers on the electronic stock exchange market. These price sequences can be analyzed as a bilateral, multiperson negotiation process. Prominence theory permits the description of the structure of these processes (Albers et al. 1998). This allows us to draw conclusions from observed data on the influences of market struc-tures on the exactness of price setting.

Scales by Relative and Absolute Exactness

A helpful tool to analyze the responses of the decision maker involves the levels of relative and absolute exactness:

$S(r,a)$ is the set of all numbers with absolute exactness $\geq a$ and relative ex-actness $\geq r$. Two numbers, x, y, of $S(r, a)$ belong to the same class, if their distance is $|x-y| < a$, or if their relative distance is $|x-y|/\max(|x|, |y|) < r$.

Sets $S(r, a)$ describe possible choices of persons under given levels of relative and absolute exactness. Sets $S(r, a)$ can include pairs of responses that cannot be separated by the decision maker. For example, $a = 20$ permits the responses $70 = 50 + 20$ as well as $80 = 100 - 20$; however, these responses have a differ-ence of 10 and can thereby not be separated under an exactness level of 20. The second condition puts such pairs of numbers into one class. Such classes in

---

[10] Note that the exactness of price setting is highly correlated with the extension of the spread and thereby provides information as to the liquidity of the market.

$S(r, a)$ can contain at most two elements, namely (20, 30) or (70, 80) or the multiples of these pairs with integer powers of ten.

PERCEPTION OF UTILITY

Perception of Utility and Evaluation of Prospects

The basic idea of this approach is that decision makers measure utility by means of scales with a step structure in such a way that the differences between any two neighboring steps of the scale are perceived as equal, and interpolation of the distance between neighboring steps is possible. For scales on the money and on the probability space, interpolation is modeled as linear with respect to the respective space.

Steps of these scales are related to the full-step numbers: for a given task there is a task-dependent "finest perceived full-step number" (FPF) with the property that all full-step numbers that are greater than or equal to FPF are steps of the scale, while all finer full-step numbers are not steps of the scale. The idea is that full-step numbers that are finer than FPF are not perceived as steps. Below FPF the next step of the scale is zero.

If negative values are possible, the steps in the range of negative numbers are obtained from the steps in the range of positive numbers by multiplication with −1. For the money scale, steps in the range of negative numbers are valued twice.

The probability scale is a union of two parts. Part A has steps in the range between 0% and 50% (probabilities in the narrower sense). They are constructed as above with task-dependent FPF and zero, but they are restricted from above by 50% as maximal element. Part B has the steps in the range between 50% and 100% (counterprobabilities in the narrower sense). These steps are obtained by subtracting the steps of Part A from 100%.

For monetary amounts, the finest perceived full step is the crudest full-step number that is more than one full step below the maximal absolute value of the numbers given in the task. For probabilities, the finest perceived full step is the crudest full step that is finer than or equal to all probabilities and counterprobabilities given in the task.

Examples: When 10 is the finest perceived full step, one obtains the steps ..., −100, −50, −20, −10, 0, 10, 20, 50, 100,... This permits us to measure the difference between −50 and 10 as seven steps (valuing steps in the range of negative numbers twice), or to obtain the distance of −50 and 15 as 7.5 steps by using linear interpretation between full steps. When 1% is the finest perceived probability, we obtain the probability scale 0%, 1%, 2%, 5%, 10%, 20%, 50%, 80%, 90%, 95%, 98%, 99%, 100%. On this scale, 1% is one step above zero, and the total distance from 0% to 100% is 12 steps. Accordingly, 1% is perceived as 1 of 12 steps, i.e., as 1/12, whereas 99% is perceived 11/12. If 10% is the finest perceived full step of probability, we obtain the scale 0%, 10%, 20%, 50%, 80%,

90%, 100%, in which 10% represents 1 of 6 steps, i.e., in a binary lottery with probabilities 10% and 90%, 10% is perceived as 1/6, and 90% is perceived as 5/6. In general, the values of two probabilities p and $1-p$ generally add up to 1. Therefore, the evaluation of binary lotteries is not rank-dependent; 50% is evaluated as 1/2.

Below, the perceived values of monetary amounts are represented by $u(.)$ and the perceived values of percentages by $\pi(.)$. Both evaluation functions describe the results of evaluation processes. They are strongly task-dependent and are thus different from utility functions and probability evaluation functions of traditional utility theory.

Binary lotteries (payoffs x, y with probabilities p, $1-p$) are evaluated by using a weighted utility model:

$$u\left[p, x; 1-p, y\right] = u\left(x\right) \cdot \pi\left(p\right) + u\left(y\right) \cdot \pi\left(1-p\right).$$

The certainty equivalents of the lotteries are obtained by applying u^{-1} as:

$$ce\left[\,p, x;\left(1-p\right), y\right] = u^{-1}\left[u\left(x\right) \cdot \pi\left(p\right) + u\left(y\right) \cdot \pi\left(1-p\right)\right].$$

Since, in prominence theory, 50% is evaluated as 1/2, 50%–50% lotteries are evaluated by the midpoint of the two payoffs on the utility scale.

For lotteries with more than two alternatives, we have conducted only initial series of experiments. The results indicate that subjects' evaluations are generally in accordance with the theory but are also influenced by spontaneous emotional judgments that are performed on a crude level of analysis, such as counting the cases of positive and negative payoffs. It seems that subjects apply different evaluation concepts that interact with each other. However, our knowledge is not yet sufficient to extend prominence theory to these cases. As a general principle, I presently recommend the application of rank-dependent utility, as used in prospect theory, along with our probability evaluation function.

Range of Application

The utility approach of prominence theory has been successfully applied in various fields, including the evaluation of prospects, the explanation of paradoxes in the evaluation of prospects, the description of fairness criteria in Nash-bargaining problems, Kalai–Smorodinsky situations, principal agent problems, and equilibrium selection. The step structure has also proved to be a necessary descriptive tool for negotiations in characteristic function games and multipersonal agreements.

The theory is parameter free and does not adjust to individual characteristics. It describes median behavior over large sets of subjects and thereby models that part of utility perception which is common to all subjects. As a result of the simplicity of its conditions, it may have served as a focal point for cultural evolution. The concept has descriptive aspects, since it models observed behavior;

however, it also has normative aspects, since it describes a rule system that can be recommended.

As presented above, prominence theory models the perception of money in "substantial" amounts; for low amounts of money, however, perception tends to be more linear. For high monetary amounts, saturation in money restricts the validity of the concept. For students, these two effects can be avoided if the highest absolute payoff is around 2000 to 20,000 DM (ca. U.S. $1000 to $10,000). This conforms to restrictions of Kahneman and Tversky (1979) and Tversky and Kahneman (1992).

Both prominence theory and prospect theory (Tversky and Kahneman 1992) model the monetary equivalents of lotteries (1/2, 0; 1/2, x) as constant proportions of x. However, my experimental results indicate that the monetary equivalent as a proportion of x is a monotonically decreasing function whose median over all subjects is about 1/2 for x = 10 DM, and about 1/4 for x = 100,000 DM. Accordingly, both approaches can adequately model the utility function only within a restricted range. When errors are restricted to at most 10% of the prediction, the range has an extension of about a factor of 10 between its upper and lower limits. Prominence theory can be improved upon by introducing FPF as a decreasing function of the maximum absolute payoff involved in the task. For prospect theory, the exponent of the utility function can be adjusted in a like manner.

Another effect that restricts the validity of the concept (and of other approaches as well) is the utility of chance. When subjects are asked whether they prefer a "sure payoff of 10,000 DM," or "sure payoff of 10,000 DM plus a lottery [1/2, x; 1/2, $-x$] where they can choose x," the clear majority selects the second alternative with median x = 1000 DM. Albers et al. (2000) have shown that this is a separate effect that is distinct from traditional utility approaches. It can be explained by the preference for tension and the excitement induced by the unsolved problem. This effect influences subjects' evaluations of binary lotteries with monetary amounts x, y when the difference $|x - y|$ is small compared to $|x|$ and $|y|$. In addition, it seems to influence the evaluations of lotteries with small payoffs.

While these three effects refer to the modification of the perception of utility, other effects concern the process under which the decision is made. Kahneman and Tversky (1979) describe several such effects, which may be termed "framing effects." These effects modify the structure of the decision before the theory is applied.

Relations to the Weber–Fechner Law

Our approach has some similarity to the Weber–Fechner law. This law gives two rules for the perception of psychophysical stimuli as loudness or brightness: (a) equal relative physical differences are perceived as equal absolute differences, and (b) there is a finest perceived stimulus (Fechner 1968).

The full-step structure introduced by prominent numbers is such that equal relative differences of stimuli are perceived as equal absolute differences of perception (two subsequent prominent numbers as stimuli differ roughly by a factor of two); finest perceived stimuli exist that are, however, dependent on the task. The similarity to the Weber–Fechner law makes sense if one assumes that the numerical stimuli characterizing monetary amounts or probabilities can be viewed abstractly as emotionally perceived quantities that induce psychophysical reactions similar to those caused by the brightness of light or the loudness of sounds.

Our idea is that perception below FPF does not possess an emotional component. Nevertheless, the decision maker is able to perceive rationally the numerical information of such small terms. Although the decision maker is unable to transform the information into emotional reactions, she transforms the stimuli to the perception space by using rational methods of interpolation between the emotionally perceived reference points "zero payoff" and "finest perceived full step."

The two main differences between numerical and psychophysical stimuli are: (a) for numerical stimuli, the exactness of perception is adjusted to the respective task by the selection of the finest perceived full step, and (b) perception of numerical stimuli is also possible for amounts below the FPF.

Relations to Prospect Theory

Although prominence theory and prospect theory possess similar ranges of validity, several substantial differences should be noted. First, the approach of Kahneman and Tversky describes individuals, while prominence theory (presently) describes only mean behavior and needs an additional theory to explain individual deviations. Thus, we can compare prominence theory only with the predictions of prospect theory when median parameters are applied.

Second, prominence theory does not predict a universal utility function but rather assumes that perception of utility depends on the finest perceived monetary unit, which is task-dependent. This task dependence could be used specifically to predict and explain phenomena that cannot be explained by prospect theory (see next section).

Third, Tversky and Kahneman's evaluation function of probabilities assumes rank- dependent evaluation. For example, for binary prospects the probability 50% is devaluated to 40% for the alternative with the higher payoff. Prominence theory predicts no rank-dependent devaluation for binary lotteries. In the lottery [1/2,10,000;1/2,0] both theories predict about the same certainty equivalent, which is below the expected value 5,000. However, while prominence theory explains the entire devaluation as caused by the concavity of the utility function, prospect theory explains 50% of the reduction by the concavity of the utility function, and the other 50% by rank-dependent devaluation of the lottery.

Monetary equivalents of 105 binary lotteries $[p, x; (1T-p), y]$ were investigated with p = 1%, 10%, 20%, 50%, 80%, 90%, 99%, and x = 10000, y = 5000, 1000, 500, 0, –500, –1000, –5000, –10,000, and y = –10,000, x = 5000, 1000, 500, 0, –500, –1000, –5000. To explain the median of the observed evaluations, the predictions of prospect theory (with the median parameters a = 0.88 and γ = 0.61 reported by Tversky and Kahneman [1992]) were worse than those of prominence theory, while both theories were about equally accurate when the probability evaluation function of prospect theory was replaced by that of prominence theory (see Albers 1998a).

Two Crucial Experiments

The following experiments test predictions that are uniquely devied from prominence theory. They address the main point of the theory, namely that subjects neglect the steps below the finest perceived full step. It is my intent to show that subjects — although they generally perceive these steps — neglect them when they are confronted with a task that creates a finest perceived full step cruder than these steps.

Experiment 1 (new kind of *preference reversal paradox*): Consider the lotteries $A = [1/2,5000;1/2,-1000]$ and $B = [1/2,1000;1/2,0]$.

1. Decide which of the two lotteries you would prefer.
2. Then determine the certainty equivalents of both lotteries.

Result: The majority of subjects prefer B to A, but evaluate A higher than B.

How can this be explained? Under the comparison condition, both lotteries are evaluated in a combined task. The finest perceived full step is two steps below the maximum of the absolute values of all payoffs, i.e., two steps below 5000 or 1000. The values of the 50%–50% lotteries are obtained via the midpoints on the utility scales. For lottery A, the steps are –1000, 0, 1000, 2000, 5000. Since the steps in the range of negative payoffs are counted twice, one obtains the midpoint after 2.5 of 5 steps, i.e., the certainty equivalent of A is 500. For Lottery B, we have the steps 0, 1000. The certainty equivalent of B is at the midpoint of this step, i.e., 500 (by linear interpolation). Thus, the two lotteries have the same values, and subjects may prefer B to A since it does not involve negative payoffs. When both lotteries are evaluated separately, they are evaluated in separate tasks, and the finest perceived full steps are determined separately. For Lottery A, the finest perceived full step does not change, since it contains the maximum absolute value of both lotteries. Its certainty equivalent is still 500. For Lottery B, the maximum absolute payoff is 1000. This gives the finest perceived full step of 200. The payoffs of Lottery B are evaluated on the scale 0, 200, 500, 1000. On this scale, the midpoint of 0 and 1000 is 350. Thus, the monetary equivalent of Lottery B is 350, which is smaller than that of Lottery A. This explains the different evaluation of Lottery B under the condition of comparison and the condition of individual evaluation (for further details, see Albers 1997b).[11]

Experiment 2 (*preference construction paradox*): When a person receives an amount of money, she experiences a feeling of pleasure. Different amounts of money induce different levels of pleasure.

1. Construct a sequence of monetary amounts possessing the following property: for any three subsequent amounts, x, y, z, the additional pleasure obtained by switching from x to y equals the additional pleasure obtained by switching from y to z. Start with the numbers 0, 100, and construct a sequence of twenty elements (including 0 and 100).
2. Write down the last number of this sequence and label it as z^*. Give that amount y^* with the property that the additional pleasure of receiving y^* instead of 0 equals the additional pleasure of receiving z^* instead of y^*.
3. Take z^* as above and give the amount y' with the property that the additional pleasure of receiving y' instead of $z^*/4$ equals the additional pleasure of receiving z^* instead of y'.

Result 1: Let s^* be the step of y^* on the self-constructed scale. Then the median of s^* over all subjects is between steps 16 and 17. This indicates that some of the 20 steps are not taken into consideration at the time that the "midpoint" y^* between z^* and 0 is determined. This strongly supports prominence theory's prediction that full steps below FPF will collapse and contradicts the approach of prospect theory. It also does not conform with any utility theory that I know.

Result 2: For the "midpoint" y' of z^* and $z^*/4$, the number of steps in the self-constructed scales between $z^*/4$ and y' equals the number of steps between y' and x^*. This result holds for the median across all subjects and shows that steps in the self-constructed scale above $x^*/4$ are not neglected. Steps are neglected only in the range below $z^*/4$. This again conforms with the prediction of prominence theory.

These two experiments clearly support the idea of task-dependent utility functions. They support the approach of prominence theory even in the structural details of the function. The two paradoxes are not explained by any other utility approach I know.

---

[11] I believe that preference reversal can, in general, be explained using arguments that follow along these lines.

AGGREGATION OF UTILITY ON ONE DIMENSION

Below we consider individual and interpersonal choice conflicts that can be described by numerical variables as payoffs of different persons under different conditions, or opinions of different persons concerning state outlays, or estimates of different persons of probabilities of events. We only consider the case that all variables of a given problem are on the same dimension. We present a collection of rules of boundedly rational aggregation of the utility of such variables. The key tool is the utility approach of prominence theory. The approach could meanwhile be successfully applied to a variety of different interpersonal conflict situations.

Principles of Aggregation

As standard task we consider the decision between two alternatives, *A, B*. The decision is performed via a preference function $P(A, B)$, which measures the preference of alternative *A* over *B*. *A* is preferred to *B*, if $P(A, B) > 0$, and *B* to *A* if $P(A, B) < 0$; these inequations are denoted as the preference criterion. Sometimes it makes sense to split the preference criterion up into two terms of which each aggregates the arguments for one alternative as $P(A, B) = P'(A) - P'(B)$, then $P(A, B) > 0$ is equivalent to $P'(A) > P'(B)$. In two-person situations it can also make sense to split the arguments according to the persons *i, j* as $P(A, B) = P''(i) - P''(j)$. The function $P(A, B)$ is constructed according to:

Principles of Aggregation of Utility on One Dimension

(1) utility is measured according to prominence theory
(2) utility is aggregated in an additive way
(3) the utilitiy of a variable has weight $+1, -1$, or 0
(4) no variable can be selected twice
(5) $P(a, b)$ can be presented as a sum of differences of utility values

The restriction to additive aggregation is surprising, since the literature offers criteria of the type $(u(x) - u(a))/(u(y) - u(b))$. On the other hand, the combination of linear and logarithmic elements in the utility function[12] suggests that subjects do not distinguish relative and absolute differences, and therefore only use one kind of operator, here the addition.

The restriction of weights to $+1, -1$, or 0, and the condition that every variable can be used at most once are formally identical to the conditions of the construction of numerical responses. We assume that every important attribute has nonzero weight. The dependence of this evaluation on individual judgments could be confirmed under experimental conditions. In situations where two persons

---

[12] For example, the step structure 0, 10, 20, 50 indicates linear shape in the range of 0, +10, +20, and logarithmic shape in the range of +10, +20, +50.

could decide whether to use a conflict payoff as an argument, we observed that some pairs of subjects considered the possible conflict as an important argument, while others did not use it at all. Thus corresponding predictions must either use the variable with full weight or not (see Vogt and Albers 1997a, b).

$P(A, B)$ is obtained as a sum of differences of utility values if one assumes that the utility function only serves to measure differences and that there are no meaningful general cardinal levels of utility. This condition is fulfilled when $P(A, B)$ can be split into two subterms with identical structures: as $P'(A) - P'(B)$ or $P''(i) - P''(j)$.

Fairness Criteria

Below we apply the principles of aggregation of utility to situations that have been addressed by classical solution approaches connected with the names of Nash, Kalai–Smorodinsky, and Harsanyi–Selten. Each situation addresses the question of which of the two n-tuples of payoffs should be selected when certain alternatives (conflict payoffs or bliss points) are given.

Fair choice should depend on the utility of the players for the different alternatives; however, it is not possible to ask the players for their utilities, since they would deviate from the true values in order to influence the decision in their favor. In this situation the approach of prominence theory suggests itself. If we assume that prominence theory models those principles of utility measurement that are common to all subjects, then it makes sense to assume that subjects have internalized the rules of prominence theory and thereby know how to evaluate payoffs from a neutral point of view.

In fact, our experimental results indicate that all presented boundedly rational criteria seem to be the presently best predictors for subjects' choices in the respective conflict situations (see Vogt and Albers 1997a, b and Vogt 1999b, c).

In our approach, we reformulate the concepts such that they decide between pairs of alternatives. In each case we assume that all variables of the model are considered equally important (otherwise we would be in another model). The signs $+1, -1$ of the variables follow the natural direction of the argument. If the preference $P(A, B)$ of A over B increases when the value x_i of a variable increases, then the value x_i gets positive weight; if the preference decreases, the weight is negative. (Below we assume that $x_i > c_i$, $y_i > c_i$, $x_i > m_i$, $y_i > m_i$, $b_i > x_i$, and $b_i > y_i$ for all i. In two-person situations we assume that $x_1 > y_1$, i.e., player 1 prefers (x_1, x_2) to (y_1, y_2), and that $y_2 > x_2$, i.e., player 2 prefers (y_1, y_2) to (x_1, x_2)).

Nash problem: A group of players must decide between two alternatives with payoffs $x = (x_1, ..., x_n)$, $y = (y_1, ..., y_n)$. If all payoffs are considered equally important, all weights are obviously $+1$. Preference is given in the form $P'(x) <> P'(y)$ as $u(x_1) + ... + u(x_n) <> u(y) + ... + u(y_n)$. In two-person situations the criterion can be aggregated personwise as $P''(i) <> P''(j)$ as $u(x_i) - u(y) <> u(y_j) - u(x_j)$.

Nash problem with conflict point: This uses the same problem as described above, but if there is no agreement, players receive the conflict payoff $(c_1, ..., c_n)$. In the two-person case, it is easy to present the preference criterion in the form $P''(i) <> P''(j)$ as $u(x_i) - u(y_i) + u(c_i) <> u(y_j) - u(x_j) + u(c_j)$, which adds the terms $u(c_i)$ and $u(c_j)$ on both sides of the inequation obtained from the paragraph above. The form $P'(x) <> P'(y)$ is obtained as $u(x_i) + u(x_j) + u(c_i) <> u(y_i) + u(y_j) + u(c_j)$, where every alternative is supported by the conflict payoff of the player who supports it. This two-person approach cannot be easily transfered to the n-person case, since the idea of adding the values $u(c_i)$ of the players i who prefer the respective alternative to the respective side of the inequality, does not need to fulfill the fifth principle of aggregation (see above). Specifically, the fifth principle cannot be fulfilled when the number of players is odd.

Harsanyi–Selten problem: As above, but here the players must decide simultaneously, each player for one of the alternatives. If both players select the same alternative, they receive the corresponding payoff. If both of them select their best alternative, they receive the conflict payoff (c_1, c_2). If both of them select the best alternative of the respective other player, they receive the miscoordination payoff (m_1, m_2). The preference criterion in the form $P''(i) <> P''(j)$ is obtained as $u(x_1) - u(y_1) + u(c_1) - u(m_1) <> u(y_1) - u(x_2) + u(c_2) - u(m_2)$.

Kalai–Smorodinsky problem: As the Nash problem with conflict point, but here there is also a "bliss"or "utopia" point (b_1, b_2), which has the property that agreement between subjects (b_1, b_2) would be the adequate payoff pair if the sum $b_1 + b_2$ could be paid ($b_i > x_i$, and $b_i > y_i$ for both players). In this case the preference criterion can be presented as $u(b_1) - u(x_1) + u(x_2) - u(c_2) <> u(b_2) - u(y_2) + u(y_1) - u(c_1)$. The terms on the two sides of the inequation can be interpreted as the concessions of the players. At point (x_1, x_2), player 1 has made the concession $u(b_1) - u(x_1)$ on her payoff scale by reducing her payoff below the bliss point; moreover, she made the concession $u(x_2) - u(c_2)$ by increasing the opponent's payoff above the lowest possible level c_2. A similar description holds for the concession of player 2 in (y_1, y_2). The criterion measures which of the two players made the higher concession.

Optimal solutions: The criteria above can also be used to define optimal solutions of a set of alternatives (which is usually assumed as convex): an alternative is optimal with respect to a set of alternatives, if it is preferred to all other alternatives of the set. For the Nash problem, the optimal solution is characterized by $u(x_1) + ... + u(x_n) = max!$. For the Kalai–Smorodinsky problem, it is the payoff pair (x_1, x_2) for which $u(x_1) - u(x_2)$ is nearest to $(u(b_1) - u(b_2) + (u(c_1) - u(c_2))/2$.

Recent studies by Vogt applied the principles of utility aggregation to ultimatum games, certain reciprocity games, and certain sequential combinations of these two types, including the principal agent conflict. For the analysis of these games he added an additional principle of aggregation:

(6) a stronger player does not receive less than a weaker player from a joint payoff.

(This kind of condition can be also found in the equal share analysis approach of Selten [1972] for characteristic function games.) The games were solved by the boundedly rational version of the Kalai–Smorodinsky approach. An important finding of these experiments was that the motives of sequentially combined games can be separated, such that the solution of the combined game is obtained as the sequential combination of the solutions of the partial games (for details see Vogt 1998a, b, c, 1999).

Relations to Traditional Concepts

The situations described in the preceding section have been extensively addressed in the literature. The names connected with the problems stand for axiomatic traditional solution concepts (see Nash 1950, 1953; Harsanyi and Selten 1988; Kalai and Smorodinsky 1975; Kalai 1977). The criteria of these concepts are given by:

- Nash problem: $x_1 \cdot ... \cdot x_n <> y_1 \cdot ... \cdot y_n$
- Nash problem with conflict point:
  $(x_1 - c_1) \cdot ... \cdot (x_n - c_n) <> (y_1 - c_1) \cdot ... \cdot (y_n - c_n)$
- Harsanyi–Selten problem: $(x_1 - c_1)/(y_1 - m_1) <> (y_2 - c_2)/(x_2 - m_2)$
- Kalai–Smorodinsky: $(b_1 - x_1)/(x_2 - c_2) <> (b_2 - y_2)/(x_1 - c_1)$

The transformation from the traditional to the corresponding boundedly rational concept can also be obtained by evaluating payoffs by their values according to prominence theory and transforming the operators "+" to "+," "–" to "–," "·" to "+," "/" to "–." For each of these concepts, the modified boundedly rational approach seems clearly to be a better predictor than the corresponding classical solution concept (see Vogt and Albers 1997a, b).

Negotiations for a Joint Agreement

The following experiment provides an example of finding a compromise for a group: Subjects were asked for their individual opinions on several questions, such as "How much money should Germany spend per year on the development of weapon systems?" Opinions were collected, and groups of 4–5 subjects were formed such that within each group, diversity of viewpoints was maximized. Next, the subjects discussed the topic without mentioning actual sums of money. They then revealed their individual opinions to each other and negotiated a joint agreement. Communication was performed via terminals, and it took approximately 30–60 minutes to secure an agreement.

The result was that subjects gave their responses as spontaneous numbers and made their concessions in such a way that they made equal numbers of

concession steps in both directions (downward and upward). They thus minimized the sum of concessions or equivalently selected the mean on the step scale
of prominence theory. The principle is again immediately obtained from the
principles of aggregation of utility, if one assumes that the initial positions of all
players should be used.

ACKNOWLEDGMENT

I thank Reinhard Selten for many discussions, comments, and ideas during the
process of developing the theory.

REFERENCES

Albers, W. 1997a. Foundations of a theory of prominence in the decimal system. III.
    Perception of numerical information, and relations to traditional solution concepts.
    Working Paper No. 269. Institute of Mathematical Economics, Bielefeld.
Albers, W. 1997b. Foundations of a theory of prominence in the decimal system. IV.
    Task-dependence of smallest perceived money unit, nonexistence of general utility
    function, and related paradoxa. Working Paper No. 270. Institute of Mathematical
    Economics, Bielefeld.
Albers, W. 1998a. Foundations of a theory of prominence in the decimal system. VI.
    Evaluation of lotteries with two alternatives — A model that predicts median
    behavior, and serves as a normative benchmark of risk neutrality. Working Paper No.
    284. Institute of Mathematical Economics, Bielefeld.
Albers, W. 1998b. The complexity of a number as a quantative predictor of the frequency
    of responses under decimal perception — An empirical analysis of price level
    responses based on the theory of prominence. Working Paper No. 288. Institute of
    Mathematical Economics, Bielefeld.
Albers, W., E. Albers, L. Albers, and B. Vogt. 1997. Foundations of a theory of
    prominence in the decimal system. II. Exactness selection rule, and confirming
    results. Working Paper No. 266. Institute of Mathematical Economics, Bielefeld.
Albers, W., and G. Albers. 1983. On the prominence structure of the decimal system. In:
    Decision Making under Uncertainty, ed. R.W. Scholz et al., pp. 271–287. Amsterdam:
    Elsevier.
Albers, W., and A. Güntzel. 1998. The boundedly rational decision process creating
    probability responses — Empirical results confirming the theory of prominence.
    Working Paper No. 286. Institute of Mathematical Economics, Bielefeld.
Albers, W., R. Pope, R. Selten, and B. Vogt. 2000. Experimental evidence of the theory of
    chance. *German Econ. Rev.*, in press.
Albers, W., A. Uphaus, and B. Vogt. 1998. Stock price clustering and numerical
    perception. Working Paper No. 280. Institute of Mathematical Economics, Bielefeld.
Fechner, G.T. 1968. In Sachen der Psychophysik. Amsterdam: E.J.Bonset.
Harsanyi, J.C., and R. Selten. 1988. A General Theory of Equilibrium Selection in
    Games. Cambridge: MIT Press.
Hertwig, R., U. Hoffrage, and L. Martignon. 1999. Quick estimation: Letting the
    environment do the work. In: Simple Heuristics That Make Us Smart, G. Gigerenzer,

P.M. Todd, and the ABC Research Group, pp. 209–234. New York: Oxford Univ. Press.

Huttenlocher, J., L. Hedges, and V. Prohaska. 1988. Hierarchical organization in ordered domains: Estimating the dates of events. *Psych. Rev.* **95**:471–484.

Kahneman, D., and A. Tversky. 1979. Prospect theory: An analysis of decision and risk. *Econometrica* **47**:263–291.

Kalai, E. 1977. Proportional solutions to bargaining situations: Interpersonal utility comparisons. *Econometrica* **45**:1623–1630.

Kalai, E., and M. Smorodinsky. 1975. Other solutions to Nash's bargainging problem. *Econometrica* **43**:513–518.

Nash, J.F. 1950. The bargaining problem. *Econometrica* **18**:155–162.

Nash, J.F. 1953. Two person cooperative games. *Econometrica* **21**:128–140.

Schelling, T.C. 1960. The Strategy of Conflict. Cambridge, MA: Harvard Univ. Press.

Selten, R. 1972. Equal share analysis of characteristic function experiments. In: Beiträge zur experimentellen Wirtschaftsforschung, ed. H. Sauermann, vol. III, Contributions to Experimental Economics. Tübingen: J.C.B. Mohr (Siebeck).

Selten, R. 1987. Equity and coalition bargaining in experimental three-person games. In: Laboratory Experimentation in Economics, ed. A.E. Roth et al., pp. 42–98. New York: Cambridge Univ. Press.

Tversky, A., and D. Kahneman. 1992. Advances in prospect theory: Cumulative representation of uncertainty. *J. Risk Uncert.* **5**:297–323.

Uphaus, A., B. Vogt, and W. Albers. 1998. A model of the concession behavior in the sequence of offers of the German electronic stock exchange trading market (IBIS) based on the prominence structure of the bid ask spread. Working Paper No. 287. Institute of Mathematical Economics, Bielefeld.

Vogt, B. 1998a. Connection between bargaining behavior and reciprocity in a combined ultimatum-reciprocity game. Working Paper No. 287. Institute of Mathematical Economics, Bielefeld.

Vogt, B. 1998b. Criteria for fair divisions in ultimatum games. Working Paper No. 281. Institute of Mathematical Economics, Bielefeld.

Vogt, B. 1998c. The strength of reciprocity in a reciprocity game. Working Paper No. 279. Institute of Mathematical Economics, Bielefeld.

Vogt, B. 1999. Full information, hidden action and hidden information in principal agent games. Working Paper No. 315. Institute of Mathematical Economics, Bielefeld.

Vogt, B., and W. Albers. 1997a. Equilibrium selection in 2×2 bimatrix games with preplay communication. Working Paper No. 267. Institute of Mathematical Economics, Bielefeld.

Vogt, B., and W. Albers. 1997b. Selection between pareto-optimal outcomes in 2-person bargaining. Working Paper No. 268. Institute of Mathematical Economics, Bielefeld.

18

Goodwill Accounting and the Process of Exchange

Kevin A. McCabe and Vernon L. Smith

Economic Science Laboratory, University of Arizona,
Tucson, AZ 85721–0108, U.S.A.

ABSTRACT

Since the brain of any organism is a scarce resource, we expect to see specialization of cortical fields to solve content-dependent problems that occurred frequently over evolutionary time. We expect these solutions to exhibit bounded rationality in so far as the amount of information processing engaged on any problem is limited by the opportunity cost of cortical fields devoted to this problem. In this chapter we hypothesize that personal exchange is one of these problems. We begin by proposing a strategy called Goodwill Accounting for implementing reciprocal behavior that has been observed in both "Trust" and "Punishment" games. We hypothesize that this strategy represents a fast and frugal heuristic for tracking individual reputations without conscious awareness. We provide evidence for mental modules, studied by evolutionary psychologists, which together support this heuristic. These modules include friend-or-foe detection, cheater detection, and shared attention. We then examine the results from an agent-based simulation of this strategy in an ecology of prisoner's dilemma games. These simulations demonstrate the basic robustness of the strategy and suggest desirable parameter settings. We conclude with a discussion of the role of institutions as extensions of the mind's capacity for exchange.

INTRODUCTION

Economics is the study of exchange. Many things are exchanged: ideas, goods, services, information, and access rights, to name a few. In fact, the ubiquity of trade raises the following question: Why do people trade? Economics teaches that people trade because they differ in their circumstances, abilities, interests, knowledge, wants, and what they own. Since everyone is different, they place different values on different things, and so when a trade occurs, each party exchanges something of lower value for something of greater value.

Because exchange is most often sequential it involves risk. For example, I give you my credit card number and you then ship me the good; however, you might send me something of lesser value than I thought I was going to get. This raises the question we are interested in: How is risk managed in exchange relationships in order to make exchange possible? Most economists would say that people do not cheat because they desire to have "good" reputations. Yet, why is a "good" reputation valuable, what is the microstructure of reputation formation, and how does it reduce the riskiness of exchange?

Answers to these questions have implications for the design of institutions. For example, the Internet gives individuals the ability to choose any degree of anonymity and/or personae in their market interactions. Therefore, what prevents self-interested people from cheating on their trading partners? The *New York Times* (November 12, 1998) quotes one Internet market provider as saying, "sometimes people are too trusting, " and quotes an assistant director in the Federal Trade Commission as saying, "complaints about person-to-person on-line auctions is one of the largest categories of Internet complaints we receive."

Overlooked, or at least understated, in this article is that the vast majority of Internet exchanges are free from cheating. Just as people previously solved the problem of trust in "snail" markets, people are now solving the problem of trust on the Internet. But not all solutions are equal, and solving for exchange risk adds to transaction costs. It seems clear that existing institutions that currently prevent cheating on exchanges will not work as efficiently on the Internet. Can our current institutions be adapted for this purpose, or will new institutions have to be created?

Why Is Game Theory Alone Not Sufficient for Institutional Design?

The work on reciprocity by experimental economists differentiates between negative reciprocity (punishing the behavior of others that hurts you) and positive reciprocity (rewarding the behavior of others that helps you.) Negative reciprocity is currently the most often studied and is found to have a strong effect on behavior in "ultimatum" games, negotiations in other two-person bargaining games, and as an enforcement mechanism in "public goods" games that examine free-riding behavior in the commons. Positive reciprocity has been most often studied, and was also found to have a strong effect on behavior in "investment" and "trust" games, where defection in exchange cannot be punished.

Game theoretic models of exchange behavior are not sufficient. In one-shot investment/trust games, we observe the play of strictly dominated strategies by second movers who reward trusting behavior even though it is personally costly. In one-shot ultimatum games, we also observe second movers who punish "cheating" behavior, even though this also is personally costly (and thus strictly dominated). Furthermore, we observe behavior by first movers that suggests they rationally expect these rewarding and punishing behaviors in choosing their own strategies. McCabe and Smith (1999) summarize games in which the subjects who play cooperatively earn more money than if they played the subgame perfect equilibrium. If subjects are irrational, or naive, then how do we explain this empirical observation? In this chapter, we present a model of goodwill accounting as a tool in the adaptive social toolbox that allows individuals to engage in reciprocal behavior in order to achieve self-interested outcomes.

Basic Reciprocity Games

In this chapter we consider two simple examples of reciprocity games. The basic *trust game*, shown in Figure 18.1a, is played as follows: Player 1 must decide whether to move right, and get $10 for sure, or to move down and, depending on what player 2 does, either get $15 or nothing. The game can be interpreted as a sequential exchange. By moving down, player 1 initiates a trade but leaves himself vulnerable to cheating by player 2. By moving to the right, player 2 reciprocates and the exchange is consummated. The problem for player 1 is whether or not to trust player 2, while the problem for game theory is to predict the beliefs and consequent actions of player 1. A solution concept, based on backward induction, for this class of games was first suggested by Kuhn (1953). This approach makes a strong assumption about player 1's belief about player 2, and consequently player 1's actions. Using Kuhn's solution concept we derive the following analysis: if player 2 gets a chance to move, he or she should always move down to get the $40 (since $40 is preferred to $25), and player 1 realizing this, should play right.

The basic *punishment game*, shown in Figure 18.1b, is played as follows: Player 1 must decide whether to move to the right and get $20 for certain, or to move down and, depending on what player 2 does, either get $30 or nothing. The game can be interpreted as a bargaining over 40. By moving to the right, player 1 gives player 2 an equal split; however, by moving down, player 1 makes player 2

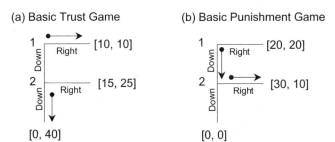

Figure 18.1 Basic reciprocity games. Arrows indicate choices predicted by game theory.

a more demanding offer but leaves himself open to punishment by player 2. By moving to the right, player 2 accepts the unequal offer and the deal is consummated. The problem for player 1 is whether or not player 2 will punish the more greedy demand by refusing the offer and giving them both zero. Using Kuhn's solution concept, we arrive at the following analysis: if player 2 gets a chance to move, he or she should always move to the right to get the $10 (since $10 is preferred to $0), and player 1, realizing this, should play down.

Why Are "Good" Reputations Valuable?

In personal exchange we hypothesize that reciprocity is used to reduce the risk of exchange. In Figure 18.2a, player 1 gives player 2 the good, G_t, at time t in return for a promise (perhaps specific) by player 2 to repay player 1 with something of value in the future. Suppose, in the future player 2 reciprocates by giving player 2 the good H_{t+1}. What does player 1 now give player 2 in return? Player 2's original promise? Not likely, since it was not really player 1's to begin with; not at least without a highly developed legal system. Instead, player 1 credits 2 with "goodwill" making it more likely that 1 will trust 2 in future trading.

Figure 18.2b shows how the trust game in Figure 18.1a can be extended to include "goodwill" decisions. Player 1 comes into the game assessing two kinds of risk. First, just looking at the game itself and the incentives created by moves and payoffs, player 1 evaluates the subjective risk of playing this game; this evaluation results in a number x^1. At the same time, player 1 uses any information he or she has on player 2 to assess 2's "goodwill"; this evaluation results in a number g_t^{12}. Goodwill accounting can now be used to play the memory-dependent, state transition, strategy shown in Figure 18.2b. If $g_t^{12} < x^1$, at any point in time, t, then player 1 chooses to play right (defect from cooperation). If $g_t^{12} \geq x^1$, player 1 chooses to cooperate by playing down.

Given this strategy player 1 updates player 2's goodwill as follows. If player 1 chooses to cooperate and player 2 reciprocates, i.e., chooses to cooperate by moving right, then 1 credits 2 with additional goodwill:

$$g_{t+1}^{12} = g_t^{12} + \alpha .$$ (18.1)

If, however, player 2 defects by playing down, then player 1 debits 2's goodwill:

$$g_{t+1}^{12} = g_t^{12} - \beta .$$ (18.2)

Note that more goodwill in the future increases trading opportunities. Let us define $V(g_{t+1}^{12})$ as the presented discounted dollar value of having goodwill in the amount of g_{t+1}^{12}. If

$$V(g_t^{12} + \alpha) - V(g_t^{12} - \beta) > 15 ,$$ (18.3)

then player 2 will cooperate by playing right. Why is this not the whole explanation? Because logically, in one-shot games, $V(g_{t+1}^{12}) = 0$. Therefore, the fact

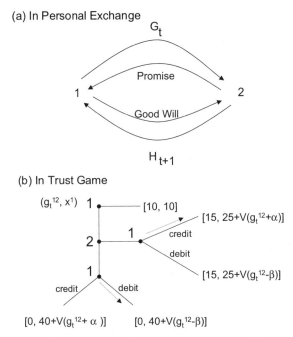

Figure 18.2   Goodwill accounting in (a) personal exchange and (b) trust game. Goodwill accounting strategies are shown with dotted arrows.

that people reciprocate in one-shot games supports the hypothesis that goodwill accounting is invoked automatically as a boundedly rational adaptation for an environment where most trading is repeated, i.e., the agent does not mentally alter the computation conditional on the anonymous interaction being a one-shot event.

Why Do People Punish?

Not only do people keep track of the goodwill they have towards others, they must also predict how much goodwill others have towards them. One can argue that players are more likely to punish other players when their defection is a surprise. For example, if I believe we have an exchange relationship worth nurturing, and you defect, then I am more likely to punish you than if I do not believe we have such a relationship. In the latter case, I offered to cooperate to test you and gather information. Your decision shows that you failed the test, so why incur the cost of punishing you? I should choose to save what I can and debit your goodwill account. The basic punishment game with goodwill accounting, shown in Figure 18.3, illustrates this point. Suppose player 2 believes his goodwill with player 1 is high, but player 1 then defects on him by playing down. Player 2 now has two options. First, player 2 can move right and at the same time

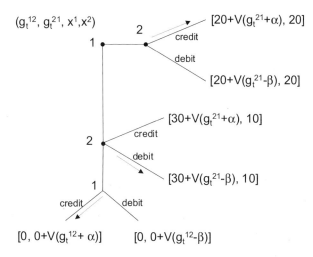

Figure 18.3 Goodwill accounting in basic punishment game. Goodwill accounting strategies are shown with dotted arrows.

lower player 1's goodwill, but this means less trading opportunities in the future. Alternatively, player 2 can move down and punish, giving both players an immediate payoff of zero. Under this option, player 2 does not decrement player 1's goodwill, $g_t^{12} - \beta$, but instead expects player 1 to increment player 2's goodwill, $g_t^{21} + \alpha$, thus bringing it more in line with player 2's goodwill assessment of player 1. This second option has two effects: (a) it makes both players better trading partners in the future, and (b) if player 1 anticipates that player 2 will punish for this reason, then player 1 is less likely to defect. In fact, punishment at time t followed by a renewed effort to cooperate at time $t+1$ is a common strategy (reported by McCabe and Smith 1999) in the punishment version of the games we have studied with the same partners matched in each trial.

HOW DOES THE MIND SOLVE THE PROBLEM OF EXCHANGE?

Clearly, a subject who, acting as player 1, moves down, must have a strong belief that player 2 will reciprocate (at least two-thirds of the time.) Noncooperative game theory cannot explain where these beliefs come from, but evolutionary psychology offers an explanation (see Hoffman et al. 1998). According to evolutionary psychologists, the mind is a complex organization of specialized mental algorithms, each designed by natural selection to solve a specific problem of reproductive success. We hypothesize that such a system of mental modules exists for solving the problem of personal exchange.

Figure 18.4 describes the mental modules that we hypothesize are used by the mind to reason about the riskiness of exchange. At the core of our cognitive

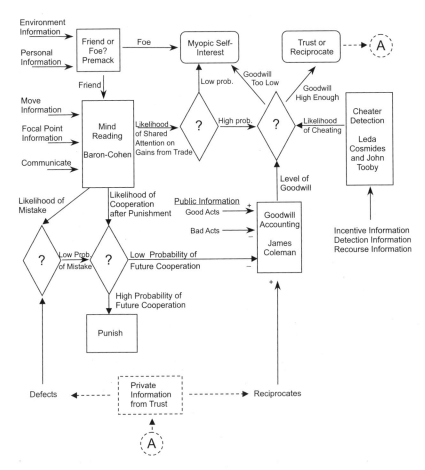

Figure 18.4 Cognitive model of exchange.

model is the idea that people engage in mental goodwill accounting of others. The more goodwill a person has, the more they are to be trusted to reciprocate in an exchange. When individuals interact with a new person, in-group and out-group information as well as any public information will be used to determine the initial stock of goodwill that we extend. The greater the initial goodwill, the more likely trust will be extended to initiate an exchange. However, this leaves people vulnerable to cheating. Therefore, as an aid to a mental accounting module we model a number of supporting mental modules: cheater detection; friend-or-foe detection; and a theory of mind system that attributes mental states to others. However, once an exchange is initiated, a person's goodwill is incremented or decremented based on our perception of their reciprocal response. Through this process, goodwill becomes a form of personal capital that allows a reciprocator greater trading opportunities in the future. Coleman's (1990) idea of social capital has an immediate interpretation in this theory. For a fixed amount of goodwill, social capital increases the amount of trade by reducing the likelihood of defection.

The Friend-or-Foe Module

The friend-or-foe module is modeled (although not by this name) by David and James Premack (1995) in their work on human social competence in infants. They observe that infants at a very early age distinguish between physical and animate objects. Furthermore, infants assume that those animate objects which seem self-propelled have intentions based on specific goals. They theorize that infants place either a positive or negative value on the interaction between intentional objects and try to avoid negative interactions. Initially, the value placed on an interaction is based on intensity, thus striking, fast movement and loud noises result in the interaction being given negative value, while caressing, slower movement and softer sounds result in the interaction being valued as positive. Later, as infants perceive that other intentional objects have goals, they begin to value the interactions with another intentional object as positive, if the object is helping another object (perhaps themselves) achieve its goal, or negative, if the object is hindering another object (perhaps themselves) from achieving its goal. It is this valuation process that determines whether an intentional object is friend or foe.

The Premacks further argue that infants conceptualize groups of intentional objects of equal power as having additional in-group properties. The infant expects group members (a) to act alike, (b) to engage in both negative and positive reciprocity, and (c) to have mostly positive interactions. Note that this later expectation may indicate certain evolutionary predisposed biases to a priori value interactions among in-group members as positive and to value interactions among out-group members as either negative or neutral.

The first module, friend-or-foe, is most likely an early warning/screening module for the priming of the decision to behave either cooperatively or noncooperatively. We see noncooperative behavior as taking one of two forms. In its first form, noncooperative behavior leads to the decision to avoid the other person or persons. Orbell and Dawes (1993) have run laboratory experiments that demonstrate the value of this behavior for subjects in prisoner's dilemma games. In its second form, noncooperative behavior results in sub-game perfect, strategizing, and belief formation, subject to the complexity of calculating continuation values that incorporate reasoning about others.

Cheater Detection Module

One aspect of intentions that must be constantly monitored is the likelihood of cheating. Cosmides (1989) and Cosmides and Tooby (1992) have done extensive behavioral research on the existence of a cheater detection module, which they postulate has had strong adaptive value in small group interactions of Pleistocene humans.

Cosmides and Tooby developed a computational theory for the adaptive problem of exchange. This theory predicts that subjects in trading environments will try to acquire information to answer the following questions: what are the gains from trade, and where are they largest; what is my counterpart trying to achieve; what is the implicit contract, if any, that I have with my counterpart; will cheating on this contract be detected; and how will my counterpart behave if I am caught cheating? Cosmides (1989) provides experimental evidence for the existence of specialized human modules for cheater detection.

Cheater detection is invoked to estimate the likelihood that someone has cheated. This calculation is then used either to punish the individual or to debit their goodwill account. It has not yet been resolved whether cheater detection or some other module acts to evaluate the riskiness of the situation in order to come up with the risk assessment number x^i.

Shared Attention Module

Once a person has formed some initial expectation about the likely value of a trading relationship with another person, he or she will continue to gather additional information to better understand the intentions of the other person in the specific trading instance. At this stage, individuals are likely to use what Simon Baron-Cohen (1995) calls the shared attention mechanism. Such a mechanism is used to convert a dyadic understanding of intentions, such as "he is hungry," to a triadic understanding, such as "he knows, that I know, that he is hungry." Triadic knowledge becomes the basis for reciprocity. For example, offering food as a way to "help" him meet his goal now implies a promise of reciprocity to keep the value of the relationship positive.

Baron-Cohen hypothesizes mental modules, or mechanisms, whose existence is consistent with a variety of evidence he summarizes. These modules enable inferences to be made about mental phenomena in other agents based on their actions or words: (a) an intentionality detector (ID); (b) an eye direction detector (EDD); (c) a shared attention mechanism (SAM); and (d) a theory of mind mechanism (TOMM) thought to be interconnected so that ID and EDD are inputs to SAM with the latter an input to TOMM. The implications of this work for the analysis of strategic interaction differ substantially from the underlying postulates of game theory.

In game trees involving two-person anonymous interactions, such as those discussed in this chapter, shared attention will operate on two kinds of information: (a) focal points as discussed by Schelling (1960) are features of the strategic setting, such as symmetry and Pareto dominance of payoffs, which are likely to be observed by the other player and consequently promote triadic understanding; (b) move information is another way to promote triadic understanding since it communicates intentions through both foregone opportunities, and what payoffs remain as admissible future opportunities.

THE GOODWILL ACCOUNTING STRATEGY

One goal of this area of research is to develop models of goodwill accounting that have predictive success in the laboratory. Figure 18.5 shows an intelligent agent representation of the goodwill accounting strategy. The agent is labeled, i, and is playing agent j. Strategies shown in octagons represent agent i's choice: C for cooperate, D for defect, A for avoid, P for punish. Strategies in brackets $\{\}$ represent agent j's choices as seen by agent i. The addition of U for unknown indicates that agent i may not see agent j's strategy either during activation of the choice rule or later in the updating rule. Not modeled is the activity necessary to convert any exchange context into this symbolic form.

As described above, the choice component of the goodwill mechanism is given by the relationship $g_t^{ij} \geq x^i$, which results in cooperation by i. Of course at the same time, j is choosing what to do based on $g_t^{ji} \geq x^j$. Notice that confusion between i and j can arise from two sources. First, they may disagree on the intrinsic risk of the game, i.e., $x^i \neq x^j$. Second, they may disagree in how much goodwill each gives the other. Such confusion can result in less cooperation and thus provides a role for a mind-reading system.

In Figure 18.5 mind reading is modeled in two ways. First, we model mind reading by treating x^i and x^j as random variables. We can determine the degree of agreement that agents i and j reach on X by how tightly x^i and x^j are distributed around X. This precision is determined by the individual specific parameter of the uniform distribution, z^i. A second form of mind reading is to give an individual the ability to predict his or her goodwill with someone else. For example, h_t^{ji} is agent i's prediction of his or her goodwill with agent j, i.e., g_t^{ji}. The precision of h_t^{ji} is again treated as a random variable drawn from a uniform distribution around the true goodwill account g_t^{ji}, with individual specific parameter, y^i.

The effect of h_t^{ji} is that agent i can now form some expectation about agent j's likely behavior. If, for example, $h_t^{ji} < x^j$, then agent i would realize that agent j is likely to defect under these circumstances because i does not yet have enough goodwill with j for the degree of risk in the current situation. If agent i can avoid the situation, then agent i can avoid the resulting mutual loss of goodwill. This helps explain the previously cited work by Orbell and Dawes (1993). However, mind reading provides agents with imperfect predictions of their goodwill with others. If in fact agent i does not yet know what agent j is doing, given by U^j, then i will use his or her judgment prior to deciding on an action. In Figure 18.5, if $h_t^{ji} < x^i$, and agent i cannot avoid an interaction with agent j, then i will defect, D^i, unless i sees that j has cooperated, $\{Cj\}$, in which case i will then check j's goodwill $g_t^{ij} \geq x^j$ in deciding whether or not to reciprocate with C^i or defect D^i.

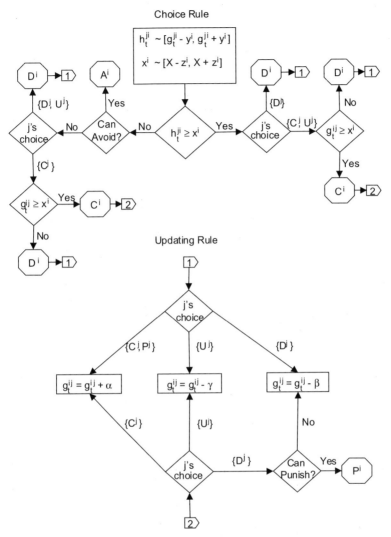

Figure 18.5 Goodwill accounting strategy. See text for a full description of the model.

The role of mind reading on goodwill can explain why researchers observe differences in behavior between normal form and extensive form games even though theory predicts isomorphic behavior. For example, in the trust game shown in Figure 18.1a, when player 1 moves down player 2 now knows for sure that $g_t^{12} \geq x^1$. If however, player 2 had to move simultaneously with player 1, player 2's choice would be based on the relationship, $h_t^{12} \geq x^2$, which has greater potential for error.

AGENT-BASED SIMULATIONS OF THE GOODWILL
ACCOUNTING STRATEGY

A classic approach to studying cooperation is to examine behavior in the prisoner's dilemma game shown in Figure 18.6. In this game there are two players
denoted row and column. Each player can choose to either cooperate, C, or defect, D. Depending on what each player does they each receive one of the payoffs, a, b, c, d. We denote a play as an ordered pair with row's choice first, and
then columns choice, e.g., [C, D] is the play where row cooperates, chooses C,
and column defects, chooses D. We denote players' payoffs from the game as an
ordered pair with row first and column second, e.g., for the play [C, D], the payoff is (d, a) where row gets d and column gets a. However, if [D, C] is played the
payoff reverses to (a, d). Alternatively, both players could choose to cooperate,
i.e., play [C, C], resulting in the payoff (b, b), or both players could choose to defect, i.e., play [D, D], resulting in the payoff (c, c). Payoffs satisfy, a > b > c > d,
which gives each player a dominant strategy to always play defect, D. For example, [D, C] is better for row than [C, C], since a > b, and [D, D] is better for row
than [C, D], since c > d. This is what makes the game a dilemma. Both players
would be better off cooperating and getting (b, b), but they each have a dominant
strategy to defect and thus they only get (c, c). To sharpen the nature of this

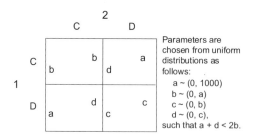

Figure 18.6   Simulating goodwill accounting in an ecology of prisoner's dilemma
games.

dilemma we further require that a + d < 2b. This implies there does not exist a weighted average of the plays [C, D] and [D, C] which would make both players better off compared to always cooperating by playing [C, C].

In a series of tournaments organized by Robert Axelrod, well known game theorists were asked to submit their favorite strategy for playing the repeated prisoner's dilemma. Axelrod (1984) found that a very simple behavioral strat- egy known as Tit-for-Tat (TFT) often won these tournaments. A person who plays TFT always cooperates in period one, and then in subsequent periods plays whatever his or her partner played in the previous period. Why was TFT so suc- cessful? Axelrod notes that all of the successful strategies, including TFT were nice, i.e., were never the first to defect, and were reciprocal, i.e., they always met cooperation with cooperation, and defection with defection.

The goodwill accounting strategy is nice when it starts with a high initial level of goodwill, g_0^{ij} relative to the distribution of subjective risks, x^i. Figure 18.6 shows the distribution of payoff values a, b, c, d used in this chapter. We as- sume that for every prisoner's dilemma game (a, b, c, d) encountered players evaluate the subjective risk as,

$$x^i = (a - b) + (c - d) \quad . \tag{18.4}$$

Figure 18.7 shows the distribution of subjective risks for 5000 randomly drawn games. The goodwill accounting strategy is reciprocal but only indirectly through the updating of goodwill. Depending on the parameters, α and β, the goodwill accounting strategy will be more or less contrite and generous, attrib- utes found to be important in strategies which must cope with noisy play in the

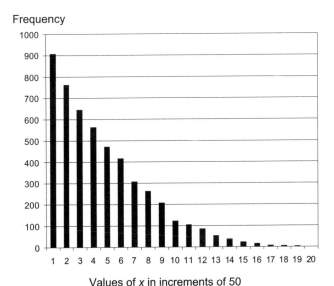

Figure 18.7   Histogram of *x* values.

repeated prisoner's dilemma. See Axelrod (1997). Generosity allows a certain number of defections to go unpunished. The goodwill accounting strategy accomplishes this by decreasing goodwill slowly, i.e., a relatively small β. Contrition means that one should not be provoked by the other player's response to an unintended (or misdirected) defection. The goodwill accounting strategy accomplishes this through mind reading.

Preliminary simulations of the goodwill accounting strategy are reported in this chapter. In these simulations agents are placed on a 25 square grid (one agent per grid) which is then mapped onto the sphere so that each agent has exactly eight neighbors as shown in Figure 18.6. One iteration of the simulation has each agent (starting with agent 1 and proceeding consecutively to agent 25) play a randomly chosen neighbor (with each neighbor equally likely) in a randomly chosen game (a, b, c, d). The simulation is stopped at 200 iterations. At the beginning of the simulation each agent is given a random set of parameters (an initial level of goodwill extended to all neighbors, GW, and updating parameters, α and β). In all of the simulations α is drawn uniformly between 0 and 50, and β is drawn uniformly between 25 and 75.

Table 18.1 shows the stopping values of a simulation involving relatively low initial goodwill values, GW, i.e., all values were drawn between 0 and 300. So, for example, agent 1 initially gives all neighbors a starting goodwill GW = 174, increases a neighbor's goodwill by 36 if he or she cooperates, and reduces a neighbor's goodwill by 51 if he or she defects. Goodwill values are truncated at 0 (defect in any game) and 1000 (cooperate in any game). The next two columns under the label *Self* indicate that agent 1 cooperated 114 times and defected 288 times. The next two columns under the label *Neighbor* indicate that a neighbor cooperated 105 times with agent 1 and defected 297 times with agent 1. Agent 1's total payoff from all plays is 91,662. Finally, the last eight columns give agent 1's goodwill towards his or her neighbors. Agent 1 has maximum goodwill towards neighbors 6 (agent 10) and 8 (agent 7) and zero goodwill towards everyone else. This means that agent 1 will always cooperate with agents 10 and 7. Furthermore, if we look at rows 10 and 7 we see that these agents have also given agent 1 goodwill of 1000. (Note for agent 7, agent 1 is neighbor 1, while for agent 10, agent 1 is neighbor 3.) Figure 18.8 summarizes strong trading partners ($g_{200}{}^{ij} > 800$) after 200 iterations with solid arrows, and weak trading partnerships after 200 iterations with dotted arrows ($g_{200}{}^{ij} < 500$). Agents with more than one trading partnership are circled.

Note that agent 14 has the most trading partners (5) and has the highest starting value (300) for his goodwill accounts for his neighbors. This is consistent with Axelrod's findings that nice strategies do well. However, nice is more complicated for goodwill accounting strategies since updating rules also matter. Agent 3 also uses a high starting goodwill value (245) but does much worse than average due to a very low $\alpha = 1$ and a very high $\beta = 63$. Note that agent 3 is the opposite of Axelrod's generous or contrite strategies. Instead, agent 3 gives very

Table 18.1 200 iterations
$0 \leq g \leq 300$.

ID	GW	α	β	Self		Neighbor		Payoff	Goodwill Accounting towards Neighbors							
				#C	#D	#C	#D		1	2	3	4	5	6	7	8
1	174	36	51	114	288	105	297	91,662	0	0	0	0	0	1000	0	1000
2	233	15	40	77	342	69	350	91,002	0	0	0	0	0	0	0	878
3	245	1	63	32	385	36	381	77,858	0	0	0	0	0	0	0	0
4	125	36	27	101	291	96	296	89,327	0	0	1000	0	1000	0	0	0
5	113	44	64	39	362	43	358	88,522	0	0	0	1000	0	0	0	0
6	17	49	68	2	405	8	399	73,203	0	0	0	0	0	48	0	0
7	158	48	43	105	286	102	289	94,135	1000	0	0	0	1000	0	0	0
8	178	39	27	185	220	174	231	105,973	1000	0	0	1000	1000	0	0	430
9	187	24	39	174	232	177	229	107,244	0	0	1000	1000	1000	0	1000	0
10	84	33	38	120	239	127	232	97,337	0	0	1000	1000	0	897	0	0
11	177	42	66	17	377	18	376	72,524	0	0	42	0	0	0	0	0
12	69	50	70	7	399	11	395	78,311	0	0	0	0	0	0	0	0
13	74	35	74	57	344	68	333	89,258	0	0	0	0	0	0	1000	0
14	300	27	30	221	189	198	212	118,407	351	1000	804	0	0	1000	0	1000
15	173	34	25	25	383	16	392	80,685	0	0	0	0	0	0	0	0
16	240	6	30	72	323	71	324	87,434	0	0	0	0	0	450	0	0
17	89	15	27	20	390	26	384	82,659	0	0	1000	0	0	0	0	0
18	285	20	40	137	262	121	278	97,415	0	1000	1000	0	0	0	0	0
19	84	49	45	12	380	17	375	74,062	0	0	0	0	0	0	0	0
20	194	9	33	75	317	79	313	85,176	494	0	0	0	0	0	0	0
21	214	21	45	41	388	37	392	87,641	0	0	0	0	0	0	0	0
22	63	17	56	28	349	44	333	77,461	0	0	0	0	0	0	0	0
23	25	10	54	7	407	16	398	74,894	0	0	0	0	0	0	0	0
24	79	23	70	17	361	29	349	72,819	0	0	1000	0	0	0	0	0
25	87	40	43	101	295	98	298	87,448	0	0	0	0	0	1000	0	0

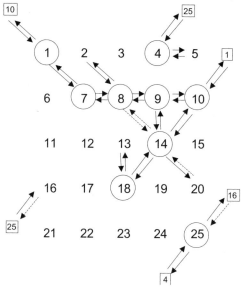

Figure 18.8 Trading partners.

little additional goodwill to cooperators and decreases defectors' goodwill very quickly. What we can conclude is that even in a fairly low initial goodwill environment subsets of the populations can find long-term trading partners using goodwill accounting.

Table 18.2 shows what happens as we increase the propensity of strategies to be nice by drawing initial goodwill values between 0 and 900. We see many more long-term trading partnerships developing and much higher payoffs to participants. Notice agent 3 now starts with an initial goodwill account of 734. Even though this is very high, the bad updating parameters again make it difficult for agent 3 to do as well as players with lower initial goodwill but with more even updating parameters. To see the importance of good updating parameters that place a high value on cooperation, contrast agent 6 (who has initial goodwill of only 51 and updating parameters $\alpha = 49$, $\beta = 68$) with agent 23 (who has a slightly higher initial goodwill of 73, but poorer updating parameters $\alpha = 10$, $\beta = 54$). In a high starting goodwill world, even low goodwill agents can develop many trading partners as long as they put a high enough value on cooperation.

In another simulation we decided to see how invasion-proof nice (high initial goodwill) strategies are. To this end we created a checkerboard pattern of strategies with every even agent playing a nice strategy and every odd agent playing a strong noncooperative strategy, i.e., initial goodwill of 0 with updating parameters, $\alpha = 1$, $\beta = 50$. Table 18.3 reports the results from this simulation. As expected, the nice strategies have developed long-term trading partnerships with

Table 18.2 200 iterations $0 \leq g \leq 900$.

ID	GW	α	β	Self #C	Self #D	Neighbor #C	Neighbor #D	Payoff	Goodwill Accounting towards Neighbors 1	2	3	4	5	6	7	8
1	522	36	51	400	2	394	8	152,441	1000	1000	1000	1000	1000	1000	1000	1000
2	698	15	40	375	44	355	64	146,235	1000	1000	0	1000	1000	1000	1000	1000
3	734	1	63	368	49	357	60	144,202	270	0	788	783	725	792	727	774
4	373	36	27	345	47	339	53	142,180	0	1000	1000	1000	1000	1000	1000	1000
5	337	44	64	268	133	267	134	133,808	0	1000	1000	1000	1000	1000	0	0
6	51	49	68	249	158	269	138	129,421	0	1000	1000	1000	1000	1000	1000	0
7	473	48	43	386	5	379	12	154,365	1000	1000	1000	1000	1000	1000	1000	1000
8	534	39	27	401	4	403	2	154,992	1000	1000	1000	1000	1000	1000	1000	1000
9	561	24	39	405	1	403	3	153,490	1000	1000	1000	1000	1000	1000	1000	1000
10	252	33	38	257	102	268	91	129,962	0	1000	1000	1000	0	1000	1000	1000
11	531	42	66	388	6	379	15	144,805	1000	1000	1000	1000	0	1000	1000	1000
12	205	50	70	240	166	250	156	132,257	0	1000	1000	1000	0	1000	1000	0
13	220	35	74	288	113	291	110	139,312	1000	1000	1000	1000	1000	1000	1000	1000
14	900	27	30	410	0	402	8	164,423	1000	1000	1000	1000	1000	1000	1000	1000
15	518	34	25	402	6	394	14	154,951	1000	1000	1000	1000	1000	1000	1000	1000
16	719	6	30	390	5	375	20	148,979	989	1000	857	977	869	1000	1000	599
17	267	15	27	255	155	262	148	137,977	915	0	972	1000	897	1000	0	0
18	854	20	40	399	0	367	32	142,179	1000	1000	1000	1000	1000	1000	1000	1000
19	251	49	45	293	99	292	100	132,930	0	1000	1000	1000	1000	0	1000	1000
20	582	9	33	387	5	384	8	146,649	1000	927	897	972	969	1000	885	1000
21	642	21	45	400	29	386	43	164,522	1000	1000	1000	1000	0	1000	1000	1000
22	187	17	56	221	156	251	126	126,025	677	0	1000	0	0	918	947	492
23	73	10	54	66	348	115	299	97,982	0	693	0	0	0	0	0	0
24	236	23	70	288	90	297	81	130,671	1000	855	1000	0	1000	1000	1000	0
25	261	40	43	391	5	393	3	151,527	1000	1000	1000	1000	1000	1000	1000	1000

Table 18.3 200 iterations $0 \leq g \leq 900$. Checkerboard cheating.

ID	GW	α	β	Self #C	Self #D	Neighbor #C	Neighbor #D	Payoff	1	2	3	4	5	6	7	8
1	0	1	50	1	394	21	374	76,614	0	0	0	0	0	0	0	0
2	522	36	51	174	242	140	276	100,576	0	1000	0	0	0	1000	0	1000
3	0	1	50	2	403	39	366	79,167	0	0	0	0	0	0	0	0
4	698	15	40	214	188	144	258	97,682	0	1000	0	0	0	1000	0	1000
5	0	1	50	6	390	34	362	80,533	0	0	0	0	0	0	0	0
6	734	1	63	188	207	143	252	95,365	0	0	783	721	0	0	0	588
7	0	1	50	1	406	19	388	80,775	0	0	0	0	0	0	0	0
8	373	36	27	227	154	198	183	109,201	1000	0	1000	0	0	1000	0	1000
9	0	1	50	2	396	29	369	85,530	0	0	0	0	0	0	0	0
10	337	44	64	173	233	163	243	103,026	1000	44	0	0	1000	1000	0	0
11	0	1	50	0	396	29	367	78,165	0	0	0	0	0	0	0	0
12	51	49	68	191	216	203	204	116,627	1000	0	1000	0	0	1000	0	1000
13	0	1	50	6	387	24	369	76,203	0	0	0	0	0	0	0	0
14	473	48	43	235	171	207	199	107,045	1000	0	1000	0	0	1000	0	1000
15	0	1	50	1	383	40	344	84,242	0	0	0	0	0	0	0	0
16	534	39	27	218	187	151	254	106,130	0	0	1000	1000	0	0	0	1000
17	0	1	50	4	430	34	400	87,226	0	0	0	0	0	0	0	0
18	561	24	39	226	169	186	209	109,792	1000	0	1000	0	0	1000	0	1000
19	0	1	50	3	392	25	370	73,136	0	0	0	0	0	0	0	0
20	252	33	38	140	252	128	264	97,273	1000	0	0	0	1000	1000	0	0
21	0	1	50	1	394	30	365	83,466	0	0	0	0	0	0	0	0
22	531	42	66	155	212	127	240	85,771	1000	0	1000	0	0	0	1000	0
23	0	1	50	1	415	38	378	82,659	0	0	0	0	0	0	0	0
24	205	50	70	158	237	150	245	107,665	1000	0	1000	0	0	0	1000	0
25	0	1	50	3	416	28	391	88,182	0	0	0	0	0	0	0	0

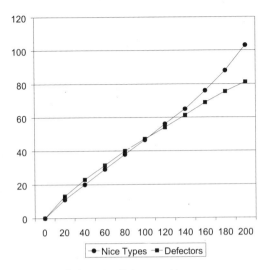

Figure 18.9   Average cumulative payoffs by agent types.

other nice strategies while almost always defecting against their noncooperative neighbors. The nice strategies all have higher payoffs with the exception of agent 22. Figure 18.9 plots the average cumulative earnings of the nice strategies versus the defectors. As we see, defectors do better in the beginning; however, by period 112 the cooperators have had enough time to work out their goodwill accounting to pull ahead. So far we have not done simulations that make use of mind reading, but we predict this is likely to reduce the time over which noncooperators benefit.

INSTITUTIONS AS EXTENSIONS OF MIND

Exchange is governed by rules, both formal and informal, which define individual rights and responsibilities. These rules make up our social institutions, which in turn shape our incentives to increase trading opportunities. We hypothesize that our economic institutions serve as extensions of our minds' capacity for exchange as our economic environment has moved increasingly from personal to impersonal exchange settings. For example, in personal exchange individuals choose who they want to trade with based on their "goodwill" accounting. We call this right a "minimal property right," since it seems necessary for personal exchange. One augmentation of the mental "goodwill" system is the use of reputational institutions, for example, credit reporting. These reputational mechanisms allow the "minimal property right," normally found in personal exchange to extend to impersonal exchange. We propose that new behavioral experiments be carried out to study the extension of mental "goodwill" accounting systems to institutions that overcome the anonymity problem in Internet transactions.

Money as an Extension of Mind

As group sizes continue to increase, institutions begin to emerge that augment modern humans' ability to trade. To understand how our cognitive adaptations for trade would shape these institutions, we start with the historical transition from personal to impersonal exchange documented by Douglas North (1990). In impersonal exchange, an important institutional innovation is the introduction of a generally accepted medium of exchange, i.e., money, which overcomes the inter-temporal trust problem. In Figure 18.10b, A gives B the good, G_t, while B gives A money, m_t. As long as money keeps its value over time (McCabe 1989), the use of money reduces the subjective risk of the exchange, x^A. Consequently, for the same amount of goodwill, g_t^{AB}, player A is able to exchange with player B over a larger set of exchanges. Thus money acts as an extension of the mind's capacity for personal exchange to impersonal exchange settings. As monetary theory tells us, additional functionality then comes from using money since it solves the double coincidence of wants problem at low cost and thus promotes even greater specialization.

It is unreasonable to expect much specialization in the brain for monetary exchange since this activity has had a very short evolutionary history. However, monetary exchange probably builds on specialized modules in the brain used for personal exchange, an activity that has had a very long evolutionary history. Note, for example, that the use of money does not reduce the risk of exchange to zero. Therefore we would expect the goodwill accounting system to still be invoked even in impersonal exchange situations. Consider someone who wishes to sell their used car through the classified ads. Consider the difference in risk assessment between someone who says they will bring a certified check to a local bank at noon versus someone who says they will bring a certified check to a crossroads in the countryside at midnight.

Minimal Property Right Systems and Public Good Provision

Another example of an institution that acts as an extension of the mind's goodwill system is minimal property rights, i.e., the right to choose with whom one trades. What makes trade possible is that over the duration of our dealings with someone else, our institutions provide us with some degree of reliability that we are dealing with whom we think we are dealing with, and provides some accountability when deals go wrong.

Most laboratory experiments using the voluntary contributions mechanism (VCM) show initially high public good provision followed by a characteristic decline in contributions over time. Consider the following game theoretic

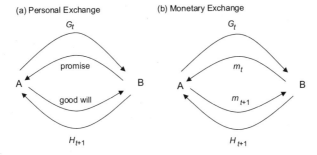

Figure 18.10 Comparison of personal and monetary exchanges.

analysis of incentives in the linear VCM. There are $i = 1, \ldots, N$ players each with endowment, w_i. Players choose a level of contribution g_i such that $0 \le g_i \le w_i$. Let G be the sum of the player contributions and r the group return on G. Private return is normalized to 1. Let g_{-i} be the vector of contribution by everyone but player i. The payoff function for player i is given by:

$$\prod_i(g_1, g_{-i}) = (w_i - g_i) + \frac{rG}{N}. \qquad (18.5)$$

Assuming that $r/N < 1 < r$ we have the following two results: (a) each player i has a dominant strategy to set $g_i = 0$; and (b) $g_i = w_i$ for all i is Pareto optimal, and Pareto dominates $g_i = 0$, for all i. Note that r/N is called the marginal per capita return on the group investment, or more briefly the MPCR.

Game theory does not explain the high initial contributions but does seem to explain the incentives observed in the characteristic decline in contributions over time. This has led some observers to conclude that relatively naive subjects must learn the dominant strategy property of the linear VCM. However, Ameden et al. (1999) hypothesize that the characteristic decline occurs because the standard experimental design introduces free riders, which forces subjects to decrease the goodwill they assign to their group. In particular, previous VCM experiments show that individuals vary widely in their willingness to contribute to a public good. In these experiments subjects are preassigned to a group, which forces a heterogeneous mix of individuals (including free riders). Over time, if contributors do not see their levels of investment in the public account reciprocated, they will reduce the amount of goodwill assigned to their group and invest less. In four person groups, with an MPCR of 0.5, Croson (1998) finds strong support for "middle-matching" reciprocity, i.e., subjects try to match the middle (or average) contribution of the other contributors. The existence of free riders reduces this average making it more likely for reciprocity behavior to spiral downwards.

When Ameden et al. (1999) model goodwill accounting in the public goods game they hypothesize that changing the assignment to groups so that the four highest contributors are matched together, then the next four highest, and so on, will find much higher (often-sustainable) contributions to the public good, and that this will occur even though the subjects themselves are not informed as to the nature of the assignment rule. The data support this hypothesis. The four highest contributors experience high group contributions and find it natural to reciprocate; the four lowest contributors observe others behaving like themselves and free riding is more frequent.

REFERENCES

Ameden, H., A. Gunnthorsdottir, D. Houser, and K. McCabe. 1999. Free-riders and cooperative decay in public goods experiments. Working Paper. Economic Science Lab., Univ. of Arizona.

Axelrod, R. 1984. The Evolution of Cooperation. New York: Basic.

Axelrod, R. 1997. The Complexity of Cooperation: Agent-Based Models of Competition and Cooperation. Princeton, N.J.: Princeton Univ. Press.

Baron-Cohen, S. 1995. Mindblindness: An Essay on Autism and Theory of Mind. Cambridge, MA: MIT Press.

Coleman, J. 1990. Foundations of Social Choice Theory. Cambridge, MA: Harvard Univ. Press.

Cosmides, L. 1989. The logic of social exchange: Has natural selection shaped how humans reason? Studies with the Wason selection task. *Cognition* **31(3)**:187–276.

Cosmides, L., and J. Tooby. 1992. Cognitive adaptations for social exchange. In: The Adapted Mind, ed. J. Barkow, L. Cosmides, and J. Tooby, pp. 163, 228. New York: Oxford Univ. Press.

Croson, R.T.A. 1998. Theories of altruism and reciprocity: Evidence from linear public goods games. Working Paper. Dept. of Management, Univ. of Pennsylvania.

Hoffman, E., K. McCabe, and V. Smith. 1998. Behavioral foundations of reciprocity: Experimental economics and evolutionary psychology. *Econ. Inq.* **36(3)**:335–352.

Kuhn, H.W. 1953. Extensive games and the problem of information. In: Contributions to the Theory of Games, ed. H.W. Kuhn and A.W. Tucker. Princeton, N.J.: Princeton Univ. Press.

McCabe, K. 1989. Fiat money as a store of value in an experimental market. *J. Econ. Behav. Org.* **12**:215–231.

McCabe, K., and V. Smith. 1999. Strategic analysis by players in games: What information do they use? Economic Science Lab., Univ. of Arizona.

New York Times. 1998. Opportunism on the Internet. Nov. 12.

North, D. 1990. Institutions, Institutional Change, and Economic Performance. Cambridge: Cambridge Univ. Press.

Orbell, J., and R. Dawes. 1993. Social welfare, cooperator's advantage, and the option of not playing the game. *Am. Sociol. Rev.* **58**:787–800.

Premack, D., and J. Premack. 1995. Origins of human social competence. In: The Cognitive Neurosciences, ed. M. Gazzaniga, pp. 205–218. Cambridge, MA: MIT Press.

Schelling, T. 1960. Strategies of Conflict. Cambridge, MA: Harvard Univ. Press.

Standing, left to right: Phil Tetlock, Wulf Albers, Kevin McCabe, Axel Ockenfels
Seated, left to right: Peyton Young, Joe Henrich, Rob Boyd

19

Group Report: What Is the Role of Culture in Bounded Rationality?

Joseph Henrich, Rapporteur
Wulf Albers, Robert Boyd, Gerd Gigerenzer,
Kevin A. McCabe, Axel Ockenfels,
and H. Peyton Young

As a research program, "bounded rationality" aims to understand the actual cognitive processes that humans use to arrive at their behavioral repertoire. The assumptions of bounded rationality depart from the traditional assumptions of omniscient, "Laplacean Demons" with unlimited information, time and processing ability, and instead assume that individuals possess fast, frugal algorithms which allow individuals to solve a variety of difficult problems under ecologically realistic circumstances without incurring substantial information-gathering or processing costs. In this chapter, we explore three ways in which sociocultural processes produce adaptive (or boundedly rational) algorithms. First, simple imitation or social learning heuristics allow individuals to save the costs of individual learning, experimentation, and search by exploiting the information available in the minds of other individuals. Second, over cultural-evolutionary time scales,[1] these algorithms give rise to complex sets of motivations, decision processes, rules, cues, and procedures that are adaptive in particular socio-ecologies (yet quite maladaptive in others). Third, cultural and socio-interactional processes can combine to give rise to adaptive group processes that distribute cognition, knowledge, skill, and labor (institutions, governing processes, markets, etc.). We argue that these three types of processes form the essential elements in a wide range of human decision-making and

---

[1] Cultural–evolutionary time scales are, on average, longer than individual-level adaptive learning processes, but shorter than genetic–evolutionary time scales.

behavioral patterns. Consequently, any effort to understand the patterns requires an exploration of how each of these sociocultural processes works.

WHAT ARE CULTURE, CULTURAL TRANSMISSION MECHANISMS, AND SOCIAL DECISION MECHANISMS?

"Culture" is information, stored in people's heads, that can be transmitted among individuals. This information can be thought of as the ideas, values, beliefs, behavioral strategies, perceptual models, and organizational structures that reside in individual brains, which can be learned by other individuals through imitation, observation (plus inference), interaction, discussion, and/or teaching. Culture is not institutions, technology, or social structure but is inextricably related to the evolution and functioning of each.

Technology, for example, is often considered a part of culture; however, this interpretation fails to understand that the essential part of technology (its function, use, and design) resides in people's heads and is not embodied in the artifacts themselves. The glass coke bottle was originally designed to store Coca-Cola, but people unfamiliar with carbonated beverages find that it's an excellent musical instrument, portable mini-club, water container, nut grinder, or even a fire starter. What it is (meaning its function or what it's "good for") depends on what is in the mind of the user, and is only constrained by the physical form of the object itself.

People often have the sense that culture must, by definition, be shared among some group of individuals. This intuition arises because individuals within social groups tend to believe similar things and behave in similar ways, and thus they share a large amount of culture. However, populations may share certain components of culture more or less: there may be subcultures within the population that share some things, but not others; there may be clines of cultural traits carving out regions through populations, etc. In each case, we want to be able to ask why a certain distributional pattern exists. One cannot ask why individuals share certain traits, and not others, if "shared" is part of the definition of culture.

Cultural transmission mechanisms are cognitive information processors that allow individuals to acquire information (or infer information) in some fashion from other individuals, often via observation, imitation, and interaction (Cavalli-Sforza and Feldman 1981; Durham 1991; Boyd and Richerson 1985; Sperber 1996). Many researchers think of these as species-specific, mental mechanisms constructed by natural selection to search, select, and acquire information from the distribution of different behaviors available in the social world. Cultural transmission capacities allow individuals to shortcut the costs of search, experimentation, and data processing algorithms, and instead benefit from the cumulative experience stored in the minds (and observed in the behavior) of others.

CULTURAL TRANSMISSION MECHANISMS AND THEIR CULTURAL-EVOLUTIONARY PRODUCTS ARE FAST AND FRUGAL HEURISTICS THAT HAVE ALLOWED HUMANS TO ADAPT TO AN INCREDIBLY WIDE RANGE OF DIFFERENT HABITATS

Taken as a whole, human populations display three interesting patterns: (a) humans have the largest variety of habitats and adaptations of any animal; (b) humans belonging to the same group tend to behave in similar ways, while members of different groups often behave quite differently (i.e., most studied behavioral variation occurs *between* human groups)[2]; and (c) even in identical and overlapping environments, human groups display *quite* different behavioral patterns. In an effort to explain these three facts about human behavior, researchers have suggested that individuals rely heavily on certain forms of imitation and/or cultural transmission mechanisms. Here we will briefly describe the operation of two such cognitive algorithms: prestige-biased transmission and conformist transmission (see Boesch and Tomasello 1998; Gil-White and Henrich 1999; Cavalli-Sforza and Feldman 1981; Boyd and Richerson 1985; Henrich and Boyd 1998; Sperber 1996; Boyer 1994 for more detail on other mechanisms).

A substantial amount of cross-cultural ethnography (e.g., Dove 1993; Hammel 1964; Rogers 1995; Moore 1957) and laboratory psychology (for a summary, see Gil-White and Henrich 1999) suggests that humans everywhere possess a tendency to copy prestigious individuals, i.e., those who receive the most displays of respect/deference from others. This mechanism embodies two shortcut heuristics. First, by preferentially copying a "bundle" of cultural traits from prestigious individuals (prestige correlates with skill/knowledge and often wealth) copiers can rapidly acquire a repertoire of fitness-enhancing or success-oriented traits (i.e., better-than-average solutions to the problems of life). Second, rather than gradually learning via individual experience who the most successful, knowledgeable, or skillful individuals are, copiers rely on honest ethological and sociolinguistic signals of respect that other individuals display toward such high status individuals. Ethologically, lower status individuals unintentionally indicate who are the high status individuals by watching them, paying attention, maintaining proximity to them, and by their diminutive body position relative to the prestigious individual. Sociolinguistically, high prestige individuals can also be recognized by how rarely they are interrupted, how often it's their "turn" to speak, how lower status individuals ask questions, and by the ingratiating compliments that prestigious individuals receive. These signals cue

---

[2] A "group" is composed of individuals who frequently interact socially, but not necessarily by individuals who share similar cultural beliefs/behaviors (not by definition). Baboons, for example, live in social groups, yet they do not have any cultural capacities.

copiers as to who they should begin imitating, i.e., who, for example, is likely to be the most highly skilled hunter. Lower status individuals interested in acquiring information from high status hunters must provide these signals and deferential displays — both because these copiers want to improve their learning (by watching and listening closely), and because they need to supply a kind of payment to the high status individuals for allowing them to hang around, interact, and learn. Failure to show such signals causes high status individuals to avoid interactions with such disrespectful imitators. Because copiers continually update their initial assessments of who is prestigious (i.e., worthy of respect) with information that can be gradually accumulated through life experiences (which may cause them to switch among potential models), the aforementioned correlation between prestige and skill/knowledge is maintained (for a detailed discussion, see Gil-White and Henrich 1999).

Unlike prestige-biased transmission, conformist transmission causes individuals to preferentially copy the most common behaviors in a population. Under conformist transmission, individuals use the frequency of a behavior as an indirect measure (or cue) of the behavior's quality. Theoretical evolutionary modeling suggests that individuals should rely heavily on this heuristic (and a little bit on individual learning) under a wide variety of circumstances, even when environments vary both spatially and temporally, but especially when circumstances provide ambiguous or uncertain cues about the environment (Henrich and Boyd 1998).

Both laboratory and field data provide some confirmation of the predictions generated by these models. Laboratory work by psychologists studying conformism confirms that, as the uncertainty of environmental information rises, individuals rely more heavily on socially transmitted information (Baron et al. 1996). Further, the fact that individuals within social groups tend to behave in similar ways, even when these behavioral patterns cannot be enforced by social sanctions or punishments, suggests that some kind of conformist mechanism is at work.

Both ethnographic data and computer modeling suggest that innate, individually adaptive processes, such as prestige-biased transmission and conformist transmission, will accumulate and stabilize cultural-evolutionary products that act as effective decision-making algorithms, without the individual participants understanding how or why the particular system works. Systems of divination provide interesting examples of how culture provides adaptive solutions. Among the Kantu of Kalimantan (Indonesian Borneo) swidden farmers rely religiously on a complex system of bird omens that effectively randomizes their selection of garden sites (Dove 1993). Each Kantu farmer selects a new garden location based both on the type of bird observed there, and the type of call the bird makes after it is first observed. This prevents individuals from committing the "gambler's fallacy," which would increase their chances of crop failure from periodic floods, and diversifies the types of gardens across community members, which spreads risk among households. As a quick and thrifty heuristic, this cultural system suppresses errors that farmers make in judging the chances of a flood, and substitutes an operationally simple means for individuals to randomize their garden site selection. In addition, by randomizing each farmer's decision independently, this belief system also reduces the chance of catastrophic failures across the entire group — it decreases the probability that many farmers will fail at the same time. All this only works because the Kantu believe that birds actually supply supernatural information that foretells the future and that they would be punished for not listening to it.

Theoretical work by Hutchins and Hazlehurst (1991) suggests that gradual cultural evolutionary processes can accumulate effective mental models of complex problems — that is, sufficiently difficult problems that no single individual could solve on her own. In the past, these inland-living, native Californians evidently visited the coast to harvest nutritionally important shellfish. To facilitate this, these people acquired an effective cultural model of the relationship between lunar phases and tides. Hutchins and Hazlehurst's simulation shows how, with a small bit of individual learning and observation, and the ability to transmit this information across individuals and through the generations, populations would eventually produce an accurate, effective lunar-tide model. From the bounded rationality perspective, such processes can generate simple rules that are quite hard for individuals to figure out — like when to travel to the ocean to harvest shellfish.

Perhaps as a consequence of the interaction of cultural evolution and social processes that occur among individuals and groups, humans are also affected by higher-level processes which produce things like institutions, political systems, firms, markets etc. These things allow groups to aggregate information, skill, and processing power (each of which may be distributed among group members) in adaptive ways (e.g., group decision making, democratic structures, a division of labor, Micronesian navigation) without individual participants necessarily understanding how or why the total system works. One theory suggests that cultural transmission mechanism, like conformist transmission can give rise to a higher-level selective process called *cultural group selection*. This process can build increasingly adaptive, more accurate, and more efficient systems at the group level, which involve both distributed cognition and complex divisions of labor (Boyd and Richerson, this volume, 1990; Soltis et. al. 1995). This process is the sociocultural analog to the genetic group-selective processes which have been suggested to explain the evolution of the highly effective "new nest" search algorithms among bees (Seeley, this volume).

HOW DOES CULTURE INFLUENCE IMPORTANT HUMAN DECISIONS?

In an effort to explore how culture influences human behavior and decision making, we will examine empirical data from three different cases: reciprocity and cooperation, mate selection, and food choice. We use these concrete cases to: (a) demonstrate that many important human decisions cannot be understood as products of built-in cognitive algorithms, devoid of cultural input; (b) delineate the debates about how to approach such issues; and (c) suggest lines of future research.

Does Culture Influence Decision-making Related to Reciprocity and Cooperation?

Evidence from cross-cultural experimental economics strongly suggests that cultural differences can substantially affect the patterns of reciprocity and cooperation found in different social groups. In recent experimental work from the Peruvian Amazon, Henrich (2000) has shown that Machiguenga horticulturalists greatly deviate from the behavior of typical western subjects in both the ultimatum and a common pool resources game. In the ultimatum game, Machiguenga proposers yielded an average offer of 26% of the total pot, and a modal offer of 15%, while typical ultimatum proposers (those found in urban, industrial societies) produce a mean around 44% and a mode of 50%. Similarly, in the common pool resources game, Smith and Henrich found that Machiguenga players yielded a mean contribution of only 23% to the common pool and a modal contribution of 0% (complete defection) as compared to typical U.S. mean contributions of between 40% and 60%. Henrich also found quite different results (as compared to westerners) among the Mapuche, an indigenous group of small-scale peasant farmers in the agricultural plains of central Chile (Henrich and Smith 1999).

Even in places as culturally similar as East and West Germany or Israel and Pittsburgh, we find more similar, but still significantly different, results in these games. In a study of solidarity and cooperation experiments conducted in eastern and western Germany, it was observed that eastern subjects behave in a significantly more selfish manner than do western subjects. The solidarity game, which was invented by Selten and Ockenfels (1998), is a three-person game in which each player independently wins DM 10 with probability 2/3. Before the random decisions are made, each player has to decide how much he or she is willing to give to the losers in the group in the case of winning. Ockenfels and Weinmann (1999) observe that the conditional gifts made in anonymous experiments in eastern Germany are dramatically smaller than the corresponding gifts in western Germany. Moreover, average expectations about the conditional gifts of the other group members match average gifts within each population (but, of course, not across populations). Analogous effects are observed in standard public goods games. The authors conclude that cooperation and solidarity behavior depend on different culture-specific norms resulting from opposing economic social and economic histories in the two parts of Germany. Ultimatum game experiments performed by Roth et. al. (1991) have also demonstrated that significant cultural differences exist between Israeli students from Hebrew University (with a mean proposer of 0.36) and American students from Pittsburgh (with a mean proposer offer of 0.44).

In these cases, simple heuristics like "give half" or "take almost everything" operate quite well, given that others in your group possess similar and complementary rules. Such rules allow people to make pretty good decisions without any computation and without knowing much about how others will behave. In general, people's heuristics seem well calibrated with other members of *their* group.

A variety of approaches may account for these data. There seem to be two basic starting points. Starting point 1: people come into the world with a propensity to reciprocate and behave "fairly" with anyone (kin, friend, or anonymous person), but they are sensitive to socio-environmental cues, which allow them to adjust or calibrate their degree of trust and trustworthiness and their expectations of fairness and punishment in adaptive ways (ways that fit with the current pattern of social interaction so they avoid being exploited). Such cues may be social interaction or cultural. Social interaction cues mean that either individuals rapidly learn from small samples of failed or successful interactions, or they use some ethological signal (e.g., narrow eyes, hunched shoulder, downturned head) to update or adjust the relevant parameters (like degree of trustworthiness). Culture users would ignore ethological cues (at least innate ones) and save the costs of failed interactions by copying the dispositions, degree of trust, or behavioral patterns of others. From an evolutionary perspective, however, it remains unclear how this tendency toward generalized reciprocity could have evolved, although Richerson and Boyd (1998) have suggested one coevolutionary possibility.

Starting point 2 maintains that humans come predisposed to cooperate/reciprocate with *only* kin and "close friends" (i.e., "reciprocal altruism" or repeated interaction with known individuals).[3] This assumption derives from empirical work in simple horticultural and forager societies. In these places, people do not interact with, trust, or expect anything from anonymous individuals who are not friends or relatives. Even when governments, missionaries, and locally inspired leaders attempt to conduct group projects that would surely benefit the entire community, individuals do not cooperate or fail to reciprocate. Even imposed sanctioning methods fail to maintain cooperation and reciprocity in many cases.

From an evolutionary perspective, interacting and cooperating with anonymous individuals is probably a recent problem (last 10,000 years). Thus the development of anonymous exchange and cooperation results from cultural evolutionary processes, and requires that each individual acquire an entire behavioral model about how to deal with specific types of situations. This has three implications: (a) humans are probably heavily reliant on cultural transmission

---

[3] Both cooperation with kin and reciprocal altruism are also found among other primates, although the data on reciprocal altruism remains sparse.

(so reliant that cultural input can fundamentally structure one's basic eco-nomic-interactional behavior); (b) behavioral rules and mental models will be specific to certain cultural domains, and will not translate across all coopera-tive/exchange possibilities; and (c) people who achieve effective cooperation in different societies may possess entirely different decision-making algorithms or heuristic models. Both allow their possessor to navigate effectively, but each embodies entirely different assumptions about the world.

One line of evidence that bears on this debate comes from recent work by ex-perimental economists on signaling in exchange interactions. Ockenfels and Selten (1998) examined involuntary truth-signaling with the help of a simple two-person bargaining game with face-to-face interaction. Players bargain about the division of a fixed sum of money. Each bargainer could either have costs subtracted from his or her bargaining agreement payoff or not. The cost sit-uations were neither known by the opponents nor by onlookers who observed the bargaining. It is shown that the cost guesses of the onlookers are somewhat more accurate than chance. However, this effect is entirely explicable by the on-lookers' information about "objective features" of the bargaining process and not due to involuntary physical cues. Also, onlookers were not able to discrimi-nate between liars and truth-tellers among those bargainers who explicitly as-serted to have costs. The authors conclude that there is no evidence for involuntary truth-signaling in their bargaining experiments. Psychological stud-ies suggest that the hypothesis of involuntary truth-signaling may have some merits in different contexts. However, people's ability to detect lies is quite modest (Zuckerman et al. 1981; Gilovich et al. 1998).

If these researchers are correct, and this result can be generalized, then we can eliminate ethological signaling as one of the potential cues that might calibrate an individual in the generalized reciprocity model (starting point 1). This leaves us with two potential cues: individual experimental samples or direct cultural transmission of behaviors and/or dispositions.

How Are Cooperation, Reciprocity, and Fair Exchange Maintained within Groups?

This is a large topic so we'll just sketch the debate and make a few comments. Cooperation among anonymous, unrelated individuals is notoriously difficult to explain. Most researchers believe that cooperation is maintained by an appropri-ately sized threat of punishment, such that deviations from cooperative behavior incur sufficiently large penalties that defections "don't pay." However, invoking punishment creates a new problem: how to explain punishment. Punishers can be exploited by nonpunishing cooperators (NPCs) when punishing has a cost. NPCs always cooperate, but cheat when it comes time to punish noncooperators, and therefore get higher payoffs than punishers do (Boyd and Richerson 1992).

Theorists have attempted to solve this problem in three ways:

1. Some ignore it by assuming that a State or some other overarching institution does the punishing.
2. Others incorporate a recursive punishing method in which punishers punish noncooperaters and other punishers who fail to punisher any nonpunishers, etc., in an infinite regresss.
3. Still others assume punishing is costless.

Solution 1 just moves the problem back to why we have States and institutions, and in answering this question one gets hung back up on the horns of the same old dilemma. The second solution seems entirely unrealistic to many people. Do people really punish people who fail to punish other nonpunishers? Solution 3 seems unrealistic too. Any attempt to inflict costs on another must be accompanied by at least some tiny incremental cost.

Cultural transmission mechanisms, however, may provide a fourth means to solve the problem of cooperation and punishment. A mechanism like conformist transmission, which creates a directional force that maintains common behaviors, can act to maintain cooperative behaviors in populations — when they are common — by reducing the appeal of rare noncooperative and nonpunishing behaviors. Because second- and third-order defections (not punishing rare nonpunishers) have such small differential payoff advantages, conformist transmission can act to eliminate the replicatory viability or advantage of such strategies effectively, as long as they remain rare. This makes cooperation possible and reduces the cost or frequency of the punishment required to maintain cooperation.

Some empirical evidence supports this argument by suggesting that cooperation levels are too high, given the potential for and cost of punishment. The legal system, for example, often ends up to be more costly than simply ignoring the transgression. Courts recognize this, e.g., small claims, etc., but individual opportunity costs are not taken into account. In this sense, courts are a threat that are not used very often — low frequency of use keeps costs down. However, if the threat were credible so that large numbers of law-breakers went to court, then the system would be too costly and would fail. Similarly, tax compliance in the U.S. is too high, given the probability of being caught for cheating and the size of the penalty — particularly in comparison to other nations where people cheat more, get caught more, and receive stiffer penalties.

Our discussion suggests several lines of future work. First, the relative importance of specific culturally evolved models of exchange/cooperation vs. a genetically evolved generalized reciprocity can be tested by performing experimental games with different, culturally appropriate mediums of exchange. If foragers, for example, were to behave the same when the stakes are paid with meat (or honey) instead of money, then a generalized reciprocity would seem likely. If people behave differently (and predictively) with different mediums, then this suggests that people have special sets of rules for exchanging different mediums — which supports the cultural models line of reasoning.

Second, the "protection game" should be further incorporated into our arsenal of experimental games, so we can differentiate behavioral orientations or decision algorithms related to exchange from those consistent with other social contexts (and establish if and how context matters). In general, testing people's behavior under different contexts will allow researchers to identify the cues that individuals use to select among different rules or strategies.

Third, experimentalists should team up with geneticists to figure out what proportion of the variation within experimental game samples can be explained by genes, common-family environments, and other factors, like the cultural milieu. Experimentalists could administer economic games to subsamples from the existing data bases that geneticists use to sort out the genetic and environmental components of personality, behavior, and preferences.

Fourth, experimentalists need to incorporate further study of their subjects' behavior and decisions outside the laboratory — in the real world — to determine how performance in these games maps onto actual behaviors. Perhaps experimental economists should team up with anthropologists and sociologists who can observe and interview experimental subjects in real-life socioeconomic interactions — in their jobs, homes, volunteer work, and economic dealings.

Mate Selection

Mate selection is a very old problem. One might think that, given the evolutionary importance of this problem and the amount of time natural selection has had to work on it, humans would have innate, highly refined cognitive algorithms for picking mates. It turns out, however, that while there are some regularities like women's preferences for wealthy, powerful men, and men's preferences for some physical features in women, people living in different groups select mates in an extraordinarily wide variety of ways. Among the Kipsigis (e.g., Borgerhoff Mulder 1988), for example, brides are sold for cows in a marriage market. Brides are priced just as one would guess: the fattest ones fetch the most. This contrasts with our own societies where most things are openly sold on the market, except of course wives. In other places, parents select marriage partners for their children and, depending on the place, the children may or may not be able to decline. Among many Amazonian groups, the ideal partner is someone who does not speak your native language (Jackson 1983), or someone who is your mother's brother's daughter (i.e., your first "cross-cousin"; Johnson 1986). To understand how someone in a particular place picks a mate, one needs to understand the cultural models acquired by individuals from those around them.

How Does Culture Influence Food Choice Decisions?

Selecting a food, like selecting a mate, is an important evolutionary problem that natural selection has had a long time to perfect. However, unlike mate selection, which most do only a few times per life, food choices are amenable to repeated trials and small improvements, which — one might think — make it more likely to be solved through some individual sampling algorithm that would allow humans to find food fast in any environment. However, with the exception of innate preferences for the taste of salt, sugar, and fat, and certain food avoidance learning responses, humans possess an incredibly diverse culinary repertoire that is highly dependent on cultural input.

Some comparative examples of food preferences will illustrate the diversity of human food choice. Many people in the Midwest of the U.S. will not eat lamb, ostensibly because they have some vague notion that it causes disease. Meanwhile, people elsewhere in the U.S., with access to the same sheep, love to eat lamb. In the U.S. most people would not think of eating horse, despite the fact that it's lower in cholesterol and fat than most other red meats, favorable characteristics for many Americans. Meanwhile, the Mapuche of Chile, who rely on horses as their primary mode of transportation, frequently eat horse meat, although they prefer pig because it has more fat (horse is way too lean for them). Many Germans believe that drinking water after eating cherries is deadly; they also believe that putting ice in soft drinks is unhealthy. The English, however, rather enjoy a cool drink of water after some cherries, and Americans love icy refreshments.

In Peru we find an interesting comparative case. Among the Machiguenga of the Peruvian Amazon, nobody ever eats snake meat. If you ask people what happens if you eat snake, they say that you will throw up blood and die. Nobody admits to ever having eaten snake, and they say that they do not know anyone who has ever eaten it. Meanwhile, just down river from this Machiguenga village is a Mestizo village inhabited by immigrants from the Andean highlands who have retreated into the tropical forest in search of arable land. These Mestizos, who have periodic contact with the Machiguenga, believe snake meat is fine to eat, and do consume it, when the occasion presents itself — although they do not hunt snakes or raise them, like the Chinese do.

The Machiguenga have another curious dietary preference (besides stopping along the trail to snack on the fat-rich larva found under decaying logs). The recent sedentization of Machiguenga families into communities has depleted the availability of wild foods, which have traditionally supplied the Machiguenga with critical sources of vitamin A and C. Recognizing the rising problem, protestant missionaries planted lemon and grapefruit trees throughout the community, and these trees have subsequently multiplied. Presently, despite their ongoing deficiencies in vitamins A and C, few Machiguenga have adopted the practice of consuming these abundant fruits. When asked, Machiguenga will explain that they do not consider the fruits a food and find it strange that outsiders seem to like them so much.

Except in its ritual form during Christian ceremonies, consuming human meat, blood, or bone marrow is rare among Westerners, but many peoples consume these for symbolic and perhaps even for nutritional reasons. The Foré people of New Guinea, for example, consume the brains of dead relatives (Durham 1991). In Mexico, Aztecs distributed the choice limbs and organs of sacrificial prisoners-of-war to valorous warriors for ritual consumption (Price and Feinman 1993). In the Amazon, the Yanomana consume the bone marrow of deceased relatives in a rite of ancestor worship (Chagnon 1992).

Few mammals ever eat their own kind, presumably because this meat may carry harmful microorganisms that are well adapted to the consumer. Despite this strong aversion to cannibalism in most mammals, humans, because of their immense reliance on culture transmission, may acquire a taste for their own kind, and cultural evolutionary processes may maintain these preferences through time under certain socio-environmental conditions.

Culturally transmitted preferences are so powerful that they can overcome physiological aversion. For example, capsicums (e.g., chili peppers) possess the chemical equivalent of pain. When anyone eats them for the first time, it's an unpleasant experience. Yet, under certain ecological conditions, particularly in tropical regions, the habit of eating capsicums, often with every meal, is widespread. Evidence suggests that eating capsicums, storing food in their marinades, and applying capsicum sauces to foods generates a number of adaptive results. In places where food cannot be stored and bacteria infestation is likely, capsicums supply vitamins (especially vitamin C) in a form that can be stored for long periods. Actually eating capsicum probably helps control parasite loads, which are a primary cause of death among children throughout the developing world. Food stored in, or "treated" with, a capsicum sauce lasts longer and is much less likely to spoil. Here we find an adaptive behavior using what should be an aversive food, yet most of these people think they just like to eat chilies.

Human children do not arrive in the world being disgusted by any particular foods or classes of foods, although they will react negatively to very bitter things (Rozin and Fallon 1986). Children will happily eat bloodworms or solidified chunks of bacon fat. It seems that children connect the emotional reaction of disgust to particular foods by observing the disgust reaction of other individuals. Often, as we all probably know well, no amount of nutritional information or well-meaning recommendations can change these emotional connections once they are solidly in place.

As a learning heuristic, cultural information channeled by social learning algorithms acts to limit choices and direct attention to certain reliable dietary options. It solves the otherwise difficult and costly problem of figuring out what to eat in widely varying environments that range from the Arctic tundra and the Amazon. Cross-cultural evidence clearly indicates that human tastes are incredibly flexible, and people seem to rely enormously on imitating the taste preferences of those around them.

ARE CULTURAL PREFERENCES, CUES, AND DECISION PROCESSES ADAPTIVE?

A survey of the cross-cultural data yields a large number of cases in which human cultural practices seem well adapted to their environments, yet we still find a substantial number of clearly maladaptive cases (Edgerton 1992). We will begin with two illustrations.

Favism, a genetically transmitted disorder, provides a good example of how culture can be both adaptive and maladaptive. Fava beans are an important food in many parts of Europe that border the Mediterranean compared to other areas in Europe. According to Katz and Schall (1986), fava bean use coincides with the areas in which malaria was prevalent during historical times, an intriguing result in light of the fact that fava beans contain a chemical which acts as a malarial prophylactic. It also turns out that an X-linked genetic condition called G6PD deficiency is also common in the same areas in which malaria was endemic. Women who are heterozygous for the G6PD allele are also resistant to malaria. Thus it is plausible that fava bean consumption and G6PD deficiency both represent evolved responses to malaria: one cultural and the other genetic. However, there is an interesting interaction between these practices that shows how culture can be maladaptive as well. Men who carry the G6PD-deficient gene get sick when they eat fava beans because, in effect, they overdose on their malaria medicine. This disease, called favism, is a significant health problem in places like Sardinia in which fava beans are an important part of the cuisine, and in which G6PD deficiency is common. Thus, the cultural heuristic "fava beans are good to eat — include a lot in your diet" causes many people to avoid malaria, but at the same time causes the G6PD deficient to suffer serious health consequences.

It's also interesting that people living in these areas believe malaria is caused by "bad air" (and thus the name "mal" [bad] aria [air]). One locally prescribed measure that helps to prevent this "bad air" condition is to keep all the windows shut, especially at night. This preventive scheme has the fortunate side effect of also keeping mosquitoes out.

Among the Foré people of New Guinea, the practice of eating the brains of dead relatives has maladaptive and dire consequences, especially for women. While preparing the raw brains of a deceased relative for cooking, a woman sometimes contracts Kuru (a human version of Mad Cow Disease) from contact with brains.[4] Months later, this disease eventually produces a horrible death, as the victim gradually goes violently insane. Then, while her female relatives repeat the ritual in preparing her brains, they too may contract the disease and

---

[4] Eating the brains may be a secondary means of disease transmission, as this virus is particularly resistant to heat and may sometimes survive the cooking process.

continue the cycle. Women were also forced to eat the brains more often, because men believed that human flesh diminished their combat prowess, and thus they preferred to eat pork (Durham 1991). Interestingly, southern Foré women apparently came to prefer to eat Kuru victims and found them particularly tasty, as they were more tender and fatty than other recently deceased individuals (Glasse 1963, p. 13).

When complex cultural practices and preferences spread incompletely or too rapidly from one place to another, we often find quite maladaptive cultural practices. Amazonian Indians have long cultivated bitter manioc in the infertile, acidic soils of the Amazon basin where sweet manioc cannot grow. To remove the cyanide from this long root crop, indigenous Amazonian groups have a routinized preparation, which involves grating, boiling, and repeatedly rinsing the manioc. Eventually Europeans brought bitter manioc to Africa, where it spread rapidly into regions where agriculture had previously been impossible. Unfortunately, the processing model was transmitted incompletely or, in some cases, not at all. The sad result is that many African cultivators of manioc die quite young — once the cyanide has accumulated beyond toxic levels (Frechione 1998).

When are cultural products (i.e., fast, frugal algorithms) adaptive and when are they maladaptive? This question will go largely unanswered; however, four things are relatively clear. First, cultural products can rapidly become maladaptive when environments change too quickly, or when individuals migrate into environments that are too different from their previous environments. Second, groups vary immensely in their concern for and punishment of norm violations, which affects the operation of within-group cultural evolutionary processes. Sometimes cultural groups adopt very high levels of norm enforcement that severely suppress the individual variations, innovations, and "errors" that innate cultural transmission mechanisms require to generate adaptive evolutionary processes within groups — although slower between-group selection processes may eventually sort this out (e.g., the Foré are gradually disappearing).

Third, historical and archaeological evidence indicates that group size (population size) and degree of interconnectedness or contact with surrounding groups strongly affect cultural evolutionary rates. For example, eight thousand years ago a technologically sophisticated, stone-age group of Australian aborigines settled on the island of Tasmania, where they were subsequently isolated for thousands of years. When the Europeans arrived in 1835, they found the most technologically simple people on earth. The Tasmanians had lost a vast repertoire of complex technologies including fishhooks, canoes, nets, and even the knowledge of how to make fire (Diamond 1978). This is certainly not an isolated story.[5] The ethnographic, historical, and archaeological record is full of cases in

---

[5] It is probably also no coincidence that the most technologically sophisticated and complex societies on earth have all arisen from the world's largest and most interconnected continent, Eurasia (see Diamond 1997).

which small, isolated groups began to lose the cultural knowledge that allowed them to adapt. Large, interconnected populations, if nothing else, allow populations to resist the long-term effects of random cultural drift by storing many copies of the relevant information throughout a dispersed metapopulation (through several populations)

Fourth, social structure, together with innate biases about who to imitate, and certain cultural beliefs may eliminate valuable innovators, experimenters, and error-makers from being viewed as people to copy. For example, in the case of food choice, innovation is suppressed because "innovators" and "experimenters" are usually young children, or because "novel" food choices are observed only among individuals from ethnically or social disenfranchised groups.

FURTHER RESEARCH

Understanding how and why cultures change requires understanding the details of why certain ideas or practices spread, and why others do not. Understanding and analyzing the factors that influence how rapidly novel beliefs, preferences, cues, decision models, and values diffuse through populations, demands detailed laboratory and field research in which individual ideas, decision methods, or preferences are tracked as they spread through populations.

We close by briefly summarizing the decision-making challenges confronted by cultural transmission mechanisms, cultural-evolutionary products, and social decision mechanisms, and how this is accomplished.

1. Cultural transmission mechanisms speed up learning by skipping costly individual experimentation, sampling, and data processing.
2. Cultural-evolutionary products limit choice sets. For example, norms of fairness in ultimatum games (when played in industrial societies) provide players with a quick, easily-calculated method of getting a pretty good answer. Yet, similar norms would perform poorly among the Machiguenga.
3. Cultural-evolutionary products limit choices in explicit decision making by providing simple mental models, built upon our most basic cognitive abilities (e.g., spatial and temporal representation), which may effectively exploit features of the environment to simplify processing and improve accuracy. The medieval tidal computer is one such example.
4. Social decision mechanisms solve adaptive problems that individuals could not by distributing memory, computations, and skills among individuals. Micronesian navigation (Hutchins 1980) is one example; others include decision-making institutions and governance structures.

REFERENCES

Baron, R.S., J. Vandello, and B. Brunsman. 1996. The forgotten variable in conformity research: Impact of task importance on social influence. *J. Pers. Soc. Psych.* **71(5)**:915–927.

Boesch, C., and M. Tomasello. 1998. Chimpanzee and human cultures. *Curr. Anthro.* **39(5)**:591–614.

Borgerhoff Mulder, M. 1988. Kpisigis bridewealth payments. In: Human Reproductive Behavior, ed. L. Betzig and P.W. Turke, pp. 65–82. Cambridge: Cambridge Univ. Press.

Boyd, R., and P.J. Richerson. 1985. Culture and the Evolutionary Process. Chicago: Univ. of Chicago Press.

Boyd, R., and P.J. Richerson. 1990. Group selection among alternative evolutionarily stable strategies. *J. Theor. Biol.* **145(3)**:331–342.

Boyd, R., and P.J. Richerson. 1992. Punishment allows the evolution of cooperation (or anything else) in sizable groups. *Ethol. Sociobiol.* **13(3)**:171–195.

Boyer, P. 1994. The Naturalness of Religious Ideas. Berkeley: Univ. of California.

Cavalli-Sforza, L.L., and M. Feldman. 1981. Cultural Transmission and Evolution. Princeton, NJ: Princeton Univ. Press.

Chagnon, N.A. 1992. Yanomamo. Fort Worth: Harcourt Brace Jovanovich College Publ.

Diamond, J.M. 1978. The Tasmanians: The longest isolation, the simplest technology. *Nature* **273**:185–186.

Diamond, J.M. 1997. Guns, Germs, and Steel: The Fates of Human Societies. New York: Norton.

Dove, M. 1993. Uncertainty, humility and adaptation in the tropical forest: The agricultural augury of the Kantu. *Ethnology* **32(2)**:145–167.

Durham, W.H. 1991. Coevolution: Genes, Culture, and Human Diversity. Palo Alto: Stanford Univ. Press.

Edgerton, R.B. 1992. Sick Societies: Challenging the Myth of Primitive Harmony. New York: Free Press.

Frechione, J. 1998. The Root of the Problem: Cassava Toxicity in Amazonia and Central Africa. Pittsburgh: Univ. of Pittsburgh.

Gilovich, T., V.H. Medvec, and K. Savitsky. 1998. The illusion of transparency: Biased assessments of other's ability to read one's emotional states. *J. Pers. Soc. Psych.* **75**:332–346.

Gil-White, F., and J. Henrich. 1999. The evolution of prestige: Freely-conferred status as a mechanism for enhancing the benefits of cultural transmission. webuser.bus.umich.edu\~henrich.

Glasse, R.M. 1963. Cannibalism in the kuru region. Reissued by National Institutes of Health, Bethesda, MD. Territory of Papua and New Guinea. Mimeo.

Hammel, E. 1964. Some characteristics of rural village and urban slum populations on the coast of Peru. *Southw. J. Anthro.* **20**:346–358.

Henrich, J. 2000. Does culture matter in economic behavior: Ultimatum game bargaining among the Machiguenga of the Peruvian Amazon. *Am. Econ. Rev.*, in press.

Henrich, J., and R. Boyd. 1998. The evolution of conformist transmission and the emergence of between-group differences. *Evol. Human Behav.* **19**:215–242.

Henrich, J., and N. Smith. 1999. Cross-cultural experimental economics: Ultimatum and public goods games in four cultures. webuser.bus.umich.edu\~henrich.

Hutchins, E. 1980. Culture and Inference: A Trobriand Case Study. Cambridge, MA: Harvard Univ. Press.

Hutchins, E., and B. Hazlehurst. 1991. Learning in the cultural process. In: Artificial Life II, ed. C. Langton, C. Taylor, J. Farmer, and S. Rasmussen, pp. 689–706. SFI Studies in the Sciences of Complexity X. New York: Addison-Wesley.

Jackson, J.E. 1983. The Fish People: Linguistic Exogamy and Tukanoan Identity in Northwest Amazonia. Cambridge: Cambridge Univ. Press.

Johnson, O.R. 1986. Interpersonal Relations and Domestic Authority among the Machiguenga of the Peruvian Amazon. Ph.D. diss., Columbia Univ., New York.

Katz, S.H., and J. Schall. 1986. Favism and malaria: A model of nutritional and biocultural evolution. In: Plants in Indigenous Medicine and Diet, ed. N.L. Etkin. Bedford Hills, NY: Redgrave.

Moore, O.K. 1957. Divination: A new perspective. *Am. Anthro.* **59**:69–74.

Ockenfels, A., and R. Selten. 1998. An experiment on the hypothesis of involuntary truth-signaling in bargaining. Working Paper. Magdeburg: Univ. of Magdeburg.

Ockenfels, A., and J. Weinmann. 1999. Types and patterns — An experimental East–West German comparison of cooperation and solidarity. *J. Publ. Econ.* **71(2)**:275–287.

Price, T.D., and G.M. Feinman. 1993. Images of the Past. Mountain View, CA: Mayfield Publ. Co.

Richerson, P.J., and R. Boyd. 1998. The evolutionary dynamics of a crude super organism. www.sscnet.ucla.edu/anthro/faculty/boyd.

Rogers, E.M. 1995. Diffusion of Innovations. New York: Free Press.

Roth, A.E., V. Prasnikar, M. Okuno-Fujiwara, and S. Zamir. 1991. Bargaining and market behavior in Jerusalem, Ljubljana, Pittsburgh, and Tokyo: An experimental study. *Am. Econ. Rev.* **81(5)**:1068–1095.

Rozin, P., and A.E. Fallon. 1986. A perspective on disgust. *Psych. Rev.* **1**:23–46.

Selten, R., and A. Ockenfels. 1998. An experimental solidarity game. *J. Econ. Behav. Org.* **34**:517–539.

Soltis, J., R. Boyd, and P.J. Richerson. 1995. Can group-functional behaviors evolve by cultural group selection? An empirical test. *Curr. Anthro.* **36**:473–494.

Sperber, D. 1996. Explaining Culture: A Naturalistic Approach. Oxford: Blackwell.

Zuckerman, M., M. Bella, and R. Rosenthal. 1981. Verbal and nonverbal communication of deception. *Adv. Exp. Psych.* **14**:1–59.

Subject Index

Subject Index 369

Name Index